readings
on the
family
and
society

prentice-hall international, inc., London
prentice-hall of australia, pty., ltd., Sydney
prentice-hall of canada, ltd., Toronto
prentice-hall of india (private) ltd., New Delhi
prentice-hall of japan, inc., Tokyo

readings on the family and society

William J. Goode

Columbia University

prentice-hall, inc./englewood cliffs, new jersey

prentice-hall readings in modern sociology series
Alex Inkeles, Editor

Printed in the United States of America C-75692

Library of Congress Catalog Card Number: 64-7569
Current printing (last digit):
12   11   10   9   8   7

preface

Since World War II, sociologists have produced many readers in a wide variety of fields—a handful in the field of the family. Professors and students use them, often instead of a standard textbook. Evidently they fill a need. What is it?

Perhaps the prime service they perform is to put within easy reach many good articles and sections of books. As teachers, we may properly ask students to be diligent in searching the library for materials on a special topic as part of an individual project. But we impose a needless burden if we ask them to search out a dozen articles in half a dozen journals as part of an ordinary assignment in class reading. Moreover, most libraries have only one copy of a journal, which then makes a class assignment a problem in scheduling and a nuisance for an already overworked library staff.

Readers do not substitute for a good textbook, but that fact suggests still another service they perform. The textbook presumably summarizes the main body of factual materials and presents a theoretical framework in which to analyze them. However, many teachers decide that this theoretical approach is faulty or insufficient. They prefer instead to use their own lectures for deeper theoretical analysis and to assign materials in readers as the proper supplement.

In addition, the complaint is widespread that in an effort to reach a mass market, the textbook writer achieves a bland conformity without intellectual challenge. By contrast, the selections in a reader have been written by professionals for professionals. Thus individual sections may be more difficult to read than the usual textbook, but they show the craftsman attempting to resolve difficult issues of research technique as well as trying to present a sharp theoretical analysis. The student can thereby more easily understand the craft of sociological investigation and learn more quickly to be critical of research findings. Working through the inquiry *with* the professional sociologist, he is more likely to be inspired to attempt to surpass him, to push beyond these frontiers.

It is partly for these reasons that I have not sought to collect the classical articles on each subtopic in this reader. True, I have included articles by Kingsley Davis and Judith Blake, Robert K. Merton, and William N. Sewell, which summarize the available material, integrate it theoretically, and suggest further lines of inquiry. However, I have been more concerned with locating articles that challenge received opinion, that open an intellectual door, even when I believe that the author was not able to demonstrate fully his assertions.

This reader also looks forward to a change now taking place in American sociology, which must eventually recognize that, as Durkheim put it, comparative sociology is sociology *itself*, not a separate discipline. If our generalizations are correct, they apply to other societies, too. If not, then we must correct or qualify them. Thus the selections about other family systems are not to be viewed as exotic descriptions, but as part of the solid core of family sociology.

My colleagues in the field will see that I have also laid considerable stress on the family as an element in the larger social structure—shaping it, and being shaped in turn—rather than focusing only on the internal relations of the family. Research has not, I believe, charted these relations adequately, but the explorations contained in this reader deserve the student's attention.

Finally, since each selection is but one individual's special choice, the professional may of course decide that a "better" article on a given topic might have been chosen. I can only hope that such judgments will be made about no more than a few of these selections. More important, I shall hope that as against such lapses, the student and professional will find other selections that raise new issues, suggest different pathways to be explored, or present fruitful data to be analyzed —in short, selections that point to some of the exciting problems in this field that need to be studied.

WILLIAM J. GOODE

table of contents

Part 1 biological foundations of familial elements

one **intrahuman "family" relations   1**
Intragroup Relationships, C. R. CARPENTER   2

two **social relations as a developmental need in monkeys   6**
Social Deprivation in Monkeys, HARRY F. HARLOW AND MARGARET K. HARLOW   7

three **a biological basis for the incest taboo   11**
The Incest Taboo and the Mating Patterns of Animals, DAVID F. ABERLE, URIE BRONFENBRENNER, ECKHARD H. HESS, DANIEL R. MILLER, DAVID M. SCHNEIDER, AND JAMES N. SPUHLER   11

Part 2 societal recognition of the family unit

four **legitimacy and illegitimacy   21**
Illegitimacy and the Social Structure, KINGSLEY DAVIS   21

five **cultural differences in the disapproval of illegitimacy   32**
Cultural Relativism and Premarital Sex Norms, HAROLD T. CHRISTENSEN   33

six **high illegitimacy rates as a consequence of cultural destruction   37**
Illegitimacy, Anomie, and Cultural Penetration, WILLIAM J. GOODE   38

seven   **caste elements in marriage   56**

Intermarriage and the Social Structure: Fact and Theory, ROBERT K. MERTON   56

eight   **upward mobility through economic exchange   64**

Changing Patterns of Mobility, ELINOR G. BARBER   65

nine   **arranging the marriage in rural ireland   68**

The Irish Countryman, CONRAD M. ARENSBERG   68

ten   **the marriage in modern japan   71**

The Go-Between in a Developing Society: The Case of the Japanese Marriage Arranger, EZRA VOGEL   72

eleven   **similarity of beliefs and complementarity of needs in the choice of mate   83**

Value Consensus and Need Complementarity in Mate Selection, ALAN C. KERCKHOFF AND KEITH E. DAVIS   83

twelve   **how the social and cultural patterns affect fertility   90**

Social Structure and Fertility: An Analytic Framework, KINGSLEY DAVIS AND JUDITH BLAKE   90

thirteen   **premarital sexual experience as a cause of sexual adjustment in marriage   96**

Premarital Experience and the Wife's Sexual Adjustment, ROBERT L. HAMBLIN AND ROBERT O. BLOOD, JR.   96

Part 3
the social
and market
processes
in family
formation

Part 4
the
determinants
of fertility

Part 5
marital
adjustment

fourteen   **sex in the lower-class english marriage   104**

Sex Life in Marriage,   ELIOT SLATER AND MOYA WOODSIDE   *104*

fifteen   **husband-wife interaction in a matrilineal system   108**

Marriage, Matriliny, and Social Structure Among the Yao of Southern Nyasaland, J. CLYDE MITCHELL   *108*

sixteen   **how the wife's working affects husband-wife interaction   115**

Dominance and the Working Wife,   DAVID M. HEER   *115*

seventeen   **the formation and maintenance of friendships   124**

The Primary Relations of Middle-Class Couples: A Study in Male Dominance, NICHOLAS BABCHUK AND ALAN P. BATES   *124*

eighteen   **love in puritan marriage   132**

Puritan Love and Marriage,   EDMUND S. MORGAN   *132*

nineteen   **class differences in child-rearing patterns   136**

Social Class and Childhood Personality, WILLIAM H. SEWELL   *136*

twenty   **the effect of maternal employment on adolescent children in town and country   143**

Maternal Employment and Adolescent Roles: Rural-Urban Differentials,   PRODIPTO ROY   *144*

Part 6
parents
and
children

twenty-
one
the influence of peers and parents on mobility aspiration 152

Parental Influence, Anticipatory Socialization, and Social Mobility, RICHARD L. SIMPSON *152*

twenty-
two
the achievement motivation in the united states and brazil 158

Socialization and Achievement Motivation in Brazil, BERNARD C. ROSEN *158*

twenty-
three
extended kin networks in the united states 170

Kin Family Network: Unheralded Structure in Current Conceptualizations of Family Functioning, MARVIN B. SUSSMAN AND LEE BURCHINAL *170*

Part 7
family
and larger
kin groups

twenty-
four
extended kin in an arab village 176

The World of Kin in Lebanon, ANNE H. FULLER *176*

twenty-
five
extended kin ties in a mexican town 180

The Extended Family in Mexico, OSCAR LEWIS *180*

twenty-
six
moving the young man into the larger society 184

The Function of Male Initiation Ceremonies: A Cross-Cultural Test of an Alternative Hypothesis, FRANK W. YOUNG *184*

Part 8
interplay
between
familial
and other
role behavior

twenty-
seven
the breakdown of a society into separate family units 189

A Predictive Hypothesis, EDWARD C. BANFIELD *190*

twenty-eight   **the family as a training ground for political participation   193**

Agencies of Socialization into Politics, HERBERT HYMAN   *193*

twenty-nine   **social structures and high divorce rates   196**

Marital Instability Among the Kpelle: Toward a Theory of Epainogamy,   JAMES L. GIBBS, JR.   *196*

thirty   **the factors generating higher divorce rates among the lower social strata   203**

The Meaning of Class Differentials in the Divorce Rate,   WILLIAM J. GOODE   *204*

thirty-one   **unwilled major role failure in the family   207**

Family Organization and Crisis,   BERNARD FARBER   *207*

thirty-two   **in-laws and marital conflict among jewish families   213**

Laterality and Conflict in Kinship Ties, CANDACE L. ROGERS AND HOPE J. LEICHTER   *213*

thirty-three   **the machine as a factor in family change   219**

The Approximate Effects of Machinery on the Workman,   KARL MARX   *219*

thirty-four   **the family as an independent factor in industrialization   224**

Contrasting Factors in the Modernization of China and Japan,   MARION J. LEVY, JR.   *225*

Part 9
family
dissolution:
internal and
external
factors

Part 10
interaction
between
familial
and societal
factors in
social change

thirty-
five

changing patterns of child rearing in russia 230

Social Change and Social Character: The Role
of Parental Mediation,   ALEX INKELES   *231*

thirty-
six

changing role relations of the japanese wife 237

The Changing Social Position of Women in
Japan,   TAKASHI KOYAMA   *237*

readings
on the
family
and
society

Part 1

biological
foundations
of familial
elements

intrahuman "family" relations

one

Since man's family life is determined by his culture and that of the lower animals is not, how can the sociologist profitably use data about the behavior of even the four manlike apes (gibbon, gorilla, orangutan, chimpanzee)? After all, the gorilla does not "marry" or "divorce." The aging male gibbon does not complain that his grown son is treating him with little respect. In short, human and animal family patterns differ radically in that the former are based on a moral system, a set of values transmitted by socialization from one generation to the next.

The reasons for extending our view are primarily the following:

1. An increasing body of data shows that when the social experiences of primate infants are distorted or lacking (for example, when the mother is absent) the adult monkey or ape is not normal. The higher apes are social, and we can observe and analyze their group structures. Thus we find similarities in the developmental needs of apes and men.

2. The debate as to which part of man's behavior is determined by his biology and which by his culture will continue for decades. New facts suggest, however, that the limits are less clear and definite than once seemed likely, that biological, psychological, social, and cultural elements interpenetrate in many ways. Understanding human behavior requires knowledge about this borderline area.

Unfortunately for an understanding of the social or family patterns of our manlike relatives, few investigators have carried out *field* studies of their behavior in the natural habitat, where—not surprisingly—their group structure is different from that in the zoo.

C. R. Carpenter's study of the gibbon, part of which is presented below, is a classic. Recent work shows that the family patterns of the gorilla differ from those of the gibbon. Adequate data for the other two anthropoid apes, the chimpanzee and the orangutan, are not available.

Intragroup Relationships

C. R. CARPENTER

* * * * *

Male-Female Relationships

The grouping pattern characteristic of gibbons suggests that their courtship and mating activities differ from the mating relationships of the New World monkeys, . . . of gorillas, of chimpanzees, and . . . of macaques. . . . The association in gibbons is structured around a *pair* of animals which evidence strong bonds of attachment and form the core of the group. Although it is impossible to observe the establishment of bonds of mating in detail during field observations, nevertheless, by organizing large numbers of observations, the process of mating can be reliably reconstructed.

In the first place, given a parental family with a maturing male, the question arises as to how he obtains a mate. There are several possibilities; either he mates with one of the other siblings in the family, sister or half sister, or he mates with a suitable female from another semiclosed group. Also, he may mate with his mother, if the dominant male is by some means eliminated from the group. The maturing female has similar possibilities of mating with male siblings or with the father.

An example of mating within the group seemed to have been taking place in Group 1 with the two black young adults. These animals, as far as I could learn, were male and female siblings, although I could not have proved their sex without collecting them, and

C. R. Carpenter, "A Field Study of the Behavior and Social Relations of the Gibbon (*Hylobates lar*)," *Comparative Psychology*

this was impossible because they lived within the temple reservation. It was clearly observable that they were strongly attached to each other and were more closely associated than with others of the group. In fact, during some days for many hours this subgroup of young gibbons would be separated from the rest of the family (male, female, and infant) for many hours and by distances of several hundred yards. Perhaps in this case, a new family was *budding off* from the parent family in an incest type of mating.

If the young maturing male mates outside of his parent group, he must go through processes of breaking away from the original group, of exploring and of making contacts with many other groups in his search for a suitable mate. . . . Following this mating comes a process of establishing reciprocal bonds of attachment through what might be broadly viewed as mechanisms of conditioning. The probabilities are that in gibbons the mating bonds are fixed gradually over weeks or even months and that, once established, they are not ended by the completion of any phase of the sexual or reproductive cycle.

It is possible for a young male to find a suitable mate in some group of an adjacent territory during times when the parent groups come near each other. Sometimes neighboring groups actually intermingle for short periods of time.

Monographs, **16** (December, 1940), 127-129, 135-136, 143-145, 150-151. We are grateful to the author and *Comparative Psychology Monographs* of the University of California Press for permission to quote.

During such periods, a young male may find a suitable female and begin the initial stages of the mating process. Some young males may be completely cut off from the parent group and live temporarily as wanderers who go from group to group, exploring and eventually finding a mate while living tangentially to other groups. This would account for observed young males which were temporarily separated from groups. Similar contacts to those observed may be repeated many times before a pairing is made, since mating depends upon a specific state of maturity and physiological condition.

The foregoing description should not lead to the conclusion that the males are more aggressive in this respect than the females. I have no observations to support this fact. On the contrary, observations in the field and on my captive gibbons tentatively indicate that the males and females are about equally aggresssive both in pugnacity and in reproductive behavior. In fact, in two instances of pairings of captive gibbons, females took the initiative. Thus maturing young female gibbons may go through a parallel process of becoming more explorative with an increased drive for mating, breaking away from the parent group and eventually finding a suitable mate. This would lead to the prediction that in a gibbon population one might expect to find temporarily solitary young females as well as young males, and there [are] some data to support this assumption. The breaking away from the parent group by either the maturing male or female is believed to be mainly a result of the heightened sex drive, frustration of this and other drives, and the subsequent exploratory behavior.

The behavior of mated gibbons contrasts sharply with that of males and females in macaque groups or in hordes of baboons. In groups of primates which are organized on the mosaic, harem patterns with several males and many females in the large troop, tribe, or clan, there is competition among the males for the females and each male has his particular dominance status. Also, there is competition among the females during estrus for close relations with males and for maintenance of a female hierarchy of dominance. In the gibbon family, the dominance gradient is found between the mated male and female and among the young adults of the family. The activities of the adults may be said to be coaxial, perhaps cooperative, with reference to each other rather than competitive in most social activities.

* * * * *

Male-Young Relations

Very young gibbon infants stimulate the adult males to inspect, manipulate and groom them. Mild play between a male and an infant, in which the latter is usually the aggressor, may be observed throughout the period of growth.

One of the male's psychosocial functions is that of guarding the infants or juveniles of his family against animals from other groups, against enemies, and against other disturbances, such as hunters or observers. A few alarm calls by a young one will bring the male of a family swinging rapidly to its location. Even within the group, the guarding function is shown. During rough play or play fighting, an adult male may interfere while the young ones are struggling.

In a group of captive gibbons which I had assembled in Penang, Straits Settlements, in the summer of 1938, there was a male *Hylobates agalis* which had permitted a small juvenile to adopt him. The little fellow was carried much of the day by the adult, and this behavior suggests that there may be considerable *paternal* care in this species under conditions which may require it.

Furthermore, in a colony of captive gibbons I found that the males uniformly would attack vigorously any individual who tried to catch a young associated animal. These attacks would go further than mere biting at the keeper and would involve complex patterns of interference, such as holding the net or hand of the keeper or placing themselves between the keeper and the small animal which he was trying to catch. Behavior patterns which are usually judged to be expressions of extreme "jealousy" are shown. This type of aggressive behavior for the protection of other individuals deserves more careful study.

It may be concluded that a gibbon male plays with, grooms, and guards the young of his group when the necessity arises.

Sometime during early adulthood, a change occurs in the relational behavior of a developing young male and the dominant male of the family. Gradually the relationship seems to shift from that of compatibility to antagonistic responses characteristic of gibbons which are strange to each other. The conditioning stimuli which bring this about are little known. Perhaps sexual approaches to the mother are involved, and since gibbons are very "jealous," a situation would arise which would induce fighting. This fighting, in turn, would weaken the bonds of attachment and establish instead antagonistic relations.

One part of the greeting responses which occur between gibbons almost invariably involves visual, olfactory, and tactual inspection of the genitalia. When a strange animal is introduced into a group, this inspection is prepotent over every other kind of behavior. Perhaps with the maturation of the young males, rather specific genital stimuli become functional in arousing antagonistic responses in the adult males. In this greeting pattern, the approach is exploratory and neutral until the inspection takes place; then the activity takes on a fairly definite quality of friendliness or antagonism. The antagonistic responses are seen clearly in the actions of the adult males when this stage in the greeting pattern is reached.

* * * * *

Female-Infant Relationships

Almost invariably gibbons carry their infants low down over the pelvis, more or less to one side or the other and sometimes almost over one leg as it is held in a sharply flexed position. Occasionally the infant varies its form of grasping from that of holding around the mother's body and grasping her hair with its hands while holding on to the hair of the groin with its feet, to a position much lower down on the mother's belly where it grasps the legs of the mother from underneath. *Not once did I see a young gibbon being carried on its mother's back.*

When females carrying young infants stop to rest during the day, the infants usually leave their mothers and engage in various kinds of exploratory activity, such as pulling at leaves and flowers, trying out all kinds of swinging postures and locomotor gaits and generally playing "solitaire." When the infant nurses, the mother is usually seated with her body bent slightly forward. If the infants needs rest or sleep while the mother is quiet, it takes a position somewhere in the flexure of the mother's trunk and is further protected by the mother's long arms and legs. A furry enclosure is thus arranged which may be of considerable importance as a temperature-regulating arrangement for the young infant. In a sense, the mother forms a nest for her young from her own trunk and limbs.

As the infant gibbon matures, changes occur in its activities with reference to its mother. During the first month or six weeks, when it is still very spiderlike with long, thin, spindly legs and arms and short, downy hair, it rarely if ever leaves its mother; it maintains an almost continuous contact with her. Its first movements away from the mother occur when she is resting and other young animals of the group approach the infant and coax it to play, or at least try to use it as a play object. Beginning by reaching out with its long, thin arms and equally slender legs, it advances to a second stage involving momentary release of contact with the mother, movement away for short distances, and then hurried returns at the slightest provocation. The focus of behavior for the early infant is its mother; all activities are carried out with continuous reference to her and dependence on her.

The mother in turn usually shows solicitude for the infant. Frequently before a female starts to travel when her infant is a short distance away from her, she will pull it in and arrange it in a suitable position for carrying before she begins to brachiate. This greater handling of infants in gibbons as compared with platyrrhine types is perhaps a function in part of the anatomical differences; their lack of a tail, their upright posture, and the infants' less capable hands for manipulations, as well as the slower rate of maturation in the infant gibbon.

Decreasing dependence and increasing independence in the female-infant relationship consists of gradual changes in a number of important behavior patterns. Most important among these are the following: Even the very young infant is almost continuously exploring for foods, reaching, grasping, and carrying objects to its mouth. During the first few weeks of life, the intake of solid foods begins to supplement the mother's milk. Just as the getting of food from the breasts and warmth from her body conditions the infant toward its mother, so the getting of food away from her, accompanied by maturation of motor capacities, stimulates the infant to extend its explorations and become more active. Its need for warmth decreases as it grows a coat of hair. Frequent contacts with other young animals stimulate the infant to play and hence to establish a web of social bonds away from the mother. Increased locomotor capacities make the infant gibbon less dependent on the mother for movement from one place to another. Maturation of communicative behavior, involving movement patterns and sound signals, makes less necessary the *actual contact control* by the mother. These and other factors lead to a gradual weakening of the female-infant bond and finally to actual repulsion by the mother during the weaning period.

* * * * *

Infant-Infant Interaction

These observations show, in summary, that young gibbons pass through a stage during which they play alone, exploring, trying various forms of movement and postures. They play by themselves, with their hands and feet, and repeat over and over various postures and movements. Play patterns of the social type consist of chasing, catching, wrestling, and biting. Frequently the juveniles chase each other over a circuitous route which has jumps or swings that are repeated many times as the young gibbons engage in a kind of follow-the-leader game.

The amount of play varies in several ways. The diurnal variations include an early morning period of play which takes place before the group begins to move out to feeding places. The next period of most active play behavior occurs as the older animals settle down for the midday interval of rest. There is a third maximum about four or five o'clock in the afternoon as the group settles into a proper abode tree for the night. However, at any time when the group is relatively stationary, young animals may be seen playing. When the group is disturbed, and often the playful juveniles are the first to sense a disturbing object, play stops and the young give alarm calls and dash away.

From the point of view of the life cycle, the amount of play increases up to the stage of development classified as juvenile 3 or young adult. With maturation, the amount of play decreases and the decrease seems to be correlated with periods of inactivity in old animals. In addition to other basic physiological factors associated with age and the maturation of sexual behavior, play fighting seems to function to reduce the amount of social play and of general activity. These activities give way to greater differentiation and specialization of behavior and social attachments.

*　*　*　*　*

social relations as a developmental need in monkeys

two

The rare "isolated" human child, given physical care but little or no social experience, does not grow up normally. Lacking speech, exhibiting awkward or inept bodily adjustments to physical things, unable to initiate human contact, such a child proves to us how necessary the child's social relations are for normal development. Interestingly, the rhesus monkey can mature *physically* when he is deprived of a real mother but given a substitute terry cloth or wire form with a bottle for a breast. The infant monkey prefers the terry cloth mother. However, the monkey reared with such a substitute does not become a normal adult and cannot function in an adequate fashion.

The following section reviews this research and shows that monkeys *can* develop normally without mothers if they are allowed to experience enough social interaction with other young monkeys.

Social Deprivation in Monkeys

HARRY F. HARLOW   MARGARET K. HARLOW

*   *   *   *   *

Our investigations of the emotional development of our subjects grew out of the effort to produce and maintain a colony of sturdy, disease-free young animals for use in various research programs. By separating them from their mothers a few hours after birth and placing them in a more fully controlled regimen of nurture and physical care, we were able both to achieve a higher rate of survival and to remove the animals for testing without maternal protest. Only later did we realize that our monkeys were emotionally disturbed as well as sturdy and disease-free. . . .

Having separated the infant from its mother, our procedure was to keep it alone in a bare wire cage in a large room with other infants so housed. Thus each little monkey could see and hear others of its kind, although it could not make direct physical contact with them. The fifty-six animals raised in this manner now range in age from five to eight years. As a group they exhibit abnormalities of behavior rarely seen in animals born in the wild and brought to the laboratory as preadolescents or adolescents, even after the latter have been housed in individual cages for many years. The laboratory-born monkeys sit in their cages and stare fixedly into space, circle their cages in a repetitive streotyped manner, and clasp their heads in their hands or arms

Harry F. Harlow and Margaret K. Harlow, "Social Deprivation in Monkeys," *Scientific American*, **207** (November, 1962), 138-144. Reprinted with permission. Copyright © 1962 by Scientific American, Inc. All rights reserved.

and rock for long periods of time. They often develop compulsive habits, such as pinching precisely the same patch of skin on the chest between the same fingers hundreds of times a day; occasionally such behavior may become punitive, and the animal may chew and tear at its body until it bleeds. Often the approach of a human being becomes the stimulus to self-aggression. This behavior constitutes a complete breakdown and reversal of the normal defensive response; a monkey born in the wild will direct such threats and aggression at the approaching person, not at itself. Similar symptoms of emotional pathology are observed in deprived children in orphanages and in withdrawn adolescents and adults in mental hospitals.

William A. Mason, now at the Yerkes Laboratories of Primate Biology, compared the behavior of six of these animals, which were then two years old and had been housed all their lives in individual cages, with a matched group of rhesus monkeys that had been captured in the wild during their first year of life and housed together in captivity for a while before being individually housed in the laboratory. The most striking difference was that all the animals that had been born in the wild— and not one of the laboratory-born animals—displayed normal sex behavior. That the laboratory-born animals were not lacking in sex drive was indicated by the fact that the males frequently approached the females and the females displayed part of the pattern of sexual presentation. But they did not orient themselves correctly, and they did not succeed in mating. Moreover, the monkeys born in the wild had apparently learned to live with others in a stable hierarchy of dominance, or "pecking order"; consequently, in the pairing test they fought one another less and engaged more often in social grooming. They would also release a companion from a locked cage more frequently than did the laboratory-born animals, which usually ignored their caged partner's plight.

The severity of the affliction that grips these monkeys raised in the partial isolation of individual wire cages has become more apparent as they have grown older. They pay little or no attention to animals in neighboring cages; those caged with companions sit in opposite corners with only rare interaction. No heterosexual behavior has ever been observed between male and female cagemates, even between those that have lived together for as long as seven years. When efforts have been made to bring about matings, by pairing animals during the female's estrus, they have sometimes fought so viciously that they have had to be parted. Attempts to mate the socially deprived animals with sexually adequate and experienced monkeys from the breeding colony have been similarly frustrated.

In the summer of 1960 we undertook to devise a group-psychotherapy situation for nineteen of these animals—nine males and ten females—by using them to stock the monkey island in the municipal zoo in Madison, Wisconsin. This was their first experience outside the laboratory, and they had much to learn in order to survive. They had to learn to drink water from an open trough instead of from a tube in the wall of a cage, to compete for food in a communal feeding situation, to huddle together or find shelter from inclement weather, to climb rocks and avoid the water surrounding the island. Most dif-

ficult of all, they had to learn to live together. Within the first few days they made all the necessary physical adjustments. The three casualties—a male that drowned and two females that were injured and had to be returned to the laboratory—resulted from the stress of social adjustment. Fighting was severe at first; it decreased as effective dominance relations were established and friendship pairs formed. Grooming appeared in normal style and with almost normal frequency. A limited amount of sex behavior was observed, but it was infantile in form, with inadequate posturing by both females and males. In the hope of promoting therapy along this line we introduced our largest, strongest, and most effective breeding-colony male to the island around the middle of summer. He immediately established himself at the head of the dominance order. But in spite of his considerable persistence and patience he did not succeed in starting a single pregnancy.

Back in the laboratory these animals ceased to groom and fought more frequently. In pairings with breeding-colony monkeys, not one male has achieved a normal mount or intromission, and only one female has become pregnant. After two years we have had to conclude that the island experience was of no lasting value.

As the effects of the separation of these monkeys from their mothers in infancy were first becoming apparent in 1957, we were prompted to undertake a study of the mother-infant affectional bond. To each of one group of four animals separated from their mothers at birth we furnished a surrogate mother: a welded wire cylindrical form with the nipple of the feeding bottle protruding from its "breast" and with a wooden head surmounting it. The majority of the animals, sixty in all, were raised with cozier surrogate mothers covered by terry cloth. In connection with certain experiments, some of these individuals have had both a bare wire and a cloth-covered mother. The infants developed a strong attachment to the cloth mothers and little or none to the wire mothers, regardless of which one provided milk. In fright-inducing situations, the infants showed that they derived a strong sense of security from the presence of their cloth mothers. Even after two years of separation they exhibit a persistent attachment to the effigies.

In almost all other respects, however, the behavior of these monkeys at ages ranging from three to five years is indistinguishable from that of monkeys raised in bare wire cages with no source of contact comfort other than a gauze diaper pad. They are without question socially and sexually aberrant. No normal sex behavior has been observed in the living cages of any of the animals that have been housed with a companion of the opposite sex. In exposure to monkeys from the breeding colony, not one male and only one female has shown normal mating behavior and only four females have been successfully impregnated. Compared with the cage-raised monkeys, the surrogate-raised animals seem to be less aggressive, whether toward themselves or other monkeys. But they are also younger on the average, and their better dispositions can be attributed to their lesser age.

Thus the nourishment and contact comfort provided by the nursing cloth-covered mother in infancy does not produce a normal adolescent or adult. The surrogate cannot cradle the baby or communicate monkey sounds and gestures. It cannot punish for misbehavior or attempt to break the infant's bodily attachment before it becomes a fixation. The entire group of animals

separated from their mothers at birth and raised in individual wire cages, with or without surrogate, must be written off as potential breeding stock. Apparently their early social deprivation permanently impairs their ability to form effective relations with other monkeys, whether the opportunity was offered to them in the second six months of life or in the second to the fifth year of life.

One may correctly assume that total social isolation, compared with the partial isolation in which these subjects were reared, would produce even more devastating effects on later personality development. Such disastrous effects have been reported in the rare cases of children who have been liberated after months or years of lonely confinement in a darkened room. We have submitted a few monkeys to total isolation. Our purpose was to establish the maximum of social deprivation that would allow survival and also to determine whether or not there is a critical period in which social deprivation may have irreversible effects.

In our first study, a male and a female were housed alone from birth for a period of two years, each one in its own cubicle with solid walls. Their behavior could be observed through one-way vision screens and tested by remote control. The animals adapted to solid food slowly, but they had normal weight and good coats when they were removed from the isolation boxes at the end of two years. Throughout this period, neither animal had seen any living being other than itself.

They responded to their liberation by the crouching posture with which monkeys typically react to extreme threat. When placed together, each one crouched and made no further response to the other. Paired with younger monkeys from the group raised in partial isolation, they froze or fled when approached and made no effort to defend themselves from aggressive assaults. After another two years, in which they were kept together in a single large cage in the colony room, they showed the same abnormal fear of the sight or sound of other monkeys.

We are now engaged in studying the effects of six months of total social isolation. The first pair of monkeys, both males, has been out of isolation for eight months. They are housed, each monkey in its own cage, in racks with other monkeys of their age that were raised in the partial isolation of individual wire cages. For twenty minutes a day, five days a week, they are tested with a pair of these monkeys in the "playroom" of the laboratory. This room we designed to stimulate the young monkeys to a maximum of activity. It was not until the twelfth and twenty-seventh week, respectively, that the two totally deprived monkeys began to move and climb about. They now circulate freely but not as actively as the control animals. Although frequently attacked by the controls, neither one has attempted to defend itself or fight back; they either accept abuse or flee. One must be characterized as extremely disturbed and almost devoid of social behavior. The other resembles a normal two-month-old rhesus infant in its play and social behavior, and the indications are that it will never be able to make mature contacts with its peers.

A considerably more hopeful prognosis is indicated for two groups of four monkeys raised in total isolation for the much shorter period of eighty days. In their cubicles these animals had the contact comfort of a cloth-covered surrogate. They were deficient in social behavior during the first test periods in the playroom. But they made rapid gains; now, eight months later, we rate them as "almost normal" in play, defense, and sex behavior. At least seven of the eight seem to bear no permanent scars as the result of early isolation.

Our first few experiments in the total isolation of these animals would thus appear to have bracketed what may be the critical period of development during which social experience is necessary for normal behavior in later life. We have additional experiments in progress, involving a second pair that will have been isolated for six months and a first pair that will have been isolated for a full year. The indications are that six months of isolation will render the animals permanently inadequate. Since the rhesus monkey is more mature than the human infant at birth and grows four times more rapidly, this is equivalent to two or three years for the human child. On the other hand, there is reason to believe that the effects of shorter periods of early isolation, perhaps sixty to ninety days or even more, are clearly reversible. This would be equivalent to about six months in the development of the human infant. The time probably varies with the individual and with the experiences to which it is exposed once it is removed from isolation. Beyond a brief period of neonatal grace, however, the evidence suggests that every additional week or month of social deprivation increasingly imperils social development in the rhesus monkey. Case studies of children reared in impersonal institutions or in homes with indifferent mothers or nurses show a frightening comparability. The child may remain relatively unharmed through the first six months of life. But from this time on the damage is progressive and cumulative. By one year of age he may sustain enduring emotional scars, and by two years many children have reached the point of no return.

*　*　*　*　*

a biological basis for the incest taboo

three

For generations, sociologists and anthropologists have developed theories and gathered facts about the nearly universal prohibition against both marriage and sexual relations among all members of the conjugal family except husband and wife. Freud wrote an elaborate speculation about its origins, since the incest taboo is so important an element in his Oedipus theory. An examination of the consequences that would follow from violation of the taboo shows that there would be much confusion of family roles (e.g., father *vs.* lover); a turning inward of the family, away from ties linking it with other families; serious problems in the allocation of tasks and responsibilities; an undermining of the rules of legitimacy; and so on.

However, the aversion and moral objection to incest do not arise from a rational calculation about its consequences. Young people acquire these feelings long before they learn any reasons justifying them. Moreover, since so many societies approve many actions that seem self-destructive or unproductive, it is not out of place at least to speculate about the origins or bases of the incest taboo, other than the recurring transmission of these feelings from parents to children. The following article attempts to link this family pattern to certain biological processes among the higher mammals.

The Incest Taboo and the Mating Patterns of Animals

x

Error

DAVID F. ABERLE
URIE BRONFENBRENNER
ECKHARD H. HESS

DANIEL R. MILLER
DAVID M. SCHNEIDER
JAMES N. SPUHLER

*   *   *   *   *

The incest taboo in any society consists of a set of prohibitions which out-

David F. Aberle, Urie Bronfenbrenner, Eckhard H. Hess, Daniel R. Miller, David M. Schneider, and James N. Spuhler, "The Incest Taboo and the Mating Behavior of Animals," *American Anthropologist*, **65** (April, 1963), 253-264. We are grateful to the authors and *American Anthropologist* for permission to quote.

law heterosexual relationships between various categories of kinsmen. Almost always, it includes prohibitions on sexual relations between brother and sister, father and daughter, mother and son. Invariably, where any prohibitions are present, other, nonprimary relatives are tabooed as well. There are rare cases where the taboos seem to have been abandoned. In the main, these

the incest taboo and the mating patterns of animals   **11** involve very small groups in some way or other isolated from other populations to a degree which makes it impossible to maintain the taboo if the group is to reproduce at all. There are other cases where sexual relations between brother and sister or father and daughter are permitted or prescribed for special categories (e.g., chiefs, kings) or under special circumstances (e.g., ritual). It must be emphasized, however, that in the very societies where these sexual relations are permitted to some people, or under some circumstances, they are forbidden to the bulk of people and under most circumstances. Incest prohibitions are not always obeyed, but we will not attempt here to discuss rates, causes, or consequences of transgressions.

Most theories about the incest taboo attempt to account for its origin and persistence, but especially for the origin and persistence of the taboo on sexual relationships within the nuclear family. (Here and elsewhere, the phrase "sexual relationships within the nuclear family" will refer to sexual relationships between brother and sister, father and daughter, and mother and son. The phrase "familial incest taboo" will refer to the prohibition of these relationships.) It is hard to provide satisfactory support for any theory which attempts to account for a universal phenomenon. (Thus far, almost no theory of the origin of the incest taboo which has any currency has attempted to utilize the exceptions to universality noted above to account for origins. For all practical purposes, virtually all theories treat the familial taboo as a universal in discussing origins.) With a little ingenuity, virtually any universal phenomenon can be explained by, or be used to explain the existence of, any other universal phenomenon in the realm under discussion. There are no criteria save aesthetics and logical consistency for

choosing among theories, since there is no possibility of demonstrating that A varies with B, if both A and B are universally and invariably present. Futhermore, most of the theories about the incest taboo provide a demonstration that in one or another sense it is adaptive, and thereby often confuse the question of origin and the question of persistence. It is not logically admissible to assert that a phenomenon has come to exist because it is adaptive: that men grew noses because they support spectacles. It can be said only that if something comes into existence which has superior adaptive potential, it is likely to be perpetuated or to spread. The question of the cause of its origin, however, remains unsolved.

Our concern, then, was to account for the origin of the incest taboo and to find a range of phenomena such that the familial incest taboo need not be treated as a universal. This range of phenomena was the mating behavior of humans and certain other animals. Before this mating behavior is discussed, it is necessary to outline some of the theories respecting the origin and persistence of the incest taboo.

1. *The inbreeding theory.* This theory asserts that the mating of close kin produces bad results, such as abnormal, enfeebled, or insufficiently numerous offspring. The incest taboo is therefore adaptive because it limits inbreeding, and arose on that account. . . .

2. *The socialization theory.* This theory asserts that the regulation and control of erotic impulses is an indispensable element in socialization—that it serves to maintain the growing child's motivation to accept the roles that he is taught. These roles include extrafamilial and societywide roles as well as those in the nuclear family. Since societies must be larger than a single nuclear family to be viable, and since

nonfamilial roles are different from family roles, these roles in the wider society must be learned by the child. In order for this learning to occur, the socializing agent must control but not directly gratify the child's erotic impulses. Therefore it is necessary that these impulses be frustrated and directed outside the nuclear family. The incest taboo does this.

3. *The family theory.* This theory asserts that unregulated sexual competition is disruptive for any group, that the family is a crucial group, and that the incest taboo is needed to maintain the family intact. The theory asserts that the incest taboo originated because it served this function. Freud, one of the proponents of this theory, made a vigorous effort to imagine the series of events which could have led from promiscuity and unregulated, lethal competition to the final promulgation of nuclear family taboos.

4. *The social and cultural system theory.* This theory asserts that, left to their own devices, human beings would prefer to mate within the family, but that the advantages of a wider group for mutual aid, collective economic security, internal peace, offense and defense, and of a wider group for the sharing of cultural innovations make family and suprafamily exogamy highly adaptive as a device for joining families or larger kinship groups. These advantages would be marked in any kinship-based society but were crucial in early human history. This is so because the first ordered human group to emerge was the family, and the incest taboo and exogamy permitted a society built on existing materials: these devices linked families by bonds developed within the family—the ties of parents and children and of siblings. Because of the strong tendency to mate within the family, the familial incest taboos were necessary to insure exogamy. . . .

5. *The indifference or revulsion the-ory.* According to this theory, the incest taboo is either a formal expression of the sexual indifference of kinsmen toward each other, or a formal expression of an instinctive horror of sexual relations among kinsmen. . . .

6. *The demographic theory.* This theory holds that for early man, the short life span, small number of offspring to reach maturity, spacing of those offspring, and random sex ratio made intrafamilial inbreeding a virtual demographic impossibility. Hence very early man bred out by necessity. Later, when technological improvements made for larger families and longer life, and intrafamilial mating became possible, the already existing pattern of familial exogamy was given normative backing through the creation of the familial incest taboo. This taboo sustained a practice advantageous from the point of view of group cooperation. . . .

We omit various theories which center on the role of religious or mystical ideas in determining the specific prohibition on incest. . . . We do not explicitly consider the numerous composite theories, most of which combine various elements from Theories 1-4 to arrive at their conclusions.

We will now discuss various criticisms that have been, or might be, directed at each of the six theories. The criticisms themselves are of three types. (1) The adaptive value claimed by the theory for the incest taboo may be rejected. (2) The adaptive value claimed by the theory for the incest taboo may be accepted, but the possibility that the adaptive quality gave rise to the taboo may be disputed. (3) The adaptive value claimed by the theory may be accepted, but the necessity to achieve this result through the incest taboo may be denied.

The inbreeding theory in its simplest

form has been rejected for decades because it was thought to be wrong. In its pregenetic form the inbreeding theory asserted that inbreeding caused a weakening or deterioration of the stock. The facts of genetics provided a simple corrective to this notion. It was found that inbreeding could not produce "deterioration" but could only bring to expression what was already present in the stock, by producing offspring homozygous for some recessive character. Therefore, it was argued, if deleterious recessives were present, they would appear with greater frequency as a result of inbreeding, but if advantageous recessives were present, they would also receive full expression. Thus the disadvantages of inbreeding were offset by the advantages.

This simple corrective, however, does not stand up in the face of new information from the field of population genetics. . . . First, it has become clear that the ratio of deleterious and lethal recessive genes to selectively advantageous genes is very high indeed. This results from the random character of mutation. Second, as we move from (biologically defined) second cousin matings to first cousin matings to parent-child or sibling matings, both the models of population genetics and the experimental and observational evidence from animals indicate that the reduction of heterozygocity increases rapidly, and hence that the percentage of individuals homozygous for lethal or deleterious recessive genes also rises sharply. The same is true of course for adaptive recessive forms. Provided that the species in question can stand the loss of many offspring, close inbreeding can provide a superior strain—superior either from the point of view of adaptation to the environment or from the point of view of a human being practicing the selective breeding of some plant or animal domesticate. But where births are widely spaced, where the animal produces few offspring at a time, or only one, and where the animal reaches reproductive maturity only slowly, the closely inbred population may not be able to stand either culling or natural selection. The abortions, stillbirths, animals incapable of surviving to reproductive maturity, and the animals whose breeding period or capacity to rear their young is drastically shortened, through the inheritance of homozygous, disadvantageous recessive genes, may so reduce the total effective breeding population as to make its survival impossible, or as to result in its expulsion from its niche by an expanding, neighboring population. Close inbreeding of rats is possible over many generations; with chickens the process becomes more difficult; with cattle it seems to be impossible. Thus, in the perspective of population genetics, close inbreeding of an animal like man has definite biological disadvantages, and these disadvantages are far more evident as respects the mating of primary relatives than as respects other matings. Hence the biological advantages of the familial incest taboo cannot be ignored.

It is difficult to see, however, how primitive man would come to understand the connection between familial inbreeding and low net reproductive rate or the production of monstrosities. We will return to this point.

It is often argued, however, that since many simple societies regard the marriage of first cross-cousins as highly desirable, the incest taboo by no means eliminates fairly close inbreeding. In this connection we must stress the fact that the familial incest taboo is virtually universal, and that familial inbreeding shows far more effects from the point of view of population genetics than cousin inbreeding.

The socialization theory is difficult to deal with. Fundamentally, it rests on psychoanalytic hypotheses of fixation and regression and regression which have not yet been fully demonstrated. For this reason we will not attempt to discuss it further here.

The family theory has certain empirical difficulties. It rests on the supposed acute conflict that would arise out of sexual rivalries between father and son over mother and sister, between mother and daughter over father and brother, between brothers over sisters, and sisters over brothers. Yet father and son, mother and daughter, brother and brother, sister and sister do in fact share sexual partners in a number of societies. With polyandry, father and son sometimes share the same wife (but not the son's mother), or brothers share the same wife (but not their sister). With polygyny, mother and daughter sometimes share the same husband (but not the daughter's father), or sisters share the same husband (but not their brother); there are a large number of instances of institutionalized sharing of sexual favors outside the marital bond, as well.

These objections to the family theory do not lead to the conclusion that the family could tolerate *unregulated* intrafamilial sexual relations. There is ample evidence that sexual competition is disruptive. But there would seem to be two solutions to the problem of maintaining order within the family, rather than one. The first solution is of course the interdiction of sexual relations except for the parents: the familial incest taboo. The second, however, is the institutionalization of sexual access in the family. This would define the time, place, and rate of access of each member of the family to every other. This institutionalization could not be a complete solution for all families. In some families there would be no male offspring, and in others no female. Cohabitation with the parent of opposite sex would temporarily solve this problem, but since children normally outlive their parents, the solution would be only temporary. Nevertheless, it would be possible to adopt this sort of institutionalization as the primary pattern, with secondary alternatives available. Thus societies with other preferential, or even prescribed, mating patterns, must ordinarily afford alternatives to these patterns, or redefine the groups suitable for prescribed alliances over time.

The family theory has one distinctive advantage. It is easy to see how human groups might evolve rules to deal with immediate and obvious potential sources of disruption of social life. If indeed jealousy threatened the integrity of the family, it is possible to conceive of the development of norms to cope with this. And the incest prohibitions of any society constitute a set of conscious norms.

The social and cultural system theory, especially in its evolutionary form, as stated by White, does not raise serious empirical difficulties. It is clear that the advantages postulated by White exist, and that, given a tendency to choose the most easily available mates, a complete prohibition on familial sexual relations is the simplest device for forcing ties between families. His theory seems to assert that because this shift was advantageous, it came into being. Yet, like the family theory, this theory requires a movement in opposition to certain strong trends. It requires the elimination of some younger members from the family, in spite of emotional attachments, and entrusting these members to groups where stable relationships do not yet exist. It also requires that primitive men understand the advantages of the exchange—or else must assume that familial exogamy and the familial taboo arose as a chance "mutation" and survived because of their adaptive character.

The indifference theory has both logical and empirical difficulties. It is hard to see why what is naturally repugnant should be tabooed, and the evidence for sexual attraction among kinsmen is quite adequate for rejecting the theory. We mention it only for the sake of completeness.

The demographic theory makes certain assumptions about the life span, breeding period, etc., of very early man. If these assumptions are correct, most of the rest of what is said in this presentation is irrelevant and unnecessary. But if any of its assumptions about age of maturity or spacing of births or length of breeding period can subsequently be shown to be wrong, this theory would also face difficulties. It serves to remind us of the number of implicit or explicit assumptions about the time and conditions of the emergence of the incest taboo which are made in the case of each theory. M. K. Slater assumes a cooperative group and normal breeding population larger than the family; L. A. White and our work group assume a situation where family cooperative relationships have become reasonably firm, whereas interfamily relationships are fluctuating and unstable. Either approach, and various others, make assumptions about the biology and social life of our ancestors which cannot be fully validated at present. More primatological and archeological data may still make it possible to choose more carefully among these assumptions.

Thus far, for all of these theories except the demographic and the socialization theories, there are either empirical objections as regards their validity, or logical difficulties in understanding how the function that the taboo supposedly fulfills would have led to institutionalization of the taboo, or both.

It should be noted that the empirical objections do not apply to the inbreeding theory or to the social and cultural system theory; in each case it seems fair to say that the advantages postulated would have resulted from the familial taboo, and that, for primitive man, it is hard to see what other device might have been an effective alternative.

In order to broaden the range of phenomena to be considered, let us now turn to the realm of animal behavior. We will here restrict the term "animal" to birds and nonhuman mammals. There is a wide range of behavior as regards inbreeding among animals. At one end of the spectrum there is no restriction on matings except opportunity. At the other end, there is no intrafamilial mating whatever, except for the parental pair. (An animal family will be defined as a relatively stable grouping of two generations of animals, of both sexes, including at least one sexual partnership, and smaller than a band of animals.) The most spectacular limitation on familial inbreeding is found in the case of the Canada Goose and the Graylag Goose. The behavior of the Canada Goose will be described here, based on observations by E. H. Hess.

The young geese hatch in the spring. The following spring they are not sexually mature, but are driven away from the family group while the parents rear the new brood. When the new brood is a few months old, the young from the previous year's brood rejoin the family group. During the next spring, the parents again drive off the older broods while they rear the current brood, and the older broods again join the family group a few months later. Hence, quite a large family develops. In the third year, the goslings from the first brood are sexually mature. They mate with individuals from other families. They will not mate with siblings or with the opposite-sex parent. The newly formed pairs may join either family of orientation, making one of the families even larger, or they may start their own family groups. Thus in the Canada Goose, parents and children tend to remain in the same larger group after the young mature. These ties are very stable. Indeed, mating tends to be for life.

Experimental work on the Canada Goose indicates that this fastidious behavior is the result of sexual imprinting. It is necessary to emphasize that the reaction persists without external sanctions. The luckless breeder who takes a male and a female from the same brood to raise geese is doomed to disappointment: the pair will not mate even if no other partners are available. If, however, two members of the same brood are separated before hatching occurs and are subsequently reintroduced to each other, having been raised in different families, they may become mates.

There is no evidence to suggest that asexual imprinting occurs among mammals. There the principal mechanism limiting inbreeding in animal groups with families—where there is such a mechanism—seems to take the form of competition between the parent and its same-sex child when this child approaches or reaches sexual maturity. The older animal's superior size and strength normally result in the expulsion of the young animal from the family, so that it is forced to mate elsewhere. In the course of time, an older animal becomes enfeebled and may be overcome, so that some intrafamilial mating will occur, but on a statistical basis this mechanism of intergenerational competition does insure a large amount of outbreeding. It is particularly effective where most births are single births, so that two siblings of opposite sex rarely become sexually mature at the same time. The beaver seems to expel its sexually mature young, and this may be true of the gibbon.

Among animals with apparent complete promiscuity may be mentioned the rat, the spider monkey, and the macaque. (By "promiscuity" we refer to patterns which result in the animal's mating indifferently with siblings, parents, or others. Since there are more "others," promiscuity involves a preponderance of outbreeding as regards primary relatives. Promiscuity need not imply truly random mating. Size, strength, age, and so forth always result in some departure from randomness, if only in the ordering of the sequence of copulatory partnerships.)

Sexual behavior among animals, as has been said, varies from complete promiscuity to complete elimination of familial inbreeding. Under what circumstances is elimination of familial inbreeding likely to occur? It would seem that, on a cross-species basis, restriction of inbreeding, whether by competition or by asexual imprinting, is found among the larger, longer-lived, slower-maturing, and more intelligent animals. On a cross-species basis, these are also relatively late evolutionary products. Those species which limit inbreeding are among those which form families, although not all species that form families limit inbreeding. It would appear that a certain level of intelligence and length of life are necessary for animals to form stable attachments —that otherwise they will breed with kin or nonkin indifferently. When stable attachments are combined with familial groupings, however, they give rise to the potentiality for close inbreeding. Thus there seems to be an empirical tendency for barriers against close inbreeding to be found where close inbreeding would otherwise be most likely to occur. Finally, it should be mentioned that, among birds, asexual imprinting is particularly common in species which have both stable families and larger than familial groupings —a feature which we have not tried to account for.[1]

We will now bring the animal and human data into juxtaposition and define the range of mating behavior which we will attempt to explain. Some animals have no barriers which prevent parent-child, brother-sister matings. Some animals have barriers which reduce or prevent such matings. Humans drastically limit such matings through the familial incest taboo. Thus human beings share with some animals a limitation on familial inbreeding, even though the mechanism of limitation differs from those of all animal species. Only humans have any limitations on mate choice beyond the nuclear family: in no human society is the incest taboo limited to the nuclear family, whatever its range of variation may be.[2]

Let us first consider these facts in the light of the genetic theory. It has been suggested above that close inbreeding might not be deleterious to animals which mature quickly and have numerous offspring. It is in such cases that promiscuity is most likely, and promiscuity itself tends to reduce inbreeding, on a purely statistical basis. So even here, close inbreeding is unlikely. Where intensive inbreeding is most likely to occur, barriers are common. The more intelligent, slower-maturing animals living in family groups, where stable attachments are likely, and human beings, who also live in family

groups where stable attachments are likely, manifest patterns which limit familial inbreeding: asexual imprinting, intergenerational competition, and the familial incest taboo. We suggest that with the emergence of culture, if not before, relatively stable family groupings in the human evolutionary line required *some* limitation on familial inbreeding. From this inference alone, however, one cannot predict the familial incest taboo.

Asexual imprinting would be an equally effective mechanism—but it does not seem to occur in man, the apes, the monkeys, or even in more remote mammalian species. It is plausible to assume that this adaptive device was simply not available—not a part of the genetic equipment of man's ancestors or relatives. Intergenerational competition, however, would seem, at first blush, to be a feasible alternative. Competing with others to get and to keep mates is a widespread mammalian pattern, though not a universal one. Nothing is required to bend it in the service of limiting inbreeding except that it be directed to maturing members of the family as well as to outsiders—and this does not represent a change in pattern, but merely the preservation of the mechanism as family life develops.

If, for any reason, a gap develops between the point at which the young animal is sexually mature and the point at which it is capable of fending for itself, expulsion becomes an unsuitable mechanism. There is such a gap in all known human groups—or at least in no known human group does the onset of sexual maturity coincide with *full* assumption of adult economic and social responsibilities. Even where marriage occurs at a very early age—indeed, especially where it does—the youthful marital partner, or pair, remains under the direction of senior members of the

---

[1] The socialization theory would profit from the examination of animal cases where the young learn a fairly large part of their response repertory from their parents.

[2] Here and at other points we must except those rare cases where the familial taboo has been partially or wholly abrogated for the sake of the propagation of the group.

kingroup. In early human or proto-human society, a gap of even a year between sexual maturity and the capacity to operate independently would create problems for a family unit which used intergenerational competition and expulsion to limit inbreeding. If expulsion continued, the young would be exposed to dangers—unless they could find acceptance in another group, which would presuppose no intergenerational competition in the other group. If expulsion were abandoned, the family unit would be exposed both to an increase of the impetus toward inbreeding and to unregulated sexual competition within the familial unit. A gap between sexual maturity and full capacity could occur either through changes of maturational pattern or through the development of culture and the consequent need for time to transmit cultural information, information about the local scene, and so forth, or both. The incest taboo is a cultural phenomenon, and we must therefore assume that it emerged concomitantly with, or subsequent to, the beginnings of culture. We cannot, however, be certain whether the gap between sexual maturity and full performance was a matter of culture, physical maturation, or both.

What we seek is a situation which will result in the normative definition of the nuclear incest taboo. If, as can safely be assumed, unregulated sexuality is incompatible with a stable family unit, and if expulsion of the sexually maturing human animal is not possible, then the problem of maintaining order within the family posed by sexual competition would have to be solved. As has been said, two solutions are possible: institutionalized sexual access within the family, or the familial incest taboo. Either solves the competitive problem. Either is within the scope of a human animal with language and limited culture. The problem of order within the nuclear family would also be observable as a pressing problem, on a day-to-day basis, and the sources of the problem in sexual competition would be equally evident. Either mechanism might be adopted: regulation of sex, or its elimination from the family. But whereas either mechanism would solve the problem of order, only one mechanism, the familial taboo, would solve the genetic problem. Hence that group, or those groups of human beings which adopted a taboo on intrafamilial mating would have an advantage both over those groups which could not solve the problem of order and over those groups which solved the problem by institutionalized intrafamilial sexual activity, thereby encouraging close inbreeding. Hence, over time, only the familial incest taboo could survive, because of its superior selective advantages.

We suggest, then, that man, along with certain other animals, is particularly vulnerable to deleterious effects arising out of close and continuous inbreeding, and that he shares with these animals the characteristic of having a mechanism which limits or prevents inbreeding within the family. We suggest that this problem may have been the underlying cause for the development of the familial incest taboo, since man shares a limitation on familial inbreeding with other animals which are not cultural, which socialize their young far less elaborately than do humans, which do not have to educate them for role systems in a wider cultural order, and which do not have to cope with the problem of ordering the relationships of a number of potential sexual competitors in the same family. This suggestion of a common core shared by the various devices of animals and humans which limit familial inbreeding has the advantage of theoretical parsimony. It is also open to partial test, since there are a large number of studies of animals which could be carried out to demonstrate whether the variations we suggest on the basis of somewhat piecemeal evidence in fact occur. But the human device, the familial incest taboo, is unique to humans, and is both required by and made possible by culture. The incest taboo requires symbols, but it becomes significant only when expulsion from the family is impossible: a state of affairs largely, though perhaps not wholly, dependent on the existence of a corpus of cultural tradition which must be fully transmitted for adequate functioning as an adult to occur.

The familial taboo has of course the *de facto* result of linking families, as well as of solving the problem of order within the family and the genetic problem. The stable attachments between individuals long associated in family units which make intrafamilial mating so potent a possibility also create ties of interest and sentiment between members of an original family of procreation as they disperse. The advantages of ties between families have been clearly pointed out . . . : an enlarged circle of cooperation, sharing, offense, and defense. These advantages, in turn, generate the last phenomenon to be accounted for: the fact that in no animal group are there restrictions on inbreeding except for the family unit, whereas in no human group are incest taboos limited to the nuclear family. Once the familial taboo is in existence, extensions of the taboo to other categories of kin become a simple evolutionary step. Whether this step is made by stimulus generalization, planning, aesthetic reactions, or whatever, its adaptive value is such as to perpetuate the extensions, which increase the circle of cooperation still further.

Extensions of the incest taboo beyond the family sometimes involve permitted, preferential, or theoretically prescribed matings between first cousins. Hence the extensions may involve no further genetic advantage. Once again we must point out that the results of the familial inbreeding are genetically far more deleterious than those of first cousin matings.

* * * * *

In sum, we propose that the adoption of the familial incest taboo was adaptive primarily because of the genetic results of close inbreeding, and that man's familial taboo is to be considered part of the class of devices which limit familial inbreeding among intelligent, slow-maturing animals which bear few offspring at a time and which live in family units. The selection of the taboo, however, we hypothesize, occurred through efforts to solve the problem of sexual competition within the family in a cultural animal with an organized family life. Among the available mechanisms, the incest taboo solved this problem and the genetic problem. Other alternatives solved only one of these problems. Hence it had high selective value. We suggest that it might not have come into being as a response to needs for cooperation between families, but that, once it existed, it did promote this cooperation, which had an adaptive function of little significance for animals. Finally, the familial taboo could be extended, by a simple evolutionary step, to a wider group of kinsmen, with great selective advantages. To date, some combination of the various advantages imputed to the nuclear and more extended incest taboos has resulted in their perpetuation, even in postindustrial societies organized as states. The taboo in some form or other is likely to survive so long as the family remains a significant part of the social order.

Part 2

societal
recognition
of the
family
unit

legitimacy and illegitimacy

four

All societies "forbid" illegitimate births, each following its own definition of what is legitimate. In spite of varying definitions, all succeed in pinning responsibility for the maintenance, socialization, and social control of the child on a definite family unit. Illegitimacy as an individual case or as a social category arouses moral disapproval, yet societies do not seriously consider all the possible solutions to this "problem." Here one of the foremost family sociologists examines the phenomenon of legitimacy and its mirror image, illegitimacy, in order to see how much the society might have to sacrifice in order to rid itself entirely of the latter.

Illegitimacy and the Social Structure

KINGSLEY DAVIS

The bastard, like the prostitute, thief, and beggar, belongs to that motley crowd of disreputable social types which society has generally resented, always endured. He is a living symbol of social

Kingsley Davis, "Illegitimacy and the Social Structure," *The American Journal of Sociology*, **45** (September, 1939), 215-233. Reprinted by permission of The University of Chicago Press.

irregularity, an undeniable evidence of contramoral forces; in short, a problem —a problem as old and unsolved as human existence itself.

Down the ages this problem has remained a matter of morals and policy rather than of scientific theory. It has been viewed as an evil occurrence, calling in each case for a distribution of blame, a manifestation of repentance, and an adjustment of rights and duties.

Such moral preoccupation has contributed a great deal to the efficient operation of the institutional system, but it has given little to science except an added object of study. Scientific interest in a social problem emerges only when the moral norms by which the thing is judged evil are themselves subjected to analysis rather than taken for granted. In other words, the early preoccupation of social science with the irregular and contramoral aspects of human life was generally unscientific. It was the "problem approach." Not until the regular and moral aspects themselves were subjected to scrutiny could scientific validity be achieved, for the contramoral is always functionally related to the moral, illegitimacy to legitimacy.[1]

The Question of Causation

Even today the literature on illegitimacy is mainly a problem literature. It is true that it relies upon statistical findings and seeks objectively to discover causes; but since the principal aim of the causal investigation is simply to find more intelligent ways of handling, or remedies for, the "problem" (thus taking for granted the values which define it as a problem), the usual analysis of causes seems theoretically unsound.

Willystine Goodsell declares that "with almost complete unanimity social investigators agree upon a variety of causes, both personal and social, for the prevalence of illegitimacy." She then cites the lists of alleged causes given by Mangold, Kammerer, and Lundberg.[2] These include such factors as "ignorance and low ideals," "defective home life," "vicious neighborhood conditions," "demoralizing education," "mental abnormality," and so forth. She seems unacquainted, however, with another, less current type of analysis, which controverts her opinion of "almost complete unanimity." This second approach is represented by the works of Brinton, Malinowski, Robbins, and Deak.[3] Its central thesis is epigrammatically stated in Brinton's words:

Bastardy and marriage in this world are quite supplementary—you cannot have one without the other. In another world, you may indeed separate the two institutions and eliminate one of them, either by having marriage so perfect—in various senses—that no one will ever commit fornication or adultery, or by having fornication so perfect that no one will ever commit marriage. But these are definitely other worlds.[4]

There are thus really two different approaches to the study of the causation of illegitimacy. One we shall call the "social welfare" interpretation; the other, the "sociological" approach.

Social Welfare Approach

The social worker's point of view toward societal phenomena is that of a person required to achieve practical, immediate goals by dealing with concrete situations. The causes of illegiti-

---

[1] For an analysis of the nature of social problems and a critique of the usual approach to them, see Willard Waller, "Social Problems and the Mores," *American Sociological Review*, 1 (December, 1936), 922-933. The early preoccupation with the irregular in society as against the regular is illustrated by *The Encyclopedia of the Social Sciences*, which contains two lengthy articles on illegitimacy but nothing on legitimacy.

[2] *Problems of the Family*, rev. ed. (New York: Appleton-Century-Crofts, 1936), p. 365.

[3] Crane Brinton, *French Revolutionary Legislation on Illegitimacy 1789-1804* (Cambridge: Harvard University Press, 1936); Bronislaw Malinowski, "Parenthood," *The New Generation*, V. F. Calverton and S. D. Schmalhausen, eds. (New York: Citadel Press, 1930); H. H. Robbins and Francis Deak, "The Familial Property Rights of Illegitimate Children: A Comparative Study," *Columbia Law Review*, 30 (March, 1930), 308-329.

[4] Brinton, *op. cit.*, p. 83.

macy from this standpoint, such as low mentality or bad home conditions, are not so much causes of the total phenomenon as explanations of why particular women become illegitimate mothers.[5] An understanding of the total phenomenon requires that we get behind the personal motives in particular cases and penetrate to the system of norms on which personal motives are premised. We must analyze the very sentiments which define a birth as legitimate or illegitimate—in short, the institutional norms of reproduction.[6]

Interpretation in terms of specific factors, such as mental abnormality, bad home conditions, or bad employment situations, generally assumes a stable institutional system (and the values that go with it) without which the factors could not operate. But this system is assumed only unconsciously and is hence left unanalyzed. Therefore the degree of generalization obtained is quite low; as soon as the discourse shifts to another society—or even another social class or epoch—the conclusions do not follow.

This becomes clear if we ask why certain factors are seized upon as important. Is it that sheer scientific curiosity finds certain traits to be common to large numbers of cases of illegitimacy? If so, why are so many uniformities in these cases ignored? Actually it would seem that certain factors strike the attention of the welfare theorist because they are culturally abnormal or disapproved. The welfare worker tends to regard as determinants of illegitimacy those events which, like illegitimacy itself, are considered unfortunate and in need of remedy. Being in the habit of focusing attention upon things that require remedial work anyway, it is natural that he should fall into a species of the like-causes-like fallacy—in this case, the theory that evil causes evil. Thus he is likely to observe that in a large number of cases the illegitimate mothers were so situated in their work that clandestine sexual advances could easily be made, and he then records as a factor in illegitimacy "demoralizing employment conditions." But there is another common factor in these same cases that escapes notice: the mothers did not practice contraception, or they practiced it inefficiently. Why is this not equally a cause? Because, presumably, failure to use contraception is not an "evil," while "demoralizing employment" is.[7]

---

[5] This approach resembles that found in much of the literature on prostitution, where attention is largely confined to the question of why girls enter the profession. See Kingsley Davis, "The Sociology of Prostitution," *American Sociological Review*, 2 (October, 1937), 749-755. It should be realized that just as it takes two to make an act of prostitution, so it takes two to procreate an illegitimate child. If one is to reason in terms of the motivation of becoming an illegitimate parent, the father as well as the mother must be considered. The preoccupation with the female in the discussion of "causes" reflects not only the difficulty of studying illegitimate fathers, but also the double standard of morality.

[6] It is understandable that the social welfare interpretation has been too restricted to concrete cases and practical goals to do a good job of abstract analysis. Remedial workers cannot be expected to construct abstruse scientific theories. But this being true, no one should make the mistake of regarding social welfare literature as the authoritative approach to illegitimacy (or any other social phenomenon). Above all, social-work authors cannot legitimately take their own analyses for complete scientific statements and blind themselves to any other discussions as being "too theoretical."

[7] Since many things are regarded as evil because of their evil effects, this reasoning tends to become circular. P. G. Kammerer, e.g., *The Unmarried Mother: A Study of Five Hundred Cases* (Boston: Little, Brown & Co., 1918), p. 320, gives as one of the causes of illegitimacy "evil companions." Obviously, companions are judged to be evil by what they do and what they lead others to do.

Once the factors are chosen on this evil-causes-evil principle, a search is begun for measures which, if taken, will reduce the extent of illegitimacy. The primary aim is to prevent the entrance of women into the ranks of illegitimate mothers, but, as so often happens, the remedial purpose limits the theoretical understanding to such an extent as to defeat the achievement of the purpose. One striking example of this type of reasoning is the failure to distinguish immoral sex relations from the procreation of illegitimate children. Illicit sex relations are generally a matter of inclination and intention; the procreation of bastards a matter of neither, but an undesired and unintended accident. An explanation of the former is by no means an explanation of the latter, nor is prevention of the former necessary for the prevention of the latter. Yet since illicit sexuality is considered an evil, it is considered in welfare thought to be not only a necessary, but also a sufficient, cause of illegitimacy.

Sociological Approach

The second approach tries to understand the institutional norms and public sentiments which define certain births as illegitimate and fix the status of the parties concerned. At the same time it tries to explain why, in spite of these norms and sentiments, illegitimacy does occur.

In another article[8] a functional explanation of attitudes toward illegitimacy is briefly sketched. The gist of the theory is that the function of reproduction can be carried out in a

socially useful manner only if it is performed in conformity with institutional patterns, because only by means of an institutional system can individuals be organized and taught to cooperate in the performance of this long-range function and the function be integrated with other social functions. The reproductive or familial institutions constitute the social machinery in terms of which the creation of new members of society is supposed to take place. The birth of children in ways that do not fit into this machinery must necessarily receive the disapproval of society, else the institutional system itself, which depends upon favorable attitudes in individuals, would not be approved or sustained. Since the reproductive institutions embrace several different principles and are structurally related to the other major institutions, it is possible to violate the prescribed patterns in several different ways, making possible nine different kinds of illegitimacy, some more severely condemned, some occurring more frequently, than others.[9]

The present article tries to expand this functional approach and to apply its conclusions to current reform proposals. Assuming that the first of two major theoretical questions has now been answered—why there should be

---

Thus the man who has illicit relations with a woman becomes automatically an "evil companion." No one would dispute that he is a causal agent in the resulting illegitimacy; but, on the other hand, no one would regard this fact as a profound scientific discovery.

[8] Kingsley Davis, "The Forms of Illegitimacy," *Social Forces*, **18** (October, 1939), 77-89.

[9] The nine forms, grouped under the five norms which they violate, are as follows: (A) cases violating the simple rule that procreation should come *after* the parties are married: (1) illegitimacy as a result of simple fornication; (B) cases offending the rule of nonadulterous procreation: (2) one-sided adultery with the illegitimate mother married, (3) one-sided adultery with the illegitimate father married, (4) symmetrical adultery; (C) cases disobeying the law of nonincestuous procreation: (5) brother-sister incest, (6) father-daughter incest, and (7) mother-son incest; (D) cases violating the rule of caste endogamy: (8) intercaste illegitimacy; (E) cases violating the principle of nonreproduction of celibate groups: (9) celibate illegitimacy.

socially prescribed norms, departures from which are illegitimate—we shall move on to the second: Why does illegitimacy actually occur in spite of the norms and sentiments against it? This question must really be divided into two distinct parts: (1) Why does forbidden intercourse take place? (2) Why does this intercourse sometimes lead to illegitimate births?

In explaining why all men and women are not continent before marriage and faithful after it, it is usually considered sufficient to invoke the "imperiousness of the sex urge." Undoubtedly this urge is imperious and does play a part in illicit sexuality, but since it is a universal biological factor, it cannot be used to explain deviate behavior without reference to the cultural setting. The urge could doubtless be taken care of, as an organic appetite, by letting everybody marry at puberty and remarry at the death of the partner. But the fact remains that human beings universally, even when married, have never been willing to satisfy the sex impulse exclusively with the marriage partner, as is shown by the existence of adultery in all societies. There is more to sexual conduct than a mere urge. The emotions are involved, and these are compounded of organic and cultural processes, for they are aroused, defined, and expressed in cultural situations with reference to meaningful or symbolic events. Implicit in these cultural situations and meaningful events are the regulatory norms of society; hence deviate behavior is not to be explained solely in terms of biological factors, but also in terms of the very institutional system of which the deviate behavior is a violation.

Inherent in societal motivation are certain inconsistencies which, taken in conjunction with the dynamic nature of the human organism, explain the fact of deviate sexuality. Our own culture extols quick and violent love for the accidental object of one's fancy in courtship but expects the person to forget such love after marriage. It defines intercourse as a mystical and important thing, and yet requires restraint during the period when youthful vigor is at its highest. It describes adulterous behavior as one of the "joys of the flesh," and yet decrees that no one shall have a secret hankering to partake of these joys. It praises and encourages variety in regard to other appetites, but elects to remain blind to the advantages of variety in regard to sex. Such inconsistencies (which are not mentioned for purposes of criticism) could be cited indefinitely. The list varies in different societies, but each society has many of them; in fact, they are apparently inherent in the nature of human association and illustrate how the intricate dynamic of social motivation itself is responsible for man's socially deviate behavior. Not the flesh alone, but the flesh and society, make the devil.

Since society itself connives at engendering pent-up sexual emotions, it must also provide sanctioned modes of release. Though it counts upon fitting a minority almost perfectly into the ideal patterns, it prepares for the great majority customary outlets, hedged round always with cultural taboos to keep them from going too far. Some cultures permit, at certain carefully restricted times and places, veritable orgies; others allow vicarious thrills in drama, music, and literature, or unconsummated release in bodily contact and dancing. Always for some individuals, however, the vicarious thrills are not enough; they must push beyond the bounds to illicit consummation. When this emergency happens, the social system has several lines of retrenchment. It provides certain customary measures for handling "problems." The patterns for dealing with bastards and their parents are of this character. People are not supposed to have illegitimate children, but when they do, an emergency machinery is set into operation to give the child a status (though an inferior one) and to define the positions of the parents. In this way society continues. No one ever completely transcends the institutional boundaries. If he did, he would not be human. On the other hand, no one ever remains completely within the narrowest institutional boundaries. If he did, he would not be human. The fundamental explanation of nonconformity to the marital institutions is the same as the explanation of institutional nonconformity in general.

Too much of the thinking about illegitimacy, however, has been concerned with illicit relations. We must now raise the ridiculously obvious question of why illicit intercourse sometimes leads to the birth of bastards. Since intercourse does not necessarily bring conception, or conception bring parturition, illicit sexuality is a necessary but not a sufficient cause of the occurrence of illegitimacy. One could with more truth assert that the cause of illegitimacy is the suppression of contraception and abortion. Indeed, if our obvious question is to be answered, it must be answered by an explanation of the social taboos against the use of these two devices—and again we are drawn back to the institutional structure of society. The norms of reproductive institutions motivate persons to bear children, and they control sexual behavior to this end. If the connection between sexuality and the bearing of offspring were entirely broken, then a powerful factor in the motivation to procreate would be lost. Seldom do societies permit the connection to be entirely broken, although many of them possess such solidaristic social organiza-

tions in other respects that they can afford to relax somewhat on this point. Our taboos against contraception and abortion are at one with our taboo against extramarital intercourse—they both function to maintain a motivational connection between sexual gratification and procreation.[10]

The sociological approach to the causation of illegitimacy attempts to show, in brief, that reproductive norms, whose violation constitutes illegitimacy, exist because social functions can be performed only through institutional patterns; that these norms are broken because the emotional life of man in society inevitably leads him to fall short, and leads some individuals to fall far short, of perfection; and that, finally, illegitimate children are born of illicit relations because the measures that would prevent their being born (encouragement of contraception and abortion) constitute in themselves a violation of the mores.

Why Is the Child "Victimized"?

It is easy to understand in these terms why illegitimacy, along with the acts leading to it, should be socially condemned. But one may well ask why the innocent child should suffer.

As far back as the Middle Ages there were men (theologians among them) who argued that all offspring, being God-given, are by nature neither legitimate nor illegitimate, and that it is ir-

---

[10] So ingrained is the connection between intercourse and reproduction in our institutions that it constitutes an integral and unconscious part of our thinking. Malthus, e.g., in formulating his theory of population, assumed that because the sex urge is strong, population would inevitably press upon the means of subsistence. The deliberate practice of contraception and abortion never occurred to him as a real possibility, because this "artificial" separation of the sex urge from procreation was to him contrary to human nature (i.e., contrary to our institutions).

rational to punish innocent children for the sins of the parents. The logic of these gentlemen, as of their successors, was excellent, but their premises and conclusions were unrealistic. The medieval church, though liberal on the matter of legitimation, never doubted the reality of bastards.

The question as to why the child is punished for the sins of its parents is wrongly put. It assumes an explanation of what has yet to be explained. It should read: What is the status of the illegitimate child, and why is he given this status? Perhaps his status is partly explicable in terms of punishment, but not primarily. For one thing, the sociological identification of parent and child, which furnished the ancient *raison d'être* for punishing the offender in the person of his offspring, is present in illegitimacy only to a very limited degree. In the second place, illegitimacy is disapproved even in societies where premarital and extramarital intercourse is sanctioned—in which case the motive cannot be a wish to punish the parents for illicit acts, because there are no illicit acts. The only way in which the punishment theory can make sense is in terms of procrastination and tangibility. Though illicit intercourse in our culture is disapproved officially, it is usually winked at or ignored in practice—by persons, indeed, who heartily disapprove of illegitimate children— partly because it is difficult to detect and control. The illegitimate child comes as a tangible and inescapable consequence of a clandestine act; it comes as a climax, a point at which public indignation can self-confidently boil over. The public attitude, thus born of procrastination, seems vindictive rather than preventive. But punishment for parental sin is not the sole motive for the treatment of illegitimate children and does not deserve the primacy generally given it. The inquiry must be pushed to a deeper level which will explain both the legal disabilities (concerning descent, inheritance, support, and domicile) and the social disabilities (concerning public opinion, folkways, and mores).

Legal Disabilities

The illegitimate child presents a grave dilemma. On the one hand, the community must preserve the reproductive institutions and hence must not allow him to compete with actual or potential family ties. On the other hand, it must find some way to support the child and naturally tends to fix this responsibility on those who brought him into the world. The two necessities —that of segregating the child from his procreators and that of attaching him to these procreators—are in conflict.

Descent, inheritance, and succession. A universal rule is that the illegitimate child does not acquire full membership in the family group or family line of his parent. He can begin a family line but cannot continue one. This rule of nondescent protects the parents' established family (if it is a case of adulterous procreation) or the parents' future legitimate family (if it is a case of simple fornication). It also maintains the caste division (if it is a case of intercaste procreation) and continues the celibate organization (if it is a case of illegitimate procreation by members of a celibate class). The disabilities upon descent, therefore, are better explained by reference to their institutional functions than by the hackneyed reference to the difficulty of identifying the father.

If the bastard cannot descend legitimately (except through the special mechanisms of acknowledgment, adoption, or legitimation), then to which parent will he be socially attached for domicile and other necessary matters? He will be attached, as between the two parents, to the one that is not lineally significant. Thus in a patrilineal system, a child who cannot descend patrilineally is (if socially connected with either parent) attached to the mother. This derives partly from the close physical attachment of the child to its mother, rendering it difficult for the mother to hide her connection with the child, and partly from the logic of patrilineal institutions. When the system of descent revolves around the male, the principle of nondescent revolves around the female. By placing the illegitimate child's relationship, if any, on the shoulders of a woman, the male line—and hence the family system—is protected.[11]

The same general rule also holds for the inheritance of property. The natural child is wholly or partially prohibited from inheriting from his father.[12] Again the explanation rests on the necessity of protecting the legitimate family connections of the natural parents. Since the child does not descend from the father and does not bear his name, it follows that the father's family (or indeed his whole clan) will scarcely wish, as a family, to see the property inherited by a *filius nullius*. This would injure the brothers of the father and their legitimate children; and if the father were married, it would also injure his wife and his legitimate children who are entitled to inherit through him. Thus the rule of noninheritance is a corollary of the rule of nondescent, both being part and parcel of the reproductive structure.

Support, domicile, and custody. If the illegitimate child is to live at all, it must be supported and kept.[13] Since the normal care of children is familial, the first plan occurring to a community is some sort of family or semifamily home for the bastard. Hence the mother or an adoptive parent is granted its care, the community often showing itself quite careless and hasty in its efforts to get the child off its hands. The community sometimes undertakes to elicit money from the putative father for the child's support, because the mother cannot be expected to support it in a world organized on the principle of feminine dependence. Such support, however, constitutes merely a minimum claim upon the father. The community, unwilling to attach the illegitimate child to him too closely, usually permits many loopholes and prosecutes only upon the initiative of the mother.

Domicile and custody of the illegitimate child generally follow the mother.

---

[11] For a summary of past English law on the subject see S. P. Breckinridge, *The Family and the State* (Chicago: University of Chicago Press, 1934), pp. 415ff. The author states that the illegitimate child belonged to his mother more fully than did a legitimate one, and that the mother's custody was protected against the father and against the outside world.

[12] A bastard may be prohibited from inheriting from his mother, but in strict patrilineal societies such a prohibition is meaningless, because inheritance does not pass through females anyway. Where inheritance is somewhat bilateral, the child's inheritance is limited with reference to both parents; but with the weakening of the whole kinship structure in an urban civilization, the child may be permitted to inherit from his mother. . . .
The disabilities are not always absolute. Thus a bastard may be entitled to some inheritance, but less than a legitimate child. Different kinds of bastards may suffer varying degrees of disability. . . .
The disabilities do not necessarily affect a child adversely. In some cases it may be a positive advantage to a child not to acquire the name and status of his natural father. The illegitimate child of a migratory laborer is probably better off, e.g., if adopted by a wealthy couple than if entitled to rights by his actual father. Contrariwise, it is in some instances better to be born the illicit child of a member of the upper class who will provide good support but no inheritance than to be born a legitimate member of a lower-class family.

[13] Many societies solve their problem by killing illicit children, exposure "in the bush" being a favorite method.

Since women are not economically independent to the same degree as men, the rule constitutes a hardship penalizing both the child and the mother; it thus forms part of the double standard of morality which is an integral feature of patrilineal reproductive institutions.

In short, if attached to either parent, the child is attached to the mother. This secures the care of the child without interfering with the patrilineal family system as represented by the male line. The minimum obligation upon the father is the duty of support, enforced only in a limited and desultory manner because otherwise it would defeat the principle of paternal nonattachment to the illegitimate child.

Disabilities in Public Opinion— Folkways and Mores

Since legal controls form only a framework of social life, one can say that were it solely a matter of law, illegitimacy would constitute no great hardship for bastards and their mothers. But legal disabilities are sustained and supplemented by attitudes that enter into the texture of daily life, coloring in countless ways the subjective feelings of the unfortunates. These attitudes attack the mother even before her confinement, because she and her family and friends all feel a moral horror at the idea of unwed pregnancy. In scarcely any other way can a woman lose status so completely. She reads her disgrace in the expressions of others and feels it in her own conscience.

These attitudes next attack the newborn child. Not only is its presence a disgrace to the whole family, but its support may fall upon them as well. In some cultures there are superstitions concerning the ill fate of an illegitimate child. During the child's life his indiscreet peers and whispering superiors constantly reiterate his moral inferiority. This is true no matter what the method of caring for him—whether by adoption, placement in an orphanage, or custody of the unmarried mother.

Given our institutional patterns and the sentiments supporting them, the position of the illegitimate child seems inevitable. Poetry, art, and religion weave into the mind the sentiments of the normal family, which implies in most civilized societies physical as well as social kinship. A child whose physical parents are not his full sociological parents because not married to each other, or who is living with adoptive parents, must necessarily feel different from other children, even though he is never directly insulted. He is supposed, for example, to cherish his mother and to view as an outrage any reflection upon her virtue; but illegitimate pregnancy is in itself a great blotch upon a woman's virtue. Hence, insofar as the child identifies himself with his physical mother—as he is bound to do in our culture—he will be profoundly affected by the knowledge of his illegitimacy. The very rationalizations with which we discuss illegitimacy show the inevitability of its constituent sentiments. Lundberg and Lenroot, for example, begin a statement in this fashion: "The instinctive yearning of every child for a mother and father and kin of his own is shown. . . ." This attitude, this rationalization of the matter, emphasizes the inescapable emotional conflict that must result for the person whose "real" parents are not what they should be.[14]

Can Illegitimacy Be Abolished?

Popular opinion vaguely holds that illegitimacy, like most major evils of long standing, is capable of abolition, but that human nature being what it is, the proper solution will never be dis-

[14] E. O. Lundberg and K. F. Lenroot, *Illegitimacy as a Child Welfare Problem* (Washington, D.C.: U.S. Government Printing Office, 1921), pp. 60-61.

covered and applied. On the other hand, a considerable body of social-welfare thought, somewhat divorced from lay opinion, regards abolition as possible. Persons holding this latter view, however, make two outstanding errors: (1) They tend to think purely in legalistic terms and to overlook the connection between illegitimacy and the reproductive institutions. (2) They confuse illegitimacy with illicit intercourse.

Preoccupation with law in illegitimacy reform. A common belief is that abolition can be achieved by passing statutes granting natural children the same rights as other children. . . . It is doubtful if bastards could ever be given complete legal equality, or that such equality, if given, would eliminate illegitimacy. The latter is a matter of public opinion and attitude, as well as of law; its elimination as a legal concept (if such were possible) would not alter the customary attitudes and sentiments. Legal fiat cannot abolish the acts, or the condemnation of the acts, which lead to illegitimate procreation—namely, fornication, adultery, incest, intercaste union, etc. The stigma that these acts draw to the parents must necessarily fall to some degree upon the child as well, since he, being dependent upon them for his social role and status, will suffer when they suffer.

The natural child, moreover, necessitates special and deliberate community measures. In a complex society these can be provided only in the form of legal rules. Thus in the same breath that reformers praise the abolition of illegitimacy as a legal concept, they mention the *new* legal rules required to put this abolition into effect. For example, it may be legislated that the illegitimate child is entitled to support from its natural father just like the ordinary child; since, however, its father may be missing, special legislation must

be provided for his apprehension, trial, etc., all of which again sets the illegitimate child apart, an object of special attention and special procedures—an illegitimate child in the legal sense of the word.

To think of illegitimacy purely in legal terms is to overlook the complete societal picture. Since there is a prescribed procreative structure, any reproduction outside this structure will inevitably provoke retaliatory and restorative measures. These measures will be in part punitive because the event is the result of willful acts, and in part remedial because it is an immediate problem which must be met. Whatever the remedy, it must be such as will not endanger any existing family or encourage further illegitimate procreation. Unless these institutional facts are taken into account, illegitimacy cannot be understood—much less abolished.

Confusion of illicit intercourse with illegitimacy. It becomes obvious that reform proposals operating *after* the child's birth are superficial. Any thoroughgoing reform must keep bastards from being born in the first place. But though the proposals seeking to prevent illegitimate conception show more insight than the purely *post partum* (e.g., legal) programs, they fall into another interesting error; for it seemingly fits nicely into the moralistic logic of most reformers to believe that in order to stop illegitimacy it is necessary to stop illicit intercourse. Otherwise why stop illegitimacy? The crusade against the latter is really a crusade against immorality—which, however, is a far greater and more invincible enemy. So invincible is the latter, in fact, that to make the abolition of illegitimacy contingent upon elimination of vice insures failure.[15] Yet so dominant

---

[15] In relation to reproduction, society is much less worried about illicit sexuality than

is the evil-causes-evil type of reasoning that practically all discussions of reform automatically fall into this error.[16]

A Hypothetical Method of Abolishing Illegitimacy

The legalistic and moralistic errors are better exposed by further consideration of possible abolition measures. According to the sociological analysis of causation, for example, there is one sure way of abolishing illegitimacy—namely, by eliminating marriage and the family. The welfare theorists have not thought of this because they unconsciously assume the reproductive institutions and hence ignore them in their causal analysis. But such a course has been actually advocated by radicals who are more logical, but less practical, than the humanitarians. . . . But though this method would successfully abolish illegitimacy, it would also, according to our analysis, abolish society, because according to our analysis, reproductive institutions (though no particular type) are necessary for societal existence.

It is possible, however, to imagine a means of abolishing illegitimacy without resorting to such drastic measures (though the ultimate effect upon the reproductive institutions might be similar). At the most it would require four, and only four, measures, as follows: (1) Every citizen to be given a thorough, scientific, compulsory education concerning the nature of sex, reproduction, and contraception. (2) The state to advertise, furnish, and distribute contraceptive techniques to all individuals, thus insuring that failure to use these techniques could not be excused on grounds of poverty or circumstance. (These two measures alone would go a long way toward reducing the number of illegitimate children, because bastard offspring are generally the result of accident and ignorance rather than of deliberate planning. Given free contraceptive knowledge and techniques, most people would not reproduce outside of wedlock, whatever else they might do. But in order to make society doubly secure, two additional measures would be in order.) (3) Abortion to be performed freely and scientifically, and perhaps compulsorily, upon all pregnant women not married to the partner in conception. (4) A fine of $5000 or a long period in jail to be posted for anyone procreating an illegitimate child (scientific means to be used in determining parentage).

It is safe to say that, in a country where such measures were put into effect, the jails would not be crowded with unwed mothers and fathers, nor would illegitimate offspring constitute a palpable percentage of the total birth rate. There would still be a few cases, but illegitimacy as a social problem would disappear. The matter is astoundingly simple—once the moral preoccupation is dispensed with.

Then why is this simple scheme not immediately adopted? Primarily because the moral preoccupation cannot

---

is the moralist. For instance, it is an almost universal principle that a child conceived out of wedlock but born in it is legitimate. G. B. Mangold [*Children Born out of Wedlock* (Columbia: University of Missouri Press, 1921), p. 38] states that in Australia, 1910-12, the number of children born in the first six months of marriage practically equaled the number born outside of marriage, but he says nothing about any condemnation of these children born within wedlock but conceived immorally. The primary motif in illegitimacy attitudes is not the punishment of the parents for illicit intercourse, but the regulation and protection of the reproductive institutions.

[16] F. H. Hankins, in the article on "Illegitimacy" in *The Encyclopedia of the Social Sciences*, p. 581, affords an illustration of the basic reasoning: "Where illegitimacy suffers social stigma its causes must obviously be those conditions which result in unregulated premarital intercourse."

be dispensed with. Society is a moral universe; to extract the moral sentiments (i.e., the mores) is to extract society. Our hypothetical scheme makes two unrealistic assumptions: first, that the abolition of illegitimacy is the supreme goal, and, second, that human reproduction can be guided by logico-empirical science. Obviously there are other goals, and these limit the means that can be used to abolish illegitimacy. Thus the taboo against abortion is for us more ultimate than the taboo against illegitimate procreation, since our mores forbid the use of the former to prevent the latter; and the taboo against illicit relations is equally important, since reformers cannot envision reducing illegitimacy without first reducing immorality. Furthermore, the reproductive institutions are not subject to completely rational control, because they lie deep in the texture of society and deep in unconscious thought. Like other basic institutions, they rest upon firmly imbedded, socially engendered sentiments, far removed from the surface of purely rational behavior.

In the last analysis, our hypothetical scheme is not far removed from the radical proposal to abolish marriage. If we were so emancipated from the mores as to sanction contraception and abortion, why should we worry about illegitimacy? The attitudes toward the illegal mother, father, and child, though understandable, are as irrational as any. If we look at social matters so objectively that we could eliminate illegitimacy by deliberate planning, we would cease to abhor illegitimacy itself and would feel no necessity of putting our plan into effect. Illegitimacy and marriage would both have disappeared. We may conclude, therefore, that such a bizarre plan will not be adopted, and that the future changes in our reproductive institutions, whatever they may be, will not embrace among their fruits the abolition of illegitimacy, but merely alterations in the amount, kind, and circumstances of it.

cultural differences in the disapproval of illegitimacy

five

One element in the cultural disapproval of illegitimacy in Western countries is the disapproval of premarital sexual relations, especially strong in countries with a Puritan tradition. However, cross-culturally it can be seen that illegitimacy is disapproved even when young people are given much sexual freedom. Obviously, most societies view the consequences of illegitimacy as greater than those of premarital sexual freedom.

The more liberal sex codes of Scandinavian countries do not arise only from a modern philosophy of freedom. They also have roots in an ancient farmer tradition, widespread in Europe, which allowed rather free courtship. Since all belonged to about the same social stratum, a landholding class, the young man was not likely to run away and a marriage was fairly certain. Thus a fairly high rate of premarital conceptions or births did not mean that many young mothers were abandoned or their children cast out of decent society.

In present-day Scandinavia, premarital conception occurs primarily between couples who are deeply involved with one another and who expect eventually to marry. In the United States, as Christensen shows, couples immediately rush to marry when they learn that the girl is pregnant. Thus many marriages are based on little more than fear of social disapproval. This, in turn, results in much higher rates of divorce among such couples than in Denmark.

Cultural Relativism and Premarital Sex Norms

HAROLD T. CHRISTENSEN

* * * * *

Effects upon Timing of the Wedding

The tendency to be philosophical about a premarital pregnancy when it happens, so as not to be stampeded into a marriage, seems to be much more characteristic of Denmark than of Indiana or Utah. It is suggested, perhaps, by the higher Danish illegitimacy rates. . . . In the Utah and Indiana samples, the modal time of conception is one lunar month after marriage, in the Danish sample it is five lunar months *before* the marriage. As a matter of fact, the Danish data show many more couples conceiving about five months before the marriage than at any other time; in that culture, therefore, premarital conception coupled with subsequent delayed marriage must be considered as the norm. The Indiana curve is bimodal, with the peak for premarital conceptions at two lunar months

Harold T. Christensen, "Cultural Relativism and Premarital Sex Norms," *American Sociological Review*, **25** (February, 1960), 35-39. We are grateful to the author and the American Sociological Association for permission to quote.

prior to marriage—suggesting a tendency to get married as soon as possible after the second menstrual period has been missed and the doctor's positive diagnosis has been given. The Utah curve starts low and moves up regularly until the time of marriage and immediately thereafter, when it is the highest of all three.

The fact just noted is . . . evidence of Utah's pattern of early conception following the wedding. Of the three cultures here compared, Utah has not only the lowest rates of premarital conception, but [also] the highest rate of *early* postmarital conception.

Apparently in Denmark there is little pressure to hurry marriage merely because of pregnancy.[1] In Indiana the tendency is to marry immediately after the pregnancy is definitely known so as

[1] In attempting to explain this situation to the writer, several Danish scholars have pointed to the current great housing shortage in Copenhagen—which means waiting for a place to live, thereby discouraging any rush into marriage. When reminded that the figures used here are for 1938 marriages, however, these observers were quick to admit that the argument doesn't apply, since there was little housing shortage then.

to hide the fact from the public. Couples who have premarital sexual intercourse in Utah, on the other hand, seem to hurry marriage because of that fact alone, without waiting for pregnancy to force them into it (religious guilt is a sufficient sanction once the "law of chastity" has been broken).[2]

As Kinsey has pointed out, "The psychologic significance of any type of sexual activity very largely depends upon what the individual and his social group choose to make of it."[3] Since in Danish culture there is less stigma placed on premarital conception and on illegitimacy than in Indiana, and especially in

[2] Although this latter explanation is speculative, it is plausible. Chastity is so stressed in Mormon culture that the religiously oriented offender may panic and try to ease his conscience by getting married.

[3] Alfred C. Kinsey, et al., Sexual Behavior in the Human Female (Philadelphia: W. B. Saunders Company, 1953), p. 320.

Utah, the differences in timing pattern for the wedding once pregnancy has occurred may be explained in cultural terms.

Effects upon the Divorce Rate

This type of explanation may also apply to possible variations in divorce rate differentials of premarital pregnancy vs. postmarital pregnancy cases. We would hypothesize that the more liberal the culture the less likely is premarital pregnancy to be followed by divorce. This hypothesis is tested with data from the Indiana and Danish samples.[4]

For Tippecanoe County, it has been reported . . . that the divorce rate is

[4] Unfortunately, in our Utah sample, record linkage was limited to marriage and birth data; whereas in the Indiana and Denmark samples, divorce data were also included.

TABLE 1   Divorce Rate Comparisons by Interval to First Birth
(For Births Occurring Within Five Years of the Wedding)

Classification	COPENHAGEN, DENMARK			TIPPECANOE COUNTY, INDIANA		
	Number of Cases	Number Divorced	Per Cent Divorced	Number of Cases	Number Divorced	Per Cent Divorced
Interval Between Marriage and First Birth						
1. 0-139 days (premarital pregnancy, marriage delayed)	176	60	34.1	71	14	19.7
2. 140-265 days (premarital pregnancy, marriage hurried)	129	31	24.0	276	39	14.1
3. 266 days-4.99 years (postmarital pregnancy)	572	111	19.4	1174	84	7.1
Percentage Difference Between Divorce Rates						
4. Between lines 2 and 1			42.1			39.7
5. Between lines 3 and 2			23.7*			98.6*

* No direct formula has been located for testing the statistical significance of this intersample difference between differences in proportions. However, an approximate equivalent test is to consider $p1 - p2 < p3 - p4$ (where $p1 = 24.0$, $p2 = 19.4$, $p3 = 14.1$, and $p4 = 7.1$). When the p-values are changed according to the arcsine transform, they have been placed on a comparable scale, and the use of the normal probability table is permitted. This procedure yields a probability for a one-tailed test of .12. Alternatively, we may approximately test $\frac{p1}{p2} < \frac{p3}{p4}$ if we assume $\frac{p1}{p2} - \frac{p3}{p4}$ is normally distributed, and use an approximate variance formula. Since the hypothesis is stated in terms of the greater ratio for the United States than for Denmark, a one-tailed test is permissible, yielding a probability of .038. There is no way to evaluate the assumption of a normal distribution for this test.

significantly higher for premarital than postmarital pregnancy couples.[5] For marriages occurring in Copenhagen during 1948, Holm has shown that, with age controlled, the divorce rate is not significantly different for couples bearing a child within the first nine months of marriage than for all other cases.[6] At first glance, this seems to bear out our hypothesis.

It is to be noted, however, that Holm did not compare premarital pregnancy cases with postmarital pregnancy cases, as was done for Tippecanoe County, but rather with all nonpremarital pregnancy cases, including childless couples. Since those who become divorced are less likely to have children than those who do not,[7] the inclusion of childless cases in the nonpremarital pregnancy category would raise the divorce rate for that category and, in this way, would obscure the true comparison. What is needed is a comparison between divorce rates of premarital and postmarital pregnancy cases; for unless nonconceivers are excluded, it is impossible to determine the effects of conception timing.

Table 1 is designed to compare the Copenhagen and Tippecanoe County samples concerning possible effects of premarital and postmarital pregnancy upon the divorce rate. As noted above, these two samples are not strictly com-

parable, but they are approximately so.[8] It seems probable that the following generalizations are at least tentatively justified:

1. In both populations there is the clear tendency for the divorce rate to fall as the length of interval between marriage and first birth increases. This means that premarital pregnancy cases are more likely to end in divorce than are postmarital pregnancy cases,[9] and that those premarital pregnancy couples who delay marriage for a considerable time after the knowledge of pregnancy have the highest divorce rate of all—in Denmark as well as Indiana.

2. The *relative* difference in divorce rate between premarital pregnancy couples who hurried marriage and those who delayed it is essentially the same for both populations. Thus Copenha-

[5] Harold T. Christensen and Hanna H. Meissner, "Studies in Child Spacing: III—Premarital Pregnancy as a Factor in Divorce," *American Sociological Review*, 18 (December, 1953), 641-644.

[6] Henry F. Holm, *Statistisk Maanedsskrift*, 33, No. 4 (Copenhagen: Statistical Office, 1957), Table 12, p. 117.

[7] In the writer's Copenhagen sample of 1938 marriages, for example, 57 per cent of the childless marriages ended in divorce or separation as compared with 20.9 per cent of the fertile marriages. A primary explanation for this differential is that many of the divorces occur relatively soon after the wedding, before the couple has decided to start a family.

[8] See descriptions of the two samples, above. Calculations for Table 1 are based uniformly on cases having a first child born within five years of the wedding. Although absolute divorce rates cannot be compared across the two samples—since they would be influenced in distinctive ways by differential emigration and differential lengths of time of exposure to the divorce possibility—there seems to be no good reason why the *relative* rates by pregnancy timing cannot be compared.

[9] There is an interesting parallel finding from the Copenhagen data: marriages in which the wife had borne an illegitimate child previously showed a divorce rate of 45.7, as compared with 20.9 for childbearing marriages where she had not. A partial explanation of course may be that a selective factor is operating, which may mean that the least stable personalities are the ones most likely to become pregnant before marriage and also to be divorced later. But another possibility is that, through such things as resentment about the necessity to marry, guilt feelings, and poor preparation and unsuitable personality matching because of a hasty or pressured marriage, the premarital pregnancy may itself help to bring about divorce. In the Tippecanoe County study, the writer controlled other divorce-producing factors, through matching, and still found premarital pregnancy to be significantly associated with high divorce; see Christensen and Meissner, *op. cit.*

cultural relativism and premarital sex norms   35

gen figures show a 42.1 per cent difference between these two rates as compared with a difference of 39.7 per cent in Tippecanoe County, an intersample difference that is not significant.

The facts that both samples show substantially higher divorce rates for couples who delay marriage after knowledge of pregnancy and that the differentials in this respect are about the same in the two cultures suggest universal tendencies for certain pregnant couples to marry under the pressure of social responsibility (for example, sympathy for the lover, consideration for the future child, or parental influence). The data also suggest that, statistically speaking, such "shotgun" marriages do not turn out well.

3. The *relative* difference in divorce rate between postmarital pregnancy couples and the premarital couples who married soon after the discovery of pregnancy is four times greater in the Indiana sample (98.6 per cent compared with 23.7 per cent), an intersample difference that by some tests is statistically significant. (See footnote to Table 1.)

The fact that the postmarital pregnancy divorce rate is lower in both cultures is evidence that premarital pregnancy—even when associated with an early wedding—tends generally to make marriage's survival chances less than even. This may be because some marriages take place under pressure from others and are therefore accompanied by resentment, or because in their haste to escape public scorn the couple marries without adequate preparation, or in the absence of love, or in the face of ill-matched personalities. But the fact that the postmarital-premarital pregnancy divorce rate differential is substantially less in Denmark gives strong support to our hypothesis. It seems probable that in Denmark, where sexual relations outside of marriage are more or less accepted, premarital pregnancy will have less negative effect upon marriage than in Indiana, where it is expected that sexual intercourse and pregnancy be confined to marriage.

Summary and Theory

Premarital sex norms in Utah, Indiana, and Denmark stand in sharp contrast—with Utah being very conservative or restrictive and Denmark being extremely liberal or permissive. As might be expected, therefore, premarital pregnancy rates were found to be lowest in the Utah sample and highest in the Danish sample, with the difference being considerable. Furthermore, certain consequences of premarital pregnancy were found to vary from culture to culture. Thus permissive Denmark, at the time of the study, showed the longest delay between premarital conception and the wedding, and the smallest divorce rate differential between premarital pregnancy and postmarital pregnancy cases.[10] In all three cultures the same factors were associated with premarital pregnancy:

---

[10] As noted above, divorce rate comparison does not include the Utah sample since data were not available. It is believed, however, that the Utah divorce rate differential (between premarital and postmarital pregnancy cases) probably is the greatest of the three areas—because premarital sexual intimacy is most strongly condemned there.

This unestablished assumption can be argued by an analogy. The drinking of alcoholic beverages is also strongly condemned in Utah (and in the rest of Mormon culture). Research shows that Mormon college students have the lowest incidence of drinking among religious groups, but that, of the drinkers, Mormon students have a very high rate of alcoholism. This suggests that cultural restrictions can lower the incidence of the condemned practice, but that for those who indulge, the negative effects are apt to be extreme. Cf. Robert Strauss and Selden D. Bacon, *Drinking in College* (New Haven: Yale University Press, 1953).

namely, young age at marriage, a civil wedding, and a laboring occupation.

In some respects our data give support to the idea of cultural relativism. It has been shown that both the rates and effects of premarital pregnancy are to a considerable extent relative to the cultures involved. The most liberal culture was found to have the most premarital pregnancy, but also the least negative effects therefrom; in Denmark there is less pressure than in the American cases either to speed up the wedding or to resort to divorce when premarital pregnancy occurs. Thus the relationship is not simply a matter of how premarital pregnancy affects subsequent behavior, considered in a vacuum, but rather how it affects this behavior in the light of particular norms. Cultural norms represent an intervening variable.

But there are also *regularities* among the cultures studied. In all of them, pregnancy usually takes place within marriage. In all of them also, premarital pregnancy is found to be associated with young age, a civil wedding, and a laboring occupation. Finally, the Indiana-Denmark comparisons reveal a parallel phenomenon of higher divorce rates for premarital pregnancy than for postmarital pregnancy cases. These rates are especially high, and in similar magnitude within both cultures, for couples who delay marriage until just before the child is born. Forced marriage, in other words, seems to work against marital success regardless of the culture. All of this suggests the existence of certain universals which are to some extent independent of the cultural variable.

The present analysis is concerned with *inter*cultural comparisons. The next step is to see if the theory applies to the *intra*cultural level, that is, when interpersonal differences are taken into account. We hypothesize both regularity and variability at that level also, with personal values having very much the same effects as cultural norms are found to have in this report.

high illegitimacy rates as a consequence of cultural destruction

six

In an earlier article, the author demonstrated that in the Caribbean countries the high illegitimacy rates are neither a native "tradition" nor a new "cultural alternative" fully approved by the whole society. Investigators who make either assertion report many behavioral patterns and attitudes which contradict that claim, and prove instead that a legitimate marriage is approved. However, both familial and extrafamilial social structures create a social setting in which the young girl must risk pregnancy in order to obtain a man, with the opportunity eventually of a marriage.

Here the author follows up that inquiry by looking more broadly at other high illegitimacy countries, and suggests that in the New World and industrializing sub-Saharan Africa the destruction of the native cultures—and of the social structures that supported them—creates the social settings in which such high rates are likely.

Illegitimacy, Anomie, and Cultural Penetration

WILLIAM J. GOODE

Since the family is a prime instrumental agency through which the needs of various institutional needs are met and legitimacy is the keystone of the family system, an examination of family systems with high illegitimacy rates should yield useful data on the integration of societies. Analysis of high illegitimacy rates indeed suggests that some modifications may be profitably made in several segments of sociological theory: (1) the cultural and social conditions under which high illegitimacy rates occur; (2) the classical theory of the assimilation of both native rural and foreign-born immigrants in the United States; (3) effective procedures for destroying cultural and social systems; and (4) the relation between social and cultural integration.

Illegitimacy rates are, or have been, relatively high in three major areas: Northwestern Europe, industrializing sub-Saharan Africa, and the New World, from Tierra del Fuego to the nonwhite Southern population of the United States. To consider these in turn, let us note that Iceland and particular regions in Sweden, Germany,

William J. Goode, "Illegitimacy, Anomie, and Cultural Penetration," *American Sociological Review*, 26 (December, 1961), 910-925. We are grateful to The American Sociological Association for permission to quote.

and Austria have had rates of about 20 to 30 per cent in recent years.[1] In special studies of native urbanizing areas in sub-Saharan Africa, rates of 40 per cent or more have been reported.[2] In

[1] Iceland's rate was 27.9 per cent in 1950 (Meyer F. Nimkoff, "Illegitimacy," in *Encyclopedia Britannica*, 1954). The Swedish illegitimacy rate has been dropping over the past generation. The highest rates have been found in Stockholm (1841-1860, 43 per cent illegitimate; 1901-1910, 34 per cent; 1921-1925, 28 per cent), but presumably these include many rural mothers. However, the regions of Gävleborgslän and Jamtlandslän have continued to be relatively high (23 per cent and 21 per cent in 1921-1925; 17.6 per cent and 18.5 per cent in 1956). In Steiermark in Austria, the rate was 19 per cent in 1956. Oberbayern in Germany had a rate of 18.5 per cent in 1954. I have recently found that certain regions of Portugal (Lisbon, Beja, Evora, and Setubal) have rates of 20 per cent to 30 per cent, but I have found no special reports on them.

[2] The best surveys of recent changes may be found in *Social Implications of Industrialization and Urbanization South of the Sahara* (Paris, UNESCO, 1956) and *Survey of African Marriage* and *Survey of African Marriage and Family Life*, Arthur Phillips, ed. (London: Oxford University Press, 1953). Twenty-three per cent of all unmarried women in certain Kxatla groups had borne children, 19 per cent among the Ngwato and 17 per cent among the Kwena [I. Schapera, *Migrant Labour and Tribal Life* (New York: Oxford University Press, 1947), p. 173]. An analysis of Bantu attitudes toward illegitimacy may be

the New World, particular provinces may have rates over 80 per cent, a handful of mainland countries have rates over 70 per cent, and a majority of all the political units have rates over 30 per cent. The nonwhite populations of the Southern states in the United States had rates of 20 to 30 per cent in 1957.[3]

Why did the New World rates become so high? They cannot be "survivals of native customs," since neither the native Indian groups nor the New World immigrants, whether white or African, had especially high rates of illegitimacy.[4] Moreover, they had many

different family patterns—patriliny and matriliny, low and high divorce rates, polygyny and monogamy—but the rates are generally high.

Another common explanation is that the consensual union, out of which such high rates grow, is part of the "development of a new subculture." That is, the union without benefit of wedlock is the "native," normatively supported equivalent of a legalized union. Consequently, Malinowski's Principle of Legitimacy, according to which every society has a rule condemning illegitimacy, is to be discarded. This explanation is not satisfactory either. For at least the Caribbean, where this explanation has been widespread, it has been shown that both mother and child have a lower status outside the legal union, that women prefer to be married, and there is general agreement that the ideal family relationship is that of marriage. Moreover, a majority eventually do marry in the Caribbean. The Principle of Legitimacy is, then, roughly correct. But we did correct Malinowski's principle in certain respects and described the bargaining process of consensual courtship outside parental or peer group controls, by which the young girl, unprotected by a kin network, must risk an unstable union and childbirth in order to have a chance at eventually entering a legal union.[5]

That analysis seems to be generally applicable, with only minor and obvi-

found in I. Schapera, "Pre-marital Pregnancy and Public Opinion," Africa, 6 (January, 1933), esp. 83-89. Krige reported an illegitimacy rate of 59 per cent in three locations in Pretoria [Eileen J. Krige, "Changing Conditions in Marital Relations and Parental Duties Among Urbanized Natives," Africa, 9, No. 1 (1936), 4]. Janisch found that some half of the couples in a Johannesburg native township were "merely living together" [Miriam Janisch, "Some Administrative Aspects of Native Marriage Problems in an Urban Area," Bantu Studies, 15 (1941), 9]. In Capetown, illegitimacy rates of 26 per cent to 41 per cent were reported in the period 1939-44 [Ruth Levin, "Marriage in Langa Native Location," Communications from the School of African Studies (Capetown: University of Capetown, 1947), p. 41]. The rate was 30 per cent in Capetown in 1958. For Leopoldville, S. Comhaire-Sylvain reports almost half of the couples in certain native wards were living in concubinage ["Food and Leisure Among the African Youth in Leopoldville," Communications from the School of African Studies, No. 25 (December, 1950), 23]. Similar processes of "living together" have been described in the urbanizing area of Kampala [A. W. Southall and P. C. W. Gutkind, Townsmen in the Making, East African Studies, No. 9 (Kampala: East African Institute of Social Research), 1956, pp. 72, 74, 79, 174-178].

[3] Data courtesy of U.S. National Office of Vital Statistics.

[4] There are of course numerous monographs on the African societies that furnished the slaves. Because the Indian groups were, for the most part, destroyed before the anthropologists arrived, New World societies are less well known than the African, but an excellent

summary of the known South American (including the Circum-Caribbean) societies may be found in Handbook of South American Indians, Julian H. Steward, ed. (Washington, D.C.: Smithsonian Institution, Bureau of American Ethnology, Bulletin No. 143, 6 vols., 1946-1950).

[5] For details of this process, see William J. Goode, "Illegitimacy in the Caribbean Social Structure," American Sociological Review, 25 (February, 1960), 21-30. The best analysis of this process in Jamaica is by Judith Blake, et al., Family Structure in Jamaica (New York: Free Press of Glencoe, Inc., 1962).

ous modifications, to the New World south of the Mason-Dixon Line: the consensual union is not the normative equivalent of marriage. Let us now consider the larger structural conditions under which such rates *develop*, to complement our previous analysis of the processes of individual social interaction which *maintain* these rates. From such a view, Northwestern Europe, urbanizing sub-Saharan Africa, and the New World exhibit very different patterns.

Northwestern Europe: A Rural Subculture

The relatively high rates in Northwestern Europe were the product of a courtship system which permitted considerable sex freedom to the young, under indirect but effective adult and peer group supervision. The choice of sex partners and of eventual spouse was restricted to a pool of eligibles, who were children of farmers. When premarital conception or even birth occurred, the young man was likely to be known as the girl's partner, and both were likely to be acceptable to both sets of parents.[6] Illegitimacy was likely to occur mainly when there was some reason for delaying marriage (e.g., unavailability of farm or housing), rather than because either partner or set of parents had rejected the marriage.[7] Childbirth

outside of marriage was not approved. Rather, the exact *timing* of the marriage, whether before or slightly after the birth of the first child, was not a focus of intense moral concern.

This pattern was a "native," rural custom, upheld within an integrated social and cultural system of norms which was *not* integrated with those of the dominant national society. Both the national state and the Church opposed this pattern for centuries. It is not, then, a recent development, an index of "disorganization" in an urbanizing epoch. It is a subcultural difference, which has gradually been disappearing as isolated, rural cultural and social systems have become more closely integrated with national cultural and social systems.

Classical Assimilation Theory

Studies of United States rural-urban migrants and of immigrant populations in the period 1910-35 outlined a theory of assimilation and a theory of cultural destruction which fit both these cases of migration but which must be modified to fit the other two great cases of culture contact being analyzed in this paper, Africa and the New World south of the Mason-Dixon Line.

These migrants entered as *individuals* and families, so that their initial social systems were undermined. Thus their cultural patterns could not be maintained by those social systems and were dissolved by an open-class, individualistic, secular culture which gave substantial rewards to those who assimilated. The in-migrating populations were culturally absorbed by the dominant, numerically larger group. In the transitional period, they also became somewhat anomic: they lost their allegiance to their native cultural patterns but for a while felt no great commitment to the norms of the dominant group. To

---

[6] The most complete description of this pattern, and of its temporal and geographical distribution, is to be found in K. Rob. V. Wikman, *Einleitung Der Ehe*, Abo, *Acta Academiae Aboensis; Humaniora*, 1937. He asserts, however, that the pattern was not found in Iceland.

[7] And consequently, the rate of divorce for such marriages would be lower than for "forced" marriages in the United States. See Harold T. Christensen (above, p. 34). See also Sidney H. Croog, "Aspects of the Cultural Background of Premarital Pregnancy in Denmark," *Social Forces*, **39** (December, 1951), 215-219.

some extent, in various cities[8] they developed new social subsystems and kept some of their cultural integration by living in ghettos, from which individuals moved out as they became acculturated into the larger society. Younger and older generations were in conflict, since each was oriented to different cultures. Some people lived as "marginal men," being accepted by and accepting neither culture and neither social system fully.

These in-migrants typically entered society in the United States at the bottom of the class structure, where they were somewhat freed from both the older social controls and the controls of the new country. Some customs were difficult to obey under urban conditions and lost their force. Younger people could use either set of norms as a justification for any desired course of action. Generally, the native-born generation became acculturated, and the grandchild generation was *both* socially and culturally integrated in the larger society.

The cultural and social systems of the in-migrating peoples were undermined by these factors: (1) the dispersion of the immigrating social systems, (2) the political power and prestige standards of the receiving populations, which judged the migrants as belonging at the bottom of the class system, (3) the economic and social opportunities in the new system, which gave rewards to those who became acculturated and punished those who refused to do so, (4) the sheer numerical superiority of the receiving populations, and (5) the irrelevance of older customs to the new social situation.

---

[8] Mr. John Western has pointed out to me that there may be considerable difference in the assimilation patterns of those who "just landed" in the cities and stayed there and those who deliberately chose to migrate to the city.

Transitional populations exhibited of course relatively high rates of deviation in such areas as juvenile delinquency, adult criminality, desertion, illegitimacy, and so on. Unfortunately, the studies of that time did not make independent measures of "anomie," or "social disorganization," and correlate them with the usual rates of deviation in various areas of action. However, their findings do add corroboration to the modifications of Malinowski's principle, offered in the paper on the Caribbean: (1) its foundation is not primarily the protection which the male gives the child, but the social importance which a kin or family line enjoys (i.e., it focuses on status placement), and (2) the strength of the norm commitment will vary with the importance of the kin line and thus will be higher toward the upper strata, where the proportion of important kin lines is greater and where, as a consequence, illegitimacy rates will be lower.[9]

African Illegitimacy: Breakdown of the Cultural and Social Systems

Classical assimilation theory was, then, an outline of the processes by which a given "native" system moves from (a) being internally integrated both socially and culturally to (b) being internally nonintegrated or anomic *both* socially and culturally and then (c) eventually absorbed. *Individuals* moved from state (a), their original situation in their native region, to (b), losing their position in their native social system, but gaining one in the new United States social system and, for a considerable time, being part of the older cultural system but not part of the new one. Ultimately of course they became integrated in the new social and cultural system. That set of phases

---

[9] William J. Goode, *op. cit.,* 27ff.

must be modified somewhat to fit urbanizing or industrializing sub-Saharan Africa and still more to fit the New World. On the other hand, both the suggested modification of Malinowski's principle and the anonymous "bargaining" pattern of Caribbean courtship may be applied to the African situation.

The African anomie is like the older United States rural and foreign immigration in these respects: (a) African individuals have been greatly dispersed in the urban locations, (b) native customs are often irrelevant and inconvenient in urbanizing areas, and (c) white standards and customs have higher prestige. It differs chiefly in these respects: (a) the original dominance of the white group was achieved by force, (b) those being assimilated outnumber the dominant group, (c) the African cultures were much more different from that of the dominant group than were the cultures of the United States in-migrants from that of the United States, and (d) because the Africans face caste barriers they often cannot obtain substantial rewards for accepting European ways.

Important political consequences flow from these differences—for example, the inevitable creation of independent African nations throughout the continent—but here we shall confine ourselves to the matter of illegitimacy.

The natives in the African urban or industrialized locations have come from tribes in which elders were once powerful, marriages were arranged, and illegitimacy was rare. The skills and knowledge of the elders are not greatly respected in the urban areas because they are no longer effective. Social control is therefore likely to be reduced to the formal controls of the outside, white society. Although there is some tendency for people from the same tribe to cluster together, as happened in urban ghettos in the United States, such groupings achieve less social control over the individual than do the economic and political imperatives of urban life, and at every turn the native is reminded that both his parental culture and community have no prestige and can be ignored. The kin lines that his family was once at pains to preserve need not be taken seriously. A young man need not worry that a girl's elders or male siblings will bring him to account for a pregnancy outside marriage. A girl need not wait until her sweetheart has saved enough for the bride price; nor is she, unprotected by a kin network, in any position to force him to wait. White governments in Africa, like those in the United States *ante bellum* South, are little interested in maintaining legitimacy, since by caste definition African legitimacy has no relevance for white legitimacy. By contrast, United States white rural or foreign in-migrants could marry native whites so that public agencies were concerned about their legitimacy patterns.

The African couple need not bother with marriage. Indeed, marriage can no longer achieve its former manifest objectives: (1) it cannot maintain a respected lineage for yet another generation, since the kin line itself has lost its importance and because in an urban agglomeration the young man and woman may well be from different tribes, (2) it does not integrate a tribe by joining two lineages within it, since the tribe itself is disappearing and the tie may not be known to either lineage, and (3) it does not give a fully respected adult status to the young male, since under the Western caste pattern his rank will remain a lowly one, and whatever rank he does achieve will be based on his occupation and not his tribal position or the marriages he enters. Since, finally, both kin and elders

42 societal recognition of the family unit

have lost the authority on which social control once rested, both the young man and woman can and must make whatever individual role bargain with one another their circumstances permit.

In short, the political and economic dominance of the new urban world has begun to undermine that self-evident rightness of older family values which once guaranteed a legitimate position for the newborn child. The younger urban African generation has begun to feel a less intense commitment to those values, has acquired some opposing values, and in any event does not possess the means with which to achieve the older goals. The anomie of native African urban life in some centers surpasses anything observed in United States immigrant life, because the original culture of the African was more different from the Western culture, to which he must adjust, and his present deprivation is greater than that of the United States immigrant. The latter was already part of Western culture, so that the cultural destruction he experienced was minor by comparison. The native is at the bottom of a caste system and is no longer part of an integrated social group or cultural system that would permit him to assert his own worth or the worth of the family. Thus the stigma of illegitimacy becomes minor.

In the urbanizing African areas, the native patterns are neither (1) socially or culturally integrated internally nor are they (2) integrated socially or culturally with the dominant societies. In this transitional period, when the social importance of kin lines has become minimal, illegitimacy is high because of casual liaisons, promiscuity, and delayed marriage. On the other hand, the consensual union has perhaps not become the *usual* pattern of marital unions. The numerical preponderance

of the native population has prevented its being absorbed into white cultural patterns, but modern industrial and economic expansion has prevented the whites from "keeping them in their place," either in the tribes or in the stratification system.[10] As a consequence, the phases of destruction have proceeded rapidly, and perhaps reintegration will occur more swiftly than in the New World.

The New World

The conquest of the New World seems at first to exhibit a very different pattern. First, no case of cultural penetration on so huge a scale can be found since Rome, unless the Islamic conquest be excepted. From Alaska to Tierra del Fuego, aside from a few tribal pockets, the hemisphere is Western in culture. The native cultural systems have been penetrated, undermined, and destroyed, though of course some elements of the older cultures do survive.

Next, two different forms of destruction may be distinguished. One of these, shared by the Southern United States and the Caribbean, was primarily a physical destruction and overwhelming of the native population, together with the substitution of alien slaves, who were so mixed geographically that their social systems were destroyed, and thus they could not maintain their African cultural heritage. These slaves, emancipated for the most part late in the nineteenth century, became Western in culture. Their descendants generally occupy the bottom social strata in the countries in which they were introduced, but in a few countries, some occupy higher strata as well.

---

[10] The dominance of European nations is also weakened by important changes in the political philosophy of Europeans. They no longer accept colonialism as morally right.

The second major pattern of destruction, socially more complex, was found on the Latin American mainland, from Mexico southward. The main attacks were first concentrated on the three great population centers, the Aztec, Mayan, and Inca civilizations. Intent on political conquest and economic exploitation, the Iberians nearly undermined their own aims in the conquest period by wiping out from one third to one half of their subjects, through disease, overwork, and underfeeding. At first they ruled in part through native leaders, but by 1600 they had also removed this top stratum from power. Although the Church often opposed those actions, its own efforts at destroying native religions were backed by political leaders, so that even when the Church attempted to save native bodies, it persisted successfully in its goal of undermining native cults and substituting some form of Catholicism. The Iberians, like the whites in Africa, were greatly outnumbered by native Indians until relatively late in the Colonial period, but within a hundred years after the first conquests most of

the cultural destruction had already taken place.[11] The Iberians imposed their cultural patterns on the natives, unlike the Manchus in China, the Spanish in the Philippines, the Dutch in Indonesia, or the English in India.

Both the assimilation and destruction processes differed somewhat from those in Africa. The United States and the Caribbean masters dispersed the (forced, slave) immigrants, but the whites outnumbered them in the United States and did not in the Caribbean. On the mainland, the Indians outnumbered the Iberians, but their social systems were in part undermined by death and partly by forced dispersion and relocation in villages. There was no industrial expansion, and little economic expansion, so that there was little need (in contrast to modern Africa) to use the natives in higher-level jobs. Native African customs are essen-

---

[11] See the estimates of the proportion of destruction by certain dates in Sol Tax, et al., *Heritage of Conquest* (New York: The Free Press of Glencoe, Inc., 1952), p. 264. Most of these groups are among the less acculturated peoples in the New World.

TABLE 1   Comparison of Cultural and Social Destruction and Assimilation Patterns: Modern United States Cities, Modern Industrializing Sub-Saharan Africa, and the Past New World

Patterns	Immigration to United States Cities, Rural or Foreign	Modern Africa	NEW WORLD: PRE-1900		
			Ante-Bellum U.S. South	Caribbean	Mainland Iberian Countries
1. Physical destruction of acculturating population	No	Some	Little or none	Some	Considerable at first
2. Dispersal of social groupings	Yes	Yes	Yes	Yes	Yes
3. Numerical preponderance of population being acculturated	No	Yes	No	Yes	Yes
4. Prestige dominance of absorbing population	Yes	Yes	Yes	Yes	Yes
5. Caste system	No	Yes	Yes	Yes	Yes
6. Industrial expansion	Yes	Yes	Yes	No	No
7. Economic expansion	Yes	Yes	Yes	No	No
8. Relevance of native customs to new situation	No	No	Yes	Yes	Yes
9. Situation of culture contact	Urban	Urban	Rural	Rural	Village and Urban

tially irrelevant to the problems faced in urban and industrial situations, but since in the New World the natives or slaves were used primarily in an agricultural setting, their customs might have been maintained had the whites not opposed them. In all these cases, the rule of the whites was based to a considerable degree on face-to-face interaction rather than indirect rule.[12]

The destruction pattern in these major cases are summarized in Table 1:

Before analyzing the consequences of these different patterns, let us comment further on the situation of the mainland natives. Although the Iberian rulers attempted to hold the Indians in economic, and therefore political, subjection and thus sought to keep a rigid caste line between the two groups,[13] the emergence of two new classes in the stratification system had considerable effect on the subsequent development of the family system. One new class, eventually to become the top stratum, was the Creoles, those born in the New World as legitimate offspring of Iberian families. As in the colonial United States, these rulers gradually loosened their ties with the Old World and led the revolutions which, in one country after another, freed all these possessions, except Puerto Rico and Cuba, from Mexico southward, during the first quarter of the nineteenth century. The second class, which began at first from illegitimate unions between Iberians and Indians, were the *mestizos*, who gradually came to be a majority of the population in most Latin American countries. Likely to be intermediate in both appearance and culture between the rulers of pure descent and the Indians, this class reduced the strength of barriers against mobility.

More important for our understanding of cultural penetration, the mainland caste patterns permitted mainly only one form of mobility, what is called "passing" in United States white-Negro relations. This pattern is still found in the so-called caste relations between Ladinos and Indios in Guatemala[14] and in the Andean Highlands of Bolivia, Ecuador, and Peru. That is, the individual could enter the Iberian world, for the most part in urban areas, only by becoming Iberian in all observable cultural characteristics, by ceasing to be Indian. He might starve as easily being all Iberian as being Indian, but without becoming Iberian the way upward was entirely closed. This structural pattern permitted some upward mobility without softening the low evaluation of Indian culture and without eroding the social barrier between Indian and Iberian.

In the New World, then, the native social and cultural systems were undermined by the steady economic and political pressures of a *closed*-class system, rather than by the open-class, expanding, industrializing system of the modern world. The destruction was greatest among the slaves of the antebellum South, less in the Caribbean,

---

[12] Of course the whites first ruled indirectly in Africa through native chiefs, but this becomes impossible in industrial and urban locations.

[13] The Creoles faced similar restrictions also: only four viceroys in Spanish America up to 1813 were American born, and these were sons of Spanish officials; 601 of the 706 bishops and archbishops came from Spain. Moreover, the restrictions had become more severe in the eighteenth century [C. H. Haring, *The Spanish Empire in America* (New York: Oxford University Press, 1957), p. 209]. It can be argued that the first *social* revolution in Latin America was the 1910 Mexican Revolution [Robin A. Humphreys, *The Evolution of Modern Latin America* (New York: Oxford University Press, 1946), pp. 119-122].

[14] Melvin M. Tumin, *Caste in a Peasant Society* (Princeton: Princeton University Press, 1952).

and least on the Iberian mainland. Southern slaves were "seasoned" in the Caribbean first and were further dispersed on arrival in the United States. Indians were able, especially in areas of less economic and political interest to the Iberians, to maintain some part of their social and cultural integration for many decades, and a few tribes still exist in remote regions, such as the upper Amazon. An index of the disorganization of Caribbean slaves is their failure to reproduce,[15] so that slave-running continued to be profitable almost until the end of the slavery period. In general, the illegitimacy rates of former slave areas are still higher than the nonslave areas; and on the mainland countries rimming the Caribbean, the coastal provinces where Negro slaves were introduced have higher rates than the interior.

The caste barriers were most severe in the ante-bellum South, somewhat less severe in the Caribbean non-Iberian islands, and least severe on the Iberian mainland. As Tannenbaum has shown, the Iberian treatment of even Negroes was less rigid than the treatment by any of the other New World settlers.[16]

The Iberians also made the most conscious effort to indoctrinate their subject peoples, the Indians, in Western norms, especially those relating to religion. However, in all these cases the inculcation of the new, Western values proceeded slowly and inconsistently. It is difficult to socialize an individual unless he is assured of acceptance as a full member of the social system, but the Iberians refused to accept the Indian anywhere until recently. *Village* controls were weak, because norm commitment to either native or Iberian values was weak and because the local social system was truncated: the locus of economic and political power was in the Iberian world, and the religious system accepted the Indian as parishioner, not as priest. Rewards for becoming Iberian were low or nonexistent. For example, the Indian might be exhorted to work hard, but he would be subjected to economic exploitation if he acquired any wealth. Learning to read would help little, since there were few positions open to him if he became literate. The Iberian pressures were directed toward keeping the Indians docile, not toward transforming them into Iberians.

In the slave areas, primarily the United States, Brazil, and the Circum-Caribbean, neither master nor slave had any concern about illegitimacy, since the slave kin line had no social importance: slavery undermines the status of the male as family head more than that of the female,[17] and it is precisely the male elders who would be (in an independent society) the guardians of the family honor. It was to the interest of the conquerors or masters to prevent the development of native systems of social control, whether family or community, for therein lay a potential threat to their dominance. Even in the twentieth-century United States South, whites have opposed the "pretensions" of Negroes in seeking certificates of marriage and divorce. Slavery was abolished only late in the nineteenth century, and we could expect that where the caste barriers against Negroes were stronger, especially outside the Iberian regions, concern about Negro legitimacy among both whites and Negroes would develop only slowly.

[15] For an analysis of one attempt to solve this problem, see J. Harry Barnett, "The Problem of Slave Labor Supply at the Codrington Plantations," *Journal of Negro History*, 37 (April, 1952), 115-141.

[16] Frank Tannenbaum, *Slave and Citizen* (New York: Alfred A. Knopf, Inc., 1947).

[17] Ruth Landes, "Negro Slavery and Female Status," *Les Afro-Américains* (Dakar: Institut Français d'Afrique-Noire, 1952), pp. 265-266.

Illegitimacy and the Structure of Community Integration

Our review to this point suggests that it is the *community*, not the individual or the family, that maintains conformity to, or deviation from, the norm of legitimacy. The community defines and confers legitimacy. The individual decision, his or her role bargain, determines whether illegitimacy will be risked, and both family and individual may lose standing if illegitimacy results, but there is little stigma if the community itself gives almost as much respect for conformity as for nonconformity. Lacking integration, the community cannot easily punish the deviant. In any population, the maintenance of a high individual or family commitment to a given norm or conformity to the norm is dependent on *both* the commitment of the community to the *cultural* norm and the strength of its *social* controls. In the New World during the Colonial period and the nineteenth century, as in contemporary industrializing sub-Saharan Africa, both native community controls and the commitment to the norm of legitimacy were weak. Correlatively, neither conquerors nor masters were concerned, since such deviations had little effect on their primary interests, power and economic exploitation.

The failure of community social integration means, then, a high rate of illegitimacy, since (a) it is likely to occur along with a weakening of norm commitment and (b) even if norms are not greatly weakened, controls are weak. However, the nature of this community integration or nonintegration must be *specified*. We cannot fall back on the frequent alternative term, "anomie." The classical definition of "anomie," *normlessness*, is not adequate because such a state is so extreme: almost no cases of it, perhaps

none at all unless we accept the examples of Nazi concentration camps and of United States prisoners of the Chinese during the Korean War, have been described by modern investigators. Here we can more usefully think of anomie or nonintegration as a matter of *degree*. However, sociological theory has not agreed on a clear meaning for "nonintegration." Moreover, most analysts have viewed New World villages as "communities," i.e., as integrated. Thus it is fruitful to specify the *several* structural points where "integration" may or may not exist.

We are asserting that for a period of about two centuries most of the slave and peasant populations of the New World lived in relatively stable, *non*-integrated settlements, kept from integration by United States, Iberian, and other European rulers. They were kept from either being integrated into the Western cultural and social systems *or* establishing independent, *internally* integrated cultural and social systems of their own. Here of course we necessarily go beyond the available data, but some of the specific descriptions can eventually be tested.

The points of nonintegration can be outlined as follows:

I. These villages were not internally *culturally* integrated. This statement also holds of course for the United States Southern Negro population, only a few of whom ever lived in separate communities. Without even a geographical basis, cultural integration is most difficult to achieve. This general assertion means:

A. There was a commitment, though relatively weak, to a wide range of norms from *both* cultures: religious elements from both cultures, allegiance to both languages, songs, and music, or local and "national" loyalties.
B. There was relatively low norm commitment to various *instru-*

mental norms, such as literacy, Western languages, skills in economic activities, etc., which might have been useful in fulfilling *other* Western norms to which there was some commitment.

C. Conditions for the achievement of norms in the villages were difficult (contradictions of norms and conditions).

1. Costs of church marriage were high.
2. Masters or conquerors were little interested in facilitating formal marriage.
3. Costs of the *fiesta*, or reception, after marriage were high.
4. There were few means for economic expansion, literacy, and even learning Church beliefs precisely.
5. Conquerors and masters opposed native or slave efforts to pretend to the status honor enjoyed by rulers.
6. European goods were urged on them, but prices were high.
7. Responsibility for debts or labor was encouraged, but caste prohibitions against mobility were strong.[18]

II. These villages were not internally *socially* integrated. Of course where there is very low norm commitment, social integration may be low: there is little to be integrated *about*. Again the Southern Negro population obviously fits this description, which means:

A. White rulers prevented the development of local leadership or self-rule, thus hindering community controls.

B. Natives were not generally permitted to participate in Church activities as priests or officials (the cofradías may be viewed as a partial exception, but they were organized to insure proper contributions to the Church).

C. Any local community pressures, decisions, or rules were subject to being overridden by the whites.

III. The village *cultural* patterns were not integrated with "national," white patterns. This means:

A. The two patterns were differently oriented toward various important norms: the value of working and owning agricultural land, the value of living in the city, nationalism-patriotism, or belief in the details of Church doctrine.

B. Whites viewed the native, or Negro, patterns as alien, rather than as merely lower class or a variant of the dominant culture.

C. Whites viewed the native, or Negro, people as requiring acculturation or training (even when they wasted little energy on the task), not as having a different culture of equal validity.

IV. The villages were not *socially* integrated with the dominant social system of the whites or the larger social system of the nation.

A. Natives did not generally feel part of the nation and had little interest in the changing political fortunes of the élite.

B. Relatively few intercommunity relations existed.[19]

C. The native was not viewed as a "citizen" everywhere in the nation, and many barriers to free movement existed.

D. The economic system was locally oriented for the most part.

E. The wishes of the local villages were little taken into account in national planning or action.

---

[18] See an examination of these contradictions by George Kubler, "The Quechua in the Colonial World," in *Handbook of South American Indians, op. cit.,* Vol. 2, pp. 374-375 *et passim.* Indians in Peru were not even allowed to own horses, though there were many of them: Bernard Mishkin, "The Contemporary Quechua," *ibid.,* p. 427.

[19] Mishkin (*ibid.,* p. 448) reports this of the Quechua today. The "isolation" of New World villages south of the Rio Grande has been commented on by most observers.

All four structural connections have been specified, in order to avoid needless debate as to whether these populations were "anomic," or "nonintegrated." The outline is thus partly a summary of the preceding analysis but emphasizes the special character of the nonintegration of these populations, which also applies *mutatis mutandi* to the Negro population of the Old South in the United States. The caste pattern of India is different in that the local village is *internally* both socially and culturally integrated; and it is culturally integrated with the larger Indian cultural pattern in that the local caste norms and patterns are viewed as a legitimate part of the national moral fabric. It seems doubtful, however, that until recently such local village castes were *socially* integrated with the national social system except through a lengthy series of intermediate steps. Under such circumstances, social control remains strong locally and so does the commitment to the norm of legitimacy.

Consequently, in the New World, from the Old South in the United States to Cape Horn, the nonwhites assimilated only slowly into the social and cultural patterns of the West. They accepted the superiority of these patterns or at least did not assert the contrary. However, the barriers to integration into the nationally dominant patterns and the forces arrayed against local social or cultural integration failed to yield the rewards which are necessary for effective acculturation, so that the process did not accelerate in most countries until the twentieth century.[20] Consequently, both low norm commitment to legitimacy and weak com-

---

[20] It is worth noting that Alexander von Humboldt also commented on the relation between the Indian's anomie and lack of motivation (see Haring, *op. cit.*, pp. 201-202).

munity controls maintained relatively high illegitimacy rates.

Phases of Assimilation: Rural-Urban Illegitimacy Differentials

Although the foregoing outline of nonintegration in the New World seems both theoretically and descriptively correct, it goes far beyond available data from individual community studies, which would test whether any large proportion of existing or historical villages were in fact nonintegrated. However, some further conclusions can be derived and tested in this analysis, so that we are not left merely with speculations.

The first of these concerns the *phases* of nonintegration. If the line of theory pursued so far is correct, then in the conquest period in the Iberian world the illegitimacy rates first began to increase in the urban centers where contact was first made and the primary undermining of the Indian patterns began. Thereafter, however, because urban centers were the source of westernizing forces and the urban Indians were more likely to assimilate, the norm of formal marriage was more likely to be followed. In addition of course, the cities contained Iberians who would usually follow this norm. Thus while the rural areas were kept in a relatively nonintegrated state or forced gradually into it as Iberian dominance spread, the urban regions moved toward Western norms.

We should therefore suppose that in most cases the urban illegitimacy rates would now be *lower* than the rural rates, even though the modern rapid urbanization of Latin America may be creating all those disruptions of social and cultural patterns which have elsewhere been recorded when rural peo-

TABLE 2 Differences in Illegitimacy Rates Between Capitals and Remainder of Country, Mainland Independent Countries South of the Rio Grande[21]

Political Unit	Year	Federal Capital Major Urban Province	Per Cent	Remainder of Country (23.8% for whole)	Highest Rate in Any Department or Province (Per Cent)
Argentina	(1957)	Federal Capital	10.4	27.0	60.3 (Formosa)
Brazil	(1952)	Capital Territory	12.4	15.0 (Total for Country as a Whole)	
Chile	(1958)	Valparaiso Province	16.3	25.2	30.2 (Coquimbo)
Uruguay	(1943)	Montevideo	18.4	27.5	66.7 (Florida)
Paraguay	(1946)	Capital	62.4	56.5	(No Figure Obtainable)
Colombia	(1956)	Cundinamarca Section	20.2	30.1	69.1 (Córdoba)
Ecuador	(1947)	Pichincha Province	22.3	34.7	84.9 (Los Rios)
Peru	(1953)	Callao Department Lima & Callao Departments	30.9 46.4	43.9 43.0	59.6 (Loreto) 54.7 (Lambayeque)
Venezuela	(1954)	Federal District	47.2	58.3	74.9 (Yaracuy)
Nicaragua	(1947)	Managua Department	57.5	62.3	70.4 (Chinandega)
Honduras	(1957)	Francisco Morazán	68.4	69.3	80.3 (Colón)
Costa Rica	(1957)	Province San José	14.2	28.1	49.1 (Limón)
Mexico	(1956)	Distrito Federal	12.9	23.9	27.9 (Sinaloa)
El Salvador	(1955)	San Salvador Urban Area	30.8	59.3	67.6 (Santa Ana)
Guatemala	(1956-57)	Urban Areas	64.5	76.1 (Rural Areas)	
Panama	(1958)	Urban Areas	64.5	79.6 (Rural Areas)	

ples enter an urban milieu.[22] In Table 2, the rural and urban rates are presented.

As can be seen, the conclusion is validated, except for Paraguay. If our theory of phases in disintegration and reintegration is correct, this means that Paraguay, the socioeconomically least developed of independent Latin American countries, has not yet entered the phase in which urban rates have begun to drop below rural ones. It should do

---

[21] Data from official sources.

[22] I am of course aware of the difficulties in interpreting illegitimacy rates in countries where recording procedures are undeveloped: (1) Official urban rates might be higher than rural rates, because recording procedures are more thorough. (2) In some rural areas, those classed as "Indios" may be generally ignored by officials. (3) Where social services are available in the city, as in San Juan, Puerto Rico, some illegitimacies may be recorded there, although the mothers come from rural villages. (4) The disorganization of urban slums may lead to much promiscuity and thus *override* any of the factors presented in my analysis (e.g., Caracas, Venezuela). (5) It is difficult to obtain true "rural-urban" breakdowns, because the political subunits (provinces, departments, sections) of Latin American nations typically contain both an urban center and a surrounding rural countryside, and the data are recorded for the subunit as a whole. Nevertheless, all of these except the last (whose effect is unknown) would bias the official rates *against* my hypothesis. Consequently it seems safe to use the data. Many analysts have claimed that consensual unions, and therefore illegitimacy, are more common in rural areas. As we shall see, however, that assertion is correct only for mainland, independent Latin America. [See, for example, Kingsley Davis and Ana Casís, *Urbanization in Latin America* (New York: Milbank Memorial Fund, 1946), pp. 39-40.]

Included under "illegitimate" are those born of a consensual union, whether or not the offspring are "recognized," as well as those born outside of any continuing marital relationship. These are official rates.

so in the future. Correspondingly, of the seven independent Iberian countries with very high rates (over 50 per cent) all are little developed, and still show very low differentials between urban and rural rates. Finally, in the more advanced countries, such as Uruguay and Mexico, the differences should *diminish* in the future.

The mainland *dependent* countries do not fit this phase pattern (British and Dutch Guiana, British Honduras), nor do the Caribbean island countries. Of the three Caribbean countries that have been independent for more than half a century, Haiti, Cuba, and the Dominican Republic, we have been able to obtain rural-urban breakdowns for only one, the Dominican Republic, where the rural rate *is* slightly higher but has become so only recently (65.1-63.9 per cent, 1958).

In the Caribbean political units, the rural rates are almost the same as the urban and are very slightly *lower* in over half of them. This region differs from the mainland Iberian lands pri-

marily in these characteristics: (1) Almost all their population is descendant from slaves: caste restrictions were more severe against Negroes than on the mainland against the Indios; (2) almost all of them have been dependencies until this century, so that there has been little basis for national integration; (3) most important, the phases which apply to the mainland Iberian countries do not apply here, since the initial disorganization *was as intense in rural as in urban regions*. The Indians were everywhere destroyed. The slaves who replaced them were no longer members of a community, and the bulk of them were used in agriculture. We should not expect the Caribbean, then, to follow all the phases of the mainland development, though we predict that the urban rates will become lower than the rural. Several of the differentials are given in Table 3. The United States Southern Negro rates are also included, as following the Caribbean pattern.

TABLE 3 New World Rural-Urban Differentials in Illegitimacy Rates, Selected Mainland Dependencies and Caribbean Countries[23]

ILLEGITIMACY RATES

	Urban (Per Cent)	Rural (Per Cent)
U.S. South, Nonwhite (1957)	18.6-32.7	18.6-32.1
Puerto Rico (1956)	34.6 (San Juan)	27.4 (Rest of Country)
British Guiana (1955)	43.8	33,6
Trinidad and Tobago (1956)	47.3	47.4
Dominican Republic (1958)	63.9	65.1
Surinam (Dutch Guiana) (1951)	43.0 (Paramaribo)	38.0 (Rest of Country)
Jamaica (1954)	73.1 (Capital)	71.5 (Rest of Country)
British Honduras (1956)	52.9 (Capital District)	49.8 (Rest of Country)
Barbados (1955)	65.2 (Capital Parish)	59.3 (Rest of Country)

Illegitimacy and Degree of National Integration

A second conclusion may be drawn from our earlier analysis. The New

[23] Rates calculated from figures furnished by Caribbean Commission and from U.S. National Office of Vital Statistics.

World countries have succeeded to varying degrees in integrating their formerly Indian or slave populations into the national cultural and social systems. Since their illegitimacy rates are in part a function of this variable, countries which have moved *further* toward such an integration should have

illegitimacy, anomie, and cultural penetration **51**

lower rates. The degree of this type of integration is greatly dependent on the extent of industrialization and urbanization, since these variables require more interconnections between different parts of a nation and offer rewards to the individual for entering the cultural systems. Thus it becomes both easier and more desirable to conform to the norm of legitimacy. However, the rank order of the illegitimacy rates has a Spearman-Brown coefficient of correlation of only .50 with the rank order of urbanization as measured by the percentage of the national population living in the major metropolitan areas.

In Table 4, most of the New World political units are ranked by the degree to which their formerly slave or Indian populations have been brought into the dominant cultural and social systems. As can be seen, with few exceptions the conclusion holds: in general, where the formerly slave or Indian populations have been more fully integrated into the national cultural and social systems, the national illegitimacy rates are lower.

Illegitimacy and the Internal Integration of Communities

A third deduction from our earlier analysis can be tested: because of the wide variety of geographical and sociological factors in New World history, some communities have either continued to be *internally* integrated both socially and culturally (but *not* integrated culturally or socially with the *national* systems) or else reachieved such an integration after the initial dissolution. Such communities would then be the main source of individual or family honor and rank, and would be able and willing to ensure conformity to the norm of legitimacy. Thus their illegitimacy rates would be low. Their *formal* official rates might be *high*, since the national registration system will recog-

nize only the legal, civil ceremony; but their social rates would be low, since few people will enter a union without a public marriage ceremony of some kind in which both family lines par-

TABLE 4　New World Political Units According to Their Degree of National Integration and Illegitimacy Rates[24]

Degree of National Integration	Illegitimacy Rates (Per Cent)	Date
A. Higher Integration		
Brazil	15	1952
Chile	16	1958
Uruguay	20	1954
Mexico	22.5	1956
Costa Rica	25	1957
B. Medium Integration		
Argentina	28	1957
Colombia	28	1957
Cuba	30	1939
Puerto Rico	28.5	1955
U.S. Old South, Negro	19-32	1957
C. Lower Integration		
Ecuador	36	1956
Peru	43	1955
British Guiana	34	1957
Paraguay	48	1955
Surinam	34	1953
French Guiana	65	1956
Venezuela	57	1955
Guatemala	70	1957
Panama	71	1956
Jamaica	72	1954
Martinique	48	1956
British Honduras	48	1957
D. Not Classified		
Dominican Republic	55	1956
El Salvador	59	1953
Honduras	65	1957
Nicaragua	62	1945

[24] All rates were obtained from the *United Nations Demographic Year Book Questionnaire* for the respective dates, except the figure for Puerto Rico, which was obtained from the Caribbean Commission. It was not possible to obtain recent Cuban data, and many smaller poltical units have been omitted. Bolivia has been eliminated because any birth is recorded as legitimate if the couple has been living together for two years (personal communication from Dirección Nacional de Estadística). As noted later, in Guatemala many births are classified as illegitimate because no civil ceremony preceded them,

TABLE 5 **Illegitimacy and Integration in Selected New World Communities**[25]

	High Rate of Illegitimacy	Low Rate of Illegitimacy*
High Integration:		Tzintzuntzán (Mexico)
		Cherán (Mexico)
		Cruz das Almas (Brazil)
		Tusik and Quintana Roo (Mayans of Mexico)
		Orange Grove (Jamaica)
		Nyame (British Guiana)
		Saucío (Colombia)
		Santa Eulalia (Guatemala)
		Peguche (Ecuador)
		Otóvalo (Ecuador)
Low Integration:	Rocky Roads (Jamaica)	Chichicastenango (Guatemala)
	Sugartown (Jamaica)	
	Moche (Peru)	
	Tobatí (Paraguay)	

* "Low" illegitimacy means of course relative to the level prevailing in the respective countries. Specific rates cannot be calculated from the descriptions.

though other types of marriage ceremonies may have occurred, so that its real rate is lower than its official rate.

With respect to the independent variable, there is reason to believe that this classification would for the most part be conceded by New World specialists. Several such specialists have already accepted it.

The bases for the classification are these: (1) The maintenance of caste barriers, which remain strong in Guatemala and the Andean Highlands and are weak in Brazil and Mexico. (2) Extent of ethnic homogeneity. Uruguay and Costa Rica, for example, are very "Spanish" or "European," and in Mexico, Cuba, Chile, and Puerto Rico, a thoroughgoing mixing has occurred, in contrast to Guatemala. (3) The status of political dependency. (4) The existence of national programs for education, literacy, economic development (Puerto Rico, United States, Argentina). (5) The existence of large pockets of geographically and socially isolated populations (Bolivia, Ecuador, Peru). (6) Comparison of comments by New World experts, with respect to how much the natives care about or take part in national political affairs or how long various forms of labor exploitation have continued (e.g., indentured labor was abolished in Jamaica in 1917). Too much weight may have been given to the relatively unintegrated Andean populations of Bolivia, Peru, and Ecuador. If so, they would move to "medium" integration, and their reported illegitimacy rates would "fit" better. . . .

Doubtless many observers would classify *all* those in D as "lower integration" units. I have no objection but simply have been unable to obtain sufficient data on them to be certain.

ticipate. Such communities might be found, for example, in the Andean Highlands of Peru, Bolivia, and Ecuador, or the Northwestern highland region of Guatemala, and even here and there in the Caribbean. We should find low real rates of illegitimacy in such villages and high rates in villages where such integration seems weak. In Table 5, various places which have been the object of community studies are classified by illegitimacy rates and by the degree of integration, i.e., the extent to which the village forms a self-validating social and cultural system.

As can be seen, we find relatively low

[25] The relatively highly integrated communities here outnumber the less well integrated, because anthropologists seek out the "unspoiled," the "culturally unified" village. . . . To classify a village as *non*integrated appears to be more difficult than to show its integration, possibly because there are many different ways in which a village may *not* be internally integrated. Indices such as these seem relevant: (1) how many of the young adults are attracted to city life and ways, (2) how well the elders still control the young, (3) how important is a "good name in the village," (4) how effectively nonlegal, informal relationships may decide local issues, (5) how large a portion of the village participates in ceremonies and how much of village life centers around such ceremonies.

illegitimacy, anomie, and cultural penetration **53**

rates of illegitimacy in specific communities which have achieved, or reachieved, an internal social and cultural coherence, an acceptance of themselves as the source of prestige.[26] Individuals in such communities are participants in their social systems and presumably also committed to their cultural norms. If the prestige is earned within the system, then a family line or the community as a whole will insist on conformity with the norm of legitimacy. The communities which form a self-validating social system have low rates, and the communities which are less integrated have higher rates.

Conclusion

The present paper has attempted to relate cultural penetration, cultural and social anomie, and illegitimacy rates, by considering the main areas of high rates: Northwestern Europe, urbanizing Africa south of the Sahara, and the New World south of the Mason-Dixon Line. In the first case, the community retains control, and though some children are born outside of wedlock, they are likely to be only technically and temporarily illegitimate, not socially illegitimate. In urbanizing Africa, by contrast, Western culture has undermined the native cultural and social systems, and the Western community has not created conditions which permit the native to become a full member of the Western social and cultural system.

This situation is also observable in the history of the Western Hemisphere among both United States rural and foreign immigrants, where, however, the later phases in such a massive

process of penetration have also taken place. The parallels among the United States and Latin American mainland, the Caribbean, and urbanizing Africa are striking, if we allow for the differences which the twentieth-century political situation has imposed on Africa. At the same time, apparent differences suggest theoretical reformulations of the assimilation process. We see a conquering people who first rule indirectly through native leaders, and then directly (in Africa and the New World south of the Rio Grande); considerable destruction of native populations and forced migrations; destruction of the native cultures, but the erection of quasicaste barriers to prevent the full achievement or even complete acceptance of Western norms by the native; the undermining of the *local* community as the source of prestige; bars to entrance into the conquering Western community; and the dissolution of native family systems, without granting the rewards for conformity to the new Western family norms. We have also outlined the differences among these cases.

Behind the New World, however, are 400 years of assimilation, so that it has been possible to see what happens after the initial period of cultural penetration. It is in the cities that full assimilation of the peasant is possible, and under the later industrialization that assimilation is even useful to the upper strata. Thus it is in the city that the Indian peasant may become not only culturally, but also socially, assimilated, while in the rural areas (the encomiendas) and villages he has taken over Western *culture* with less commitment, because he has been denied a part in the Western *social* community, with its concomitant rewards and punishments. Thus it is in the urban areas that the rule of legitimacy begins to be imposed more stringently by the

---

[26] Various observers have remarked on the lesser ease, openness, and friendliness of the Andean peasants who work on a *finca* or *hacienda* compared with those who have continued to live on communal lands.

community, and the *mestizo* becomes willing to pay the price of marriage, such as the wedding feast, which serves as both a community blessing and a ritual of passage.

In a parallel fashion, those countries in which strides have been taken toward integrating their populations into the national community will have lower illegitimacy rates.

And finally, where the village becomes the cosmos, usually in isolated or mountainous areas, so that the individual in it is participating in both the cultural system and the social system of a genuine community, there again we find a stronger commitment to the norm of legitimacy, and greater community and family concern about marriage. The dominant value system does not set norms which the individuals cannot achieve; there is less contradiction between norms, so that there is a stronger commitment to them; and the coherence of the community permits more effective sanctions to enforce conformity to the norm of legitimacy.

Part 3

the social
and market processes
in
family formation

caste elements in marriage

seven

In the following article, the author ingeniously ties together the facts about intercaste marriage in the United States as a way of illustrating the processes by which the larger social structure affects mate choice. Later in the inquiry, he also presents an outline of variables useful in the further study of these processes.

Intermarriage and the Social Structure: Fact and Theory

ROBERT K. MERTON

Intermarriage is a concrete action involving numerous facets, the more dramatic of which have been accorded considerable attention by students of interpersonal relations. The dramatic, however, is not always the theoretically significant; human interest and scientific relevance do not invariably coincide. Among the more prosy aspects of inter-

Robert K. Merton, "Intermarriage and the Social Structure: Fact and Theory," *Psychiatry*, 4 (August, 1941), 361-364, 370-374. Reprinted by special permission of The William Alanson White Psychiatric Foundation, Inc. Copyright 1941 by The William Alanson White Psychiatric Foundation, Inc.

marriage is the role of the social structure. Rates and patterns of intermarriage are closely related to cultural orientations, standardized distributions of income, and symbols of status. The conflicts and accommodations of mates from socially disparate groups are partly understandable in terms of this environing structure. A provisional theory of structural components in intermarriage, then, can contribute to the analysis of interpersonal relations although . . . the sociological abstractions refer to consistencies in cultural definitions rather than to the actions of particular persons. The theory of social structure complements the theory of personal interaction; from a functional standpoint, regularities in the two spheres are mutually implicative.

* * * * *

Speaking literally, all marriage is intermarriage in the sense that the contractants derive from different social groups of one sort or another. This follows immediately from the universal incest taboo, which forbids marriage at least between members of the same elementary family unit and derivatively restricts marriage to members of different family groups. Marriage contractants invariably[1] come from different elementary family groups; often from different locality, occupational, political, nationality groups; and at times from different religious and linguistic groups, races, and castes. Thus if the term "intermarriage" is used to denote all marriage between persons of *any* different groups whatsoever, without any further specification of the groups involved, it becomes virtually synonymous, with the term "marriage" and may well be eliminated. In other words, differences in group affiliation of the contractants may occur, but if these affiliations—for example, political, neighborhood, social clubs—are not defined as relevant to the selection of a spouse, then the case is one of marriage, not intermarriage. The fact is, however, that certain types of marriage are sufficiently distinctive with respect to the group affiliations of the contractants as to mark them off as a special category. Intermarriage, then, will be defined as *marriage of persons deriving from those different in-groups and out-groups other than the families which are culturally conceived as relevant to the choice of a spouse.* Thus a given marriage may be, within one frame of reference—for example, the caste—in-marriage, and within another frame of reference—for example, social class—intermarriage. The distinction is analytical.

* * * * *

The distinction between norms and practices of mate selection is . . . necessary because practices are influenced not only by the rules, but also by certain *conditions*, which facilitate or hinder conformity to the rules. In other words, the actual practices are resultants of the norms *and* specifiable conditions of group life. Among the nonnormative conditions affecting actual rates of in- and out-marriage are size of group, sex composition, age composition, and degree of contact between members of different groups. These conditions, it will be noted, are not directly matters of standardized attitudes, sentiment or cultural definitions, although they are interdependent with normative factors. Norms may affect the degree and type of social contact; as embodied in immigration laws, for example, they may influence the size of nationality groups and, indirectly, even

---

[1] "Invariably" on the basis of a study of 220 societies by George P. Murdock, "Sex Mores and Social Structure," an unpublished paper presented at the annual meeting of the American Sociological Society, December 29, 1940. "All societies prohibit sexual intercourse and marriage between mother and son, father and daughter, and brother and sister. Our 220 cases reveal no genuine exception to any of these three universal incest taboos. To be sure, in two instances brother-sister marriages are customary in the royal family, and in one case a paramount chief may marry his own daughter, but in all three societies such incestuous unions are rigorously forbidden to the rest of the population, and special factors explain their occurrence among the chosen few of highest status." Ralph Linton, *The Study of Man* (New York: Appleton-Century-Crofts, Inc., 1936), p. 125, holds that "the prohibition of marriage between mother and son is the only one universally present." Whether occasional exceptions to this taboo are "genuine" or not, the approximation to universality is not questioned.

their sex and age composition. But the conditions may best be treated as largely independent factors in the selection of mates, quite apart from the cultural norms. As Romanzo Adams has indicated in this connection, "the larger the group the higher the percentage of in-marriage, irrespective of any sentiment relative thereto."[2] Likewise, a radical disproportion in the sex ratio, as in the case of Chinese and Filipinos in this country, exerts a pressure for out-marriage. These pressures may be more than counterbalanced by in-group sentiments, but analytically it is necessary to recognize their significance. Comparisons between rates of intermarriage in different populations should take account of the relative numbers of potential in-group mates, as affected by size, sex and age composition, territorial distribution, and technologically determined opportunities for contact. Norms and actual frequencies of intermarriage, then, are not to be confused.

When, with a changing social structure, the functional significance of certain norms governing choice of a spouse diminishes, the antagonism toward violations and finally the norms themselves will tend to disappear. When the in- and out-groups are in fact progressing toward social and cultural assimilation; when pathways for group consolidation are established; when a considerable part of the population is alienated from traditional group distinctions; when social mobility is notably high; when physical and cultural marks of group distinction have largely disappeared and group "differences" persist merely as a matter of purely technical defini-

tion—as, for example, with the third generation of native-born white Americans—then a state of affairs is reached where the quadrisyllable, "intermarriage," is whittled down to a bisyllable, "marriage." . . . The circle of permissible mates is enlarged, and the change in social organization is registered by newly modified norms concerning the selection of marriage partners.

Intermarriage, whether permitted or tabooed, does not occur at random but according to more or less clearly describable patterns. Two of these patterns may be selected for special attention. The first may be called *hypergamy*, a term which we adapt from its usage in connection with the Hindu caste system to denote institutionalized or noninstitutionalized patterns of intermarriage wherein the female marries into a higher social stratum, in a system of caste, class, or estate—*Stände*. We may introduce the term *hypogamy* to denote the pattern wherein the female marries into a lower social stratum. *Institutionalized* hypergamy or hypogamy denote those instances where the practice conforms to a norm contained in the law or mores; *noninstitutionalized* hypergamy or hypogamy denote statistical uniformities of a hypergamous or hypogamous nature which are not, however, explicitly governed by a norm. Thus Hindu hypergamy is an institutionalized pattern; American caste hypogamy, a noninstitutionalized pattern or a statistical uniformity but not a normatively prescribed arrangement.

. . . These [and other] conceptual distinctions provide a framework for the observation and arrangement of relevant intermarriage data. In other words, one of the more general theses of this paper is that an explicit conceptual outfit, a part of theory, is necessary even for fruitful discoveries of fact. It

---

[2] Romanzo Adams, *Interracial Marriage in Hawaii* (New York: The Macmillan Company, 1937), p. 191. Adams has an excellent discussion of the problem of distinguishing between practices and norms in the field of intermarriage.

is our second general thesis that much of the available statistical materials on intermarriage are of relatively little value because the fact-finders, so-called, have not assembled and classified *relevant* facts and that this inadequacy is tied up with their neglect of a coherent theoretical system in terms of which relevance of facts might be determined. Studies of intermarriage which are concerned simply with "the facts" may incidentally be of some use for the scientific study of the subject, but only when they tacitly relate to a system of theory. A science without a matrix of logically interrelated propositions is a contradiction in terms. A canvass of empirical studies of intermarriage suggests that these views need to be labored, for the "factual materials" are often discrete, scattered, and arranged in what seems to be a wholly private and unusable fashion.

* * * * *

Structural and functional elements . . . appear to account for the prohibition of racial-caste intermarriage in our society. The taboo appears to be largely supported by the standardized sentiments of both Negroes and whites and, consequently, the rate of intermarriage continues to be low. But what of the intermarriages which do occur, in spite of the taboo? The most striking uniformity in the statistics of Negro-white intermarriage is the noninstitutional pattern of caste hypogamy, i.e., marriage between white females and Negro males. In our samples, such pairings are from three to ten times as frequent as the Negro female-white male combination. This uniformity has often been remarked by students of the subject. Even the collection of mixed marriages assembled from cases "personally known" to a group of students consists of eighteen caste-hypogamous unions

to seven hypergamous unions.[3] What is the basis of this uniformity?

The hypogamous pattern is clearly not attributable to nonnormative conditions affecting intermarriage. There is no significantly unbalanced sex ratio among either the Negro or white populations which can be taken to account for this pattern. Similarly, neither the etiquette of race relations nor sheer propinquity would make for more frequent contacts between white females and Negro males than between Negro females and white males.[4] We may entertain the hypothesis that hypogamy is understandable in terms of the social structure, a view which is not invariably shared by other students of the subject. Thus Baber raises the question in these nonstructural, individualistic terms: "Surely there is no more stigma attached to the white man who marries a Negro woman than to the white woman who marries a Negro. Is color difference in the mate less repulsive to the white woman than to the white man?"[5] This way of posing the problem illustrates the necessity of systematic theory if empirical data are to be made intelli-

---

[3] Ray E. Baber, "A Study of 325 Mixed Marriages," *American Sociological Review,* **2** (1937), 705-716. Reference is also made to Ray E. Baber, *Marriage and the Family* (New York: McGraw-Hill, Inc., 1939), pp. 163-173.

[4] If at all involved, the contrary is more probable since Negro females and white males are more likely to have sustained contacts than are the complementary pairs, in view of the fact that the ratio of Negro women to Negro men engaged in domestic and personal service is about 4 to 1. [It should be added, however, that this disproportion did not obtain prior to 1910, the period to which all but one of our statistics of Negro-white intermarriage refer. . . .] In any event, such contacts scarcely serve to account for the caste-hypogamous pattern, in view of the social distance deriving from both caste and class differences.

[5] Baber, "A Study of 325 Mixed Marriages," *op. cit.,* 706.

gible. An *ad hoc* common sense hypothesis such as Baber's contains no reference to social structure and ignores the fact that most illicit miscegenation involves Negro women and white men. "Repulsiveness" is not a datum; it is a cultural artifact requiring sociological analysis.

Dealing with this same general question, Park asserts that hypergamy is "one principle which seems to have been everywhere operative in determining the amount of miscegenation."[6] It appears to be true that intercaste sex relations largely involve upper-caste males and lower-caste females, but clearly "hypergamy," which denotes a form of *marriage*, is far from universal. Park further holds that hypergamy "seems to be a principle in human nature . . . which operates spontaneously." A third hypothesis holds that "the disposition of men to go abroad for wives and of women to welcome these roving strangers is probably part of original nature. Human beings are naturally exogamous." Here again, certain abstract characteristics are attributed to human nature as such and, in contrast to Park's usual analytical insight, with no regard for the role of social organization. How would one test the hypothesis that exogamy is fixed in original nature? What theoretical or factual basis exists for this hypothesis? In any case, these gratuitous assumptions do not clarify the prevalently hypogamous pattern of Negro-white intermarriage.

Donald Young[7] and Kingsley Davis[8]

have severally advanced hypotheses which may be elaborated to account for the relative frequencies of the logically possible pairings of Negroes and whites. . . . The statistics show a marked predominance of caste hypogamy. . . .

Limitations of space and the absence of sufficient concrete data prevent a detailed analysis of the multiple structural factors involved in patterns of interstratum marriage. The general lines of analysis may be briefly illustrated. In our twofold racial-caste and open-class structure, all Negro-white marriages are cacogamous, that is, they deviate from endogamous norms and are attended by the sanctions of ostracism and the ascription of lower-caste status to offspring. Within such a context [a marriage between a lower class white female and a lower class Negro male unites persons who] . . . have become, as it were, "cultural aliens" denying the legitimacy of much of the social structure in which they occupy disadvantaged positions. Interracial cacogamy is, in this instance, simply a special case of the larger repudiation of cultural means and goals. There is little in the way of mutual socioeconomic compensation between the cross-caste mates. This particular pairing, however, would not be expected to occur any more frequently than its complementary hypergamous type . . . involving a lower-class Negro female and a lower-class white male. Concubinage, rather than marriage, would be the probable type of durable sex relationship in these cases.

[Marriage between an upper-class white female and an upper-class Negro male], when it occurs, will also not involve mutual compensation with respect to socioeconomic position, since here the class positions of the upper-class mates are roughly equal. The relation is asymmetrical inasmuch as the Negro male does not compensate

---

[6] Robert E. Park, "Race Relations and Certain Frontiers," in E. B. Reuter, ed., *Race and Culture Contacts* (New York: McGraw-Hill, Inc., 1934) esp. pp. 80-81. Park's essay contains an excellent summary of comparative materials on interracial marriage.

[7] Donald Young, *American Minority Peoples* (New York: Harper & Row, Publishers, Inc., 1932), p. 409.

[8] Kingsley Davis, "Intermarriage in Caste Societies," *American Anthropologist*, **43** (1941), 376-395.

VARIABLES IN THE ANALYSIS OF INTERMARRIAGE BETWEEN PERSONS FROM DIFFERENT SOCIAL STRATA

I. *The System of Stratification*
   A. Open-class
   B. Estate or *Stände*
   C. Caste
      1. Racial
      2. Non-racial

   these may be combined in concrete social systems: racial caste-and-class in United States; estate-and-class in England, Prussia—especially 18th to 19th centuries

II. *Bases of Ascribed or Achieved Status in the System of Stratification*
   A. Membership in a kinship unit
   B. Personal qualities—including race
   C. Achievements
   D. Possessions
   E. Authority
   F. Power

III. *Types of Intermarriage*
   A. Exogamy—agathogamous intermarriage
      1. Compensatory
         a. hypergamy
         b. hypogamy
      2. Non-compensatory
         a. hypergamy
         b. hypogamy

      institutionalized or non-institutionalized

   B. Intergroup mésalliance— cacogamous intermarriage
      1. Compensatory
         a. hypergamy
         b. hypogamy
      2. Non-compensatory
         a. hypergamy
         b. hypogamy

IV. *Status of Children of Cross-Stratum Marriage*
   A. Matrilineal
   B. Patrilineal
   C. Positional (that is, status of either upper-stratum or of lower-stratum parent)

V. *Status of Conjugal Pair*
   A. Same as prior status of husband
   B. Same as prior status of wife
   C. Same as prior status of upper-stratum spouse
   D. Same as prior status of lower-stratum spouse
   E. Status of pariahs, outcaste, déclassé

for the upper-caste status of his wife. Such marriages would be expected to occur among "emancipated" persons, so-called radicals, who repudiate legitimacy of caste distinctions. The sole formal difference between [the marriages of lower-class white female with lower-class Negro male and of upper-class white female with upper-class Negro male], then, is that in the former the contractants are disadvantaged persons who relinquish social norms because of the ineffectiveness of their efforts to gear into the social structure and achieve a "respectable" status, whereas in the latter type, the contractants enjoy eminently satisfactory status as judged by conventional standards but have become alienated from the values, institutional ideologies and organization of the caste system.

We should expect [the] pairing [of a] lower-class white woman and [an] upper-class Negro man to occur most frequently, for it involves a reciprocal compensatory situation in which the Negro male "exchanges" his higher economic position for the white female's higher caste status.[9] This does not at all

_____

[9] This is the special case of hypogamy with which Kingsley Davis was primarily concerned in which the dual caste-class structure "makes it economically profitable for some white women to marry some Negro males." *Ibid.*

imply that the "exchange" is necessarily the result of an explicit utilitarian calculus in which the contractants deliberately weigh the economic and social returns to be gained from the marriage. The event may be experienced by them as simply an affectional relationship, but this psychic reaction is manifestly structured by the social organization. A comparable reciprocity pattern often emerges even more clearly in hypergamous unions in caste or estate systems of stratification. In the Hindu caste system, for example, the bride's family "[has] to pay for marrying her to a man above her in rank, whilst they also desire to make a show of wealth as a set-off to the bridegroom's social advantages."[10] In an estate system, where titles descend patrilineally, the hypergamous exchange of wealth for noble status is often quite explicit, as in the patterns involving American heiresses and foreign nobles since the middle of the last century. Thus the marriage settlement between Consuelo Vanderbilt and His Grace the ninth Duke of Marlborough was set forth in an official document in which the Duke was guaranteed for life the income from $2,500,000 of Beech Creek Railway stock.

Among the hypogamous pairings, . . . [that between a white upper-class female and a Negro lower-class male] would, on our hypothesis, occur least frequently. Here *both* the class and caste positions of the white female are superior to [those] of the Negro male, and there is no element of social or economic compensation involved. Such a marriage abjures all social and cultural considerations and this compound deviation from class-and-caste standards would be most difficult to find cul-

turally acceptable motivation. It is consistent with our interpretation that the upper-class white woman in a union of this sort . . . believe[s] that her Negro husband is "the only man who can satisfy her sexually."[11]

This brief canvass of types of caste hypogamy is avowedly hypothetical, but it involves theoretically derived hypotheses which lend themselves to empirical confirmation or refutation. Furthermore, it sets forth the particular attributes which must be included in future statistical and case materials in order to test this interpretation. Baber has apparently made a step in this direction. However, the available data are too unsystematic and fragmentary to provide an adequate test, although, so far as they go, they are consistent with our analysis. Thus Reuter observes that uniformly in intercaste marriages, the Negro "groom is of some importance and the white bride a woman of the lower class."[12]

[10] E. A. H. Blunt, *The Caste System of Northern India* (London: Oxford University Press, 1931), p. 70.

[11] Baber, "A Study of 325 Mixed Marriages," *op. cit.*, p. 708. "She comes of an excellent family and is well educated, while he is ignorant and of very poor family stock."

[12] Edward B. Reuter, *The Mulatto in the United States* (Boston: Chapman & Grimes, Inc., Publishers, 1918), p. 138. Reuter cites Hoffman's study of fifty-seven mixed unions which were predominantly between members of the lower classes of both castes . . . and included a generous proportion of criminals and prostitutes. This again concurs with our analysis, but since Hoffman does not indicate the basis on which he selected his cases, his study cannot be accorded much weight. Only twenty-three of Hoffman's cases were actual marriages. Although Reuter refers to Hoffman's canvass as a "careful investigation," it should be noted that Hoffman gives only the following indication of the source of his information and the basis of selection of cases: "I have been able during a number of years to collect information of a fairly reliable character in regard to thirty-seven mixed relations. . . ." Frederick L. Hoffman, *Race Traits and Tendencies of the American Negro* (New York: The Macmillan Company, 1896), p. 204. In view of Hoffman's bias and naïveté

We have yet to examine the structural bases for the greater frequency of caste hypogamy as compared to caste hypergamy in our society. Two aspects of the roles ascribed to males and females appear to be primarily relevant. The latitude permitted women to seek an occupational career has increased greatly, but it does not approximate that accorded men. Moreover, even in the most "emancipated" circles the status of a conjugal unit is primarily that of the male head of the family. The standardized case is one in which the social rank of the female is largely derivative from that of her husband or, prior to social adulthood, her father. In a society where this is the case, intrafamilial conflict often occurs when the wife has outdistanced her husband in the occupational sphere, since feminine careers are hedged about by conceptions of the impropriety of competition between husband and wife. Occupational achievement is still considered the usual if not the exclusive prerogative of the male, despite the larger participation of women in economic and public life. The male is "the provider," the chief source of economic status. The second difference in sex roles is contained in the prevalent code of sex morality wherein, despite some slight modifications, the female of the species is more circumscribed in the range of allowable activity. Moreover, it is commonly considered more appropriate that sex relations be initiated by the male, that the male will propose and the female dispose, and that the male will seek out the female, for examples. These definitions are not unchallenged but they exercise a discernible control.

Given these differences in role definitions, then, an upper-caste male, by virtue of his sex role, may more properly

make advances than an upper-caste female, and, secondly, he may more readily flout the caste taboos, by virtue of his upper-caste status, than a lower-caste male may dare. In short, the sex morality supports sex advances by the male; the caste morality more easily enables the dominant upper-caste member to initiate cross-caste sexual overtures. Thus the individuals who incorporate the "male attribute" and the "upper caste attribute," that is, white males, may more readily initiate cross-caste sexual relations than either the white female, who lacks the male prerogative, or the Negro male, who lacks the upper-caste prerogative. This enables us to see structural sources of the fact that most intercaste *sex relations*— not marriages—are between white men and Negro women.

It remains to be seen, then, why the durable relationships between white men and Negro women are usually extramarital. Once again, sex roles and the caste-and-class structure would appear to account for the facts. Given the dominance of the white male with his relative immunity from active retaliation by the lower-caste male, there is no pressure to legitimize his liaison by marriage. Concubinage and transient sex relations are less burdensome and less damaging to his status, since these may be more easily kept secret and, even if discovered, are less subject to violent condemnation by fellow caste members, since they do not imply equality of the sex partners. Furthermore . . . the marriage of a lower-class white male with a wealthy Negro woman is less likely than the complementary hypogamous pairing in view of the standardized role of the male as "economic provider."

We may tentatively conclude that most cross-caste sex relations will be clandestine and illicit. Within a racial-

in other respects, there is no reason to assume that this sample was representative.

caste structure, the noninstitutionalized statistical pattern of the few intermarriages which do occur will be largely hypogamous. In a nonracial caste structure, as in India, the institutionalized pattern of hypergamy may be interpreted as a system manifesting the prerogatives of upper-caste males who thus have *legitimate* access to women of their own caste *and* to women of the immediately inferior subcaste. In a racial-caste structure, the institution of hypergamy is not probable because the ambiguous position of cross-caste offspring would introduce an instability in the caste system by eventually eliminating the identification of race and caste.

The classification and interpretation presented in this paper are highly provisional and rudimentary: the one needing to be further tested for convenience, the other requiring a larger body of systemically collated data than is yet at hand. The random collection of facts will not lead to further understanding of the phenomenon of intermarriage; the collection of facts in terms of our conceptual framework may do so. Confirmed by whatever relevant facts are available, our interpretation enjoys a measure of plausibility; consistent with a wider body of theory which in turn is supported by systematic empirical inquiry, it may lay claim to a further degree of validity; stated in such terms as to be testable by freshly accumulated facts, it is, at the very least, open to further confirmation or disconfirmation.

upward mobility through economic exchange

eight

The dowry system helps to guarantee some degree of homogamy, since the potential husband cannot command a large dowry unless his own economic potential is also large. On the other hand, the bargaining process may mean that one type of marriage commodity is exchanged for another: a woman's beauty and charm for a man's money, a young man's intellectual promise for class position. In a dowry system, money may be exchanged for social rank. Note, however, that the eighteenth-century French bourgeoisie who thus moved upward socially were likely already to have acquired the manners, tastes, and style of life of the nobility.

Changing Patterns of Mobility

ELINOR G. BARBER

. . . The bourgeoise hoped for and expected a certain amount of upward social mobility. . . . Over and over again, the bourgeois revealed in words and deeds that for all their conservative acceptance of the traditional order of society, they nevertheless wished to improve their class position within that order, that their ultimate goal was nobility and the noble way of life their model. They recognized the superiority of noble status over their own, but, unlike members of a true caste society, they did not accept their position as permanently inferior; rather, they sought, with more or less courage or brashness, to leave behind them everything that stigmatized them as *roturiers*.

By definition, social classes are groups of families who treat each other as equals, and the clearest and final test of such equality is marriage between members of such a group of families. The acid test, therefore, of the successful entry of the mobile bourgeois into a higher social class than that of his parents is his marriage with a member of this higher class. The significance of such a marriage is, presumably, that by virtue of his occupation, his wealth, and his style of life in general, the mobile bourgeois has become the social equal of his marriage partner. There were, in the eighteenth century, many such marriages between men and women whose

Elinor G. Barber, *The Bourgeoisie in 18th Century France* (Princeton: Princeton University Press, 1955), pp. 99-103. Reprinted by permission. Copyright 1955 by Princeton University Press.

parents belonged to different social classes, and though the frequent designation of these marriages as *mésalliances* indicates that they had only limited approval in the society, they are nevertheless proof positive of a considerable amount of social mobility.

Even in our own society, which on the whole tends to play down the importance of class distinctions, the class relations involved in the choice of a marriage partner are the focus of considerable interest or gossip, and they arouse much hope and anxiety. Our egalitarian social values militate against too strong or open disapproval of a "bad" match, but in eighteenth-century France such disapproval was unbridled. In a society which had only limited approval of social mobility, any marriage between members of strikingly different class origins was subject to suspicion, if not to condemnation, and these sentiments were generally given full expression. Most liable to such disapproval were of course marriages between persons of noble and *roturier* origin, . . . and it was these that were most frequently designated as *mésalliances*.

In one respect, however, the marriage of people of different class origins was institutionally facilitated to a greater degree in eighteenth-century France than in American open-class society. The arrangement of marriages *with full provision for a dowry* smoothed the way for the upward marriage of young women, and of men too, belonging to families who had prospered. The dowry was of great importance in marriages between class equals within the *roturier* class, as well as in marriages between children of socially unequal families.

In the latter case especially, the mutual advantage is clear: the dowry was both a social and an economic investment. The Duchesse de Chaulnes put the case neatly and earthily for the financially embarrassed high nobility which was marrying the daughters of the socially ambitious financial élite: "to make an advantageous *mésalliance* is 'to fertilize one's soil,' and God knows the soil needs fertilizing!"

The extent to which wealth did make social mobility possible is shown by the scale of "prices" of husbands in [the] Paris of Louis XIV:

By the eighteenth century, dowries had risen further. They had always been lower in provincial towns than in Paris, so that it was remarkable when a lawyer's son in Laval now got a dowry of 10,000 livres and the son of a banker there received as much as 20,000 livres.[1] It is also revealing to trace the increase in the dowries of the daughters of successive generations of a single family, which rose in the seventeenth and eighteenth centuries from the petit bourgeoisie to the *robe*. At the beginning of the seventeenth century, a daughter of the printer Barbou received only

for a dowry of	2-6000	you got	a merchant or sergeant
" " " "	12-20,000	" "	" notary or registrar
" " " "	20-30,000	" "	" solicitor
" " " "	35-45,000	" "	" treasurer of France
" " " "	45-75,000	" "	" counselor in the *cour des aides*
" " " "	75-150,000	" "	" counselor in the Parlement
" " " "	200-600,000	" "	" *anyone you wanted.*[2]

1000-1200 livres; by 1647, a girl marrying into the Barbou family had to bring 4000 livres; and by 1748, Jean III Barbou married his daughter to a small *noble de race*, and gave her 36,000 livres. "They had come a long way since the 1000 livres given to Marie Barbou in 1606, but they readily made a sacrifice for the first gentleman entering the family."[3]

Bourgeois ambitions meshed neatly with noble financial embarrassment, especially in the *grand monde* of Paris, where noble "pride" exerted less pressure than the need to keep up a magnificent way of life, and where the costly symbols of this way of life were so much more important than the an-

cient and honorable functions attached to nobility. For financial need alone was not in all cases among the eighteenth-century nobility sufficient motivation for a *mésalliance*, i.e., for an admission that the wealthiest bourgeois, at least, must be considered their social equals. The poverty-stricken provincial nobility continued to disdain any alliance with the rich bourgeoisie, even though they might be reduced to the status of *hobereaux*. The acceptance by the Court nobility of these marriages may therefore be one more indication of its defection from a genuine noble ideology and of its espousal of a way of life no longer congruent with its older functions as a political and military aristocracy. "In Paris, a wealthy *roturière* married a duke and was 'presented' at Court; in the provinces, a *roturier*, however rich he might be, had difficulty marrying the daughter of a ruined marquis."[4] The provin-

[1] Jules-Marie Richard, *La Vie privée dans une province de l'oeust: Laval au 17e et 18e siècles* (Paris, 1922), pp. 162-163.

[2] Albert Babeau, *Les Bourgeois d'autrefois* (Paris, 1886), pp. 249ff. These prices are in livres.

[3] P. Ducourtieux, "Les Barbou, imprimeurs. Lyon—Limoges—Paris. 1524-1893," *Bulletin du Limousin*, **41** (1894), 171-172.

[4] Henri Carré, *La Noblesse de France et l'opinion publique au 18e siècle* (Paris, 1920), p. 181.

cial town of Ponthivy in Brittany seems to have been an exception, however, since daughters of merchants had no apparent difficulty in finding noble husbands. The Métayer family is only one example: they were merchants until 1740, when "they quit commerce, and one of them bought the office of King's counselor. His son married a noble girl of the town."[5]

In Paris there were, indeed, innumerable "fertilizing" marriages, with the result, as Duclos put it, that "the Court and the world of finance were often in mourning for the same person,"[6] and that ". . . the nobility have now lost the right to despise the world of finance, for only few of its members do not have blood ties with the latter."[7] The wealthy financiers of Paris saw their children make marriages of great social brilliance, marriages which involved the greatest names of the old *noblesse* as well as of the *robe*. Here are a few striking examples: Barbier reported in 1752 that "the viscount of Rohan-Chabot has married Mlle de Vervins, the daughter of a counselor in Parlement, who was the son of M. Bonnevie, a farmer general."[8] The young lady's maternal grandfather had been a cloth merchant on the rue St. Denis. Mme de la Rochefoucauld, who bore another name of great distinction, was none other than the daughter of "the extremely wealthy Proudre, the tax farmer. . . ."[9] And the same was

true of the *robe*. Mlle de la Reynière, daughter of another farmer general, married the son of Lamoignon de Blancmesnil, and brought over 700,-000 livres to the marriage. A Choiseul married the granddaughter of Crozat, a Molé the daughter of Bernard, and the daughter of the banker Laborde became no less than the Comtesse de Noailles. Descazeaux, an old shipowner of Saint-Malo, also did very well with a granddaughter of the Maréchal de Noailles.

Marriage and all the social intimacy attendant upon it should signify the complete social equality of the partners, but the kind[s] of marriages we have described fell somewhat short of such complete equality, and for that reason they were often not successful as marriages. Given the ambivalent class attitudes of the bourgeoisie, . . . and the attitudes of the nobility, which we can easily assume to have been equally ambivalent, strains and tensions in such marriages were only to be expected. To be sure, in some cases difficulties may have arisen from the discrepant ways of life of the marriage partners, but such difficulties were undoubtedly enhanced by the unconcealed public disapproval of the marriage and by the mixed feelings of the families immediately involved. In many cases, bourgeois ladies were surely as cultivated as their noble husbands, and this may have eased the situation; but it was hard to overcome the strong sentiments against *mésalliances*. The noble husband could escape from the strains of such a marriage into that faithlessness which was, in any case, much more generally accepted among the nobility than among the bourgeoisie. It was the bourgeois wife who felt the failure of the marriage most acutely.

* * * * *

---

[5] F. Le Lay, *Histoire de la ville et communauté de Ponthivy au 18e siècle* (Paris, 1911), pp. 46-47.

[6] Charles P. Duclos, *Considérations sur les moeurs de ce siècle* (Paris, 1881), p. 124.

[7] *Ibid.*, p. 125. See also Carré, *op. cit.*, pp. 34-55, for numerous examples of intermarriage.

[8] Edmond F. Barbier, *Journal historique et anecdotique du règne de Louis XV* (Paris, 1847-1856), 3, pp. 339-340.

[9] Henri Thirion, *La vie privée des financiers au 18e siècle* (Paris, 1895), p. 58.

arranging the marriage in rural ireland

nine

Compared with other European countries, Ireland has had until recently a very late average age at marriage and a high percentage of people who never marry. The ideal was not the large, extended family all living under one roof; instead, each couple was to have a farm of its own. This meant that a young man might have to wait until his late thirties before marrying. Specifically, the dowry brought in by his wife paid for the farm, and his parents then retired from it to live in the "west room" traditionally allotted to the old. Here a sensitive anthropologist describes the negotiations leading up to this change in status which made an Irish "boy" into an adult.

The Irish Countryman

CONRAD M. ARENSBERG

*   *   *   *   *

Country marriage in Ireland follows an ancient and widespread pattern. It is called "matchmaking," and it is the sort of *mariage de convenance* involving parental negotiations and a dowry which is nearly universal in Europe. In Ireland its importance is such as to make it the crucial point of rural social organization.

To describe the match one has to sink one's teeth into the countryman's way of life. For the match is made up of many things. It unites transfer of economic control and advance to adult status. It is the only respectable method

Conrad M. Arensberg, *The Irish Countryman* (New York: The Macmillan Company, 1937), pp. 72-79. Reprinted by permission of The Macmillan Company and Macmillan & Company, Ltd.

of marriage and the usual method of inheritance in the Irish countryside. It is embedded in the Gaelic tongue, in joke and story, and in folklore.

A match usually begins when a farmer casts round for a suitable wife for one of his sons. The son to be married is to inherit the farm. The farmer has full power to choose among his sons. A hundred years ago, before famine, clearances, and land reform, all the sons and daughters could hope to be provided for on the land. Such a situation is still an ideal, but little more. One cannot subdivide one's holding any longer, and new farms are hard to get. Today the farmer looks forward, ordinarily, to "settling" only one son "on the land."

"When a young man is on the lookout for a young lady," a farmer of

Inagh in mid-Clare told me, "it is put through his friends for to get a suitable woman for him for his wife. It all goes by friendship and friends and meeting at public-houses." . . . Getting married is no carefree, personal matter; one's whole kindred help, even to suggesting candidates.

"The young man," the farmer goes on, "sends a 'speaker' to the young lady, and the speaker will sound a note to know what fortune she has, will she suit, and will she marry this Shrove? She and her friends will inquire what kind of a man he is, is he nice and steady. And if he suits, they tell the speaker to go ahead and 'draw it down.' So then he goes back to the young man's house and arranges for them to meet in such a place, on such a night, and we will see about it." With this, the first step in the delicate negotiations is safely passed.

The Inagh farmer goes on: "The speaker goes with the young man and his father that night, and they meet the father of the girl and his friends or maybe his son and son-in-law. The first drink is called by the young man; the second by the young lady's father.

"The young lady's father asks the speaker what fortune do he want. He asks him the place of how many cows, sheep, and horses is it? He asks what makings of a garden are in it; is there plenty of water or spring wells? Is it far in from the road, or on it? What kind of house is in it, slate or thatch? Are the cabins good, are they slate or thatch? If it is too far in from the road, he won't take it. Backward places don't grow big fortunes. And he asks, too, is it near a chapel and the school, or near town?"

The Inagh countryman could pause here; he had summarized a very long and important negotiation.

"Well," he went on, getting to the heart of the matter, "if it is a nice place, near the road, and the place of eight cows, they are sure to ask £350 fortune. Then the young lady's father offers £250. Then maybe the boy's father throws off £50. If the young lady's father still has £250 on it, the speaker divides the £50 between them. So now it's £275. Then the young man says he is not willing to marry without £300—but if she's a nice girl and a good housekeeper, he'll think of it. So there's another drink by the young man, and then another by the young lady's father, and so on with every second drink till they're near drunk. The speaker gets plenty and has a good day."

The farmer paused here again; for the match is developing marvellously. "All this is one day's work," he continued. "After this, they appoint a place for the young people to see one another and be introduced. The young lady takes along her friends, maybe another girl, and her brother and her father and mother. The young man takes along his friends and the speaker.

"If they suit one another, then they will appoint a day to come and see the land. If they don't, no one will reflect on anybody, but they will say he or she doesn't suit. They do not say plainly what is wrong.

"The day before the girl's people come to see the land, geese are killed, the house is whitewashed, whiskey and porter bought. The cows get a feed early so as to look good; and maybe they get an extra cow in, if they want one." He said this last slyly, for to pretend to own more stock than one really has is an unfair trick in the bargaining.

"Then next day comes the walking of the land. The young man stays outside in the street, but he sends his best friend in to show the girl's father round, but sure the friend won't show him the bad points.

"If the girl's father likes the land, he

returns, and there will be eating and drinking until night comes on them. Then they go to an attorney next day and get the writings between the two parties and get the father of the boy to sign over the land." With the writings, the match is made, and the wedding can go forward.

This long statement, in fact, contains the essence of the whole of matchmaking. It serves very well as a general guide. A great deal is at stake in this elaborate negotiation. To our eyes, such a way of winning a wife seems very unromantic. It savors a little too much of hardheaded business. We should call a man a cynic who put farm and fortune ahead of personal attractions.

Yet we should be wrong to make such an evaluation of the countryman. The sentiments prompting him, and his expectations, are quite different; they must be understood in their proper setting. In matchmaking, the interests of all the members of both families are deeply involved. The match is a convention by which they are expressed and realized. We are prone to forget that a living convention can be just as joyous, even more so, in fact, than bohemian revolt.

For example, the heated, formal bargaining quickly summarized by the quotation has deep significance. It effects a necessary and balanced equality between the two families. Superficially, it seems merely a nice adjustment between the farm and fortune. But looked at more closely, it assures many things.

The girl's family know[s] that she will be well provided for. They make sure of it when they "walk the land." They make sure their standing in the countryside will not suffer. Fortune and farm must be roughly equivalent. In the scale of rural prestige, each farm is valued against the fortune it can pay out with its daughters and the fortune

it can bring in with its inheriting son's wife. In the words of the Inagh countryman quoted: "Backward places do not grow big fortunes." And as the farm is identified socially with the family whose members work it, these dowries measure the family's standing.

On the side of the family receiving the fortune, too, interests are served. The girl's dowry comes to them, to be used for their own purposes. With it, they are assured a competent "new woman," as they call the new wife and daughter-in-law. She is trained to their position in life and to their own habits and sentiments. Girl and dowry are a fair exchange for prestige and alliance.

But these are not the only values at stake. The "fortune" in the match is woven into the internal necessities of farm family life.

When agreement is finally reached between the negotiating parties, they go to a solicitor to make up the "writings," as we saw in the quotation. By this, the countryman means they cast their agreement into legal form. For the "writings" [are] a contractual instrument which unites marriage settlement and will. Reforms in land tenure have made it necessary recently to give an age-old custom proper legality, since the transfer of the farm is involved.

In the "writings" the father of the groom makes over the farm and all its appurtenances to his son. In return, the girl's fortune goes to him. The father also makes provision for his own maintenance and that of his wife. It is his abdication, and, like Charles V, he keeps only one monastery out of a vast empire for himself. He usually reserves the right to the "grass of a cow," his keep, the use of the hearth, and the use of a room in the house. That room is the "west room" . . . , the best in the house. Thus the cycle of life on the farm is completing itself. He and his wife step down from active command.

In payment for his abdication, he receives the fortune of the girl. A fair arrangement, we should say. But we should be wrong; it is much more. True to the obligations of his social role, he may not use it entirely for himself. The Irish small farmer does not retire, like the Iowan, to sunny California and the Townsend plan. He must meet the interests of the group. Ordinarily, the other children have been stalwart workers in the farm family corporation. They are not to be "settled on the land"; some other provision must be made. They may come forward now for their long due reward and their corporate share.

Here the purposes behind the match show themselves again. One daughter is ordinarily married into a nearby farm. The family makes a match for her. With her of course goes a fortune equal to that the son's bride brings in. Perhaps a son may be similarly married into a farm where there are only daughters; even though a *cliamhan isteach*, "son-in-law going-in," as he is graphically called in [Gaelic], must pay a much larger fortune. He has to overcome the anomaly felt in reversing the usual role of sons and daughters and has to compensate the family for the loss of "their name on the land."

But it is a very fortunate farmer indeed who can provide for all his sons and daughters so. Usually, only the heir and one daughter are married and dowered, the one with the farm, the other with the fortune. All the rest, in the words of the Luogh residents, "must travel."

Thus either at the match or in preparation for it comes the inevitable dispersal of the farm family. The unit must break up. Time and change are inevitable in human affairs; only an orderly social mechanism can tame their ravages.

* * * * *

the marriage arranger in modern japan

ten

In no society do the elders arrange marriages primarily for their own profit, but in most societies the choice of mate has been viewed as too serious to be left to the whim of the young. Obviously, young people in love are not likely to bargain well with one another. On the other hand, in a society in which "face," or personal dignity, is very important, if the bargaining elders reject a potential bride or groom, challenge a family's claims to rank, or carefully check on the supposed talent of the young man, the results might be embarrassing for both family lines. In Japan this task is given to a marriage arranger, a "go-between," who is often a nonprofessional.

Note that this social role has become more important with industrialization, since people are less likely to know one another's families well, but the young do not as yet engage in a completely free courtship. The activities of the marriage arranger cover a wide range, for he or she is likely to be involved in many relations with the two family lines and with the young couple after marriage.

The Go-Between in a Developing Society: The Case of the Japanese Marriage Arranger

EZRA VOGEL

* * * * *

One of the crucial problems in an industrializing society is making available a mobile supply of workers and a mobile supply of appropriate brides. In Japan this mobility was mediated by go-betweens who had some particular ties to the group from which a person came and the group to which he was going. The . . . go-between operated in such a way as to safeguard the member who was moving and both the group from which he came and the group to which he was going. [He] served to safeguard the group from which he came, because, in effect, the mobile person was required to go through channels before moving. There was not an open labor market, so that there was no widespread threat that members might suddenly leave; nor did group members threaten insubordination. Because a potentially mobile person needed the help of members of his group in achieving a new placement, he could not afford to alienate them. Similarly, by going through personal connections, the group which was taking in a new member could be assured of his loyalty and devotion, and the mobile person was assured of kind treat-

Ezra Vogel, "The Go-Between in a Developing Society: The Case of the Japanese Marriage Arranger," *Human Organization*, **20** (Fall, 1961), 112-120. We are grateful to the author and *Human Organization* for permission to quote.

ment at the hands of the new group. Often loyalty and personal connections were symbolized in a ritual kinship relationship with either the go-between or certain people in the new organization becoming, in effect, a ritual parent. If problems arose, the go-between who had made the original arrangements was available to work them out. Although placement occurred in the context of personal connections, a large number of objective considerations also governed who was to be placed where.

While the use of go-betweens in Japan has a very long history, it appears to have taken on a special importance in the period of rapid industrialization for placement of group members, and the pattern remains very important today. However, as the labor and marriage markets gradually become freer and the participants themselves have more opportunity for shopping around independently, the need for such go-betweens is beginning to decline.

The present study examines the role of the marriage go-between (*nakohdo*), who still continues to be an important figure in a large number of marriages in Japan. There are endless variations in the *nakohdo's* roles and in how much he may be involved in arranging a particular match, but, in general, he has some responsibility in introducing prospective spouses, carrying on investigations and negotiations for the marriage, officiating at the marriage, and assuming an ill-defined responsibility for the welfare of the young couple after marriage. For his services the *nakohdo* is rewarded by presents and loyalty from the young couple and his family, and general respect from the community. In rare cases, he is a semiprofessional, receiving money payments or fairly large presents for his services.

While the *nakohdo* is generally considered old-fashioned and even "feudalistic" by many Japanese themselves, in fact use of the *nakohdo* became widespread only toward the end, or after the end, of the feudal period, and in certain localities was used for the first time only in the twentieth century. While for ideological reasons there is some tendency among modern Japanese to regard the *nakohdo* as a rapidly disappearing phenomenon left over in the most feudalistic parts of Japan, it is still widespread throughout Japan, in urban as well as in rural areas, although the *nakohdo* may have more importance in introducing in cities and for carrying on negotiations in rural areas. While, in accord with the popular public image, the author's middle-class informants argued that it is rare in the lower classes, the lower-class informants gave sufficient evidence to show that it is widespread among lower classes as well, particularly in rural areas. It is difficult to estimate exactly how many marriages are now arranged by a *nakohdo*. In a national opinion survey conducted in 1952, it was found that approximately 60 per cent of couples then married had used a go-between in arranging their marriage, but unfortunately the data were not analyzed by year of marriage. One way of estimating the prevalence of the *nakohdo* is through the prevalence of marriages involving *miai* (meetings especially arranged by a go-between to introduce the couple and sometimes their respective families). Of the cases

seen in domestic courts in 1956 (total 13,733 cases), about 70 per cent had *miai*, and in no prefecture was the percentage below 65 per cent). In a 1958 survey of Tokyo area middle-class apartments where the average length of marriage was about four years, roughly one-third of the couples had had a *miai* and, when the data were analyzed by length of marriage, there was no indication of a decline in the use of the *miai*. Since these apartment dwellers are among the more modern groups in Japanese society, it would seem reasonable to accept the view of expert informants who estimated the number of current arranged marriages to be about half of all marriages in Japan. The present paper is concerned only with marriages as "arranged," but a large proportion of marriages which are not "arranged" use a variety of friends to perform various small go-between tasks, all of which would otherwise be performed by a single *nakohdo*. Nearly all marriages have a formal *nakohdo* at the ceremony, and often friends or relatives are asked to make introductions, to convey messages between the parties, or to make investigations concerning the other parties. Private detective agencies are widely used for investigations, and specialized private and public institutions are used for introductions.

Despite the widespread use of the *nakohdo*, most Japanese, especially the young people, are ideologically opposed. . . . In one Tokyo area survey, only 26 per cent of those polled thought that the *nakohdo* should continue to be used to help arrange marriages. In the mass media, the *nakohdo* is presented as a terribly old-fashioned, untrustworthy, and often comic character. Parents objecting to their child's desire to find his own spouse do not do so on ideological grounds, but on practical grounds, i.e., the proposed spouse may not be good enough, may not be reliable, and so forth. Even the *nakohdo* has no ideological objection to "love marriages," and several proudly told of their own children's love marriages. This gap between an ideology strongly against the *nakohdo* and the actual use of the *nakohdo* is something recognized by Japanese scholars and the popular press as well. . . .

The data for this study were obtained through exploratory interviews with large numbers of informants and through focused interviews of two hours or more with twenty-eight *nakohdo*. Only those . . . were included who had performed actual negotiations preceding marriage and who were considered *nakohdo* by themselves and the parties concerned. The largest single group, members of the woman's club of one of the large wards of Tokyo, was selected by the coordinator of the clubs on the basis of having the most experience as *nakohdo*. The other[s] . . . were selected because they had different types of clients. *Nakohdo* interviewed lived in several different geographical areas, fishing and farming villages, and represented upper, middle, and lower classes. While most were professional, some were semiprofessional.

The Activities of the *Nakohdo*

The *nakohdo* who performs the actual work leading to marriage is generally a person of middle age or above who is respected in his community. In the urban middle classes, the *nakohdo* who does the real work of arranging is generally a woman, but in the lower-class and rural areas it is often a man, and often a husband and wife act together as a *nakohdo* couple. There is a Japanese proverb which says that everyone should serve as a *nakohdo* three times in his life, and the *nakohdo*

regards his work as a public service. While the ordinary person may serve as a *nakohdo* two or three times in his life, some semiprofessional[s] have performed as many as several hundred matches. With rare exceptions, the *nakohdo* takes great pride and pleasure in his work, but he does not actively seek work and serves only when requested. [He] has an enormous devotion to his task, is very identified with his work, is proud of his successes and troubled by his failures to conclude satisfactory marriage arrangements.

In order for the *nakohdo* to make effective introductions, it is important for him to be well known (*kao ga hiroi*) and to have suitable contacts. No particular training is required and, in most cases, the *nakohdo* had his first experience through a request to locate a spouse by a very close friend or relative, and, since he happened to know an appropriate person, he made the necessary arrangements. After that, the *nakohdo* developed a reputation for his ability to successfully conclude matches and was approached by other people with similar requests. Frankness, honesty, tactfulness, and loyalty are considered the main virtues of the *nakohdo*, and the author's impression was that they tended to embody these characteristics.

For convenience, the activities of the *nakohdo* may be classified as: (1) introducing, (2) negotiating, and (3) ceremonializing.

Introducing

The early stages of the introduction process are clearly subordinated to the personal relationships of the parties concerned. It is usually the girl's mother who first makes a social visit to the *nakohdo*, and, as part of a social visit, she will incidentally mention that her son or daughter is approaching marriageable age. If she does not already know the *nakohdo,* she will use another informal go-between who does know [him], and they can make a social visit . . . together. This situation is clearly defined as one of no commitment, and the basic information can be gathered, and the *nakohdo* can decide whether or not to make a commitment to the case. The party to the introduction can decide whether or not to use a *nakohdo* without in any way disturbing the social relationships involved. What is casually mentioned can be casually dropped.

If the *nakohdo* decides to accept the potential bride's picture and a brief background history, he may do so with the minimum commitment of merely looking around for a possible match. He will also do his looking around within the context of personal relations, asking friends about potential candidates. One of the preferred modes is for one *nakohdo* to vouch for his party and to use a friend as a second *nakohdo* to vouch for the other party. At this early stage, before the parties are actually introduced, there may be extensive visiting back and forth between the *nakohdo* and the two parties, making further investigations where necessary. In some rural areas, the *nakohdo* may ask the mother of the bride to take her for a walk so the potential man can look her over, and, while the bride suspects what is happening, she is regarded as not knowing, thus preserving the opportunity for making judgments without commitment. In any case, before the *miai,* many factors about the spouse may be considered and decided without any great feeling of pressure to decide in one direction or another.

The official introduction is usually conducted at the *miai* in a meeting of the *nakohdo,* the potential bride and groom, and sometimes representatives of each family. This is generally regarded . . . as a serious commitment involving public recognition, and a party refused feels a blow to his prestige and status, to say nothing of the time and energy . . . involved. There are clearly limitations on the number of *miai* one may have in addition to the problems of time and expense: A reputation for refusing would make other parties hesitant to accept a *miai;* a *nakohdo* whose *miai* ended in failure may feel rebuffed and not attempt another . . . if he thinks his party unreasonable; and, as a potential spouse gets older, he has less opportunity for finding a good partner. Because of the seriousness of the formal meeting at the *miai,* the parties concerned are not likely to attempt [one] unless they feel that there is a serious chance of success, and they will do a large part of the investigating and decision making before[hand].

Despite the seriousness of the *miai,* it is clear that there is an opportunity for decision after[ward], and it is not uncommon for a person to have several *miai* before marriage. The opportunity for decision making after the *miai* is preciously guarded by playing down the seriousness of the *miai,* simplifying the *miai* itself, and keeping the atmosphere light and pleasant. In some cases the parties even maintain that the meeting is not a real *miai* but only a little get-together. Although the parties do not want the atmosphere to become so light that the other party is not taking its responsibility seriously, at a conscious level do want the atmosphere very light, and the *nakohdo* must strike a delicate balance between serious talk [and] a light casualness which will permit the possibility for decision making afterward without serious embarrassment to either party.

In recent years, there has been an attempt even to enlarge the scope of free decisions after the *miai*. While the attempt to define the *miai* as just a chance to meet someone else has not succeeded, the young people are given considerable chance to talk and make independent decisions both during and after the *miai*. An attempt is ordinarily made to give the couple a chance to talk alone, as is evidenced by the standard joke about the *nakohdo* who spends a long time in the bathroom during the *miai*. Young people, particularly those ideologically opposed to *miai* marriages, are now making an effort to discuss things frankly with a prospective spouse, and arrangements are usually made for the young couple to meet alone several times after the *miai* before making a decision about marriage.

The crucial elements of the decision about marriage have to do with objective status factors, such as the relative social standing of the two families, present and potential economic earning power of the husband, appearance and refinements of the bride, all of which can be investigated by the *nakohdo* before the *miai*. To some extent, the *miai* is crucial in telling whether the parties concerned seem to get along well together, but this getting along is vaguely defined, and, because of this vagueness, there is ordinarily elaborate preparation for the *miai* to insure that everything goes smoothly, with resulting attention to and tension about great numbers of details.[1] In the discussions between [the] *nakohdo* and the party concerned, or even in discussions between the parents and child in one party, it is difficult to describe the characteristics of

the mood, and often attention is given to such characteristics as skin defects, posture, tone of voice, and the like. In any case, these impressions are very carefully weighed, along with the more objective information obtained before the *miai* in making a decision about marriage.

Negotiating

Ordinarily the most time-consuming job of the *nakohdo* is in the negotiations between the two families. The amount of time required varies from a single visit or telephone call to each side to a major proportion of the *nakohdo*'s time for many months. In general, in the cases where the men do most of the negotiating, as in lower-class groups and certain rural areas, the negotiations tend to be briefer and more businesslike. Where women do much of the negotiation, the process is often combined with social visiting, and, in some cases, the marriage arrangements are at least ostensibly subordinated to this visiting.

In cases where negotiations are most prolonged, the mothers of the prospective mates are the ones who discuss problems in greatest detail with the *nakohdo*. However, the *nakohdo* generally insists on getting the approval of the young people concerned from the very beginning, since without it there will be great difficulty in making a successful match, and the mother often becomes a go-between, carrying messages between her own family and the *nakohdo*. Despite the *nakohdo*'s defensive denials to the contrary, there is no doubt that the *nakohdo* and parents may heavily influence decisions, but the child is ordinarily brought into discussions at all stages of negotiation, and if at any point he firmly disapproves, negotiations are broken off. . . . Particularly in rural areas, the fathers seem to

---

[1] The enormous concern about these details and the resulting embarrassments are reflected in the story of the country girl who, in order to behave properly, follows exactly everything the *nakohdo* does, including spilling a couple of peas onto the table, which is then repeated down the line by all the other guests.

have an important part in negotiations also, and in most places, even if the *nakohdo* does not speak to the father directly, it is expected that the mother will speak to him and get his general approval for her activities, although she may not discuss all the details with him and may even select which things to talk over with him, depending on how she wishes the negotiations to proceed. In some cases, the *nakohdo* will meet with [the] mother and the prospective spouse, and in other cases he may meet with both parents, or with other members of the family.

One of the major duties of the *nakohdo* is to serve as a guarantor for the other party and to conduct all the investigations necessary to establish the position of the other party. Precisely what things are thought most desirable varies greatly depending on the interests and desires of the people concerned, but, at a minimum, they wish to establish that the other family has a good reputation and social position, is not descendent from an outcaste family, does not have cases of mental illness, serious physical illness, or crime which would affect the family line. The bride's side wishes to establish that the prospective groom is capable of continuously supporting her in the style she would like, and that he is sufficiently healthy so that he will be able to work regularly and is not likely to leave her a widow at a young age. The groom's side wishes to establish that the prospective bride is in good health, will be able to work hard, is pretty, gentle, and mild in disposition. It is important that the bride be a virgin, and the groom should not be the kind of person who would waste his money on alcohol and women after marriage. The extent to which one can demand these characteristics in the spouse depends in large part of course on the extent to which one is considered desirable.

The methods which the *nakohdo* will use to investigate are designed to obtain this required information. A minimum of information about family residences is contained in the public family records (*koseki*). Using this information, it is usually possible to trace back whether the opposite family lived in a neighborhood which was inhabited by outcastes. This is getting increasingly difficult to establish by such simple methods, [for] in many cases the outcaste residences are not always in separate neighborhoods. If there is any serious doubt about whether or not one was a member of an outcaste family, however, it may be necessary to visit a family's original home, and trace back various other kinds of records. The general status and reputation of a family [are] usually established by visits to the family's original home, and this will usually include questions about mental illness, serious physical illness which might be hereditary, and crime. In general, the *nakohdo* [feels] that the neighbors [will] be quite truthful in expressing their opinion because of the importance of making a good match. However, the neighbor's opinion is often colored by his general pattern of relationships with the family, and if there is any grudge in the neighborhood and the *nakohdo* happens to go to a neighbor who has a grudge, he may get a very distorted picture. For this reason, each family ordinarily makes an effort to maintain very good relationships with neighbors, not only because they feel it is pleasant, but because it may make a very real difference in whether they will be considered desirable at the time of marriage.

If certain questionable things about a party's reputation develop, it will then be necessary to investigate this in detail. There is a certain strategy involved, however, in not investigating the family in too much detail too early in the game, because the neighbors get curious about the potential marriage, and this would make it more difficult to break off negotiations, since it would be embarrassing to the refused party. One pursues the investigation in accord with the degree of commitment of the parties at that particular time. Because of the problems involved in assessing the subtle details about a family's reputation, a *nakohdo* prefers to continue working through friends, since he can rely on their information without arousing neighbors and without having serious doubts about the validity of [the] information. He pursues the areas which seem most problematic in meeting the desired standards. If the groom-to-be has a degree from a good university and a respectable white-collar job with a well-known firm, there will probably not be any further need to investigate his occupational career, except for a routine check-up by the *nakohdo* at the groom's company to make sure that he is considered competent, reliable, and that he will continue to be promoted. The *nakohdo* will usually talk directly with the groom's superiors or, in a very large company, the personnel department, and since this is expected, the *nakohdo* is respectfully received and given the desired information. However, in case the husband did not graduate from a good university, it may be necessary to investigate his school record in more detail in order to judge his competence. If the groom is not an employee in a large company, then his future is considered much more dubious, so that a *nakohdo* is likely to investigate his bank account, the amount of goods he is likely to receive through inheritance, and to gather whatever evidence on his skill and connections would be useful in estimating his future financial success. Usually, the investigating process is one in which the *nakohdo* continually checks back with the family concerned.

If the family has more doubts, it is generally the duty of the *nakohdo* to investigate in more detail the problems brought up by the family.

If the family still has doubts, they may decide to hire a private detective to supplement the investigation made by the *nakohdo*. Ordinarily, the family pays directly for the private detective if he is used, but the *nakohdo* may also decide to employ the detective, if he himself has doubts about his own material. Private detectives seem to be used very rarely in rural areas but fairly often in cities. In some cases, the large private detective organizations may be used to gather routine information in other parts of Japan if it is inconvenient for the *nakohdo* to make a trip to investigate such things himself and if reliable personal contacts are lacking in this locality. The request by the family for the use of a private detective is ordinarily regarded as a reflection that the *nakohdo* has not turned up sufficiently reliable information, and the *nakohdo* generally disapproves of using a private detective and is a bit skeptical of their results even if he himself may advise the family to use a detective to clear up a particular point. The main reason the *nakohdo* gives for the dislike of detectives is that they are not very reliable, making reports sound definite when, in fact, there is insufficient evidence, and there are many stories in the common folklore giving support for these doubts.

While each *nakohdo* insist[s] that he himself [is] very frank and truthful in relating bad as well as good points, he [speaks] of exaggerations other *nakohdo* make, a characteristic which is the focus of public suspicion.[2] There is doubtless an element of truth in the tendency for

---

[2] The Japanese term *"nakohdo guchi"* is universally known and often used to describe talk which is so exaggerated as to be misleading.

the *nakohdo* to exaggerate, a tendency which stems from the enormous involvement [he] has in the success of his work and loyalty to his party. To the extent that he receives prestige for his work, it is in terms of his ability to conclude a successful match, and the techniques for attaining this are in many ways analogous to the techniques of salesmanship. In the large majority of cases, however, the *nakohdo* has some personal relationship with the parties concerned and expects to continue this personal relationship long after marriage, so this fact places serious limits on the extent to which [he] can distort to make a match.

The Bargaining Process

Much of the bargaining process depends on assessing the relative position of the parties. Aside from the general qualifications which need to be investigated, there are a number of other factors which determine the bargaining situation. One is the sex ratio of eligibles. For example, immediately after the war, when the number of eligible women was much higher than that of men, the *nakohdo* had hosts of applications from eligible girls. In some cases, a girl's mother would even present the girl's picture in different places simultaneously, a practice which *nakohdo* invariably try to discourage, since it can lead to many complications in making arrangements. It is felt that the man's side should initiate proposals for *miai*, but particularly in the immediate postwar period, the girl's side was using every indirect approach possible to invite a proposal. In this period, because of the sex ratio, it was common for a girl of higher social standing to arrange a marriage with a man of somewhat lower standing.

The relative bargaining position of the parties is also determined by par-

ticular Japanese values regarding marriage. For example, a girl past twenty-three or twenty-four is regarded as fairly old for marriage, and in the ordinary case it is difficult for her to find a spouse of appropriate social status when she is much beyond this age. As a result, many young girls who until twenty or twenty-one are insistent on a love marriage turn to the *nakohdo* at this age for fear it may soon be too late. Indeed, the *nakohdo* usually has an overly plentiful supply of girls in the upper age brackets. Also, when a girl is eighteen or nineteen, her family may have very high standards of what the other party should be like, but as the girl gets older these conditions gradually are lowered. Indeed, when asked how to handle the problem of a girl's family making difficult demands, the *nakohdo*'s answer [is] very simple: "wait." The demands will gradually lessen. Also, the child whose father died when he was young is at a considerable disadvantage in terms of Japanese values. It is assumed that his disciplinary training is inadequate and that his family will be in a somewhat more difficult financial situation. Hence the *nakohdo* similarly has an oversupply of pictures of prospective spouses whose fathers died when they were young, and this too is reflected in their bargaining position.

The relative position of the two parties determines not only the eventual selection, but [also] the process of negotiation.[3] The party which is most anxious to make the match must often wait for some time until the other party has made a decision, and it is the job of

---

[3] Although it involves two families and not just two people and the way of exploiting is different, the bargaining has many of the features of dating and rating. Willard Waller, "The Rating and Dating Complex," *American Sociological Review*, **2** (December, 1937), 727-734.

the *nakohdo* to convince the reluctant party. Because it is ordinarily understood that a party will not start another negotiation until one has been completely settled, this poses a serious problem if one party stalls, especially in the case of a girl in the upper age brackets, since time is very precious. In this case, the *nakohdo* tries to force a quicker decision on the part of the reluctant family and urges them to be very frank. If, however, the reluctant party refuses to make a decision, and the other party is very much interested in the reluctant party, they may wait as much as several months. On such occasions, the *nakohdo* may be called on to make estimates of the willingness of the other party and predictions about the eventual decisions, a weighty responsibility indeed. Often, indefinite stalling appears to be used as a polite way of refusal. The stalled party becomes very anxious, its pride is wounded, and in such a case the *nakohdo* tries to have a frank talk with the reluctant party to determine intentions and, if it is a refusal, the reluctant party will probably give the *nakohdo* an acceptable explanation as to the reason, usually a particular recognizable defect of the opposite party. Although the *nakohdo* may have an even closer relationship with)the refused party, he does not necessarily tell the reason, since it may be embarrassing or discouraging to the refused party. He may offer an invented reason (as, for example, that the year[s] of birth were not appropriate according to the almanac predictions), or he may give no reason. Usually, the reason is clear to the refused party, i.e., that the other party hopes for a match with a higher-status family, and the refused party will not ask to know the reason if the *nakohdo* does not give it.

* * * * *

Discussion and Conclusion

There are two general features of the role of the *nakohdo* which deserve special mention. The first is that although the *nakohdo* operates through particularistic relationships, through personal connections with both parties, the use of the *nakohdo* not only permits, but tends to maximize universalistic considerations in the decision-making process. At virtually every step in the process, the *nakohdo* is used in a way which increases rather than decreases the opportunity of making a universalistic decision, given the values regarding marriage. The *nakohdo* is originally chosen by the family because, of persons available to a family, he is felt to provide access to the widest number of opportunities for a good match. The investigation process is conducted by the *nakohdo* in order to provide as accurate information as possible about those characteristics considered most important. The nature of the items to be investigated and the interests of the parties make it impossible for the two parties to talk over frankly every possible kind of difficulty, . . . but the *nakohdo* is able, because of his particular status, to investigate such matters. Yet the nature of the items to be investigated requires an unusually high degree of confidence in the investigator, and by virtue of the *nakohdo's* position of respect and prominence in the community and his personal relationship with the parties concerned, a high degree of confidence can be placed in his findings.

As shown above, the bargaining position of the two parties and the negotiating process depend basically on their relative assets in terms of the value system, and the *nakohdo* acts to free rather than to bind the decision-making process. One block to the free negotiating process is the understanding that each

party should be negotiating with only one party at a time, but this restriction is accepted regardless of the *nakohdo's* presence, and the *nakohdo* helps break through this block by insisting on quicker decisions in case negotiations lag unreasonably. By insisting on frankness and offering an opportunity for communication of real feelings, it is possible to carry through negotiations fairly quickly and, if necessary, to begin negotiations with another party. The *nakohdo's* interest in making a successful match and the family's desire to please the *nakohdo*, who is doing so much for them, constitute the greatest danger for distorting the decision-making process. Yet the fact that he expects to have continued relationships with the parties after the marriage and will be held partly responsible for difficulties places strict limits on the amount to which he can distort the essential factors and tends to lead to decisions which are made with the hope that they will be most satisfactory to the parties concerned.

While in the United States there is a much greater opportunity for meeting potential spouses and for testing out adjustment through dating, in Japan, the *nakohdo* offers an even more universalistic basis for frank investigation of the opposite party. In the United States, objective characteristics of the couple to be married are subordinated to the personal relationship between the partners, and this limits direct investigation of bank accounts, inheritance intentions, job prospects, neighborhood reputation, and the like.[4] In Japan, the existence of the *nakohdo* makes it possible to consider all the qualifications very frankly and directly without damaging the relationship between the two parties. This same general characteristic would seem to apply to the use of the go-between in other segments of Japanese society. In the labor market, the consumption market, and in political relationships as well, it may be possible to make relatively rational decisions through personal relationships. This is not just because a balance of personal interests may lead to more universalistic decisions, but because the go-between creates sufficient distance between parties to permit universalistic decisions. This has implications beyond the topic of marriage and may help to explain the ability of Japan to modernize in line with rational considerations of industrialization even without radical disorganization of existing personal relationships. Using go-betweens, it is often possible to make rational decisions within the context of a society which is still dominated by personal ties.

While this system probably does not permit as universalistic a basis of decision as a much more open market, nevertheless, without disrupting the local ties, it has been able to achieve a reasonable approximation to the universalistic characteristics of a more open market. The use of the go-between permits a kind of detachment which makes it possible to have a relatively objective investigation.

Because of this detachment permitted by the go-between, it is possible to use the go-between for a wide range of problems other than personnel placement. The go-between's role as a mediator is extremely crucial, and this

---

[4] Of course there are limitations on this personal love relationship in the United States, but less so than in many other countries. See William J. Goode, "The Theoretical Importance of Love," *American Sociological Review*, **24** (1959), 38-47. Of course even in Western countries there may be fringe movements employing marriage arrangers. For example, Karl Miles Wallace, "An Experiment in Scientific Matchmaking," *Marriage and Family Living*, **21** (1959), 342-348.

concept, rather than the concept of two warring sides, tends to characterize Japanese legal transactions, for example. If delicate negotiations of any kind are required, it becomes possible to work them out in a fairly neutral setting without serious loss of face. The value of using third persons for planned social change, for foreigners working with Japanese when negotiations are delicate, can hardly be overestimated.

The second general comment concerns the existence of the go-between as a functional alternative to dating in modern industrialized society. With the possible exception of European Jews, no other industrialized society has marriage arranging in large segments of the population. Part of this explanation would seem to lie in the fact that Japanese society is still rather tightly structured and that movement is still channeled through personal relationships.

Through institutions like the *nakohdo*, Japan has been able to mitigate the disruptions caused by rapid social change, and the success of these institutions, in turn, in coping with the societal problems has slowed down social change. The *nakohdo*'s success in smoothing the transition has undoubtedly meant that traditional patterns of social organization have been able to persist in the face of industrialization far longer than they would have had there been no such institutions to mediate the process of industrialization. While the *nakohdo* is becoming somewhat less important as the market situation becomes freer, the *nakohdo* remains important partly because of the ability of the *nakohdo* to adjust to new conditions. The go-between system has had no trouble in adapting to the fact that young people have been given in-creased opportunity to have an important say in the decision, that they have some chance for dating, and that they have an increased opportunity to meet members of the opposite sex before marriage. But at the same time that [the *nakohdo*] has adjusted to the increasing relative power of children, he makes sure that the parents' wishes are also considered and thus he serves an integrative function for the family.

It is probably true, as modern young Japanese hope, that the *nakohdo* is weakening in power and the family-based criteria are becoming less important than the compatibility of the couple itself, but until youth is much more emancipated, the *nakohdo* will be useful in integrating the parents' wishes and the youth's wishes and in providing opportunities for matches for those who otherwise would not get married. There are certain characteristics of [the] Japanese national character which fit in with the use of the *nakohdo*,[5] but in addition, the *nakohdo* is likely to have an important role for some time to come, unless structural changes occur in Japanese society which would vastly increase the opportunities for young people to meet each other and to make reliable decisions about marriage which would be satisfactory to themselves and to their families.

---

[5] In intensive cases, studies being conducted by Suzanne H. and Ezra Vogel through the National Institute of Mental Health in Ichikawa-shi, Japan, it appears that there is a tendency for many Japanese children to be very dependent on other people's decisions and to be reluctant to make their own. This same idea is explored more systematically through the widescale use of projective tests in Japan and is reported by George De Vos, "The Relation of Guilt to Achievement and Arranged Marriage Among the Japanese," *Psychiatry*, **23** (1960), 287-301.

similarity of beliefs and complementarity of needs in the choice of mate

eleven

The massive data on homogamy show that people who marry tend to be alike in many ways. People in this society marry those with whom they fall in love, but few people fall in love with someone *because* he is Catholic, middle class, dark-haired, and so on. Evidently, then, they fall in love with people in their "circle," in the same pool of eligibles, having similar traits. But why does an individual make his particular choice? One hypothesis, Robert F. Winch's theory of "need complementarity," states that individuals have certain personality needs (e.g., the need to nurture others) which fit or fail to fit those of others (e.g., the need to be nurtured). Individuals are more likely to be attracted to one another if their needs *complement* one another, that is, if the expression of one person's psychological need gives satisfaction to another's need.

If both processes work, that of homogamy and that of need complementarity, the question arises as to how these interact in the early or later stages of courtship. Which is more important? The succeeding investigation inquires into this set of relationships.

Value Consensus and Need Complementarity in Mate Selection

ALAN C. KERCKHOFF

KEITH E. DAVIS

* * * * *

One of the continuing interests in family research has been the attempt to define the factors which lead to a

Alan C. Kerckhoff and Keith E. Davis, "Value Consensus and Need Complementarity in Mate Selection," *American Sociological Review*, **27** (June, 1962), 295-299, 301-303. We are grateful to the authors and The American Sociological Association for permission to quote.

lasting relationship between a man and a woman. The two major concerns in such research have been with the process through which mates are chosen and the characteristics of mates which are predictive of "success" in the marital relationship. A considerable body of knowledge has been assembled based on data gathered in both the premarital and postmarital periods. Although there have been somewhat inconsistent results at times, the most general conclusion suggested by these data is that individuals who are similar to each other are most likely to choose each other as mates and are most likely to be successful in the relationship. Similarities have been noted in a large number of characteristics, such as area of residence, socioeconomic level, religious affiliation and activity, and many kinds of attitudes and values. This tendency toward homogamy in mate selection, however, is not the only tendency noted in the literature. A strong case has been made, for instance, for the proposition that heterogamy or complementarity of personality needs is an important principle of selection. Winch[1] has indicated that those variables normally associated with the theory of homogamy in mate selection simply define the "field of eligibles" from which each individual then chooses a mate who is likely to complement himself on the personality level.

The present study is intended as a contribution to this body of knowledge. The major innovation it introduces is a longitudinal perspective during the selection period, so that further knowledge of the actual selection process is gained. This is in contrast to most of the earlier studies which have compared a number of cases at a single point in time. The present study attempts to examine the relationship between progress in the mate selection process in the premarital period and measures of homogamy and complementarity.

Method

In October, 1959, an attempt was made to enlist the cooperation of a number of women students at Duke University as participants in this study. This was done both through calling a meeting for this purpose and through making the study instruments available in the dormitories. Women who were engaged, pinned, or "seriously attached" were asked to participate. The latter term was used to refer to those who were seriously considering marriage even though not actually pinned or engaged. Since the women were told that the man would be asked to take part also, we assume the group was limited to those who were fairly confident of the relationship. The women filled out an extended questionnaire (including materials not reported here) and gave us the names and addresses of their fiancés or boy friends. The same questionnaire was sent to the men by mail. One hundred sixteen women filled out the questionnaire, and 103 of their boy friends returned completed questionnaires. In May, 1960, both members of the 103 couples on whom we had complete October data were sent another short questionnaire. Data for the present report on ninety-four couples were derived from these returns.

Four factors were considered in the analysis. The dependent variable was the degree of movement toward a permanent union between October and May. The two independent variables were: (1) the degree of consensus between the man and woman on family values, and (2) the degree of need complementarity. In addition, the length of time the couple had been going together was used as a control variable, since it was expected that the relationship of either or both of the independent variables with the dependent variable might differ at different stages of the mate selection process.

Two hypotheses guided the analysis:
(1) Degree of value consensus is pos-

[1] R. F. Winch, *Mate-Selection* (New York: Harper & Row, Publishers, Inc., 1958).

itively related to progress toward a permanent union.

(2) Degree of need complementarity is positively related to progress toward a permanent union.

The variables were measured as follows:

Progress Toward a Permanent Union

In May the subjects were asked: "Is the relationship (between you two) different from what it was last fall when you filled out the first questionnaire?" There were three possible responses: "Yes, we are further from being a permanent couple," "No, it is the same," and "Yes, we are nearer to being a permanent couple." Since only twelve gave the first response, the sample was divided into those who said they were *closer* to being a permanent couple (fifty-six couples) *vs.* all others (thirty-eight couples). This factor will be referred to as "progress toward permanence."

Value Consensus

Bernard Farber's "index of consensus" was used for this purpose. As in Farber's original work, both members of the couple were asked (in October) to rank . . . ten standards by which family success might be measured.[2] The rank correlation between the two sets of rankings was the index of consensus. . . .

Need Complementarity

William Schutz's FIRO-B scales were used in the October questionnaire.[3] There are six of these scales, consisting of nine items each. Each scale is concerned with one of the con-

[2] . . . "An Index of Marital Integration," *Sociometry*, **20** (June, 1957), 117-134.

[3] Schutz, *FIRO: A Three-Dimensional Theory of Interpersonal Behavior* (New York: Holt, Rinehart & Winston, Inc., 1958), pp. 58-65.

tent variables, which Schutz calls "inclusion," "control," and "affection," and each is also concerned with either the desire to have others act in some way toward oneself or the desire to act in some way toward others. These two directions are called "wanted" and "expressed" by Schultz. Before computing the complementarity scores for each couple, the scalability of the six scales was tested. It was found that it was necessary to reduce the size of the scales to five items each in order to arrive at equal-sized scales which met the scaling criteria for both men and women separately. . . .

Length of Association

For the purposes of this analysis, couples were divided into approximately equal groups, the "long-term" group having gone together for eighteen months or more, the "short-term" group having gone together less than eighteen months.

Results

Since the dependent variable was a dichotomy and since the independent variables could not be assumed to be more than ordinal scales, the form of analysis used was the test of significance of the difference in the proportions of couples showing progress toward permanence in the categories defined by the hypotheses. In all tests, the distributions of cases on the independent and control variables were dichotomized as close to the median as possible. One-tailed tests were used.

When the simple relationships between the independent and the dependent variables were tested, only that between value consensus and progress in the relationship proved to be statistically significant at the .05 level or better. Two of the measures of complementarity (inclusion and control) approached this level of significance, however, and the third relationship was in the predicted direction. . . . Although these findings lead to the tentative acceptance of the first hypothesis and the rejection of the second, further analysis presents a somewhat different picture.

* * * * *

The introduction of the control variable of length of association provides even more information about the adequacy of the hypotheses.

Discussion

If we accept the pattern of relationships discussed above as significant for the research enterprise, two further issues remain: (a) How do we interpret or explain the pattern of relationships noted? (b) How does this research fit into the body of knowledge about the process of mate selection?

Turning to the first question, it is necessary to argue on a somewhat *ad hoc* basis, since the specific pattern of relationships found ha[s] not been explicitly predicted. However, the pattern does fit rather well with some earlier work in the field of inquiry. It was noted above that Winch speaks of the "field of eligibles" from which one presumably chooses a spouse who complements one's personality needs. In his discussion of the concept "field of eligibles" Winch says:

There is a set of variables upon which homogamy has been shown to function: race, religion, social class, broad occupational grouping, location of residence, income, age, level of education, intelligence, etc. It is my opinion that these variables function to select for each of us the sort of people with whom we shall be most likely to interact, to assure that the people with whom we otherwise associate are more or less like us with respect to that set of variables and also with respect to cultural interests and values.[4]

Although neither this particular passage nor others in Winch's writings make the point explicit, he seems to be lumping social structure variables and attitude and value variables together in his discussion. The expectation that the two kinds of variables would be highly correlated is a reasonable one, but, we would argue, further understanding of the selection process might be gained if we examined the concept "field of eligibles" more closely.

The present study indicates that such a blanket statement concerning the homogamy variables may give a misleading image of the mate selection process. The homogamy variable discussed above is value consensus. However, other measures of homogamy were also made in this study, such as education, religion, and father's occupation. It is of interest to note that such social categories did not discriminate effectively among the couples. That is, the subjects of this study were very homogamous with respect to social attributes.[5]

---

[4] *Op. cit.*, p. 14.

[5] The degree of homogamy is evidenced by the following: (a) Seventy per cent of the couples had the same level of education. If we accept as homogamous those cases in which the man has graduated from college and is no longer in school and the woman is still in college, only fourteen remain. Of these fourteen, ten are cases of men in graduate school and women in college and only four are cases of women in college and men who are high school graduates. (b) Eighty-seven per cent of the couples are members of the same religious groups (Protestant, Catholic, Jew). Forty per cent report the same rate of attendance at services, and 83 per cent are within one category on a five-point scale ranging from "never attend" to "four or more times a month." (c) Using Hollingshead's seven-category classification of occupations, the fathers of the man and woman are in the same category in 45 per cent of the cases; in 76 per cent of the cases they are in the same or adjacent categories.

On the other hand, the use of the more individual measure of values reported here led to a much clearer discrimination among the couples, . . . although even here the degree of homogamy is notable.

Thus a different kind of homogamy is evidently represented by family value consensus than by similarity in social characteristics. Evidently the couples of the present study had *already* limited their field of eligibles with respect to social characteristics but were far from having limited it with respect to value consensus.

This leads us to the tentative suggestion that there are various "filtering factors" operating during the mate selection period. The social attributes presumably operate at an early stage, but values and needs are more clearly operative later on.

Our data do not fit neatly into the logic of a serial set of filtering factors, however. If they did, and if we assume that social attributes, value consensus, and complementarity operate in that order, we would expect a significantly higher proportion of high value consensus couples in the long-term group, since many of the low consensus couples would have broken up (been filtered out) in the early stages of courtship. This is not the case. What we do find is that *if* the couple survives the earlier stages despite having low value consensus, they are more likely than short-term low consensus couples to

TABLE 1   Proportions of Low Consensus Couples Showing Progress by Length of Association and Need Complementarity (Total P = .467)

	INCLUSION		CONTROL		AFFECTION	
	High	Low	High	Low	High	Low
Short term	.357(14)	.333(6)	.400(5)	.333(15)	.333(9)	.364(11)
Long term	.786(14)	.250(12)	.833(6)	.450(20)	.750(12)	.357(14)

NOTE: The n on which each proportion is based is presented in parentheses after the proportion.

progress toward permanence, and this greater likelihood is largely explained by the variable of complementarity.

This may be seen in part from the fact . . . that long-term low consensus couples show progress more often than short-term low consensus couples (.538 vs. .350). If the low consensus couples are sorted according to *both* length of association *and* one measure of complementarity, however, it is even more striking. Table 1 shows this analysis. In the case of each measure of complementarity, there is a negligible difference in the short-term row but a very sizable difference in the long-term row. Thus complementarity evidently does have a differential effect in long-term and short-term low consensus couples. What remains unspecified is the mechanism through which some short-term low consensus couples manage to stay together.

However, even if this question were answered adequately, our data raise another question about the order of influence of these filtering factors, namely: How does it happen that the filtering effects of need complementarity are not noticeable until the later stages of courtship? Although our data do not provide a wholly satisfactory answer to this question either, some light may be shed on the issue. One of the measures used in the October questionnaire was the other half of Farber's "Index of Marital Integration," the measure of value consensus being the first half. This second measure involves the rating of oneself and of one's partner on a set of personality characteristics. Some of these characteristics are "negative," such as "irritable," "stubborn," "easily excited," and so on. Scores are computed for each person according to the number and intensity of such negative personality traits he attributes to his partner. If we sum the two scores for the couple, we have a measure of negative person perception in the couple, or what Faber calls "an index of role tension."

When we analyze these scores according to the length of association, we find that short-term couples have much lower scores than long-term couples. That is, short-term couples were less likely to attribute negative personality characteristics to each other than were long-term couples. Also, there is a greater tendency for the person perception scores of short-term couples to become *more* negative between October and May, even when we hold original scores constant. This seems to be in keeping with the point so often stressed in the literature that couples go through a period of idealization and perception distortion which may lead to disillusionment (or "reality shock") at a later date.

In the light of our other findings, we would interpret this to mean that the short-term couples were likely to be responding to an idealized version of the love object which would make the effectiveness of any personality complementarity less probable. They were responding to a stylized role relationship rather than to another personality. Not until the idealization is destroyed can [one] interact at the more realistic level of personality, and only then can need complementarity "make a difference" in the relationship.

We may now turn to our other question: How does this research fit into the body of knowledge about the process of mate selection? First, the research gives

added support for both the homogamy and complementarity theories, and it provides a tentative statement of the relationship between these two during the selection process.

Second, rather than simply comparing married or engaged couples with a random pairing of other individuals in order to show greater complementarity in the couples, this study attempts to demonstrate that complementarity "makes a difference" in the actual selection process. So far as we know, this is the first time such a longitudinal perspective has been provided.

Third, this is the first study of mate selection in which paper and pencil measures have pointed to a significant contribution of complementarity in the selection process. One of the criticisms of Winch's work has been that his measures were not adequately freed of rater bias. On the other hand, one of Winch's criticisms of other attempts to test the importance of complementarity with paper and pencil instruments has been that such instruments are not sufficiently sensitive to tap the relevant need area.[6] Although there may be some disagreement over the adequacy of our operational definitions of the needs involved, the fact remains that this study has been more successful in showing a contribution of complementarity than any other of its kind.[7]

Finally, although the present study has added to our knowledge, it still

---

[6] Winch, *op. cit.*, p. 83n. Winch is referring to the Edwards Personal Preference Schedule here, but presumably his point is a more general one.

[7] We have purposely avoided a discussion of the concept "need" in this article. It is defined in so many different ways in the literature that we feel it best to let the operational definition stand on its own feet rather than attempting to add still another definition. Let it suffice to note that Schutz refers to his scales as measures of "interpersonal needs," but they are certainly a very different kind of measure [from] that provided by the TAT.

leaves many unanswered questions which are also left unanswered by earlier studies. One of the most critical of these is the question of the importance or the salience of the needs being studied. In order for complementarity to make much of a difference in the selection process, one would expect that the needs involved must be of some importance to the individuals. Neither the present study nor the earlier ones [have] provided a means of determining the salience of the needs. . . .

Summary

We have reported on the findings of a study in which measures of value consensus and need complementarity have been shown to be related to a sense of progress toward permanence during a seven-month interval in the mate selection period. Although only value consensus was related to progress toward permanence for the sample as a whole, when the sample was divided into long-term and short-term couples, value consensus was related to progress for the short-term couples and two of three measures of complementarity were related to progress for the long-term couples. These findings are interpreted as indicating that a series of "filtering factors" operate in mate selection at different stages of the selection process. Our data generally support the idea that social status variables (class, religion, etc.) operate in the early stages, consensus on values somewhat later, and need complementarity still later. Our interpretation of the delay in the operation of the complementarity factor is that such personality linkages are often precluded by the unrealistic idealization of the loved one in the early stages of courtship.

Part 4

the
determinants
of fertility

how the social and cultural patterns affect fertility

twelve

Man's biological characteristics set some of the limiting conditions for his existence and for his continuing existence through reproduction. However, in turn, man's social and cultural systems determine the reproduction rate in a given society. An interesting puzzle arises at this point. Most societies place great stress on high fertility, and many use no contraceptives or use them ineffectively. Why, then, do the rates vary so much? In the article that follows, the authors develop an extensive analysis of just how and where these family systems affect reproduction. In addition, their analytic framework can furnish the basis for still further investigations to be done in the future.

Social Structure and Fertility: An Analytic Framework

KINGSLEY DAVIS   JUDITH BLAKE

A striking feature of underdeveloped areas is that virtually all of them exhibit a much higher fertility than do urban-industrial societies. This well-documented but insufficiently analyzed fact is known to be connected with profound differences in social organization as between the two types of society and is therefore significant for the comparative sociology of reproduction. The clarity and importance of the contrast, however, should not be allowed to obscure the equally important fact that underdeveloped areas themselves differ markedly in social organization, and that these differences appear to bring

Kingsley Davis and Judith Blake, "Social Structure and Fertility: An Analytic Framework," *Economic Development and Cultural Change*, 4 (April, 1956), 211-214. Reprinted by permission of The University of Chicago Press. Copyright 1956 by The University of Chicago Press.

about variations in fertility. Though the demographic statistics of backward regions have generally been so poor as to place in doubt the validity of reported differences, there are cases in which the evidence is reliable (e.g., as between Puerto Rico and Jamaica, or Arab Palestine and Ceylon). Of equal interest are the cases in which societies with differing social organization have the same level of fertility, for they may reach this common result by quite different institutional mechanisms. All told, ample opportunity exists for the comparative analysis of social structure as it affects fertility. In view of the bearing of future population trends on economic development, the pursuit of such analysis has a practical as well as a theoretical significance.

The present paper represents an attempt to set forth and utilize an analytical framework for the comparative sociology of fertility. It first presents a classification of the intermediate variables through which any social factors influencing the level of fertility must operate. It next tries to show, in broad outline, how some types and elements of social organization, acting through these variables, appear to enhance or depress societal fertility. Our hope is that as more sociological and demographic information becomes available, the theories advanced can be refined further and tested empirically.

The Intermediate Variables

The process of reproduction involves three necessary steps sufficiently obvious to be generally recognized in human culture: (1) intercourse, (2) conception, and (3) gestation and parturition.[1] In analyzing cultural influences on fertility, one may well start with the factors directly connected with these three steps. Such factors would be those through which, and only through which, cultural conditions *can* affect fertility. For this reason, by way of convenience, they can be called the "intermediate variables" and can be presented schematically as follows:

I. *Factors Affecting Exposure to Intercourse ("Intercourse Variables")*.

    A. Those governing the formation and dissolution of unions in the reproductive period.[2]

        1. Age of entry into sexual unions.

        2. Permanent celibacy: proportion of women entering sexual unions.

        3. Amount of reproductive period spent after or between unions.

            a. When unions are broken by divorce, separation, or desertion.

            b. When unions are broken by death of husband.

[1] Although the physiologist sees more steps in the process, these can all be subsumed under the three headings given here. We are concerned only with the steps in reproduction as they may be socially recognized and utilized.

[2] Since sexual intercourse is not confined to wedlock, the term "sexual union" seems preferable to "marriage." A union is here defined as any heterosexual relationship in which either actual intercourse occurs or orgasm is produced for at least the male partner. Every society has a type of union (marriage) in which reproduction is expected, approved, and even enjoined. At the same time, every society runs the risk of unions in which reproduction is condemned, either because they lack the legal form of marriage or because they violate one or more institutional taboos [adultery, incest, caste, or class endogamy, etc. See K. Davis, "The Forms of Illegitimacy," *Social Forces*, 18 (October, 1939), 77-89]. Between the fully approved and the strongly proscribed unions, there may be other types which have a lesser grade than marriage but in which reproduction normally occurs. Such unions may be frequent, in some cases representing the majority of reproductive unions. Any satisfactory sociological analysis of reproduction must keep straight the different types of unions.

B. Those governing the exposure to intercourse within unions.
   4. Voluntary abstinence.
   5. Involuntary abstinence (from impotence, illness, unavoidable but temporary separations).
   6. Coital frequency (excluding periods of abstinence).

II. *Factors Affecting Exposure to Conception ("Conception Variables").*
   7. Fecundity or infecundity, as affected by involuntary causes.
   8. Use or nonuse of contraception.
      a. By mechanical and chemical means.
      b. By other means.[3]
   9. Fecundity or infecundity, as affected by voluntary causes (sterilization, subincision, medical treatment, etc.).

III. *Factors Affecting Gestation and Successful Parturition ("Gestation Variables").*
   10. Foetal mortality from involuntary causes.
   11. Foetal mortality from voluntary causes.

It is clear that *any* cultural factor that affects fertility must do so in some way classifiable under one or another of our eleven intermediate variables.[4] Hence the latter provide a framework in terms of which the relevance of cultural factors to fertility can be judged. In fact, attempts to explain causal relationships between institutions and fertility without such a framework have led to inconclusive and confused writing on the subject.[5] The cultural factors, or "conditioning variables," are

presumably many, and no effort is made here to classify them; but the "intermediate variables" offer a means of approach to selecting and analyzing these factors.

It is also clear that *each* of the eleven variables may have a negative (minus) or a positive (plus) effect on fertility. If by examining all societies we could find the range of influence of a given variable, any effect more negative than the midpoint of this range would be on the minus side, and any influence more positive would be on the plus side. If, for example, a society uses contraception successfully, it has a *minus* value with respect to Variable Number 8; if it uses *no* contraception, it has a plus value on this variable. The value of each variable refers to how it affects fertility in each case; so a positive use of something (e.g., contraception, abortion, abstinence) may mean that it has a "minus" fertility value.

One cannot say, as is frequently implied in the literature, that some of these variables are affecting fertility in one society but not in another. *All* of the variables are present in *every* society. This is because, as mentioned before, each one *is* a variable—it can operate either to reduce or to enhance fer-

---

[3] Means of contraception other than mechanical and chemical include the "rhythm" method (which can also be classed as voluntary abstinence), withdrawal, simulated intercourse without penetration, various "perversions," and so forth.

[4] The reader will note that our list of variables does not include infanticide or child care. The reason for this omission is that our analysis is focused on factors affecting fertility strictly defined. Infanticide does of course affect family size and natural increase and may serve as an alternative to factors affecting fertility. It is therefore discussed briefly at a later point.

[5] For instance, Frank Lorimer, *Culture and Human Fertility* (Paris: UNESCO 1954), by failing to make clear the ways in which fertility *can* be affected, gives in some ways a confused picture of how it *is* affected. The reader may wish to compare our framework with a half-page outline of direct and indirect factors affecting fertility given by Raymond Pearl at the end of an article on "Biological Factors in Fertility," *Annals of*

the *American Academy of Political and Social Science*, **188** (November, 1936), 24.

tility. If abortion is *not* practiced, the fertility value of Variable Number 11 is "plus." In other words, the absence of a specific practice does not imply "no influence" on fertility, because this very absence is a form of influence. It follows that the position of any society, if stated at all, must be stated on all eleven variables.

Societies differing in their social organization do not necessarily have different fertility values with respect to all the variables. On some of the variables they may exhibit quite similar values. A nomadic tribe may have the same age at marriage as a settled, agrarian village; a primitive group may practice the same rate of abortion as an industrial society. Two contrasting societies are not likely, however, to manifest similar values for all the variables; they are not likely to do this even when their general fertility level is practically the same. The actual birth rate depends on the net balance of the values of all the variables. Though societies which generate a high fertility tend to be predominantly on the plus side, no society has the highest plus value on all eleven variables; and societies with low fertility turn out to be amazingly positive on a number of them.

It should of course be mentioned that cultural influences affecting our eleven variables do not necessarily represent rational attempts to govern fertility. Many fertility consequences stemming from sociocultural conditions (especially in underdeveloped regions) are byproducts, being unanticipated and unrealized by members of the society. Surely by now social scientists know that they cannot confine their attention only to rational actions or treat nonrational actions as somehow defying systematic analysis. The requirements of a given society can be met just as well, and just as ill, by an unintentional level of fertility as by an intentional one.

Institutional Patterns and the Intermediate Variables: A Preliminary Analysis

From the standpoint of comparative sociology, an important question is how the fertility values of our intermediate variables distribute themselves in different kinds of societies. A preliminary generalization is that underdeveloped societies tend to have high fertility values for Numbers 1, 2, 8, and 9 on the list; they *may* have high values for 3a, 3b, and 10; and they often have *low* values for 4 and 11. As for the remaining variables—5, 6, and 7—it is hard to prove that there are any consistent differences between preindustrial and industrial societies. If this generalization is roughly accurate, then it becomes meaningful to regroup the eleven variables as follows:

The Intermediate Variables According to Their Values in Preindustrial Societies

Usually High Values

1. Age of entry into unions.
2. Permanent celibacy.
8. Contraception.
9. Sterilization, etc.

Usually Low Values

4. Voluntary abstinence.
10. Foetal mortality—involuntary

High or Low Values

3a. Time between unstable unions.
3b. Postwidowhood celibacy.
11. Foetal mortality—voluntary.

Indeterminate

5. Involuntary abstinence.
6. Frequency of coitus.
7. Involuntary sterility.

* * * * *

[After analyzing in detail how each of these factors may influence the fertility of industrial and nonindustrial societies, the authors proceed to an important conclusion.]

Conclusion: The General Pattern

Any analysis of institutional factors in fertility must first explain the well known fact that underdeveloped societies in general have a higher rate of reproduction than industrial societies. The explanation, in brief, is that the pre-industrial peoples, in the face of high mortality, have had to develop an institutional organization which would give them sufficient reproduction to survive. However, analysis at this level does not carry us very far. In order to study the effects of institutional factors, one needs to break down the reproductive process itself so as to distinguish clearly the various mechanisms through which, and only through which, any social factor *can* influence fertility. In trying to do this, we have found eleven "intermediate variables." When analysis is made along those lines, it can be seen that the generally high fertility of underdeveloped areas does not mean that these areas encourage high fertility in every respect. As we have seen, they do not have high plus values on *all* the intermediate variables. Why, then, do they have low values in some respects and not in others?

It is possible to discern a systematic difference between underdeveloped and developed societies with reference to the eleven variables. In general, the pre-industrial societies have high fertility-values for those variables farthest removed from the actual moment of parturition and which, therefore, imply an overall outlook favorable to fertility. To a much greater degree than industrial societies, they tend to encourage early exposure to intercourse—exhibiting a far younger age at marriage and a higher proportion married. They thus lose little potential fertility by delaying or avoiding the formation of unions. After unions have been formed, these societies tend to enjoin more abstinence than industrial societies do (and therefore have lower values on variable number 4), but such "sexual fasting" arises from religious and magical motives rather than as a deliberate fertility control measure, and it does not appear to be great enough to have a substantial negative effect on fertility.

Underdeveloped societies also have high fertility-values for the conception variables. They practice little contraception and virtually no sterilization. Consequently, the tendency is to *postpone* the issue of controlling pregnancy until a later point in the reproductive process, which means that when a couple wishes to avoid children, those methods nearest the point of parturition—abortion and infanticide—are employed. These have the advantage, in societies living close to privation, of being nearer to the actual moment when the child must be supported.

Industrial societies, on the other hand, exhibit low fertility-values for those variables involving the early stages of the reproductive process, especially age at marriage, proportion married, and contraception; and they manifest high fertility-values for the variables in the later stages, especially infanticide. It follows that for many of the variables the two types of society exhibit opposite values. This is true for age of entry into unions, permanent celibacy, voluntary abstinence, contraception, and (if included as a variable) infanticide. It is not *necessarily* true of the time spent between or after unions, of sterilization, or of abortion; and it, of course, is not true of those variables characterized as "indeterminate"—involuntary abstinence, frequency of coitus, or involuntary infecundity. But the general contrast is sufficiently clear to require explanation.

A key to the position of the industrial societies lies in the fact that, as compared to pre-industrial cultures, they have achieved their lower reproduction, not by acquiring low fertility-values for *all* the intermediate variables, but by singling out particular ones as the means to that result. They took those means of reducing fertility which involved the least institutional organization and reorganization and which involved the least human cost. In the secular decline of the birth rate they relied more heavily on the mere postponement of marriage than on non-marriage. They relied less on abstinence, which makes heavy demands on the individual, and more on contraception and abortion, which do not. They dropped infanticide altogether and, in the later stages, tended to reduce abortion. In other words, they have undertaken to lower fertility, not primarily by extending further the negative effect of the variables by which fertility was lowered in the pre-industrial stage, but by using readily available institutional mechanisms with respect to marriage and by employing the possibilities of their advanced technology for conception control. Marital postponement was easily extended in the early and middle stages of industrialization because the basis for it already existed in Western society and because contraception and relatively safe abortion freed those who married late from the necessity of premarital celibacy. Gradually, in the late stages of industrial development, contraception has gained such predominance that it has made low fertility-values on the other variables (including abortion and late marriage) unnecessary.

Part 5

marital
adjustment

premarital sexual experience as a cause
of sexual adjustment in marriage

thirteen

Ever since the 1920's, when social scientists began to find out how many people engaged in sexual intercourse before marriage and when the new sexual freedom began to be preached, the debate between conservatives and reformers has continued. Aside from the moral issues, the latter have claimed that premarital sexual experience helps to create a better sexual relationship after marriage. In the succeeding study, the authors reanalyze Kinsey's data to test this possible relationship.

Premarital Experience and the Wife's Sexual Adjustment

ROBERT L. HAMBLIN   ROBERT O. BLOOD, JR.

The publishers of *Sexual Behavior in the Human Female* in an advertisement appearing in the November, 1953, issue of the *American Journal of Sociology* announced that this book would be referred to "again and again for factual information on such problems as . . . (the) relation of premarital sexual experience to the women's

Robert L. Hamblin and Robert O. Blood, Jr., "Premarital Experience and the Wife's Sexual Adjustment," *Social Problems*, **4** (October, 1957), 122-129. We are grateful to the authors and *Social Problems* for permission to quote.

sexual adjustment in marriage." The chief pertinent finding reported in the 1953 volume is that there is "a marked, positive correlation between experience in orgasm obtained from premarital coitus and the capacity to reach orgasm after marriage."[1] Otherwise stated, this finding means that a woman's orgasmic capacity in coitus before marriage is a good predictor of her orgasmic capacity in coitus after marriage. It would be

[1] Alfred C. Kinsey, *et. al.*, *Sexual Behavior in the Human Female* (Philadelphia: W. B. Saunders Co., 1953), p. 328.

surprising if this correlation were not found. (Ability to have orgasm in coitus ought to correlate highly with ability to have orgasm in coitus!)

Omitted from the Kinsey volume, however, is an analysis of the relationship of premarital coital experience *per se* and the sexual adjustment of the female in marriage. It seems appropriate that this relationship should be explored with the Kinsey data, since prior research on this socially important question has yielded contradictory results.

Fortunately there are relevant data in the Kinsey volume (as the advertisement suggests) which can clarify the relationship between premarital coital experience and sexual adjustment of the female in marriage. Harriet Mowrer has published the results of an analysis of some of these data.[2] She used indices other than orgasm rates as measures of

2 Harriet R. Mowrer, "Sex and Marital Adjustment," in Jerome Himelhock and S. S. Fava, Eds., *Sexual Behavior in American Society* (New York: W. W. Norton & Company, Inc., 1955), pp. 147-149.

sexual adjustment. Our purpose is to complement her analysis of the relevant Kinsey data by using orgasm rate as a measure of sexual adjustment.

Analysis

For a *preliminary* answer to this problem, a record of the marital orgasm rates of women with and without experience in premarital coitus is needed. . . . It is necessary to combine together all those who [have] had, and all those who [have] not [had], premarital coital experience. The results of this combination are shown in Table 1.

The data indicate that there is, in general, a small association between experience in premarital coitus and marital orgasm rate. During the first year of marriage the association is reliable at the .01 level of confidence. During the fifth year of marriage, however, the association is reduced so as to be unreliable (*P* is approximately .14). Our first conclusion, then, is that experience *per*

TABLE 1 First- and Fifth-Year Marital Orgasm Rates of Women
With and Without Premarital Coital Experience*

Per Cent of Marital Coitus with Orgasm	FIRST YEAR OF MARRIAGE		FIFTH YEAR OF MARRIAGE	
	No Premarital Coitus (Per Cent)	With Premarital Coitus (Per Cent)	No Premarital Coitus (Per Cent)	With Premarital Coitus (Per Cent)
None	27	23	17	14
1-29	11	11	12	15
30-59	12.5	13	16	14
60-89	12.5	12	15	15
90-100	37	41	40	42
Total	100	100	100	100
Number of Cases	1129	1082	784	646

* Adapted from Kinsey, *op. cit.*, Table 109, p. 406.
First Year of Marriage: Marshall's $C = 2.34$; P is less than .01.
Fifth Year of Marriage: Marshall's $C = 1.08$; P is approx. .14 (7)
It should be noted that the published Kinsey data seldom make possible rigorous comparison between homogeneous groups of subjects. For instance, we infer that the discrepancy between orgasm rates of those with and without experience in premarital coitus is reduced between the first and the fifth year of marriage. However, the former group is larger because many subjects were interviewed prior to the fifth year of marriage. Throughout this paper we have selected groups which are as nearly comparable as possible and hope that our analysis will stimulate the future publication of controlled analyses by Kinsey and his associates. Presumably the comparisons we have made are the best available basis for predicting the findings of such controlled analysis.

premarital experience and the wife's sexual adjustment **97** *se* in premarital coitus is associated with the female's sexual responsiveness during the first year of marriage. However, further analysis is indicated before it can be determined whether or not this observed association is causal in nature.

Why should females who engage in premarital coitus have a higher orgasm rate during the first year of marriage? If a reliable answer can be found for this question, we can infer whether or not the observed relationship is causal.

What theories are available which would, if substantiated, account for the observed association between premarital coital experience and the sexual adjustment of females in marriage? Kinsey gives two suggestions, and we add an obvious third. The theories themselves will be explained below as each is tested. However, since it is important to control the variables not being tested in a given test, it is appropriate to indicate in advance the crucial variables in each of these theories. These are: (1) the age at which the female begins her coital experience, (2) the amount of coital experience she has, and (3) the strength of her inhibitions about engaging in premarital coitus.

Age and Sexual Responsiveness

The first theory is taken from the Kinsey volume. If supported, this theory would account for the observed association and establish causality:

At least theoretically, premarital sociosexual experience . . . in coitus should contribute to this development of emotional capacities. In this as in other areas, learning at an early age may be more effective than learning at any later age after marriage. . . .

When there are long years of abstinence and restraint, and an avoidance of physical contacts and emotional responses before marriage, acquired inhibitions may do such damage to the capacity to respond that it may take some years to get rid of them after marriage, if indeed they are ever dissipated.[3]

Here it is hypothesized that *the sooner after puberty a female begins her coital experiences the more she will respond, since it will be easier to overcome inhibitions.*

In order to test this hypothesis it would be useful to compare the marital orgasm rates of two groups of women which have the following characteristics: (a) They ought to have the same amount of coital experience at the time of the test to control the experience variable. (b) The proportions of each group who engaged in premarital coitus ought to be the same. This would control the premarital inhibitions variable. (c) The two groups ought to differ with respect to the test variable—the average age at which coitus was first experienced.

Kinsey's data for groups of women who marry early or late may be used for this purpose. Kinsey's Table 79 shows that women married between the ages of sixteen and twenty (the "early" group) and those married between twenty-one and twenty-five (the "later" group) have similar amounts of premarital coital experience.[4] By interpolation it is possible to estimate that the median "early" bride married at age nineteen, whereas the median "later" bride married at twenty-three. At these two ages, the interpolated proportions who have ever engaged in premarital coitus are almost identical (39 per cent and 40 per cent, respectively). Moreover, the accumulative incidences of the premarital coital experience at varying ages indicate that the later-marrying women consistently tend to lag behind the early-marrying women in the age at which their first premarital coitus occurs. This implies that the

---

[3] Kinsey, *op. cit.*, p. 330.
[4] *Ibid.*, p. 337.

two groups are essentially comparable in terms both of the proportion who have ever had premarital coitus and in the length of time they had engaged in coitus before marriage. Therefore the later-marrying group on the average experienced their first coitus (whether premarital or marital) several years later than the early marrying group.

If sexual inhibitions allowed to go undisturbed for several years longer are harder to overcome, we would expect the later-marrying group to have a less satisfactory sexual adjustment after marriage than those who marry early. The figures from Table 2 . . . show

TABLE 2   First-Year Marital Orgasm Rates by Age at First Marriage*

Per Cent of Marital Coitus with Orgasm	Age at First Marriage	
	Under 21 (Per Cent)	21-25 (Per Cent)
None	34	22
1-29	9	11
30-59	10	13
60-89	12	13
90-100	35	41
Total	100	100
Number of Cases	575	1118

* Source: Kinsey, op. cit., Table 107, p. 405. Marshall's $C = 4.14$; P less than .001.

that the reverse is true, that is, that during the first year of marriage it is the later-marrying women who experience the higher orgasm rate.

We may tentatively conclude from the reversal in these data that the first theory about a causal relation between premarital coital experience and marital orgasm rate has been disproved. With proper controls, a reversal is the best possible evidence that a hypothesis is untrue. In this case, however, the adequacy of the controls is limited. This is apparent from asking, "Why should orgasm rates be negatively associated with the age at first experience?" An obvious answer is that

another factor, maturation, could be responsible for the reversal, since it was uncontrolled. Hence the early conclusion is questionable. But this much is certain, if maturation is the factor responsible, early experience is not appreciably effective in overcoming inhibitions, since its presumed effects are masked so completely by another variable. This test of the theory, then, is less than adequate for giving a reliable explanation for the original observation that premarital coital experience and marital orgasm rates are associated during the first year of marriage.

Previous Experience and Sexual Responsiveness

Perhaps *response to orgasm depends upon the development of coital skills which the female learns through experience.* Presumably these skills increase with the amount of experience, so that the observed association between female orgasm rate during the first year of marriage and premarital coital experience may result from greater experience. If verified, this theory would establish causality.

A comparison of the same early- and later-marrying females when age is held constant (both groups averaging twenty-four years of age) allows us to test this theory. At age twenty-four, the early-marrying group averages four years' more coital experience than the later-marrying groups. Hence the groups differ with respect to the test variable—amount of experience. As indicated above, the two groups are comparable in terms of the number experiencing premarital coitus and, presumably, premarital inhibitions. Also, since the averages and ranges of the ages of the two groups are the same, maturation is controlled. The other variable, age of first experience, is uncontrolled, however. It also becomes a test variable whose predicted effects are in the same direction as those of the other test variable—amount of experience. If there is no difference between the two groups with respect to marital orgasm rates, both theories may be rejected. If there is the predicted difference between the two groups with respect to marital orgasm rates, then it is impossible to tell which of the two variables is responsible. But if the predicted relationship does obtain, we shall have an indication that the observed association between premarital coital experience and orgasm rates during the first year of marriage is causal in nature.

If the amount-of-experience and/or the early-experience theories are true, then, the early-marrying group should have a higher orgasm rate. The data in Table 3 indicate, however, that the later-marrying group has a slightly higher orgasm rate. The difference is unreliable, however. (P is approximately .20.) The proper inference is that there is no difference between the two groups with respect to orgasm rates. Hence both theories considered thus far may be rejected with some confidence. An explanation of the observed association must be found in another theory.

TABLE 3   Marital Orgasm Rates at Median Age 24 for Early and Later Marrying Women*

Per Cent of Marital Coitus with Orgasm	Early-Marrying Group Married Under 21 (Md. 19) (Fifth Year of Marriage) (Per Cent)	Later Marrying Group Married 21-25 (Md. 23) (First Year of Marriage) (Per Cent)
None	21	22
1-29	14	11
30-59	13	13
60-89	16	13
90-100	36	41
Total	100	100
Number of Cases	333	1118

* Source: Kinsey, *op. cit.*, Table 107, p. 405. Marshall's $C = .82$; P approximately .20.

Inhibitions and Sexual Responsiveness

Kinsey provides the third theory that would account for the difference in marital orgasm rates of females who did and did not engage in coitus before marriage. It involves the generalization of inhibitions.

As children grow . . . it is customary in our culture to teach them that they must no longer make physical contacts, and must inhibit their emotional responses to persons outside of the immediate family. Many persons believe that this restraint should be maintained until the time of marriage. Then, after marriage, the husband and wife are supposed to break down all of their inhibitions and make physical and emotional adjustments which will contribute to the solidarity of the marital relationship. Unfortunately, there is no magic in a marriage ceremony which can accomplish this. The record indicates that a very high proportion of the females . . . find it difficult after marriage to redevelop the sort of freedom with which they made contacts as children, and to learn again how to respond without inhibition to physical and emotional contacts with other persons.[5]

Interpreted loosely, the above quotation may be condensed into the following theory: *moral scruples which inhibit*

[5] *Ibid.*, p. 328.

females from engaging in premarital coitus tend to become generalized, thereby interfering with orgasmic response in marital coitus. In order to test this theory directly, it is necessary to find marital orgasm data for two groups of women, one of which was more inhibited about premarital coitus than the other.

Since premarital coitus is tabooed in Judeo-Christian teachings, devoutly religious women ought to be more inhibited about engaging in premarital coitus than those who are less devout. In the Kinsey volume, relevant data are available for married samples of religiously active and inactive Protestant and Catholic females and moderately active and inactive Jewish females. Of the three possible combinations, Protestant and Catholic samples were chosen. The available data support the inference that devout Protestant and Catholic women are more inhibited about premarital coitus than the respective inactive groups. (See Table 4.)

TABLE 4	Experiences of Devout and Inactive Protestant and Catholic Women in Premarital Coitus*			
	Protestants		Catholics	
	Devout (Per Cent)	Inactive (Per Cent)	Devout (Per Cent)	Inactive (Per Cent)
Female Experience in Premarital Coitus Up to Age 20				
Premarital Coitus	14	25	12	41
No Premarital Coitus	86	75	88	59
Total	100	100	100	100
Number of Cases	860	887	261	122
Female Experience in Orgasm from Premarital Coitus Up to Age 20				
Coitus with Orgasm	43	48	25	63
Coitus without Orgasm	57	52	75	37
Total	100	100	100	100
Number of Cases	121	222	31	50
Female Expression of Regret Regarding Experience in Premarital Coitus, All Ages				
Regret	38	20	50	16
No Regret	62	80	50	84
Total	100	100	100	100
Number of Cases	295	490	86	90

* Sources: Adapted from Table 89, Kinsey, *op. cit.*, 342 and Table 92, *ibid.*, p. 345. The percentage of women experiencing orgasm from premarital coitus is derived by dividing the published percentage of the total sample who had experienced orgasm from this source by the percentage of the total sample who had engaged in premarital intercourse.

The data in Table 4 show that devout Protestant and Catholic women are somewhat more inhibited before marriage, in the sense that (a) they are more apt to refrain from premarital intercourse, (b) they are more apt to fail to achieve orgasm if they do engage in premarital coitus, and (c) they are more apt to regret coital experience if they have it. Hence it seems safe to conclude that the two groups differ with respect to the test variable—premarital inhibitions.

Are these two sets of groups matched with respect to other relevant variables? They are not controlled with respect to age at first experience and amount of experience. However, since these variables have been shown to be unrelated to orgasm rates, controlling them is unnecessary. Maturation of the two sets of groups is an unknown factor, but we have no reason to believe that such groups would differ with respect to maturation. Our above analysis indicates the proportion of females engaging in premarital experience is not related to age at marriage (at least for those who marry before twenty-five). Of course each set is controlled with respect to religious affiliation.

If sexual inhibitions are actually generalized from premarital to marital coitus, the orgasm rate of the "devout" women would be lower than the orgasm rates of the "inactives" after marriage. The data in Table 5 give mixed results, however. There is an unreliable difference between the orgasm rates of the devout and inactive Protestant females. (P approximates .40.) The difference between the orgasm rates of

TABLE 5   First-Year Marital Orgasm Rates of Devout and
Inactive Protestants and Catholics*

Per Cent of Marital Coitus with Orgasm	Protestants		Catholics	
	Devout (Per Cent)	Inactive (Per Cent)	Devout (Per Cent)	Inactive (Per Cent)
None	27	26	32	22
1-29	10	12	18	7
30-59	13	10	13	11
60-89	10	13	5	14
90-100	40	39	32	46
Total	100	100	100	100
Number of Cases	430	564	112	88

* Source: Table 106, Kinsey, *op. cit.* (p. 404).
Devout *vs.* Inactive Protestants: Marshall's $C = .23$; P greater than .40.
Devout *vs.* Inactive Catholics: Marshall's $C = 2.89$; P less than .005.

the devout and inactive Catholics is reliable (P is less than .01) and in the predicted direction.

What do these differential results mean? In our judgment, they may mean two things. (a) Protestant inhibitions may differ in kind from Catholic inhibitions. In Catholic doctrine, sexual pleasure is not a legitimate end in itself. Rather, such pleasure is justified only if there is a possibility of conception. Hence the Catholic position on contraceptive procedures, homosexuality, masturbation, and celibacy. It is possible that the more devout Catholic females tend to acquire scruples against sex *per se*. On the contrary, devout Protestant females apparently develop scruples against premarital coitus *per se* but feel that sexual pleasure in marriage is not only legitimate but desirable. Hence the observed discrepancy in Table 5.

The Catholic Church discourages the use of contraceptive procedures in general and forbids the use of contraceptive devices in particular. Protestant churches are more permissive in this respect. This taboo against the use of contraceptive devices may produce a conflict for many devout Catholic females which her Protestant counterpart may escape. If she adopts reliable contraceptive practices, she is likely to suffer guilt feelings. If she refrains from using contraceptives, she is likely to be anxious about excessively frequent pregnancies. The permissible Catholic method (rhythm) was found in the Indianapolis study to be less than one-tenth as effective as the diaphragm and jelly method. Insofar as anxiety or guilt is present, it would presumably distract most individuals during coitus and decrease their orgasm rates. Hence the differential beliefs of the devout Protestant and Catholic females might also account for the pattern observed in Table 5.

If either of the above explanations is valid (and both are consistent with the data in Table 5), then the third theory which would account for the association between premarital coitus and marital orgasm rates is likewise unsupported. Scruples about engaging in premarital coitus *per se* evidently do not generalize to marital coitus and hence do not depress the female's marital orgasm capacity.

Also, if either of the above explanations is valid, the association between premarital coital experience *per se* and marital orgasm rates would be predicted. Either could be a spurious factor which would account for the relationship. It is probable that more females who refrain from premarital coitus have generalized scruples against all sexual pleasure than is the case with those who engage in premarital coitus. It is also likely that more females who believe the use of reliable contraceptives is morally wrong refrain from premarital coitus than do females who believe the use of reliable contraceptives is permissible. It is impossible at present to test directly either of these theories, since the data are unavailable.

Summary and Conclusion

The purpose of this paper has been to test hypotheses about the relationship of premarital coital experience *per se* and the wife's sexual adjustment as measured by marital orgasm rates. Data from the Kinsey report were recombined and interpreted for this analysis.

A reliable association was found between premarital coital experience and wives' orgasm rates during the first year of marriage. Three hypotheses, any one of which would give direct causal significance to this association, were then tested with Kinsey data. These are:

1. The earlier after puberty a female begins her coital experience, the more she will respond (since it will be easier to overcome inhibitions).
2. Response to orgasm depends upon the development of coital skills which the female learns through experience.
3. Moral scruples which inhibit the female from engaging in premarital coitus tend to become generalized and, thereby, to interfere with orgasmic response in marital coitus.

None of these hypotheses found empirical support. Two spurious factors (generalized scruples against all sexual pleasure and internalized taboos against the use of reliable contraceptives) are consistent with and presumably account for the observed relationships. In combination, the results cast doubt on the validity of the hypothesis that premarital coital experience *per se* facilitates the wife's sexual adjustment as measured by orgasm rates. It should also be pointed out that the notion that premarital coital experience *per se* hinders the wife's sexual adjustment is also doubtful if orgasm rates are used

premarital experience and the wife's sexual adjustment   **103** as the measure. Rather, experience or inexperience in premarital intercourse seems to bear no consistent causal relationship to the wife's sexual adjustment.

Further research is needed. The three explanatory hypotheses ought to be retested in controlled *ex post facto* experiments. The relationship of generalized moral scruples to marital orgasm rates ought to be investigated more directly. The relationship of internalized taboos against the use of reliable contraceptives to marital orgasm rates should also be investigated directly. It is hoped that this paper will constitute a stimulus to such further investigations of these important questions.

sex in the lower-class english marriage

fourteen

The myth of lower-class sexuality, warmth, and naturalness has been a fruitful source of modern literature, but serious investigations (including Kinsey's) underline its mythical basis. Readers who have had informal conversations with lower-class American wives will recognize many of the following interview comments as familiar, but it seems likely that a representative sample in the United States would not yield so gloomy a picture.

Sex Life in Marriage

ELIOT SLATER   MOYA WOODSIDE

There have been several studies of sex life in marriage, but those which have taken a statistical form and relate to a normal population have all been carried out in the United States, and, before the work of Kinsey, on an upper middle-class group of well-educated people. The studies of psychoanalysis, although they have been made on neu-

Eliot Slater and Moya Woodside, *Patterns of Marriage* (London: Cassell & Company, Ltd., 1951), pp. 165-169, 174. Reprinted by permission.

rotic subjects, are also interesting for the light they throw on the amount of variability in sex behavior, the extent to which it is affected by taboos and by early education, and the effect frustration in this field may have on personal adjustment. Freud considered that it was impossible to have a neurotic illness and, at the same time, a full and satisfactory sex life. There is little doubt, however, that this is a fallacy.

The data presented here owe their interest to the fact that (apart from the husbands in the neurotic group) our informants were a fairly representative sample of the so-called working class. Information was gathered in the course of inquiries on other points, and is not of an exhaustive kind. Such as it is, it is probably reliable. The hospital setting was favorable for frankness, and a degree of confidence was won in the earlier stages of the interview which, except in unusually unfavorable circumstances, allowed inquiry on an accepted aspect of life without any particular difficulty.

The Frequency of Intercourse

The data are not sufficiently precise to allow of a statistical analysis, but the modal frequency is twice a week. The data were obtained in the course of psychiatric treatment of neurotic soldier patients. [They] show the gradual lessening frequency of intercourse with age, as well as the enormous degree of individual variation, from never to more than once daily. Even in youth and in the prime of life about 1 per cent of husbands never have intercourse with their wives at all—but that may be true only in a sample of neurotics. It is also interesting that mean figures are considerably lower than those obtained by Kinsey in an American sample. This may again perhaps be attributed to the fact that our figures were obtained from neurotic individuals; but it might also indicate a difference between British and American standards.

Even in the control cases in our main inquiry, variation in frequency of marital intercourse was very wide, from limits of more than once daily to once in several months. In our subjects, normal habits were disturbed by the war situation, as husbands were seldom in reach of home except on periods of leave. While on weekend pass from camp or hospital, intercourse might take place several times, but there would then very likely be a number of weeks before the opportunity occurred again. Nevertheless, about two thirds of the couples had experience of marriage of a normal peacetime kind and were able to report on their habits then.

Cautious and uninformative replies were often given: "just normal," "not every night," "just average," "we're just normal," "I must admit it would be more than once a week," "it varies —not excessive." A number of couples have an idea that there is a standard to which most people conform, and that other people are much the same as themselves. The idea seems to be founded on an almost total ignorance. Frequency varies with circumstances, as it depends so much on the mood of the moment and the partner's wish: "you can't lay down any hard and fast rule," "we used to come to an agreement," "just when the impulse arises." Weekends and Saturday nights are popular. On other days the husbands are tired; overtime and night work affect the times chosen.

Contrasting Attitudes of Men and Women

It was probably due to the sex of the interviewer that women were more forthcoming than men when talking on this subject. Nevertheless, men seemed to be less troubled on the subject and took it much more for granted. Sexual adaptation was in fact far more successful. For men, conjugal sex relations are a habit, a regulated indulgence, part of the marriage contract. "There's never been any trouble; I don't indulge," "we've never abused it." There is complacency, undisturbed by doubts. "My wife satisfies me and I believe I satisfy her," "it gives me great satisfaction," "I'm not a sex maniac," "I never was a beast, we've always agreed about it." Time and again, things were said to be "all right," and further inquiry was blocked. Few had much to say unless there were serious difficulties. A pattern of male dominance could be seen, and to some extent a general feeling of possessiveness and of "rights," not always agreed to: "I was never refused, but it was grudging." Responsiveness in their wives was hardly expected, and there was some suggestion that where the wife was more sensually disposed than her husband, her "hot nature" was disapproved, and even feared. Very many were unaware of their wives' feelings, and in a number of cases where the husband said it was "all right," the wife had a different view.

Women opened their hearts on this subject much more than men, and it was possible to obtain more illuminating details. For most of them it was the first opportunity for an informed discussion. A puritanical attitude was widespread. Sex is duty, and women are not trained to expect any particular pleasure. Childhood memories, the experience of their own mothers, the tales they have heard conspire against a healthy attitude. There is a barely veiled sex antagonism, and the word "they" is commonly used as a generic term for the demanding males. With this is combined an attitude of submission. Several times the phrase recurred, "I've never refused him," often said with pride. Compliance is seen as an anchor for the husband, keeping his affection at home. Passive endurance is shown in such phrases as "he's happy," "I try to be accommodating," "it's a satisfaction for him."

This negative attitude quite often reaches a low point in one of boredom, even dislike, and a desire to get it over: "I'm not keen," "I don't think there's anything in it," "sometimes it bores me," "I'm not really interested," "it's something that's got to be done, and the quicker the better," "my heart's not in it," "it's the one part of marriage I could do without." Husbands are valued in an inverse relation to sexuality: "he's very good, he doesn't bother me much," "he's not lustful," "he wouldn't trouble you at all," "he's pretty good that way; if I say no, he doesn't go on." Even where some satisfaction in sex relations is attained, consideration on the part of the husband is very welcome: "he's a thorough gentleman," "he's very thoughtful," "he's a very self-controlled man."

Libido and Capacity for Orgasm in Women

Common though these attitudes are among women, yet about half the sample found some physical satisfaction in sex relations, and to a lucky minority they were a source of real pleasure. Comments varied from "I don't dislike it," "there's a certain amount of pleasure attached," to "you've got to be playful sometimes, we're both loving like," "I do enjoy it," "that side of life is very very lovely."

Mrs. P., twenty-six (27c), says sex is "perfect." They have been married nearly five years, but intercourse is most nights, and sometimes in the day as well. She has orgasm every time. He is a perfect lover. She is highly sexed, and finds the enforced abstinence "terrible." Sex is "the only thing in life sometimes." "He need only hold my hand and I want him."

Sexual desire, the enjoyment of sex relations, and the regularity of orgasm in coitus, though distinguishable from one another, are all closely correlated. It was only possible to get satisfactory information about the last of these. About one-third of all women said they experienced orgasm always, and another fifth often or enough; one in four said infrequently or insufficiently, and about one in ten had probably never experienced it at all. There is a significant difference between the women in the neurotic and the control groups; the wives of the neurotics tended on the whole toward the extremes—more of them had a full experience, but 15 per cent, as against 5 per cent in the control group, never experienced orgasm.

These figures are not, perhaps, extremely reliable. It was difficult to word the appropriate question and doubtful sometimes how far there was sufficient self-knowledge of the physiological event. Many who said "yes" sounded unconvincing but had to be given the benefit of the doubt.

The association of these functions with other attributes of our cases shows features of interest. When the wives of the control group were rated by degree of libido, higher levels of sexual desire were found to be associated with an unneurotic test rating (r ·28), happiness of marriage (r ·24), better education, better intelligence, and absence of neurotic traits in childhood (for each ·20). All of these correlations are significant; but nevertheless none of them could be confirmed in the wives of the neurotic men. Despite this, the suggestion arises that a reasonable level of sexual appetite in women is a favorable feature and is correlated with other favorable features of very diverse kinds.

Over both groups taken together, adequacy of experience of orgasm is associated with happiness in childhood and happiness in marriage; here again,

correlations are higher in the control than in the neurotic group.

* * * * *

The Satisfied and Successful

Over half the women of the combined sample say that orgasm is sufficiently regular for sex life to be satisfactory. Like the happily married, these sexually well-adjusted women have little to add to the bare statement of their satisfaction. That there is a majority is reassuring, but it is a matter for disquiet that the minority of 30 per cent of definitely dissatisfied women is so large. The women who have been married longer than the average are rather more successful than the others; and as marriage lasts, the chances of satisfactory adjustment improve. Yet we have the impression that the younger couples have a franker and more positive attitude toward sex than their elders, and the chances will be better for them in the long run. . . . Wives are less resigned to sexual frustration, husbands are becoming more considerate; and at least among the more intelligent, inhibition is declining. Husbands and wives aim at an enjoyment that is mutual: "he won't ever have it without me getting pleasure as well," "you must satisfy the wife and at the same time if possible," "we aren't afraid to talk about it; I always get what I want," "it shouldn't become a habit, just like having your supper." Although the present state of affairs cannot be regarded with complacency, there are grounds for hope for the future.

* * * * *

husband-wife interaction in a matrilineal system

fifteen

To this point, we have not considered the type of family system in which the individual family unit is formally a part of a collective unit, a corporate group composed of a wide network of kin. In this account, the anthropologist describes both how the role obligations and rights of husband and wife differ when the main line of descent is through the wife (matrilineage) and also how they are very similar to marital interaction in our own family system. Note especially the different points of strain in family interaction under such a system.

Marriage, Matriliny, and Social Structure Among the Yao of Southern Nyasaland

j. CLYDE MITCHELL

Marriage among the Yao, as in other societies, is an institution which serves many social ends. From a sociological point of view we may see it as a formal device through which social relationships involving specific rights and responsibilities are set up between the spouses themselves, between the social groups from which the spouses come, and between these people and the children born of the marriage. Marriage apportions these rights and responsibili-

J. Clyde Mitchell, "Marriage, Matriliny, and Social Structure Among the Yao of Southern Nyasaland," *International Journal of Comparative Sociology*, 3 (September, 1962), 29-32, 35-37, 39-40. Reprinted in John Mogey, ed., *Family and Marriage* (Leiden: E. J. Brill, 1963).

ties in all societies so that they are openly stated and subject to both the informal social control of public opinion and the formal control of the legal system. In this paper I wish to examine the type of rights and responsibilities involved in marriage in a matrilineal society and how these rights and duties are formally recognized.

Matriliny, Patriliny, and Paternity

It is a truism to say that in all societies descent is traced through both parents. What is implied by stating that a society is matrilineal or patrilineal is that different kinds of relationships are customarily established with kinsmen through one of the parents as against those through the other. In the same way, descent in a bilateral society customarily establishes relations of the same sort with kinsmen through both parents.

As a rule, in unilineal systems the socially significant relationships established by descent are those of an economic and political nature. This means that in a patrilineal system a child is aligned for political action with, and acquires land and other economic rights through, his father and his patrilineal kinsmen. In a matrilineal system a child acquires these rights through his mother and her matrilineal kinsfolk. This does not imply that no rights are established through the mother in a patrilineal society and the father in a matrilineal society. These rights do exist, but they are not of the same kind as those through the parent of direct descent. A child in a patrilineal society has a jural right to assistance and support from his patrilineal kinsmen but may only obtain assistance and support from his mother's kinsmen as an act of grace on their part. Similarly, in a matrilineal society a child has claims by right to assistance and support from his matrilineal kinsmen but may obtain assistance from his father's people as an act of grace on their part. This implies that marriage in both patrilineal and matrilineal societies serves to determine what sort of rights and responsibilities are apportioned to different types of kinsmen.

The problem of descent in matrilineal systems, however, is somewhat different from that in patrilineal societies. The central problem in patrilineal descent is the uncertainty of paternity and hence the necessity of institutional devices which unequivocally establish who the pater of the child is. This derives from the necessity of determining the vitally important economic and political rights and responsibilities between the child and his father's people. Marriage is the device which achieves this. In matrilineal peoples, however, the problem of paternity takes on a different complexion. While there may sometimes be doubt as to who a child's father is, there is seldom any uncertainty about its mother. Since the most important rights and responsibilities are established through the mother, there appears to be no need for institutional devices to apportion them. From this point of view, the child's paternity appears to be irrelevant. Yet even in matrilineal societies marriage is an important institution and paternity is formally established through it. Even amongst the Nayars of Malabar, who have long been cited as an example of a people with extreme matriliny among whom marriage barely exists, the paternity of children is clearly established.

We must look at marriage therefore as a formal device through which certain rights and responsibilities between defined categories of persons are publicly stated and subject therefore to control both by public opinion and the courts of law.

Uxorial and Genetricial Rights

Analytically we may distinguish between several different categories of person involved in marriage relationships and between several different categories of rights and responsibilities set up between these people. We may distinguish the relationship set up by marriage between the spouses from those set up between their kinsmen. Marriage brings the kinsmen of the spouses into affinal relationships, so that they must adopt specific patterns of behavior toward one another. A mother-in-law among the Yao, for example, is entitled to certain services from her son-in-law, and he in turn to respect from her. Siblings-in-law, on the other hand, joke with one another. The entire group of people related to each of the spouses is thus brought into relationships with the other, and they expect specific patterns of behavior from them.

More extensive rights and responsibilities are involved in the relationship between the spouses. These may be separated into two broad categories or clusters. The first, which we may call uxorial rights, refers to the personal rights and duties of the spouses to each other. The other cluster of rights refers to the rights which an individual spouse, or the group to which he belongs, may possess or acquire over the wife as a bearer of children.

An important uxorial right is the sexual obligation of each spouse to the other. From the wife's point of view this is usually expressed as the exclusive access to her by her husband. From the husband's point of view this usually implies the obligation to beget children in his wife. But sexual rights are only part of uxorial rights as a whole. Usually a husband must also support his wife economically, provide her with shelter and protect her from harm. Likewise the wife must perform a series of domestic duties for her husband: she must cook for him, draw water for him, mend his clothes and care for him when he is ill. By the very nature of uxorial rights they are personal and individual: it is very unusual to find these rights held in common by a group of women or a group of men. They are essentially a feature of the dyadic element in the conjugal relationship.

Genetricial rights are the rights over the children which issue from the marriage and usually serve to fix the children's membership to specific kinship groups. The kinsmen of the spouses as well as the spouses themselves are implicated in these rights, and being of political significance they are frequently corporately held. It seems, however, that in some societies some rights over the children of his wife may be ac-

quired by a husband in his personal capacity. An example of such a people is the matrilineal Bemba of Northern Rhodesia. In strongly patrilineal peoples, rules of incest and exogamy demand that the males of any particular group must formally acquire the child-bearing capacities of women from other groups in order to perpetuate their lineage. This implies that there must be a legal arrangement whereby the reproductive capacity of a woman is transferred to her husband's group. The uxorial rights over the woman will be held by a man individually, but the genetricial rights will be held by his lineage as a whole. The implication of this is that whoever a woman's sexual partner may be at a particular moment, the jural relationships of her children to their pater's kinsmen are clearly defined. The levirate, for this point of view, is a mechanism whereby uxorial rights on the death of a husband pass to his younger brother (or in certain circumstances to a son by another wife), while the rights of the husband's group to the woman's issue remain unaltered. "Ghost marriage," in which a woman bears children to her deceased husband's name, is a similar device. The custom whereby a woman may marry herself a "wife" and "beget" children to her brother's lineage is a neat example of the clear separation of the two clusters of rights. The lineage of the female "husband" acquires the genetricial rights in the wife, while the uxorial rights in her may be split between herself, insofar as domestic services are concerned, and a lover, insofar as sexual services are concerned.

The formal acquisition of these rights is usually marked by the transfer of bride wealth from the husband's group to the wife's, and different parts of the bride wealth may confer different rights. Thus among the Zulu one of the payments, *mfuko* or "snuff-box," conferred uxorial rights, so that claims against an adulterer became valid only after this payment was made. Subsequent payments in the form of *lobolo* cattle fixed the rights and obligations of the children in the father's group. The genetricial rights were thus transferred by this payment, so that until it had been made, the rights to the children remained with their mother's people. The Zulu adage: "Cattle beget children," reflects this arrangement.

Amongst matrilineal peoples, the children are aligned with their mother and her brother rather than with their father. This means that the genetricial rights in a woman are held in perpetuity by her male matrilineal kinsmen as a group. Whoever her husband happens to be, her children have primary rights in, and responsibilities toward, their mother's matrilineal kinsmen. The relationships between spouses, however, contain elements which are similar to those in patrilineal societies in that they have roughly the same duties vis-à-vis one another.

In a matrilineal society therefore, the marriage transaction primarily establishes uxorial rights between the spouses, but the marriage has nevertheless clear structural implications. This may be seen in the marriage arrangements of the matrilineal Yao of Southern Nyasaland.[1]

* * * * *

Yao Marriage

A marriage . . . in Yao society sets up different relationships between the various persons and groups involved. At the same time each of the spouses does

---

[1] I lived for some twenty-four months among the Yao in Southern Nyasaland between September, 1946, and September, 1949. My observations are drawn from this experience. . . .

not by marriage cease to be a member of his own matrilineal descent group. Two matrilineal descent groups are therefore also brought into relationships through the marriage. Each of these descent groups is primarily concerned with the welfare of its own member. But they are implicated in the marriage in different ways. In the first place, in over two-thirds of the marriages the man lives in his wife's village. In these marriages therefore, the man's group is concerned with the welfare of one of its members who is living among strangers. His day-to-day care is left in the hands of the woman's group, and they are implicated only when he is seriously ill or he feels that his rights have been denied.

The woman's group similarly is interested in the welfare of its member and in protecting her rights. But in the majority of marriages she is living in her matrilineal village and is in constant contact with her kinfolk. The woman's group [has] an additional interest in the marriage, since it is through it that the woman becomes productive and contributes to the growth of the matrilineage. In other words, both parties are involved in protecting the uxorial rights of their members and in upholding their responsibilities, but only the woman's group is concerned with the genetricial rights in the woman.

Frequently in other Bantu societies, these rights and responsibilities are assumed when the marriage payments are made and the marriage is formally contracted. One of the striking features of Yao marriage, however, is that the relationship between the two matrilineal groups involved is set up without the exchange of any bride wealth or the performance of labor service by the young man. The marriage instead is legalized entirely by the public acknowledgment of the fact by representatives of each group formally appointed for this purpose and acting afterward as its agents.[2]

The husband's marriage representatives or sureties are referred to collectively as "those of the man" (*wakucilume*) and the wife's as "those of the woman" (*wakucikongwe*). These sureties stand in a particular relationship to the spouses. The senior surety, known as "the sleeping log" (*mkokowogona*), is ideally a mother's brother of the spouse. Often he is the village headman in a small village or a lineage head in one of the more complex villages. His role is to serve as mentor and counsellor to his junior kinsmen in matters arising in the marriage. His title conjures up the picture of his sitting inert at the door of his hut while his younger kinsmen bring their difficulties and troubles to him. The more active role in marriage affairs is taken by a younger man known as the "beater down of dew" (*mkupamame*). This man, who is ideally a uterine brother of the spouse, derives his epithet from the image of his beating down the dew from the grass early in the morning as he is on his way to handle difficulties which have arisen in the marriage in which he is responsible.

These marriage sureties come into the picture as soon as the couple decide to marry. They meet formally early in the negotiations and decide on a day on which the man may ceremonially come to eat his first meal with his wife's sureties and so start living "officially" in the village. After this, the marriage sureties play an intimate part in the af-

fairs of the couple. All serious domestic disputes are brought before them; they consult diviners about the illnesses of the children; they must meet formally if the wife moves to live in her husband's village; and they must be present at court cases arising out of the marriage. Finally, when the marriage ends by divorce or the death of one of the spouses, they must meet to terminate the marriage or to participate in the final mourning ceremonies, which achieves the same purpose.

This formalization of marriage is encouraged by Yao beliefs concerning the mystical danger of sexual activity. This is based on the belief that sexually inactive people, particularly the very old or the very young, will contract a dread disease called *ndaka* if they come into contact with sexually active people. When new sexual activity is introduced into the village, the sexually inactive must be protected with medicines against *ndaka*. A couple who do not regularize their relationships by arranging for their sureties to meet are likely to be named by a diviner as being responsible for the deaths of the young children and old people in the village.

These beliefs reinforce more pragmatic pressures to regularize the relationships between a couple. From a man's point of view, the meeting of the marriage sureties establishes the legality of the marriage. This means that after the sureties have met and the man has been formally welcomed into the village, his uxorial rights are secure. His claim for compensation should some other man commit adultery with his wife are then safeguarded, for the first point which the court will raise in such a case is whether the marriage sureties had met. A marriage without sureties, Yao elders told me, was merely friendship, and an action for compensation because of adultery under these circumstances was sure to fail in court.

[2] The absence of marriage payments cannot be attributed to the lack of material wealth. Like the Bemba and many other Central African peoples, the Yao have no cattle. But the amount of cash they have available is shown by the large amount which changes hands in the form of compensation when marriages end. No cash payments, however, are made when marriages are contracted.

From the woman's point of view, there are both mystical and pragmatic difficulties in her position if the arrangement with the sureties is delayed. The mystical dangers she is exposed to arise partly out of the belief that promiscuous sexual intercourse may result in prolonged and difficult parturition and partly out of the knowledge that if her child falls ill she may find it difficult to get her husband's people to cooperate in the divination of the cause of the illness. Effective divination of a child's illness requires the cooperation of both its mother's and its father's people, and if the marriage is not properly established, there will be [the] difficulties over the divination.

From a pragmatic point of view, part of the rights a woman acquires through marriage is the right to support. This means that her husband is obliged to cultivate her fields with her. It also means that the man accepts some responsibility for the support of his children. The only pressure she can bring to bear on a defaulting husband in this respect is through his kinsmen. Her correct approach to them is through her marriage surety, who is able to approach her husband's surety, who in turn is able to prevail upon him to accept his responsibilities. A person can bring sanctions to bear on his spouse most effectively through his or her marriage sureties, and until the marriage has been formally acknowledged by both sets of kinsmen, the spouses are in a weak position if a dispute concerning their rights in marriage should arise.

The mark of a legal marriage thus is its formal recognition by specifically appointed representatives of the woman's matrilineal descent group and of the husband's. The formal sharing of the meal by the new husband and a representative of the wife's group has the effect of publicly announcing the arrival of a new husband in the village. The approach between the two parties is highly formalized, and specific rituals and ceremonies serve to insure that the marriage relationship between the husband and his wife is publicly known and therefore defensible in the tribal courts.

* * * * *

Ending the Marriage

The impotence of the man, in fact, is the only formal ground on which a woman may sue for divorce in the tribal courts. She may lodge many other complaints—that he does not provide food for her, that he does not care for the children, and so on—but these points are usually raised when the woman is trying to justify her adultery. As in other matrilineal peoples, divorce among the Yao is frequent and easy.[3] By far most divorces follow an action by an aggrieved husband against an adulterer. An adulterer is considered to be a thief, and the action usually hinges around the husband's claim for compensation for the loss of rights. . . . The wife is asked whether she wishes to stay married to her present husband. If she says she does, compensation of the order of £2 or £3 will be awarded to him. If, however, she decides to marry her paramour, then the aggrieved husband may receive a higher compensation of the order of about £4 or £5. The court in addition fines the adulterer an amount of about 10s 0d and frequently also fines the woman concerned a like

_____
[3] It is difficult to produce a truly comparative measure of marriage stability among tribal peoples. . . . Some idea is given by the probability that a marriage will end by divorce within a given period. For a Yao sample, these were 38 chances in 100 that the marriage [would] be dissolved by divorce within ten years and 71 chances in 100 that it [would] be dissolved by divorce in twenty years.

amount, which her sureties usually pay.

A woman may also sue for divorce on the grounds of desertion, but her argument hinges mainly on her right to children. This sort of case arises particularly where a man has gone off to a distant labor center and has not returned or been heard of for a long time. Labor migrants are expected to support their wives by paying the taxes in the village and by sending home clothes and money. But a husband's duties are wider than this: he is supposed to provide his wife with children. The court is likely therefore to be sympathetic with a plea for divorce from a woman whose husband has been away for four or five years, even if he has been sending money and clothes to her. The more usual course is for the woman to take a lover. In this event, the husband's marriage sureties will sue her lover for compensation on behalf of their absent kinsman and formally divorce his wife on his behalf. But where a lover is not involved, the court may sanction a divorce so that the woman may remarry and satisfy her natural desire for children.

The compensation claimed is not the equivalent of the return of bride wealth, since none was paid in the first instance. It is rather compensation for the loss of rights which the husband has suffered. If his exclusive rights of sexual access to his wife have been flouted, he is entitled to a certain amount of compensation, but if he loses his entire rights to another man, he is entitled to more. I have never heard of a husband's people having to compensate the woman's people for the loss of rights, for example, when a husband is impotent.

On the contrary, when the woman's people end the marriage by "chasing the man from the marriage," even if the man is impotent he will sue for and obtain compensation of the same order as he would have obtained had he been displaced by another man.

The court awards compensation to the aggrieved husband but does not itself end the marriage. This is done by a meeting of the sureties, in which the man's people give a small amount known as *liwale* (about 2s 6d or 5s 0d) to the woman's people. The man's group make[s] the payment even if the husband has been chased from the marriage. They make it after the compensation has been awarded to them by the court, and it implies that the man's group now renunciates all uxorial rights in the woman and that she is free to remarry.

The ritual of "cutting the ropes" after the death of a spouse[4] serves the same purpose. Some months after the death of a spouse, the relict must have ritual intercourse with a stranger referred to as a "hyena."[5] The deceased spouse's people must arrange this and pay for the "hyena's" services. This act releases the widow from her obligations to her husband's kinsmen and frees her to remarry if she so wishes.

* * * * *

[4] *Kutula ngonji*. The phrase comes from the plaited ropes which widows wore around their waists as part of the mourning rites during the period of continence which followed the deaths of the husbands.

[5] So called because he removes the pollution associated with death. He is paid a fee of about 6s 0d for this service.

how the wife's working affects husband-wife interaction

sixteen

Investigations in several countries have suggested that when the wife works she has more voice in the family. On the other hand, to the extent that the husband takes more part in housekeeping tasks, clearly his decision area is increased (even if he does not wish to be bothered with such matters). The student may consider other possible factors in the relative influence of husband and wife —for example, the absence of the husband for long periods, the presence of in-laws in the household, the types of demands the wife's job makes, and so on.

Dominance and the Working Wife

DAVID M. HEER

Introduction

In recent years the proportion of families in America with working wives and mothers has markedly increased. The increasing frequency of the working-wife family makes more urgent the answer to the question: What effect does such a shift in the wife's role have on other aspects of family life? The present study was designed to help answer some parts of this broad question. Its primary focus has been on the effect of the wife's working on the decision-making process in the family.

Unfortunately, most of the existing

David M. Heer, "Dominance and the Working Wife," *Social Forces*, **35** (May, 1958), 341-347. We are grateful to the author and *Social Forces* of the University of North Carolina Press for permission to quote.

studies on the effects of the working wife on family life have been based on predominantly middle-class cases. The dearth of studies of the effects on family life of the working-class working wife is especially untoward because a far larger proportion of working-class families than of middle-class families are working-wife families. Therefore it was decided that in the present study explicit attention would be given to comparing the effect of the working wife on family decision making in the working class with its effect in the middle class.

The existing literature contains three previous studies which have dealt with the effect of the wife's working on family decision making. Kligler, in a predominantly middle-class sample of respondents from the New York area, showed that the working mother influenced family decisions on major purchases, loans, savings, and investments to a greater extent than did the nonworking mother. This difference was statistically significant at beyond the .05 level.[1]

Fougeyrollas, in a study of respondents in a suburb of Paris, France, demonstrated that the working wife had greater authority in making decisions in a variety of areas. The sample contained respondents from all social classes, but results were not published showing the effect on decision making of the wife's working for different social classes separately.[2]

The third existing study relating the effect of the wife's work status to family decision making came to publication when the present study was in progress. In a reanalysis of their data comparing 500 delinquents with 500 matched nondelinquents, Sheldon and Eleanor Glueck show that for both the delinquent and nondelinquent sample the working mother is more apt to dominate family affairs than the nonworking mother.[3] The Gluecks do not explain how they decided that either the mother or the father dominated family affairs. Apparently for the most part the information was obtained from the coding of unstructured interviews, usually with the mother alone, sometimes with the father, with both parents, or with one of the boy's older siblings or a relative. We are also told that "we had the judgment of the psychiatrist which was made following his interview with the boy."[4]

The Study

The data for the present study were gathered from the answers to 138 oral interviews with respondent couples living in the Greater Boston area. In all cases both husband and wife were interviewed together. Of the total families interviewed, approximately one-quarter were working-class, working-wife families, one-quarter working-class families in which the wife did not work, one-quarter middle-class families in which the wife was working, and one-quarter middle-class families in which the wife did not work. All families had at least one child of elementary school age and a father in the age range from twenty-six to forty-six. In order to compare middle class and working class without simultaneously being compelled to hold constant religious and ethnic differences, it was decided to interview only Roman Catholic families of Irish descent. Thus any speculative generalizations to the broader American scene of the data here presented must take into account the special peculiarities in these families engendered by their adherence to the Catholic faith and by their Irish cultural background.

The names of the respondents were selected in collaboration with the parish pastor and/or parochial school principal in eleven parishes in the Greater Boston area. The great majority of respondents were from the city of Boston. In ten of the eleven parishes, the respondents were selected from a list of families having children in the parochial school. In all, there was only one family out of the 138 in which no child attended a parochial elementary school. In all cases, both partners in the marriage were Roman Catholic.

[1] Deborah H. Kligler, *The Effects of the Employment of Married Women on Husband and Wife Roles* (Unpublished Ph.D. dissertation, Yale University, 1954).

[2] Pierre Fougeyrollas, "Prédominance du mari ou de la femme dans le ménage," *Population*, 6 (January-March, 1951), 83ff.

[3] Sheldon and Eleanor Glueck, "Working Mothers and Delinquency," *Mental Hygiene*, 41 (July, 1957), 327ff.

[4] For a discussion of the Gluecks' methodology in this regard see Sheldon and Eleanor Glueck, *Unraveling Juvenile Delinquency* (New York: Commonwealth Fund, 1950), pp. 41-53, 112.

For purposes of this study, middle-class families were differentiated from working-class families by a classification of the husband's occupation. The classification employed was that contained in the 1950 Census of Population publication, *Alphabetical Index of Occupations and Industries*. Families where the husband's occupation was classified as being that of a professional, manager, proprietor, official, sales or clerical worker were deemed to be middle-class. Families where the husband's occupation was that of a craftsman, foreman, operative, service worker, or laborer were defined as of the working class.

A working-wife family was defined as one where the wife was currently gainfully employed for at least ten hours a week and either had worked for two years or planned to remain in the labor force for a total of at least two years. In no case was a family interviewed unless the husband was also gainfully employed. A nonworking-wife family was defined as one where the wife had not been gainfully employed for at least two years prior to the interview. In almost all cases she had not been employed since the birth of her first child.

Interviewing in low-income parishes was restricted to working-class families. In relatively high-income parishes, interviewing was limited to middle-class families. In the parishes of middle income or of varied income, interviewing included both middle- and working-class respondents. Thus an attempt was made to secure middle-class respondents from middle-class neighborhoods and working-class respondents from working-class neighborhoods.

In each parish, I requested the names of all Irish families where the mother was working and which met my other requirements. In addition, I wanted an approximately equal number of names of families where the wife did not work. In about half the cases, the selection of the nonworking-wife families was made by myself by a random number process or under my direct observation with instruction from me to pick names in a successive sample. In the other half, it was made by the nun or priest, in my absence, after I had given instructions that the names were to be picked at random.

Prior to the interview a letter was sent to each prospective respondent couple. The letter informed them that their name had been given me through the cooperation of their local pastor and that when I came to call I would carry with me a letter from their pastor asking for their cooperation in my project.

The interview refusal rate was approximately one-third. However, it was approximately the same in the working-wife and the nonworking-wife groups. Probably the major reason for the high refusal rate was my stipulation that I wanted to see husband and wife together. In addition, some of the families feared that I was doing another Kinsey report and that the questions would be more intimate than they actually were.

A comparison of the four major subgroups on various demographic variables reveals that the groups are quite comparable on all but one variable: the number of children. The average number of children in the working-class, working-wife group was approximately 2½, in the working-class housewife group about 4, in the middle-class working-wife group around 3, and finally in the middle-class housewife group 4½. It is incidentally interesting that the middle-class families in both working-wife and housewife groups have more children than their working-class counterparts.

The present study tried to answer several questions relative to the effect of the wife's working on family decision making. First, there was an interest in establishing whether or not the increased influence of the working wife in family decision making would exist separately in both the middle and the working class. Secondly, there was an interest in finding out whether or not the working-class working wife would have more to say about family decisions than the middle-class working wife. It

TABLE 1   Who Usually Wins out if There Is Disagreement in Family Decision Making

Group	Both partners agree that husband usually wins out (Per Cent)	One partner says husband usually wins; other partner says decisions are mutual (Per Cent)	Both partners say decisions are mutual; or each says the other wins out (Per Cent)	One partner says wife usually wins; other partner says decisions are mutual (Per Cent)	Both partners agree that wife usually wins out (Per Cent)	Total answering	Mean score for group of husband's relative influence*
Working class, working wife	15	09	37	18	21	33	−.21
Working class, housewife	28	02	63	00	07	40	.43
Middle class, working wife	28	06	47	10	09	32	.34
Middle class, housewife	50	03	34	13	00	32	.91

RESULTS OF ANALYSIS OF VARIANCE

Source		F	
Difference between working wife and housewife groups	10.99	P is less than .01
Difference between working and middle class	8.49	P is less than .01
Interaction	0.03	

* A plus score indicates greater influence of husband.

was hypothesized that since the earnings of the working-class working wife would more nearly approximate those of her husband than those of the middle-class working wife, she would have more say in family decision making than her middle-class counterpart. Finally, there was a desire to try to answer the question: Is the presumed association between the working-wife family and increased feminine influence in family decision making a real cause-and-effect relationship, or is it due to other factors associated both with the wife's working and feminine predominance in decision making.

Let us consider first the attempts at answering our first two questions. What differences are there between working and middle class in the relationship between the work status of the wife and the degree of feminine influence in family decision making?

Husband and wife sitting down together were asked the following question: "Now I would like to know something about decisions in your family. When there's a really important decision on which you two are likely to disagree, who usually wins out?" The opinions of each spouse were then coded. The results are presented in Table 1. A mean score on relative influence in family decision making was constructed in the following way. If both husband and wife agreed that the husband usually won out, the couple received a score of plus 2. If one spouse said the husband usually won out but the other said decisions were equal, a score of plus 1 was given. If both spouses agreed that neither won out more than the other, or if each claimed the other to win out more, a score of zero was given. Similarly, if one spouse thought the wife won out while the other claimed decisions were mutual, a score of −1 was given. If both spouses agreed that the wife won out usually, a score of −2 was assigned.

For lack of a nonparametric substitute, two-way analysis of variance was used to test the two effects of work status of wife and social class upon influence in family decision making. A glance at Table 1 will show that interaction is extremely small and that both the wife's work status and social class are significantly related to family decision making at beyond the .01 level of significance.[5]

The finding that the working-class working wife has more say in family decision making than the middle-class working wife was hypothesized. However, adequate thought had not been given in advance to the decision-making process in the nonworking-wife families. *Post hoc* we may speculate that the difference is due to the following: In any serious period of crisis in family decision making during which the wife might threaten to seek a legal separation, the consequences, both socially and economically, of carrying through that threat would probably be greater for the middle-class than for the working-class wife.

A third question which the present study hoped to help answer was whether the association of feminine predominance in family decision making with the working-wife family is a mere chance coincidence or a cause-and-effect relationship. My hypothesis was that it was such a cause-and-effect relationship. To prove this one way or the other is very difficult, but perhaps this study will at least shed some light on the problem. For instance, it could plausibly be argued that the relationship is a mere association due to the fact that a woman who goes out of the home to take a job is by nature more dominant in her dealings with other individuals than is her husband. Therefore any differences found between working and nonworking wives in their relative degree of power in family decision making could be explained entirely on the basis of personality differences between the two groups.

To test this possibility, it was decided to devise a short test of dominance in general interpersonal relations but excluding the marriage relation. An orig-

---

[5] It may be worth while to speculate whether any difference in results would have occurred had the question on decision making been asked of husband and wife separately rather than jointly. There is a plausible argument that bias would be lessened if the husband and wife were asked separately rather than together. If interviewed jointly, the partner who is actually more dominant might cause the submissive partner to agree that the two have equal influence. In some cases this may have occurred. However, it is equally plausible that asking the question of the spouses jointly reduces an element of bias operative when each is interviewed alone. In our culture equality between the partners is preferred to marked dominance by one. When questioned alone therefore the dominating partner is tempted to deny greater influence, whereas in a joint interview the other partner can contradict him. I noted several instances in which a respondent who at first claimed that he did not have the greater influence admitted this fact after his spouse had pointed out examples. Thus it would appear that although questioning spouses together may in some cases introduce bias, in other cases [they] act to eliminate bias. Further research is necessary to determine which situation produces less bias.

inal set of eight items was correlated, on a sample of fifty women from Boston settlement house mothers' clubs, with the Bernreuter Personality Inven-

TABLE 2

TABLE 2   Questions Measuring the Personality Trait of Dominance in Nonmarital Roles

1. Do you usually try to convince other people to do things your way?
Yes   No   ?

2. Does your shyness ever keep you from doing things you would otherwise like to do?
Yes   No   ?

3. At a social gathering, do you take the responsibility of introducing people to the other persons they do not know?
Yes   No   ?

4. If you are interested in buying some article you saw for sale in the classified columns of the newspaper, do you frequently try to bargain down the price before you buy?
Yes   No   ?

5. Do you suffer from feelings of inferiority?
Yes   No   ?

6. Have you ever been responsible for the organization of any clubs, teams, or other groups?
Yes   No   ?

7. Do you feel ill at ease when you have to strike up a conversation with strangers?
Yes   No   ?

8. When a waitress brings you a dish at a restaurant that is not prepared the way you ordered, do you ask her to take it back rather than accept it the way it is?
Yes   No   ?

tory Test of Dominance.[6] After this pretesting of items, a revised set of eight questions was obtained and again correlated with the Bernreuter test of dominance on an additional group of 101 women also from settlement house mothers' clubs. A coefficient of .79 resulted.

The eight questions are shown in

[6] For a description of this test, see Robert G. Bernreuter, "The Theory and Construction of the Personality Inventory," *Journal of Social Psychology*, 4 (1933), 387ff.

Table 2. They were presented to the respondents on a sheet of paper, and each spouse wrote out his answers on this sheet privately.

For each of the four groups, the mean score for husbands, the mean score for wives, and the mean husband-wife score difference is shown in Table 3. As might be expected, the working

TABLE 3   Results of the Eight-Item Personality Test of Dominance in Nonmarital Roles

Group	Mean Score of wives	Mean Score of husbands	Mean husband-wife difference	Number of cases
Working class, working wife	7.48	8.33	.85	33
Working class, housewife	6.98	8.65	1.67	40
Middle class, working wife	7.91	11.18	3.27	33
Middle class, housewife	7.66	10.09	2.43	32

Results of Analysis of Variance

Source	F
I. Scores of wives	
Working *vs.* nonworking wife	0.56
Working class *vs.* middle class	1.17
Interaction	0.06
II. Scores of husbands	
Working *vs.* nonworking wife	0.48
Working class *vs.* middle class	14.6 (P is less than .01)
Interaction	1.58
III. Mean husband-wife difference scores	
Working *vs.* nonworking wife	0.00
Working class *vs.* middle class	4.05 (P is less than .05)
Interaction	1.11

women in both middle and working class score higher than their nonworking counterparts. It is surprising to note, however, that the husbands of middle-class working wives score higher than the husbands of middle-class nonworking wives. The only statistically significant differences in this table, however, are those occurring for the scores of husbands and for the husband-wife difference scores between the working and the middle class. In the former case, F equals 14.6, beyond the .01 level of significance, and in the latter, F equals 3.92, which is beyond the .05 level of probability. Thus we see that there are no large differences between working-wife and housewife families in their scores to the personality trait of dominance as here measured.

What happens to the relationship between work status and decision making when we try to hold constant the husband-wife difference in general personality dominance? Let us subdivide each of our four groups on the basis of this latter variable. By this procedure we have held constant most, if not all, of the variation between the four groups in the husband-wife difference scores. The results are shown in Table 4. We see there that for both working class and middle class, the differences in family decision making dependent on the work status of the wife still remain. In the case of the working class, the difference between working-wife and nonworking-wife groups is significant at beyond the .01 level. In the case of the middle class, this difference is significant between the .10 and the .05 level.

The major variable in which the working-wife subgroups of the sample differed from the housewife subgroups was the number of children. It was considered necesary therefore to check against the possibility that differences in the number of children might explain the association found between the wife's work status and the relative influence of each spouse in family decision making. Scatter diagrams were drawn to show the relationship in each of the four subgroups between influence in family decision making and number of children. Somewhat unexpectedly, it was discovered that in every subgroup there was a positive association between the number of children in the family and the influence of the husband in decision making. It was therefore decided to compute the degree of association between the number of children and the influence of the husband in decision making for all four subgroups combined. In computing this association, differences in decision making due to social class and wife's work status were held constant. The individual scores on family decision making were each subtracted from the mean score of their subgroup. Kendall's Tau was then computed from the rankings of these deviates and the rankings of each couple on the number of their children. The resultant value for Tau was .114, which has a two-tailed probability of less than .05. Thus holding constant both social class and wife's work status, a statistically significant positive association between the influence of the father in family decision making and the number of children in the family was found.

To determine if the number of children could account for the association between wife's work status and the relative influence of each spouse in decision making, the mean scores of the husband's relative influence in decision making for each of the subgroups were recomputed after the cases in each subgroup had been standardized for the number of children.[7] Both the standardized and the unstandardized results are shown in Table 5. It will be seen that the previous differences both by

---

[7] The component proportions for this standardization were the following five groups of families: (1) with one child, (2) with two children, (3) with three children, (4) with four children, (5) with five children or more.

TABLE 4　**Mean Scores on Husband's Relative Influence in Family Decision Making, by Wife's Work Status, Social Class, and Husband-Wife Difference in a Personality Test of Nonmarital Dominance**

	Range of husband-wife differences in personality test scores is	Mean husband-wife difference on personality test	Mean score of husband's influence in decision making*	Number of cases
Working class, working wife	From 3 to 10	6.27	— .27	11
	From — 1 to 2	0.58	— .83	12
	From — 12 to — 2	— 4.80	.60	10
Working class, housewife	From 3 to 11	6.00	.27	15
	From — 2 to 2	0.32	.47	19
	From — 8 to — 3	— 4.83	.67	6
Middle class, working wife	From 1 to 11	5.59	.27	22
	From — 5 to 0	— 1.50	.50	10
Middle class, housewife	From 3 to 12	6.06	1.06	17
	From — 7 to 2	— 1.67	.73	15

Results of Analysis of Variance

Source	F	
I. Working Class		
Husband-wife personality difference	2.76	
Working vs. nonworking wife	7.23	P is less than .01
Interaction	0.92	
II. Middle Class		
Husband-wife personality difference	0.51	
Working vs. nonworking wife	3.30	P is less than .10
Interaction	0.74	

* A plus score indicates greater influence of husband.

wife's work status and by social class remain. However, the magnitude of the difference dependent on the wife's work status has been reduced considerably, particularly so in the case of the middle-class subgroups.

What are the possible conclusions that can be drawn from these results? First it seems likely that the differential incidence of a generalized trait of personality dominance cannot account for the fact that working wives have more influence in family decision making than housewives (although to rule out this factor entirely might be presumptuous in view of the possibilities for error in the present, rather rough at-

TABLE 5　**Mean Influence of Husband in Decision Making by Wife's Work Status and by Social Class, Standardized for Number of Children in Family, and Unstandardized***

	Standardized for number of children	Un-standardized	Number of cases
Working class, working wife	— .16	— .21	33
Working class, housewife	.33	.43	40
Middle class, working wife	.39	.34	32
Middle class, housewife	.62	.91	32

* A plus score indicates greater influence of husband.

tempt to assess the personality trait of dominance).

Secondly, the association found between the number of children in the family and the husband's influence in decision making raises an interesting possibility: Not only may the work status of the wife affect the degree of her influence in family decision making, but conversely, at least for this sample of Roman Catholics, her relative influence may also indirectly affect her work status. We may first presume that among principled Roman Catholics the teachings of the Church concerning birth control are faithfully followed. This fact would imply that the only means of birth limitation available to these couples is that which can be obtained through the "rhythm method." If the periodic sexual abstinence required by the rhythm method is more irksome to the husband than to the wife, then it should follow that the requisite restraint in sexual relations might be most likely to occur in those families where the wife in general had the greater influence in family decision making. Therefore, families in which the wife had the greater influence would tend to have the fewer number of children. Having fewer children, the wife could more easily enter the labor force. Thus not only would the wife's work status exert an effect on her relative influence in decision making, but the reverse chain of causation would exist as well. Further research is needed to continue the exploration of these possibilities.

Summary

In a sample of Irish Roman Catholic families with at least one child of elementary school age, we have shown that both in the working class and in the middle class the working wife exerts more influence in family decision making than the nonworking wife. We have also shown that whether they are employed or not, wives in working-class families have more say in family decision making than wives in middle-class families. We have also tested the hypothesis that this correlation between the wife's work status and influence in family decision making could be accounted for by an association between the wife's work status and a husband-wife difference in the personality trait of dominance in nonmarital roles. The present results indicate that this hypothesis is false. An unexpected by-product of the study was a statistically significant positive association between the number of children in the family and the influence of the husband in decision making. Holding constant the number of children, the association between the wife's work status and the relative influence of each spouse in decision making was maintained, but in reduced magnitude.

the formation and maintenance of friendships

seventeen

As a bachelor, Charles Lamb once complained that he lost his friends to marriage, that their wives gradually undermined his old friendships. The power of wives to do so would seem to lie in their role as hostesses and social arrangers and their greater amount of time available for social activities. In this study, the authors not only note the influence of the husband on such friendships, but also explore the meaning of friendships among couples in our society.

The Primary Relations of Middle-Class Couples: A Study in Male Dominance

NICHOLAS BABCHUK   ALAN P. BATES

*   *   *   *   *

The status discrepancy between men and women has narrowed considerably in recent years, yet men remain dominant in many spheres. Initiative in dating and proposing marriage, the double sex standard, and a broader field of occupational choice for males are illustrative. This study deals with male dominance as it relates to friendships of middle-class American couples.

Specifically, we asked: what is the relative influence of husband and wife

Nicholas Babchuk and Alan P. Bates, "The Primary Relations of Middle-Class Couples: A Study in Male Dominance," *American Sociological Review*, **28** (June, 1963), 377-384. We are grateful to the authors and The American Sociological Association for permission to quote.

in establishing and maintaining mutual primary friendships? How many close friends do married couples have? What is the relative primariness of their friendships? To what extent do husband and wife agree on who constitutes close mutual friends?

We know that middle-class husbands and wives usually attend social gatherings and visit friends or relatives as a couple. Thus we assumed that husband and wife would see themselves as a unit vis-à-vis friends and that friends would regard them as a unit. We assumed further that if a middle-class person were asked to name primary friends, he would surely include the close friends he shared with his spouse.

We defined the primary group as one "in which members are predisposed to enter into a wide range of activities (within limits imposed by such factors as member interests, sex, age, financial resources, and so on), and their predisposition to do so is associated with a predominance of positive affect."[1] In this formulation, such sociological dimensions as smallness in size, duration in time, frequency of interaction, and homogeneity of membership (traditionally viewed as defining the concept) are seen as predisposing conditions or effects of primary groups. We tested the following hypotheses:

The husband will initiate a greater number of the mutual primary friendships shared by the couple than will his wife. (Very close friends of the male in the period prior to marriage are more likely to become mutual friends of the pair after marriage than very close friends of the female. Also, mutual friends developed subsequent to marriage are more likely to be introduced to the pair by the husband . . . than wife.)

Among primary group friendships shared by the couple, more frequent visiting will characterize friendships initiated by the husband.

The shared friendships initiated by the husband will be characterized by a stronger, positive effect.

The shared friendships initiated by the husband will involve a wider range of activities in which he and his wife participate with their friends than those initiated by the wife.

These hypotheses not only suggest that the husband is more instrumental in initiating and maintaining the couple's mutual friendships, but that the friendships initiated by him will be more primary in character. There was no prior basis for estimating the number of mutual primary friends a couple would share, since this type of information has not been sought by sociologists.

[1] Alan P. Bates and Nicholas Babchuk, "The Primary Group: A Reappraisal," *Sociological Quarterly*, 2 (July, 1961), 185.

Sample and Method

The thirty-nine couples in our sample were white and college trained. Most couples resided in Lincoln, Nebraska; several resided in suburban Omaha communities.[2] Each spouse was separately interviewed. They were given no opportunity to discuss the schedule with each other. A pretested, structured schedule was used. Respondents were asked to initial the names of persons regarded as very close mutual friends by both spouses and to exclude relatives. There was no limit on the number of units they were allowed to list. In the pretest period, we found it necessary to develop two schedule forms, one for local friendships (same city and environs) and the other for nonlocal friendships. Indeed, in the pretest phase we found that respondents included many nonlocal persons, despite the fact they had not in some instances been in face-to-face contact with such persons for a number of years. To get uniform information, the schedule was constructed in such a way that information on couples could be analyzed for each spouse separately or for the pair. This permitted us to make comparisons between unit friendships, whether such units were couples or single persons. We encountered no difficulties in identifying mutual friends of the couple through initials.

[2] The subjects were between twenty and forty years of age. Specifically, 35 per cent of the men were under twenty-five, 42.5 per cent were between the ages of twenty-five and twenty-nine, and 22.5 per cent were older than twenty-nine; 60 per cent of the women were under twenty-five, 22.5 per cent were between the ages of twenty-five and twenty-nine, and 17.5 per cent were above twenty-nine. Sixty-two and a half per cent of the couples had been married less than three years, while 12.5 per cent had been married more than a decade. Twenty-six of the couples had children, and these averaged two children per family.

Respondents communicated the information sought freely and without observable evidence of stress. Discussing their relationships with intimate friends was not seen as an invasion of personal privacy. This may have been due to the spouses' being interviewed apart and their assumption (often unwarranted) that they should agree on matters of this kind.

The Findings

Only three couples were in complete agreement in listing mutual close friends, while one couple completely failed to agree. Two categories indicated intermediate positions. There were thirteen couples in "high agreement." This category included those cases where husband and wife were in substantial though not complete harmony, but where *one* of the spouses included a friend or friends not found on the list of the other. To illustrate, in one case both spouses listed five mutual friendships, but the wife included one nonlocal couple on her list not mentioned by her husband. The "low agreement" category included those couples where *both spouses* cited one or more persons not included on the list of the other; there were twenty-two such couples. We had expected to find more consensus between spouses in their independent identification of mutual friends.

A detailed breakdown of the friendships of the thirty-nine couples revealed 277 friendship units cited by either husband or wife. Of these, both spouses included 118 friendships in common, but husbands reported eighty-seven friendship units not listed by their wives, and wives reported seventy-two not reported by their husbands. . . . On the average, the couple agreed on three friendship units, two local and one nonlocal. Husbands mentioned an average of 2.2 friendship units not cited by the wife, and wives mentioned an average of 1.8 units not included by their husbands. There was a considerable range in the number of friendships reported within the three categories where there was agreement between spouses. For example, in one case where husband and wife were in total agreement, four units were reported. In the low-agreement category, one couple agreed on three units, the husband cited one friendship not cited by his wife, and his wife cited nine not reported by the husband. Although there was considerable variance among couples, the striking fact was the paucity of close mutual friends shared by husbands and wives. The modal number of friendship units both agreed upon was 2; the mean was 3.

Lack of agreement in naming close friends was in part due to problems of recall pertaining to friends living in nonlocal areas. The interview schedule did not require information as to locale of friends. Only after couples had identified their close mutual friends were they required to indicate whether such persons were in the local community or elsewhere. Taking into account the varying lengths of time since nonlocal friends were last seen, differing frequencies of communication by letter, and personal differences in the matter of recall, we suspect that even when there was no real disagreement, one spouse may have been more likely to remember particular nonlocal friends. But even if such qualifications are taken into account, the evidence nevertheless consistently showed that middle-class couples share very few intimate friends.

. . . Lack of agreement between couples was partly accounted for by the nonlocal category of friends. . . . The ratio of local to nonlocal friends where couples agree is 2.7. For units listed by the husband but not the wife, the ratio is 1.3. Although the friendship units on which couples were least in agreement were nonlocal, the sizable number of local units listed by only one spouse underscored the fact that often there was real disagreement between husband and wife.

There was consistent support for the hypothesis that husbands initiate more mutual friendships for the couples than do wives. Typically, husbands and wives not only agreed on who initiated the friendships listed by both, but further agreed that it was the husband who was dominant. Of 118 friendship units common to both mates, both husband and wife agreed that the husband had initiated the friendship in sixty-nine cases and that the wife had done so in only twenty-three cases. In eight cases, neither spouse could be credited with initiating the friendship; finally, there were eighteen instances where the couple disagreed on who had established the friendship. A similar picture emerges when the data are organized differently. Twenty-one couples agreed that the husband's influence was greater in establishing friendships enjoyed by both, eight couples agreed that the wife was dominant, and in the remaining ten cases neither spouse was considered dominant.

Where friendships were listed by either husband or wife but not by both, a pattern emerged which suggested that the husband was more likely to initiate the establishing of close personal relations with others for the couple. Thus in 27.7 per cent of the seventy-two cases listed only by wives, the wives attribute initiation of the friendships to their husbands; of the eighty-seven listed only by husbands, only 15.9 per cent were attributed to the wives. A spouse who reported as friends persons not found on his counterpart's list, however, was most likely to attri-

bute the initiation of such "mutual friendships" to himself.

Our first hypothesis also proposed that very close friends of the male in the period prior to marriage would more likely become close mutual friends of the couple after marriage than would the close friends of the female. In addition, we hypothesized that the male would be more likely to initiate mutual lasting friendships for the couple subsequent to marriage. Both expectations were borne out. With regard to friendship units (both couple and single individuals) *listed by both spouses as very close mutual friends*, we found that seventy-one had been developed by one spouse or the other prior to marriage.[3] Of these seventy-one units, fifty-three were originally friends of the husband (twenty-seven couples, twenty-two single males, and four single females) and the remaining eighteen were originally friends of the wife (six couples, one male, and eleven females). Couples were less likely to establish close mutual friendships subsequent to marriage than they did independently prior to marriage; again, husbands were more instrumental in developing such friendships. Of the twenty-five mutual friendships developed subsequent to marriage, nineteen were attributed to the husband. Our data supported the first hypothesis and suggested explicitly that among friendships established before marriage by either the man or woman, those of the husband were more likely to survive marriage and become friendships of the married pair.

_____

[3] The seventy-one cases include units found (a) on the lists of both husband and wife, (b) where the friendships were established prior to marriage by either spouse, and (c) included only cases where both mates were in agreement that one or the other had been instrumental in introducing the unit to the pair. As a result of these qualifications, there are fewer cases than the number cited earlier in the paper.

The second hypothesis stated that among primary group friendships shared by the couple, more frequent visiting would characterize friendships initiated by the husbands. The data did not support this hypothesis. Frequency of contact between friends was approximately the same regardless of who originated the friendship. In testing this hypothesis, we limited our analysis to local mutual friends reported by both husband and wife.

Apart from its relation to the hypothesis, the evidence on frequency of contact could be seen as bearing directly upon the assumption that the relations studied were really primary. We found that in 12.8 per cent of friendships at the local level (eleven cases) the friends visited each other at least twice a week, an additional 27.9 per cent (twenty-four cases) visited at least once a week, and another 47.7 per cent (forty-one cases) visited at least once a month. In only 11.6 per cent of the cases (10 instances) did the friends get together less than once a month. Within the range of informal contact expected in the urban setting, this pattern seemed to us to represent a high frequency of visiting, a condition associated with primary relationships as both cause and effect.

Affect in the Primary Relation

Three measures were used to test the hypothesis that the shared friendships initiated by the husband would be characterized by stronger positive affect. Again our analysis was limited to units listed by both husband and wife. The first measure related to the sharing of intimate confidences between persons. This involved behavior that had already taken place. The second measure was an attitudinal one in which the respondent indicated whether he felt free to borrow a considerable sum of money from the friend should the need arise. The third measure involved naming a person as one of the three closest friends by *either* the husband or wife. These measures, although rather different from each other, all provided some qualified support for the hypothesis under test.

Shared Confidences

The spouses listed forty couples and twenty-nine persons (husband initiated) whom both included as primary friends. In seventeen of the forty *couple units*, either husband or wife claimed they had shared intimate confidences with both persons (the husband in twelve instances, the wife in five). In twenty-three cases, either husband or wife claimed they had not shared intimate confidences with *both parties* (the husband did not share confidences with both parties in five cases, the wife in eighteen).

Although our respondents included the spouses of very close friends as members of a primary group, these spouses were less likely to be in as primary a relationship to the respondents and were recognized as being somewhat less close. Stated differently, the data indicated that only rarely are both parties viewed as being equally close friends by the party making the judgment. Husbands were most likely to exchange confidences with men (twenty-three out of forty cases) and wives with women (fifteen out of forty cases), but husbands found it easier to exchange confidences with the opposite sex than did their wives. A composite picture of these relationships is presented in rows A and B in Table 1.

Throughout we found that the part played by sex roles had an important bearing on the responses given to various items on the interview schedule. There were nine cases of couple friendship units initiated by the wife. In

TABLE 1 Sharing Confidences with Friends and Borrowing Money from Friends (Restricted to Single and Couple Units Listed by Both Spouses)

	HUSBAND INITIATED		WIFE INITIATED	
	Husband	Wife	Husband	Wife
Sharing confidences with friends				
A. Couple units				
Confided in both	12	5	0	0
Confided in male only	3	2	2	2
Confided in female only	0	15	0	5
Confided in neither	5	18	7	4
B. Single units				
Confided in male friends	21	6	1	0
Confided in female friends	2	1	5	10
Borrowing money from friends				
C. Couple units				
Would borrow from both	19	22	4	5
Borrow from male only	12	5	0	0
Borrow from female only	0	0	0	1
Not borrow from either	9	13	5	3
D. Single units				
Would borrow from male friend	20	12	1	1
Would borrow from female friend	0	0	3	5

TABLE 2 Distribution of "Three Closest Friends" Choices, by Spouse Making the Choice, by Spouse Initiating the Friendship, and by Sex of Friend

	HUSBAND'S CHOICES			WIFE'S CHOICES		
	1st	2nd	3rd	1st	2nd	3rd
Husband initiated						
Couples						
Husband	13	8	2	12	6	6
Wife	1	4	5	1	6	6
Singles						
Male	10	5	5	8	4	6
Female	0	1	0	0	0	1
Wife initiated						
Couples						
Husband	0	1	2	2	1	0
Wife	1	1	2	0	2	2
Singles						
Male	0	0	0	0	0	0
Female	1	4	3	0	3	3

none of these wife-initiated friendships did husband or wife share intimate confidences with *both parties*. Indeed, even the wife had not shared confidences with *either man or woman* in four of nine cases (and the husband in seven instances). Characteristically, exchanging intimate confidences was limited to persons of like sex.

*   *   *   *   *

Closest Friends

Our final measure of affect was obtained by asking respondents to list in rank order their three closest friends from among all persons cited. Again analysis is limited to mutual friends cited by both spouses. Within our universe, 138 different persons were named as first, second, or third choice by either the husband or wife or both.

These 138 selections probably represent the very closest friends these people have. The data are presented in Table 2.

The outstanding feature of the table is the wife's tendency to identify the husband's male friends as among her own three closest friends, whether these men are married or single. Neither spouse, however, was nearly as likely to identify with the wives of couple units or, for that matter, with women.

Husband and wife frequently included the same persons as their choice of first, second, or third best friend (and, as indicated, this person was usually a male). Table 2 does not reflect the great extent to which such choices were mutual. The total enumeration of friends from whom the spouses could have selected their three closest friends included a large list of persons reported by the husband or the wife, but not by both.

The three measures of affect we utilized, namely, sharing confidences, borrowing money, and reporting a person as one of the three closest friends, all pointed to a propensity for greater affective ties to develop between husbands and wives and their mutual male friends. These males were likely to have been friends introduced through the husband. Although husbands most frequently confided in other males and their wives in other females, on balance, wives reported far more frequent exchanges with the husbands or single male friends (who were initially friends of their husbands) than they did with males whom they had been instrumental in introducing as friends of the couple. Furthermore, the exchanges between couples (individually and collectively) showed that husband-initiated friendships were *more primary* as indicated by the three measures above *for both spouses* and to be clearly recognized as such by them.

What we assumed would be the firmest measure of affect between friends (exchanging intimate confidences) proved to be a disappointing measure but an interesting datum. People who by different criteria were in a primary relation to each other often did not exchange intimate confidences despite close contact with each other over a period of years. Controlling for length of time over which the friendships had been in existence did not basically alter this last conclusion. Nor was there any major misunderstanding as to what constituted "intimate confidences" on the parts of the respondents.

The data, then, tended to confirm the hypothesis that "the shared friendship initiated by the husbands will be characterized by a stronger positive affect."

* * * * *

Discussion and Summary

When friends are separated by time and distance, friendship sometimes dies. And yet many of our respondents cited nonlocal individuals among their closest personal friends. Occasionally, our couples talked about nonlocal friends in such vivid language that we thought such persons had only recently moved to other areas and were surprised, later in the interview, to find that there had been no face-to-face contact and little correspondence between some such friends for many years. The responses often provided striking testimony to the essentially subjective character of primary relationships as formulated by Cooley, who pointed out long ago that "Persons and society must . . . be studied primarily in the imagination. . . . I do not see how anyone can hold that we know persons directly except as imaginative ideas in the mind."[4] These

---
[4] Charles H. Cooley, *Human Nature and the Social Order* (New York: Charles Scribner's Sons, 1902), p. 86.

nonlocal friendships, so vivid in the minds of our respondents, continued to be members of *suspended primary groups*. The mobility of present American society must produce many suspended primary groups.

What will happen if persons involved in one of these situationally dormant but subjectively vital relationships once again come into frequent contact with one another? Almost certainly it will be necessary to revalidate the primary character of the friendship. Crucial in this process will be the degree to which the friends continue to share the same values and interests. Should this no longer be the case, the old friends may well discover (after a period of reliving the past) that, quite without intention on their parts, the relationship has lost the primary character which it had retained in suspension over a period of years.

There are other questions which this study suggests as worthy of investigation. For instance, we deliberately focused on relations between couples and single friendship units (either couples or individuals). And while the most frequent pattern of visiting was between three- and foursomes, the interviews indicated that occasionally larger clusters of friends engaged in activities. In some ways, such larger aggregations of friends may resemble the get-togethers of extended kin groups. For some Americans, such friendship groups may have supplanted the kinship group.

Keeping in mind that not all kinship relationships are primary, the question arises as to the relative contribution of kin and personal friends to the total resources of primary experience enjoyed by married couples.

Work needs to be done to ascertain the quantitative and qualitative considerations differentiating primary friendships according to social class, sex, and stage of the life cycle. Our own analysis is limited to middle-class, relatively young couples. Several interesting lines of inquiry would investigate the relationships between the primary friendship resources of a couple and various aspects of their personal need gratification and the effectiveness of their performance in central roles.

Middle-class couples consider themselves to be a unit with respect to friends and are probably treated as a unit by most of their friends. However, husband and wife are not likely to be seen as being equally close by mutual friends, and there often are substantial differences between spouses in their separate evaluations of persons who are close to both. Middle-class couples give the appearance of being equalitarian, but in the sphere of friendships the male predominates. Finally, while our inquiry empirically endorses the major currents found in family sociology and the primary group literature, it also indicates that we still know little about the stream outside of knowing the direction of its flow.

love in the puritan marriage

eighteen

In one of the few good historical studies of the United States family, Edmund S. Morgan analyzes the peculiar quality of Puritan love within marriage. Men chose their brides on rational grounds—or thought they did—yet accepted the Puritan injunction to love their spouses. Much freedom of choice was taken for granted, and indeed Puritan parents complained that they could not control their children; but of course a marriage required attention to the virtues of character as well as to the estate which the potential spouse would bring to the marriage.

Puritan Love and Marriage

EDMUND S. MORGAN

. . . Marriage, . . . or at least proper marriage, resulted not from falling in love, but from a decision to enter a married state, followed by the choice of a suitable person. But since love formed the chief duty of marriage and since the unruly affections of fallen man might sometimes fail at once to knit themselves to the chosen object, a period of trial was necessary in which to bring the affections into the proper direction. That period was furnished by the custom of espousals. "By this meanes," said William Ames, "the minds of the betroathed, are prepared and disposed to those affections, which

in matrimony are requisite";[1] and Thomas Welde wrote in his commonplace book that "Everie Marriage before it be knit, should be contracted as is shewed. Exod. 22. 16 and Deut. 22. 28. which stay between the contract and the marriage, was the time of longing, for the affections to settle in . . ."[2] When John Winthrop had been contracted to Margaret Tyndal, he wrote her tender letters expressing his longing for her and his earnest endeavor to rest his affections wholly upon her. Bold man that he was, he suggested that she help him by refraining from the extravagant fashions and ornamentations of the period and explained that

the great and sincere desire which I have that there might be no discourage-

Edmund S. Morgan, *The Puritan Family* (Boston: The Public Library, 1944), pp. 22, 25-27. We are grateful to the author and the Trustees of the Boston Public Library for permission to quote.

[1] *Conscience, with the Power & Cases Thereof* (London, 1643), Book V, p. 204.
[2] Manuscript in the Library of the Massachusetts Historical Society, p. 87.

ment to daunt the edge of my affections, whyle they are truly labouring to settle and repose themselves in thee, makes me thus watchful and iealous of the least occasion that Sathan might stirre up to our discomfort.[3]

It might be supposed that these self-conscious and rationalistic endeavors would turn out a dry form of love indeed, but the facts belie that supposition. The love which proceeded from Christian charity, conceived in reason and conscious of God's sacred order, was warm and tender and gracious. The letters of John and Margaret Winthrop display an emotion which is all the more convincing because of its sincere restraint and lack of hyperbole. No one could call the love dry or ascetic which produced the following lines from Margaret when her husband was attending court in London:

I will not looke for any longe letters this terme because I pitty your poore handle; if I had it heere I would make more of it than ever I did, and bynde it up very softly for fear of hurting it.

John usually closed his letters with phrases such as these: "I kiss and love thee with the kindest affection, and rest Thy faithful husband"; "so I kisse thee and wish thee Farewell"; "I kisse my sweet wife and remaine allwayes thy faithfull husband"; "many kisses of Love I sende thee: farewell"; "so with the sweetest kisses, and pure imbracinges of my kindest affection I rest Thine." The possibility of achieving truly lovely feelings toward another person by force of will is demonstrated in a letter which John's father wrote to Margaret at the time of her espousal and before he (the father) had ever met her. Though it is not of course an example of conjugal love, it helps to throw light upon the manner in which

a true Christian might direct his affections toward one with whom he had entered into close relation. I quote only the opening sentence, but the whole letter possesses the same sublime quality:

I am, I assure you (Gentle Mistress Margaret), alredy inflamed with a fatherly love and affection towardes you: the which at the first, the only report of your modest behaviour, and mielde nature, did breede in my heart; but nowe throughe the manifest tokens of your true love, and constant minde, which I perceyve to be setteled in you towardes my soonne, the same is exceedingly increased in mee.[4]

Other Puritan writings demonstrate that the Winthrops were not an exceptional case. Ann Bradstreet's poems have the same depth and sincerity of affection as the Winthrop letters. The titles alone indicate the kind of feeling which produced them: "To My Dear and Loving Husband," "For the Restoration of My Dear Husband from a Burning Ague," "Upon My Dear and Loving Husband His Goeing into England," "In My Solitary Houres in My Dear Husband His Absence," "In Thankfull Acknowledgment for the Letters I Received from My Husband out of England," "In Thankfull Remembrance for My Dear Husband's Safe Arrival."[5]

The metaphorical imagery of Puritan theological works, especially those of Thomas Hooker, displays a singular sensitivity to the warmth of conjugal love. The relation of husband and wife furnished the usual metaphor by which the relation of Christ and the believer was designated. In elaborating that

---

[3] Robert C. Winthrop, *The Life and Letters of John Winthrop*, Vol. I, p. 137.

[4] The quotations in this paragraph are all from Robert C. Winthrop, *The Life and Letters of John Winthrop*, Vol. I, pp. 261, 291, 292, 197, 161, 163 and 127.

[5] John H. Ellis, ed., *Works of Anne Bradstreet* (New York, 1932) *passim*.

metaphor, Hooker showed that Puritan love, despite its restraint and care for the order of God, could delight the lovers as much as any love. The proper accompaniment to the Winthrop letters is given in Hooker's delineation of the ordinances of the church as Christ's love letters:

As a wife deales with the letters of her husband that is in a farre Country; she finds many sweet inklings of his love, and shee will read these letters often, and daily: she would talke with her husband a farre off, and see him in the letters, Oh (saith she) thus and thus hee thought when he writ these lines, and then she thinkes he speaks to her againe; she reads these letters only, because she would be with her husband a little, and have a little parley with him in his pen, though not in his presence: so these ordinances are but the Lords love letters, . . .

Hooker's picture of a husband is equally charming:

The man whose heart is endeared to the woman he loves, he dreams of her in the night, hath her in his eye and apprehension when he awakes, museth on her as he sits at table, walks with her when he travels and parlies with her in each place where he comes . . .

That the Husband tenders his Spouse with an indeared affection above al mortal creatures: This appeares by the expressions of his respect, that all he hath is at her command, al he can do is wholly improved for her content and comfort, she lies in his Bosom, and his heart trusts in her, which forceth al to confess that the stream of his affection, like a mighty current, runs with ful Tide and strength; . . .

The fact that these passages appear in a metaphorical description of the relation between man and God does not weaken the obvious authenticity of their language. Hooker was describing feelings that really existed, and in another passage he showed that he thought that these feelings arose in the orthodox manner: "If a woman," he wrote, "have with a conjugall affection taken a man to be her husband, that same taking of him to be her husband, makes her love him, ..."[6]

The Puritans have gained from their modern descendants a reputation for asceticsm that is not easily dispelled. Yet if we are to believe their own statements, they never thought of marriage as a purely spiritual partnership. When John Cotton had joined a couple in matrimony in 1694, he preached a sermon to them in which he recalled the case of

one who immediately upon Marriage, without ever approaching the *Nuptial Bed*, indented with the *Bride*, that by mutual consent they might both live such a life, and according did, sequestring themselves according to the custom of those times, from the rest of mankind, and afterwards from one another too, in their retired Cells, giving themselves up to a Contemplative life; and this is recorded as an Instance of no little or ordinary Vertue; but I must be pardoned in it, if I can account it no other than an effort of blind zeal, for they are the dictates of a blind mind they follow therein, and not of that Holy Spirit, which saith *It is not good that man should be alone.*[7]

Benjamin Wadsworth showed the same attitude: he advised married couples not to let quarrels "make you live separately, nor lodge separately neither: for if it once comes to this, Satan has got a great advantage against you, and tis to be fear'd he'l get a greater."[8] So thoroughly had these ideas permeated Puritan society that Edmund Pinson complained to the Middlesex County Court

---

[6] The quotations from Hooker are taken from the following places: *The Soules Humiliation* (London, 1638), pp. 73-74; *The Application of Redemption* (London, 1659), p. 137; *A Comment upon Christ's Last Prayer* (London, 1659), p. 187; and *The Saints Dignitie and Dutie* (London, 1651), p. 5.

[7] *A Meet Help*, p. 16.

[8] *Well-Ordered Family*, p. 33.

because Richard Dexter had slandered him by saying "that he Brock his deceased wife's hart with Greife, that he wold be absent from her three weeks together when he was at home, and wold never come nere her, and such Like."[9]

As a matter of fact the Puritans were a much earthier lot than their modern critics have imagined. The commonplace book of Seaborn Cotton, another Puritan minister, contains passages from Elizabethan and Cavalier poets which, if addressed by a modern suitor to the lady of his choice, would probably produce either a blush or a slap. Cotton apparently copied the verses while he was a student at Harvard College; yet when he became minister of the church at Hampton, N.H., he saw no incongruity in using the same copy book to take notes of church meetings. The record of one meeting in 1663 follows a receipt "For to make a handsom woman." A similar disregard for Victorian proprieties characterizes a letter sent by John Haynes to Fitz-John Winthrop in 1660. Both men belonged to orthodox and honored New England families, and the writer had graduated from Harvard College four years before. The letter indicates that Haynes had been commissioned to buy a pair of garters for Winthrop in order that the latter might present them to his fiancée. This in itself would shock a generation instructed in the notion that ladies have no legs.

In sum, the Puritans were not ascetics. They knew how to laugh, and they knew how to love. Yet it is equally clear that they did not spend their best hours in either love or laughter. They had fixed their eyes upon a heavenly goal, and whenever earthly delights dimmed their vision, they knew enough to break off. Few persons today would be willing to learn from the Puritans, for a hedonistic world denies the reality of any but earthly delights. Nevertheless, their books, their letters, and their diaries remain, ready to convince anyone who is interested that a people can live by something more than pleasures and still lead a pleasant life.

* * * * *

---

[9] Middlesex County Court Files, Folder 42, Group 3 (October, 1666).

Part 6

parents
and
children

class differences in child-rearing patterns

nineteen

In this article, the author integrates a wide body of contradictory research findings together with his own data, and comes to conclusions opposed to several popular beliefs about the type of family relations in different social strata, as well as the supposed effects of certain family experiences on the later personality of the child. He then goes on to suggest several promising directions of research in this area.

*   *   *   *   *

Social Class and Childhood Personality

WILLIAM H. SEWELL

Introduction

During the past twenty-five years there has been a great deal of interest in the relationship between social class and personality—particularly in the bearing of social class on the personality of the child and the relationship between social class and adult mental illness. Because of space and time limitations, this paper will concentrate on

William H. Sewell, "Social Class and Childhood Personality," *Sociometry*, 24 (December, 1961), 340-346, 348-351. We are grateful to the author and The American Sociological Association for permission to quote.

social class influences on childhood personality and will not be concerned with the literature on youth and adults. The product of this interest in social class influences on childhood personality has been numerous books, monographs, research articles, and essays—often with contradictory emphases and conclusions depending on the convictions, theoretical orientations, and research styles of the authors.

The theoretical basis for expecting a substantial relationship between social class and personality rests on three major assumptions upon which there seems to be widespread agreement among social scientists. The first is that in all societies some system of social stratification exists whereby the members of the society are differentiated into subgroups or classes which bear to one another a relationship of social inequality. It is further generally acknowledged that persons in the society can be more or less located in the stratification system in terms of the characteristic social roles they play. Consequently, it is possible to infer, crudely at least, the social class position of most individuals in terms of readily ascertainable criteria. The particular criteria will be dependent on the culture of the society in question. There are rather wide differences among writers as to the origins of stratification, the functions of stratification, the criteria of social classes, the meaning of the term class, the number of classes, the rigidity of any particular stratification system, and almost any other aspect of theory, substance, or measurement which could possibly be raised, but almost everyone seems agreed that some system of stratification based on social inequality is an inevitable product of organized group life. The empirical basis of this proposition is strong in that no society has yet been studied in which a stratification system, fulfilling at least the minimum requirements stated above, has not been found.

The second assumption is that the position of the child's family in the stratification system determines in considerable measure not only the social learning influences to which he will be subjected during the early period of his life, and in later life for that matter, but greatly affects also the access that he will have to certain opportunities that are socially defined as desirable. Certainly there seems to be ample evidence that this is true even in societies in which the stratification structure is not particularly rigid or the differences between the social classes extreme. While many social scientists would deny that

American society has fixed classes each with its own distinctive subculture, none would claim that the learning environment of the child whose family is highly placed in the stratification structure does not differ materially from that of the child whose social class position is low. Also it is readily apparent that the styles of life, the material comforts, the value systems and the instruction, both intentional and unintentional, which the child receives about the roles available to him in society differ depending on the social class position of his family. And finally even his treatment in the neighborhood, community, and larger society will depend, for some time at least, on his social status origins.

The third assumption on which there is general agreement is that the early experiences of the individual will be of considerable importance in determining his later social behavior. To be sure, there is rather massive disagreement about the particular psychodynamics of the relationship between early experience and later behavior, the specific or patterned experiences which produce other patterns or traits of later personality, or even the critical periods in terms of days, months, and years in which the individual is most susceptible to influence. However, these details and differences of theory and commitment have not led to any widespread rejection of the basic notion of the primary importance of early experiences in shaping later personality. The experimental evidence on animal behavior and the somewhat more inferential knowledge about human learning furnish the empirical foundation for this assumption.

On the basis of these assumptions, the reasonable expectation would be that some distinct personality traits, configurations, or types might be found which would differentiate the children of the several social classes, or at least that the incidence of certain personality characteristics would be different for the children of the various social classes. The results of research efforts to elucidate these relationships have been disappointing for a number of methodological and theoretical reasons. It would be impossible and is unnecessary to review each of the numerous writings which have direct bearing on the problem, but it does seem worthwhile to examine some of the most important of them to see if it is possible to reach any valid conclusions on the extent and nature of the relationship between social class and childhood personality, to point out some of the weaknesses of the research in the field, and to make some suggestions for future research. This is the purpose of the present paper.

An Examination of Selected Studies

A convenient point of departure might be to look at examples of studies which illustrate various approaches to the problem. As a minimum these would seem to include (a) work based primarily on typological and informal observational procedures, (b) those in which detailed observations on class-related child-training procedures have been made and personality characteristics inferred, observed, or systematically assessed, and, finally (c) studies in which some measure of social class position has been related directly to some independent assessments of personality.

Perhaps the best-known example of the first type of study mentioned is Arnold Green's. . . .[1] Green, stimulated by the neo-Freudian writers Horney and Fromm, and on the basis of his recollections of his childhood and young adulthood in a Massachusetts industrial community of about 3000

[1] Arnold W. Green, "The Middle-Class Male Child and Neurosis," *American Sociological Review*, **11** (1946), 31-41.

persons, delineated a set of social psychological conditions that he had observed in middle-class families which he believed predisposed middle-class male children to neurosis. He observed that the middle-class parent is caught up in a lifelong struggle for improvement of personal position in the class structure. The father's work takes him away from the home and involves the manipulation of others around him to further his personal career. He is ambivalent toward his son because the child takes time, money, and energy that could be used for the father's social advancement and also interferes with his role as a partner and companion to his wife. The mother, too, is ambivalent toward her child. He interferes with her career aspirations and her individual pleasures. Also, he causes worries and demands great care and attention. Despite the socially structured ambivalence of both parents toward their son, they train him to love them for the care and sacrifices they have made for him and force him to feel lost without their love. Thus the middle-class boy suffers "personality absorption" to such an extent that he cannot turn to others for genuine emotional satisfaction. Moreover, he is faced with the constant threat of withdrawal of parental love. Little wonder, then, that he feels small, insignificant, unworthy, inferior, helpless, and anxious! He can never escape his parents' norms at home, in school, or in his play groups—always he must try to live up to their high expectations of him or he will lose their love. Thus he lives "alone and afraid in a world he never made." The lower-class . . . child suffers no such fate. Although parental authority is often harsh and brutal, it is also casual and external to the "core of the self." The children avoid their parents, in fact have contempt for them and band together in common defense against their cruelty. Consequently the parents do not have the opportunity or the techniques to absorb the personalities of their children. Thus the lower-class boys do not suffer from the guilt, anxiety, and extreme sense of insecurity from which the middle-class boy suffers as a result of his extreme dependency on his parents.

* * * * *

The second type of study is perhaps most conveniently illustrated by the research done by members of the Committee on Human Development at the University of Chicago[2] . . . These studies were the first to report systematic empirical findings indicating that child-rearing practices of middle-class parents differ significantly from those of lower-class families. The findings of the Davis-Havighurst study were based on interviews with ninety-eight middle-class (forty-eight white and fifty Negro) and 102 lower-class (fifty-two white and fifty Negro) mothers and dealt with a wide variety of child-training questions and the mothers' expectations concerning their children. Perhaps the most important finding of the study was the restrictiveness of the middle-class mothers in the critical early training of the child. They were shown to be less likely to breast feed, more likely to follow a strict nursing schedule, to restrict the child's sucking period, to wean earlier and more sharply, to begin bowel and bladder training earlier, and to complete toilet training sooner than were lower-class mothers. In addition, they generally followed stricter regimes in other areas of behavior and expected their children to take responsibility for themselves earlier. From these results, the inference was drawn that middle-

class children encounter more frustration of their impulses and that this is likely to have serious consequences for their personalities. . . .

The findings of the Chicago group and the inferences made from their findings as to the personality consequences of class-related child-training practices were widely accepted and held sway without competition for some time. However, they were finally challenged by the results of two carefully designed empirical studies with quite different research objectives. The first of these was the attempt by the present writer to determine the consequences of a variety of infant-training practices on independently assessed childhood personality characteristics, and the second was the careful study of patterns of child rearing made by a group of behavioral scientists at Harvard under the leadership of Robert R. Sears.

The study of infant training and personality, published in 1952, was based on interviews conducted in 1947 with the mothers of 165 rural Wisconsin children concerning the practices they followed in rearing their children and subsequently relating the data thus obtained to the personality characteristics of the same children as these were determined from scores on both paper-and-pencil and projective tests of personality and ratings of the children's behavior by their mothers and teachers. The specific infant-training practices studied were those most stressed in the psychoanalytic literature, including feeding, weaning, nursing schedule, bowel training, bladder training, and punishment for toilet accidents. These experiences were not found to be significantly related to childhood personality characteristics as assessed in the study. Moreover, two carefully constructed factor-weighted indexes measuring permissiveness in toilet training

[2] Allison Davis and R. J. Havighurst, "Social Class and Color Differences in Child-Rearing," *Ibid.*, 11 (1946), 678-710; Martha C. Ericson, "Child Rearing and Social Status," *American Journal of Sociology*, **52** (1946), 190-192.

and feeding produced even less positive results.[3] In all, only eighteen out of 460 relationships tested in the study were significant at the .05 level, and of these seven were opposite from the predicted direction. These results, along with evidence from studies not so directly focused on the problem, tended to undermine the confidence of many who had made the inferential leap from class-determined early training practices to class-linked childhood personality characteristics and types.

Equally upsetting evidence came in 1954 with the publication of a preliminary report from the Harvard study . . .[4] and later when the more complete report of the study was published. . . .[5] Their results, based upon careful interviews with 379 New England middle-class and lower-class mothers . . . clearly indicated no differences in infant-feeding practices between the two social classes; more severity in toilet training in the lower-class families; less permissiveness in sex training in the lower-class families; more restriction of aggression toward parents and peers (and more punitiveness where such aggression took place) in lower-class families; greater imposition of restrictions and demands on the child in the lower-class family; more physical punishment, deprivation of privileges, and ridicule by lower-class parents; but no differences between the two groups on isolation and withdrawal of love. Needless to say, these results were in important respects directly contradictory to the findings of the Chicago group and provided little factual basis for continued acceptance of the stereotyped version of the middle-class mother as a rigid, restrictive, demanding, and punitive figure whose behavior can but result in frustrated, anxious, conforming, and overly dependent children.[6] Neither was there any evidence whatever to support Green's contention about personality absorption of the child in the middle-class family or its supposed consequent—the neurotic middle-class child.

* * * * *

A third type of research bearing directly on the relationship between social class and personality involves the correlation between measures of socio-economic status (henceforth referred to as SES) and children's scores on personality tests and is perhaps well illustrated by a study by the present writer and A. O. Haller. . . .[7] A comprehensive review of the studies in which SES had been measured objectively and correlated with independent assessments of the personality of the child indicated that middle-class children consistently made a better showing than lower-class children. For the most part the correlations were low or the differences were small, and often there was no indication that the association was statistically significant, that sampling was adequate, that the tests of status and personality were dependable, or that variables known to be related to status or personality or both were controlled.

Consequently, it was decided to make a rigorous test of the hypothesized relation between SES and personality using a design in which both variables were measured objectively and independ-

---

[3] For the indexes, see W. H. Sewall, *et al.*, "Relationships Among Child-Training Practices," *American Sociological Review*, **20** (1955), 144.

[4] E. E. Maccoby, *et al.*, "Methods of Child Rearing in Two Social Classes," in W. E. Martin and C. B. Stendler (eds.), *Readings in Child Development* (New York: Harcourt, Brace & World, Inc., 1954), pp. 380-396.

[5] R. R. Sears, *et al.*, *Patterns of Child Rearing* (New York: Harper & Row, Publishers, Inc., 1957).

[6] *Ibid.*, Chap. 12.

[7] "Social Status and the Personality Adjustment of the Child," *Sociometry*, **19** (1956), 114-125.

ently for a large sample (1462) of grade school children in a culturally homogeneous community with a fairly wide range of SES. Correlation analysis techniques were used to determine the relationship between SES, as measured by father's occupation and a rating of the prestige of the family in the community, and personality adjustment, as indicated by a factor-weighted score on the California Test of Personality. The zero-order correlation coefficients between the two status measures and the personality scores were determined. Then the multiple correlation coefficient of the two status measures and personality score was computed, and, finally, the relationship was determined with sibling position, intelligence, and age controlled. The results indicated a low, but significant, association between status and measured personality (.16 for father's occupation and child's personality score, .23 for prestige position and child's personality score, .25 for the multiple correlation of the two status measures and child's personality score). The combined effect of the two status measures was not significantly reduced when the controls were introduced. The direction of the correlations indicated that the lower the SES of the child's family, the less favorable his personality test score.

Certainly these results indicate that only a relatively small amount of the variance in measured personality found in this group of children can be accounted for by their SES. However, the test of the hypothesis was stringent, and the correlations might well be higher in communities with more distinct stratification systems, and if more refined measures of status and personality were used. In any event, the correlations, particularly since they are not markedly different from those reported by others who have followed similar methods, should not be dismissed. They at least help to explain some of the variance in measured personality—an area in which little measured variance has been explained by other measured variables. However, the results do not provide much encouragement for the view that social class is a major determinant of childhood personality, and they offer still another instance of evidence against the claim that middle-class children suffer greater personality maladjustment than lower-class children.

In an attempt to explore further the relationship between SES and personality, the writers next did a factor analysis of the 30 personality test items which had been found to be most highly correlated with SES.[8] The results of this analysis indicated that four factors explained approximately 90 per cent of the common variance among the items. These factors were tentatively identified as (a) *concern over status*, (b) *concern over achievement*, (c) *rejection of family*, and (d) *nervous symptoms*. Each factor was negatively correlated with SES, their respective correlations being −.31, −.18, −.12, and −.26, indicating that the lower the status of the child the greater the tendency to score high (unfavorably) on each of the factors. The intercorrelation between the factors ranges from +.25 to +.59. Thus there seems to be a tendency for children who are concerned about their social status to worry about their achievements, to reject their families, and to display nervous symptoms. The evidence from this study points to the fact that these characteristics are more common among lower- than higher-status children. Again the correlations between SES and the personality characteristics indicated by the factors, al-

[8] W. H. Sewall and A. O. Haller, "Factors in the Relationship Between Social Status and the Personality Adjustment of the Child," *American Sociological Review*, **24** (1959), 511-520.

though statistically significant, are low and offer only limited support for the notion that the position of the child in the stratification system has bearing on his personality pattern. They are, however, suggestive of a line of attack on the problem which may be somewhat more rewarding than some of the approaches employed thus far.

Conclusions Regarding Social Class and Childhood Personality

On the basis of this brief review of studies of the bearing of social class on the personality of the child, the following conclusions seem justified:

First, there is a growing body of evidence from empirical studies of several types indicating a relatively low correlation between the position of the child in the stratification system (social class) and some aspects of personality, including measured personality adjustment. The relationship has not been shown to be nearly as close as might have been expected, but there is mounting evidence that at least some of the variance in childhood personality can be explained by the social status position of the child. Possibly when better measures are used, the relationship will prove to be higher. The present crude techniques of measuring both variables doubtless result in underestimation of the correlation.

Second, the direction of the relationships found offers absolutely no support for the notion that middle-class children more commonly exhibit neurotic personality traits than do children of lower-class origins. Indeed all of the empirical evidence points to the opposite conclusion.

Third, the studies of child rearing in relation to social class, made since the publication of the Chicago studies, have found fewer class-related differences in infant training than might have been expected, and those differences that have been found tend to indicate greater permissiveness in feeding and toilet training on the part of middle-class mothers rather than lower-class mothers. The findings in relation to early childhood training indicate less impulse control, less punitiveness, less reliance on strict regime, less restrictiveness in sex behavior, and less restriction on aggression—in other words, generally greater permissiveness on the part of middle-class mothers.

Fourth, empirical studies of the consequences of child training have given a great deal of attention to such aspects of infant discipline as manner of nursing, weaning, scheduling, bowel and bladder training, but have found very little or no relationship between these experiences and childhood personality traits and adjustment patterns. Much less attention has been given to the consequences of other aspects of child training, but some low correlations have been found between such factors as patterns of punishment, permissiveness for aggression, and mother's affectional warmth for the child and such aspects of personality as feeding problems, dependency, and aggression. Although these correlations explain only a small portion of the variance in childhood personality, they cannot be entirely dismissed and, to the extent that the child-training practices are class-linked, they must be credited with having some bearing on the relationship between social class and personality. Certainly, however, the empirical evidence does not permit any lavish claims regarding the influence of the child-training variables studied on the personality of the child.

Fifth, a final inescapable conclusion from reading these and other writings on social class and childhood personality is that, with a few notable exceptions, the level of research and theoretical sophistication in this area has been appallingly low. Some of the most influential work has had little or no acceptable empirical basis. The evidence upon which widely accepted claims have been founded is sometimes from samples that are so small or so clearly biased that no reliable conclusions could possibly be reached. In fact there is not a single study that can claim to be representative of the whole society or any region of the country, and only a small handful are clearly representative of any definable social system. The statistical techniques in some of the studies are clearly inappropriate for the data. The theoretical guidelines for most of the studies are seldom specified and often are not even discernible. The chain of inference from theory to data, to conclusions, to wider generalizations is sometimes unclear, and instances can be cited in which links in the chain are entirely missing. Great lack of concep-

tual clarity, particularly concerning the two principal variables, social class and personality, is generally apparent. Thus statistical categories of socioeconomic status measured by crude techniques are treated as social classes in the broader meaning of that term, and inferences are drawn about subcultures, learning environments, value systems, and other social class characteristics without the necessary empirical evidence of their existence. Likewise the term "personality" is used in a variety of ways but with little attention to definition and specification. Often inferences are made about deeper levels of personality from more or less surface variables. Because of these weaknesses in theory and method, more definitive conclusions about the relationship between social class and childhood personality must await better designed studies.

* * * * *

the effect of maternal employment on adolescent children in town and country

twenty

Mothers have always worked—and in some countries have worked in factories for over a century—but strong arguments against maternal employment have become most pronounced in this century (possibly because women have become less dependent on men for their employment or promotion and because more middle-class women work). Fewer people were concerned in generations past, when it was mainly lower-class factory women who had to neglect their children. Moreover, growing psychological knowledge about the mother-child relationship suggests that maternal employment harms the child's development.

More rigorous research in the 1950's has cast doubt on any simple relations between maternal employment and child development. In the following article, the writer's research describes some of the complexities in this relationship.

Maternal Employment and Adolescent Roles: Rural-Urban Differentials

PRODIPTO ROY

* * * * *

The general hypothesis being tested in this study is that the addition of [the] new role [of worker] to the wife-mother position affects the roles of the children. Owing to the different rural-urban subcultural patterns that have existed, it may further logically be deduced that the employment of the mother will affect rural and urban families in different ways. *The fourfold analysis attempted in this paper is designed to manifest the effects of employment of the mother, and of residence, on certain roles played by the teenage son and daughter.*

Several rational and "common sense" fears are engendered in the minds of people whenever any institutionalized social positions are altered. Some of these fears relative to maternal employment, spelled out by Bossard and tested by Nye, are:[1]

The child feels lonely. The child feels neglected. . . .

Children exploit lack of maternal control. . . . [The child] rationalizes his own antisocial behavior.

Prodipto Roy, "Maternal Employment and Adolescent Roles: Rural-Urban Differentials," *Marriage and Family Living*, **23** (November, 1961), 340-349. We are grateful to the author, *Journal of Marriage and the Family*, and the National Council on Family Relations for permission to quote.

[1] F. Ivan Nye, "Employment Status of Mothers and Adjustment of Adolescent Children," *Marriage and Family Living*, **21** (August, 1959), 240-244. See James H. S. Bossard, *The Sociology of Child Development* (New York: Harper & Row, Publishers, Inc., 1954), pp. 282-286.

The mother is unable to render detailed services to the child.

Supervision and training of the child are neglected.

Nye found little evidence to support Bossard's conception of the neglected, maladjusted child. There are several other logical effects on the social positions of the son and daughter that may be related to the employment of the mother. First, . . . the employment of the mother would increase the amount of work that the son and daughter would do at home and consequently cut down on work they may do outside. Another consequence of the increased work at home would be a tendency to cut down on participation in school activities, out-of-school social activities, dating, and the amount of spare time. Employment of the mother, resulting in lack of supervision and training in regular study habits, would tend to lower the academic performance of children and possibly affect academic aspirations.

The general consequences of the disruptive forces in the traditional social position of the mother who has abandoned her hearth should manifest themselves in more delinquent behavior, less affection as perceived by the children, and probably less fairness of discipline. On the other hand, the employment of the mother may contribute to more democracy and cooperation in the family because of the greater sharing of work and decisions. Conservative pessimists may feel that there will be less democracy and cooperation in families with employed mothers. The hypotheses being tested in this study, stated in null form, are:

1. That the employment of the mother does not affect the amount of household work done by the adolescent daughter and son.

2. That the employment of the mother does not reduce the social activities of the daughter or son.

3. That the employment of the mother does not lower the academic performance or aspirations of the daughter or son.

4. That the employment of the mother does not affect the amount of delinquency, the affection, the fairness of discipline, the democracy, or cooperation in a family.

The statement of the above hypotheses in null form proved to be a dilemma for the investigator. . . .

Method

This study was conducted in two counties in the northeastern section of Washington. The data were gathered on a questionnaire which was filled out by high school pupils in Stevens County on March 10-12, 1958; the questionnaire was administered to all students in grades nine to twelve who were present in school. In Ferry County, the questionnaires were administered to all students from the seventh to the twelfth grades during May, 1959. A total of 1086 questionnaires, 257 of them usable, were obtained from Stevens and Ferry Counties, respectively.

The residential classification was based on two questions asked of the respondents—(a) Do you live on a farm? and (b) Do you live out of town but not on a farm? If the answer was "no" to both questions, the respondent was classified as "town." These two counties are rural counties with only one population center of about 4000 which would be classified under the census as

"urban." The respondents' definition of "town" consisted of incorporated or unincorporated places with a population of about 200 or more people. The rural-town analysis used here is not the same as the rural-urban dichotomy used by the Census of Population. It was not felt that the cutting of the rural-urban continuum farther along the rural end of the scale was a violation of the principle of rural-urban analysis. In addition, the self-conception of an adolescent as a "town" resident adds social-psychological weight to the present classification.

One condition that Mirra Komarovsky enumerates as conducive to family welfare in families with employed mothers is "the mother works short hours. . . ."[2] Three categories of employment were obtained from the data —"fully employed," "partly employed," and "not employed." Since Komarovsky raises the question that short hours may not really affect family structure, it was decided to exclude the "partly employed" group from analysis because of the logically inconclusive effect in the criterion variable. No validation was made of the children's statement regarding the employment status of their mothers, and no further questions were asked as to the number of hours worked, so that some objective cutting point may be made. It was assumed that boys or girls thirteen years or older knew the meaning of being employed "full time."

* * * * *

Results

Hypothesis 1: Household Chores

In order to find out whether or not a higher proportion of boys and girls of

[2] Mirra Komarovsky, Women in the Modern World (Boston: Little, Brown & Company, 1953), Chap. 5.

fully employed mothers were performing the household tasks, a list of household chores was provided, and each boy or girl was asked to check "What chores do you do at home? Regularly—occasionally." Twenty-one household chores were listed and a place left for others. A chore score was computed by summing a 2-1-0 rating for each chore performed regularly, occasionally, or not checked. . . . There was a consistent trend manifesting that both boys and girls of employed mothers did a little more housework. The differences observed were statistically significant in two out of the four samples. In total, the girls seemed to do more housework than boys. There was not much difference between the rural and town samples, the slight differences seeming to suggest that town boys did a little more housework than rural boys.

* * * * *

 . . . It seems that the sons of employed mothers were performing household tasks normally assigned to the expected homemaker position of mother. However, the differences were not large, and hence it should not be inferred that any radical role changes are taking place.

Corollary—Work for pay. One consequence of doing more household work would be that the girls or boys would be prevented from doing work outside for pay and earning a little money of their own. Four questions were asked to test this corollary. . . .

The pattern of responses for the boys showed results in the expected direction: that is, that boys of employed mothers do less outside work for pay than boys of nonemployed mothers. A lower proportion of employed mothers' sons worked for pay last year, a lower proportion worked for pay last summer, a lower proportion have jobs now, and the mean number of hours worked was

lower. Both the rural and town samples showed consistent predictions. The differences were greater in the rural sample with respect to the proportion of boys that have a job now and the average hours worked.

The pattern of responses for the girls was consistently *opposite* to the predicted direction. A higher proportion of the employed mothers' daughters worked for pay last year or worked for pay during the last summer. A higher proportion of the employed mothers' daughters have a job now, and on the average they work more hours per week. Both the rural and town samples were consistent in their predictions. It seems that the mother's example of working may have some direct influence on the daughter's following her example. A further hypothesis that arises out of this finding is that perhaps the breaking of the traditional feminine role by the mother makes it easier for daughters to break the traditional feminine role.

The null hypothesis may therefore be rejected, and it may be concluded that in general a higher proportion of the children of employed mothers perform household tasks than the children of nonemployed mothers. The pattern of behavior for the town boys and girls and the rural boys showed that the children of employed mothers performed household chores more often than the children of nonemployed mothers. The rural girl sample was an exception to this finding: the differences observed between the employed and nonemployed rural families were not statistically significant, and the patterns did not consistently support the above conclusion. A *corollary* derived from the above hypothesis was that as a conseqence of doing more work at home the children would be able to do less work for pay outside the home. The sons of employed mothers consistently showed that they did less work outside the home for pay. The daughters of employed mothers, however, consistently showed the reverse; that is, a higher proportion of them worked, and for longer hours, than the daughters of nonemployed mothers.

Hypothesis 2: Social Activities

The second hypothesis being tested is one that logically follows the first. If mothers are employed and the children have to do more of the household chores, it follows that they should have less time of their own for social activities. This lack of time may be manifest in such behavior as less dating, less participation in school activities or out-of-school activities, and fewer hours of spare time.

The question was asked "How often do you date?" with answer categories "frequently," "occasionally," "seldom," and "never." . . . The results show no consistent pattern of responses—the boys' predictions would support the hypothesis for the rural sample and reject it for the town sample, and the girls' predictions would reject it for the rural sample and support it for the town sample. It seems that other factors more important than the employment of the mother govern dating behavior.

Social participation was divided into school activities and out-of-school activities. Each type of social participation was measured by the number of organizations to which the person belonged and the social participation index. The social participation index was a sum of a 3-2-1-0 rating on a list of activities or organizations which were checked as "very active," "fairly active," "not very active," and not checked, respectively.

With respect to school activities, the sons of employed mothers seem to participate more than the sons of nonemployed mothers, and the daughters of employed mothers seem to participate

less than the daughters of nonemployed mothers. The differences were not very great, particularly for the town sample. In the out-of-school activities, the rural samples of both boys and girls indicated that children of employed mothers participated *more* than the children of nonemployed mothers, but the town sample of both boys and girls indicated that children of employed mothers participated *less* than the children of nonemployed mothers.

The respondents were asked to report the number of hours they had free to spend as they wished last week. The medians were computed and recorded. Three out of the four test groups showed results opposite to the predicted direction; that is, children of employed mothers did not have less spare time than children of nonemployed mothers.

The null hypothesis cannot be rejected from these data. Children of employed mothers seemed to have as much social life and spare time as children of nonemployed mothers. The data suggest that rural employed mothers' children may participate more and town employed mothers' children participate less in out-of-school activities. Further research will be needed to substantiate this rural-town differential.

Hypothesis 3: Academic Performance

The theoretical framework of analysis suggests that through lack of supervision of study hours or actual help with homework, resulting from the employment of the mother, the children of employed mothers should not perform as well in school as the children of nonemployed mothers. Low academic performance may also be a function of more household chores.

One manifestation of performance is the grade point obtained. The question was asked in this way: "On your last report card, did you get mostly: —A's,

—B's, —C's, —D's, [or] F's." More than one place could be checked. The categories and subcategories were arrayed in order from the highest to the lowest and a median grade point computed. Three out of four of the predictions were in the expected direction, but in only one were the differences observed statistically significant. The sons of employed mothers showed lower grade-point medians than the sons of nonemployed mothers; differences observed for the town sample were statistically significant ($X^2 = 11.967; P =$ less than .01). The daughters of rural employed mothers showed a slightly higher median grade point than the daughters of nonemployed mothers, but the town sample showed the opposite result. Neither of the differences was statistically significant.

It was further hypothesized that poor school performance may logically result in a low aspiration to continue studies into the college level. The results show that a higher percentage of the children of rural employed mothers plan to go to college than the children of nonemployed mothers. A lower proportion of the children of employed town mothers planned to go to college than the children of nonemployed town mothers.

. . . The town sample seemed to consistently support the hypothesis— that is, the children of employed mothers will have a lower academic performance and aspiration. The rural sample, on the other hand, seemed to refute the hypothesis—a higher proportion of the children of employed mothers planned to go to college, and the girls had a slightly higher grade-point average.

The null hypothesis in general cannot be rejected from the analyses of these data. The results seem to suggest that the employment of town mothers may lower the performance and aspira-

tion of their children, but that the employment of rural mothers may raise their academic performance and aspirations. More research will be needed to substantiate these findings.

Hypothesis 4: Disintegration of Family Values

The general hypothesis being tested is that a change in the normative role of the mother in the form of full employment will result in various disfunctional manifestations. The first and most visible manifestation would be an increase in delinquency. The Bossard statements about the child's feeling lonely or neglected should manifest themselves in less affection. Due to the time and energy expended in the new role of outside employment, the mother's understanding and disciplining of her children should suffer. Following the general disfunctional hypothesis, there should also be less democracy and cooperation in the families with employed mothers. (Logically, a case has been made in the framework of analysis for more democracy and cooperation.)

The measurement of delinquency in this study was not similar to the popular connotation of apprehended legal violations. Delinquency was measured by a checklist of delinquent-type behavior. . . .

* * * * *

The median scale scores are presented in Table 1. The medians of the delinquency scale scores showed that the rural samples for both boys and girls refuted the hypothesis, whereas the urban samples for both boys and girls supported the hypothesis. Because of the contradictory results, the null hypothesis cannot be rejected; employment of the mother does not affect the amount of delinquency for boys or for girls.

The second scale constructed was designed to measure the dimension of "affection" in the family.[3] The scale scores indicated that the rural boys with employed and nonemployed mothers rated their families equal on affection; the sons of urban employed mothers considered their families a little more affectionate than the nonemployed mothers' families. The rural sample for the girls favored the families of employed mothers, and the urban sample for girls favored the families with nonemployed mothers. The results showed differences that were not consistent in any direction. Therefore the null hypothesis cannot be rejected; the employment of the mother does not affect the amount of affection in a family as perceived by the sons or daughters.

The third scale was an attempt to measure a dimension called "fairness of discipline."[4] In three out of the four samples, the median scale scores provide results that are contrary to the hypothesis, and only in the town sample

[3] This scale and the subsequent three scales were constructed by Slocum and Stone. See W. L. Slocum and Carol L. Stone, "A Method for Measuring Family Images Held by Teen-Agers," *Marriage and Family Living*, **21** (August, 1959), 245-250. The scale included eight items: parents dislike children —no; parents are hateful—no; children are ashamed of parents—no; parents show real love and affection for children—yes; children feel "close" to parents—yes; home life is very happy—yes; parents are generous with praise —yes; and rating of family on affection— very affectionate.

[4] The scale included six items: children are punished more severely than children in other families—no; children are disciplined when they don't need it—no; rating of family on fairness of discipline—discipline very fair or quite fair; some children in the family are punished more severely than others —no; parents get all the facts before punishing—yes; and enforcement of rules is not consistent—sometimes harsh, sometimes not— no.

TABLE 1   Median Scale Scores for Delinquency, Affection, Discipline, Democracy, and Cooperation of Children of Employed and Nonemployed Mothers by Residence

	RURAL			TOWN		
	Employed	Nonemployed	Sign	Employed	Nonemployed	Sign
Boys						
Median Delinquency						
Scale Score	2.94	2.70	+	2.61	2.79	—
Median Affection						
Scale Score	6.50	6.50		6.25	6.15	+
Median Discipline						
Scale Score	4.83	4.38	+	4.00	4.75	—
Median Democracy						
Scale Score	3.00	2.88	+	3.14	2.83	+
Median Cooperation						
Scale Score	2.86	3.29	—	3.75	2.80	+
Girls						
Median Delinquency						
Scale Score	4.00	3.53	+	3.21	3.78	—
Median Affection						
Scale Score	6.70	6.38	+	6.33	6.58	—
Median Discipline						
Scale Score	5.25	4.42	+	5.09	4.57	+
Median Democracy						
Scale Score	3.80	2.46	+	2.64	3.33	—
Median Cooperation						
Scale Score	3.00	2.31	+	2.13	3.70	—

for boys did the results support the hypothesis. Therefore the disfunctional hypothesis can safely be rejected: that is, employment of their mothers does not cause children to feel that they are more unfairly punished than the children of nonemployed mothers.

The fourth scale that was constructed was an attempt to measure the dimension of "democracy" in the family.[5] The medians computed from the scale score refuted the disfunctional hypothesis in three out of four samples. Only the town sample for girls supported the hypothesis. The hypothesis that employment of mothers would lower the amount of democracy in the family can be rejected from these data.

The final scale constructed was designed to measure the dimension of "cooperation" in the family.[6] The median scale scores computed from the data seem to be contradictory on both the boy-girl dichotomy and the rural-town dichotomy. The rural sample for boys and the town sample for girls supported the hypothesis, and the town sample of boys and the rural sample of girls refuted the hypothesis. The null hypothesis therefore cannot be rejected from these data; the employment of the mother does not affect the amount of cooperation in a family.

From an overview of Table 1, it would seem that the rural families, in

---

[5] The items that constitute the scale were: rating of family on control by parents—very democratic or fairly democratic; parents listen to suggestions made by their children—yes; children are encouraged to make most of their own decisions—yes; and parents almost always respect children's opinions and judgment—yes.

[6] There were five items that constituted the scale: parents help with homework when asked—yes; quarreling between parents and children is frequent—no; parents do not understand children—no; there is bickering and quarreling in the home—no; and the rating of family on cooperation—much cooperation within the family.

general, consistently refuted the hypothesis that the children of employed mothers would manifest disfunctional tendencies. The data consistently show, in eight out of the nine cases, that families with employed mothers actually scored better than families with nonemployed mothers on the variables for which scales were constructed. The urban sample in general did not show any consistent trends.

Conclusions and Implications for Further Research

1. The children of employed mothers seem to do more household chores than the children of nonemployed mothers; the pattern for the rural girls' sample was not consistent and may well be an exception.

The corollary that because of increased work at home the children would work for pay *less* outside the home was substantiated in the role of the son but reversed in the role of the daughter.

2. The employment of the mother does not seem to have any adverse effect on the social activities of the children. There may be a rural-urban difference with respect to out-of-school activities— showing that children of rural employed mothers participate more, and urban employed mothers' children less, than their counterparts with nonemployed mothers.

3. The employment of the mother does not generally lower the academic performance or aspirations of the children. The results suggest a residential differential: the employment of town mothers lowered the academic performance and aspiration of their children, and the employment of rural mothers raised the academic performance and aspiration of their children.

4. The general fear that delinquency would increase due to the employment

of the mother was not borne out. The results indicated that rural children seemed to manifest less delinquency when their mothers were fully employed than when their mothers were not employed. The other scales devised to measure affection, fairness of discipline, democracy, and cooperation did not give consistent predictions in any one direction: that is, the employment of the mother did not seem to affect the amount of affection, fairness of discipline, democracy, and cooperation as perceived by sons and daughters in the family. The results suggest that rural families in general benefited from the employment of the mother, in that the girls and, in part, the boys showed less delinquency, more affection, more fairness of discipline, more democracy, and more cooperation in their families.

Certain general implications for further research can be made as a result of this study. First, the research design for any study attempting to test the influence of employment on the normative social positions of the family must carefully control the background factors. This was possible in the present study because of the fortuitous presence of a large number of respondents in the control group with which the experimental group could be matched. This was an expedient, because this research design was not specifically set up to study the effect of maternal employment on adolescent roles.

Second, the results of maternal employment indicate that differences between rural and town subcultures exist and need further investigation; perhaps the inclusion of a metropolitan sample would heighten the contrast. Traditional rural values of thrift and hard work *per se* may have some bearing on the theoretical framework and the hypotheses that logically follow. Since

earning money and hard work are "good," then changes in family structure and "sacrifices" made by other members when the mother is fully employed are viewed favorably and may be functional.

Third, the effects of maternal employment on the role of the son seem to be different from the effects on the role of the daughter, and these role differentiations need to be studied separately.

Finally, the definition of the criterion variable of maternal employment should be more carefully treated in a restudy: (a) the hours of work performed should be specified; (b) the regularity of work in months per year should be stipulated; and (c) the duration of the employment in the number of years should be stated *to insure that the experimental variable has been operative for a reasonable amount of time to manifest effects* in the test variables.

The hypotheses for further research should therefore be more specific and take into consideration sexual role differentiation and residence. Research hypotheses suggested from the results of this study may be stated thus:

1. That maternal employment results in less outside renumerative employment for the adolescent son and more for the daughter in both rural and urban families.

2. That maternal employment in rural areas raises the academic performance and aspiration of the son and daughter, but in towns it lowers academic performance and aspiration for both the son and the daughter.

3. Rural families show beneficial effects owing to maternal employment in that there is less delinquency, more affection, more fairness of discipline, more democracy, and more cooperation in the family.

the influence of peers and parents
on mobility aspiration

twenty-one

Many boys in the lower class want to get out, and they make effective plans to do so, thus leaving their less ambitious peers behind. Unambitious boys are also to be found in the middle classes. Parents in all classes fear that they are powerless against the influence of their adolescent children's peers. Note that these complex factors are relevant to many areas other than mobility aspiration, such as juvenile delinquency or criminality, political attitudes, or even aesthetic tastes.

Parental Influence, Anticipatory Socialization, and Social Mobility

RICHARD L. SIMPSON

Two distinct hypotheses have been proposed to explain why some boys from working-class backgrounds aspire to middle-class occupational status while others do not. According to research by Kahl, Floud and associates, and Bordua, a working-class boy is relatively likely to seek advanced education and occupational mobility if his parents urge him to do so, and unlikely to seek mobility if his parents do not exert pressure in

Richard L. Simpson, "Parental Influence, Anticipatory Socialization, and Social Mobility," *American Sociological Review*, 27 (August, 1962), 517-522. We are grateful to the author and The American Sociological Association for permission to quote.

this direction.[1] On the other hand, studies by Beilin and Wilson suggest that anticipatory socialization into middle-class values by middle-class peers at school may be the decisive factor.[2] Bei-

[1] Joseph A. Kahl, "Educational and Occupational Aspirations of 'Common-Man' Boys," *Harvard Educational Review*, 23 (Summer, 1953), 186-203; Jean E. Floud (ed.), A. H. Halsey, and F. M. Martin, *Social Class and Educational Opportunity* (London: William Heinemann, Ltd., 1956), pp. 93-95, 107-108; David J. Bordua, "Educational Aspirations and Parental Stress on College," *Social Forces*, 38 (March, 1960), 262-269. See also a summary of studies in Seymour Martin Lipset and Reinhard Bendix, *Social Mobility in Industrial Society* (Berkeley: University of California Press, 1959), pp. 237-240.

[2] Harry Beilin, "The Pattern of Postponability and Its Relation to Social Class Mo-

lin reports that working-class boys who plan to attend college, like middle-class boys, tend to participate heavily in organized extracurricular activities, and Turner feels that mobility-oriented working-class high school students should be "studied separately to discover whether or not they are incorporated into higher-level cliques. . . ."[3]

There is nothing inherently contradictory about these two hypotheses, since it is reasonable to suppose that parents and peers might independently influence the aspirations of working-class boys. However, it is also conceivable that only one of the two hypotheses might provide the true explanation for mobility aspirations, despite the evidence supporting both hypotheses when they are tested in separate studies. Conceivably the relationship between parental influence and mobility aspiration might disappear if peer group influence were controlled, or vice versa, suggesting that one of the two types of influence is more apparent than real since it has no effect unless the other type of influence is also present.

This paper will explore the effects on career aspirations of parental and peer group influences, considered separately, and will then try to see whether the relationships found are independent of each other by varying both types of influence simultaneously.

Source of Data

The data are from questionnaires administered in 1960 to the boys in the

bility," *Journal of Social Psychology*, **44** (August, 1956), 33-48; Alan B. Wilson, "Residential Segregation of Social Classes and Aspirations of High School Boys," *American Sociological Review*, 24 (December, 1959), 836-845.

[3] Beilin, *op. cit.*, 46; Ralph H. Turner, "Sponsored and Contest Mobility and the School System," *American Sociological Review*, **25** (December, 1960), 866.

white high schools of two southern cities. One school, in a city of about 25,000, provided 333 respondents, and the other, in a city of about 60,000, provided 584, for a total of 917. All boys present in homeroom period on the day when the questionnaires were given filled them out—more than 90 per cent in each school. Nonresponses and unclassifiable responses to the question on occupational plans reduced the 917 respondents to 743. The respondents omitted from tabulations because of insufficient information about their occupational plans were somewhat skewed toward the lower end of the family status range, though not markedly so. Since family background is controlled in all tabulations, the sample reduction caused by their incomplete answers probably does not distort the findings appreciably. The patterns of relationship among key variables were very similar among students at the two schools; therefore both schools are combined in the analysis.

From information on the occupations of the boys' fathers and the occupations they themselves expected to enter, they were classified into four groups. *Ambitious middle-class* boys were those whose fathers' current occupations (or last occupations, if the fathers were deceased) were nonmanual, and who were enrolled in the college preparatory curriculum and expected to enter high-ranking professional or executive occupations. . . . *Unambitious middle-class* boys had white-collar fathers but were either not enrolled in the college preparatory curriculum, not planning to enter [high-ranking or executive] occupations. . . . *Mobile working-class* boys had fathers in blue-collar occupations but were enrolled in the college preparatory curriculum and expected to enter the same high-ranking occupations as the ambitious middle-class boys. *Nonmobile working-class* boys had blue-collar fathers and failed to meet one or both of the two criteria of ambition, enrollment in the college preparatory curriculum and aspiration to enter top-ranking occupations.[4]

Parental Influence

Table 1 shows the percentages of boys in the four groups who had been advised by one or both parents to enter professions. We are considering such advice as a rough indication of parental pressure toward occupational ambition which would involve, unless the father is himself professional, upward mobility. These figures give strong support to the hypothesis that parental influence is associated with mobility aspiration among working-class boys and also with ambition among middle-class boys. Indeed, parental advice is a much better predictor of high ambition than is the boy's social class. Only 21.0 per cent of the unambitious middle-class boys and 16.0 per cent of the nonmobile working-class boys had been advised by one or both parents to enter professions; this compares with 53.1 per cent among the ambitious middle-class boys and 43.5 per cent among the mobile working-class boys.[5]

---

[4] The mobile and nonmobile working-class boys did not differ appreciably in the percentage whose fathers held skilled as opposed to semiskilled or unskilled jobs. Therefore the differences reported later between these two groups of boys cannot be attributed to heterogeneity of class background within the blue-collar category. The ambitious middle-class boys did tend to come from higher backgrounds than the unambitious middle-class boys, and the differences between these two groups would diminish (but not come close to disappearing) if our tables [were] controlled for fine gradations of background within the broad level which we are calling middle class.

[5] The superiority of parental advice to social class as a predictor of ambition appears even greater if we examine the percentages in the four groups who had been advised by

TABLE 1   Percentages of Boys in Four Groups Advised to Enter Professions by One or Both Parents

Group	Per Cent Advised to Enter Professions
1. Ambitious middle-class (N = 209)	53.1
2. Unambitious middle-class (N = 157)	21.0
3. Mobile working-class (N = 85)	43.5
4. Nonmobile working-class (N = 231)	16.0

Peer Group Membership and Anticipatory Socialization

Following Turner's reasoning, we would predict from the "anticipatory socialization" hypothesis that among working-class boys, those with middle-class friends would more often be mobile, and that among middle-class boys, those with working-class friends would less often be ambitious. Table 2 shows that this was definitely the case. The table distributes the four groups according to their answers to a question which asked them to "describe what kind of work the fathers of three of your best friends do"; the occupations they listed are classified as all middle-class (nonmanual), all working-class, or one or more of each.[6] As predicted, the ambitious middle-class and nonmobile working-class boys were at the extremes: 57.1 per cent of the ambitious middle-class boys but only 5.3 per cent of the nonmobile working-class boys mentioned only middle-class friends, while only 3.5 per cent of the former but 40.2 per cent of the latter men-

---

both parents to enter professions. These percentages, not shown in the table, are 6.4 per cent of the unambitious middle-class boys, 5.6 per cent of the nonmobile working-class boys, 28.7 per cent of the ambitious middle-class boys, and 24.7 per cent of the mobile working-class boys.

[6] The N's in Table 2 differ from those in other tables because of differing rates of nonresponse to the various questions involved.

TABLE 2   Occupational Status of
Fathers of Friends Cited by
Four Groups of Boys

STATUS OF FRIENDS' FATHERS

Group	All Middle-Class (Per Cent)	One or More of Each Class (Per Cent)	All Working-Class (Per Cent)
1. Ambitious middle-class (N = 198)	57.1	39.4	3.5
2. Unambitious middle-class (N = 133)	32.3	43.6	24.1
3. Mobile working-class (N = 83)	28.9	59.0	12.1
4. Nonmobile working-class (N = 189)	5.3	54.5	40.2

tioned only working-class friends. The unambitious middle-class and mobile working-class boys were intermediate, and the differences between them were not clear-cut, since the mobile working-class boys were more likely to mention one or more friends of each class, and the unambitious middle-class boys were more likely to mention either all middle-class or all working-class friends. However, in comparing these two intermediate groups, the unambitious middle-class boys were twice as likely (24.1 per cent *vs.* 12.1 per cent) to mention only working-class friends, but only slightly more likely (32.3 per cent *vs.* 28.9 per cent) to mention only middle-class friends. Considering the middle-class and working-class boys separately, these findings seem to give clear support to the "anticipatory socialization" hypothesis that the social class of the peer group is predictive of occupational ambition and mobility.

From the anticipatory socialization hypothesis, one would also expect mobile working-class boys to resemble ambitious middle-class boys in their extracurricular and after-school activities. Beilin's finding that those planning to attend college took part in more extracurricular activities than those not planning to attend college bears out this prediction,[7] and our data allow a further test of it. We asked the boys to list all of the "clubs and other organizations" to which they belonged. Table 3 shows that, as predicted, the mobile working-class boys approached the ambitious middle-class boys in the extent of their extracurricular participation—substantially more than the unambitious middle-class boys did and much more than the nonmobile working-class boys did. The mean numbers of clubs or organizations reported were 2.7 for ambitious middle-class boys, 1.6 for unambitious middle-class boys, 2.3 for mobile working-class boys, and 1.1 for nonmobile working-class boys.

Independent Effects

It is thus apparent that parental advice and middle-class peer group influence were both related to ambition and mobility aspiration among both middle-class and working-class boys in the two schools, and that in parental influence, peer group membership, and extracurricular activities, the mobile working-class boys resembled the ambitious middle-class boys more than the unambitious middle-class boys did. The next task is to see whether parents and peers influenced the boys' aspirations independently of each other. To test the hypothesis of independent effects, the boys were classified as "high" or "low" in the extent to which they had been subjected to each type of influence toward high occupational aspiration. They were defined as high in parental influence if either or both parents had recommended a professional career and high in peer influence if they met both of two criteria: belonging to two or more clubs and mentioning at least one middle-class friend. From this classification it was possible to define the boys

---

[7] Beilin, *op. cit.*, 46.

parental influence, anticipatory socialization, and social mobility   **155**

TABLE 3   Percentages of Boys in Four Groups Belonging to Different
         Numbers of Clubs

NUMBER OF CLUBS

Group	None or One (Per Cent)	2 or 3 (Per Cent)	4 or More (Per Cent)	Mean *
1. Ambitious middle-class (N = 209)	26.8	34.4	38.8	2.7
2. Unambitious middle-class (N = 157)	55.4	28.7	15.9	1.6
3. Mobile working-class (N = 85)	34.1	40.0	25.9	2.3
4. Nonmobile working class (N = 231)	68.8	23.4	7.8	1.1

* In computing mean, "5 or more" was counted as 5.

as high in both types of influence, high in one but low in the other, or low in both.

Table 4 supports the hypothesis of independent effects strongly and consistently for working-class boys and less strongly for middle-class boys. Among working-class boys, 71.4 per cent of those high in both parental and peer influence aspired to occupations in [the] top . . . levels, compared with only 25.6 per cent of those low in both types of influence, the boys high in one influence but low in the other being intermediate. Among middle-class boys, the rank order of the four groups in percentage aspiring to top-level occupations was the same as among working-class boys, but the differences between groups were small and statistically insignificant, with one exception: boys low in both types of influence were less than half as likely as those high in either or both influences to have high aspirations.

Table 4 also suggests that, as we have defined the two, parental influence was more strongly related to aspirations than peer influence was. Among the working-class boys high in peer influence, being high rather than low in parental influence brought the percentage of high aspirers up from 35.7 per cent to twice this figure, 71.4 per cent; and among the working-class boys low in

peer influence, high parental influence more than doubled the percentage of high aspirers, increasing it from 25.6 per cent to 55.6 per cent. The effects of peer influence on working-class boys, with parental influence controlled, were

TABLE 4   Occupational Aspirations of Middle-Class and Working-Class Boys by Extent of Parental and Peer Group Influence Toward Ambition

PER CENT ASPIRING TO HIGH-STATUS OCCUPATIONS

Source and Extent of Influence	Working Class (N)	Per Cent	Middle Class (N)	Per Cent
1. Both high	(28)	71.4	(94)	81.9
2. Parents high, peers low	(45)	55.6	(50)	78.0
3. Peers high, parents low	(70)	35.7	(109)	72.5
4. Both low	(168)	25.6	(113)	30.1

substantially less than this. Among those high in parental influence, high peer influence increased the percentage of high aspirers from 55.6 to 71.4, and among those low in parental influence, the increase due to high peer influence was from 25.6 per cent to 35.7 per cent. The seemingly greater influence of parents than of peers is also evident when we compare the percentages of high aspirers among working-class boys high in only one type of influence. Among those high in parental influence only, 55.6

per cent were high aspirers, but this percentage dropped to 35.7 among those high in peer influence only. Corresponding differences between the effects of parental and peer influence, though they were small and statistically unreliable, appeared among the middle-class boys.

It is also worth noting that when *both* types of influence were either high or low, they came close to nullifying the effects of class background on career aspiration. In every category of exposure to influence, the middle-class boys had higher aspirations than the working-class boys, but these differences were large and statistically significant only in the two middle categories, which were high in one influence but low in the other. A working-class boy who was high in either influence was more likely to be a high aspirer than a middle-class boy who was low in both.

Summary

Using questionnaire data from boys in two high schools, we have tested two alternative hypotheses concerning the factors influencing boys toward high occupational aspirations, and we have examined the simultaneous effects of the relevant variables to see whether each influences aspirations when the other is held constant. In general, the findings held true among both working- and middle-class boys, and in some respects, mobile working-class boys resembled ambitious middle-class boys more than unambitious middle-class boys did.

Among boys aspiring to high occupations, the percentage whose parents had advised them to enter professions was much higher than the percentage among low aspirers. Thus the conclusion reached by Kahl, Floud and associates, and Bordua that parental influence is a factor in the upward mobility of working-class boys, receives further confirmation and is extended to cover the ambitions of middle-class boys as well.

Mobile working-class boys were much higher than nonmobile working-class boys and somewhat higher than unambitious middle-class boys in the percentage who said that they had middle-class friends. In the number of extracurricular clubs to which they belonged, mobile working-class boys were close to ambitious middle-class boys, substantially higher than unambitious middle-class boys, and more than twice as high as nonmobile working-class boys. These findings support the hypothesis advanced by Beilin, Wilson, and Turner that anticipatory socialization into middle-class values by middle-class peer groups helps to explain the upward mobility of working-class boys. Our findings also extend the anticipatory socialization hypothesis to cover middle-class as well as working-class boys.

A working-class boy was most likely to aspire to a high-ranking occupation if he had been influenced in this direction by both parents and peers, and least likely to be a high aspirer if he had been subjected to neither of these influences. Among the middle-class boys, only those low in both influences differed significantly from the rest, though the direction of relationships in all cases paralleled those found among working-class boys. Of the two types of influence, that of parents appeared to have the stronger effect. Working-class boys influenced toward upward mobility by either parents or peers tended to have higher aspirations than middle-class boys not influenced toward high aspirations by either parents or peers.

the achievement motivation in the united states and brazil

twenty-two

Considerable research by sociologists and psychologists over the past fifteen years has pointed to a certain family constellation as crucial in the development of a high need for achievement in boys. Under some formulations, the most significant experience for the boy is asserted to be "winning" in his interaction with his father and mother, exploring without punishment, but being held to standards of performance. In most versions, the relation between mother and son is viewed as primary, so long as the father does not interfere too much. In the following report, comparing both Brazil and the United States with reference to the factors making for a high need for achievement, note that the role behavior of the father is also emphasized.

Socialization and Achievement Motivation in Brazil

BERNARD C. ROSEN

Achievement motivation has been defined as the redintegration of affect aroused by cues in situations involving standards of excellence. Children typically learn standards of excellence from parents (or their surrogates) who encourage competition with these standards, while rewarding good performance and punishing failure. In time, parental expectations become internalized, so that when later exposed to situations

Bernard C. Rosen, "Socialization and Achievement Motivation in Brazil," *American Sociological Review*, **27** (October, 1962), 612-616, 618-624. We are grateful to the author and The American Sociological Association for permission to quote.

involving standards of excellence, the individual re-experiences the affect associated with his earlier efforts. In our culture, the behavior of people with strong achievement motivation is characterized by persistent striving and general competitiveness.[1]

Several studies have shown that achievement motivation has its origins in a complex of interrelated socialization practices.[2] The first and most im-

[1] David C. McClelland, John W. Atkinson, Russell Clark, and Edgar Lowell, *The Achievement Motive* (New York: Appleton-Century-Crofts, Inc., 1953).

[2] Bernard C. Rosen, "Family Structure and Achievement Motivation," *American Sociological Review*, **26** (August, 1961), 574-585. Marian Winterbottom, "The Relation of

portant of these is *achievement training*. Parents who provide this type of training set high goals for their child, indicate a high evaluation of his competence to do a task well, and impose standards of excellence upon problem-solving tasks, even in situations where such standards are not explicit. Also related to the development of achievement motivation is another set of socialization practices called *independence training*. This type of training involves expectations that the child be *self-reliant* when competing with standards of excellence. At the same time, the child is granted *autonomy* in problem solving and decision making in situations where he has both freedom of action and responsibility for success or failure. Essentially, achievement training is concerned with getting the child to do things well, while independence training seeks to teach him to do things on his own (self-reliance) in a situation where he enjoys relative freedom from parental control (autonomy).

In an experimental study of family interaction, boys with high achievement motivation were found most often in family structures where both parents stressed achievement training, but where the parents differed sharply so far as independence training was concerned.[3] Much of this type of training came from the father, who expected his son to be self-reliant in problem solving and gave him a relatively high degree of autonomy in making his own decisions. The mothers of boys with high achievement motivation tended to stress achievement training rather

than independence training. In fact they were likely to be more dominant and "pushing" than the mothers of the boys with low motivation. But their aspirations were higher and their concern with standards of excellence greater. Observers reported that the mothers of boys with high achievement motivation tended to be strong, competitive persons who apparently expected their sons to be the same.

These data suggest that boys can take and perhaps need achievement training from both parents, but the effects of independence training and sanctions (a crucial factor determining the child's affective reaction to standards of excellence) are different depending on whether they come from father or mother. Boys appear to need more autonomy in their relationships with their father than with their mother, if they are to develop high achievement motivation. An authoritarian father may overwhelm and crush his son. He tends to deprive the boy of an opportunity to compete on his own ground, to test his skill in problem solving and to gain a sense of confidence in his own competence. A strong, authoritarian mother does not seem to have the same effect, possibly because she is perceived as imposing her standards upon the boy, while a dominating father is perceived as imposing himself. It may be that mother-son relations are typically more secure than those between father and son, so that the boy is able to accept higher levels of dominance and hostility from his mother than father without adverse effect upon his achievement motivation.

This paper is a study of family structure, child-rearing, and achievement motivation in Brazil. The questions which the investigation, reported on here, raised and sought to answer were as follows: How prevalent are achievement training and independence train-

Need for Achievement to Learning Experiences in Independence and Mastery," in John W. Atkinson (ed.), *Motives in Fantasy, Action and Society* (Princeton: D. Van Nostrand, Inc., 1958).

[3] Bernard C. Rosen and Roy D'Andrade, "The Psychosocial Origins of Achievement Motivation," *Sociometry*, **22** (September, 1959), 185-218.

ing practices in Brazil? What is the relationship of these child-rearing practices to family structure? And what effect does this structure have on the development of achievement motivation? As we report the results of our investigation, the data obtained in Brazil will be compared with those secured from a criterion group of Americans matched by age, sex, and social class. We hoped that a comparative approach would provide a more balanced perspective on family structure and socialization in Brazil.

Samples and Methods

The data for this study were collected from four independent samples: two in Brazil and two in the United States. The first Brazilian sample was selected purposively from six representative public and private schools in a major city in Brazil—São Paulo. The schools were selected in such a fashion as to insure including in the sample subjects from all social strata. This sample includes 212 boys, aged nine through eleven, and many of their mothers. An additional sample of 134 boys, representing virtually the entire universe of subjects in the nine through eleven age group enrolled in five public and private schools, and many of their mothers as well, was obtained from Rio Claro, a small city in Southern Brazil. Two separate samples were also used in the United States: the first is a heterogeneous, purposive sample of 427 boys (aged eight through fourteen) and their mothers living in four Northeastern states. The subjects in this sample were drawn from six different racial and ethnic groups: white Protestants, Italians, French-Canadians, Greeks, Jews, Negroes. This group will be called U.S. sample "A." The second American sample (U.S. sample "B") is more homogeneous and was obtained two years

later; it includes almost the entire universe of nine- through eleven-year-old boys (367 cases) enrolled in the public and parochial schools of three small Eastern Connecticut towns. These samples do not fully reflect the ethnic, regional, or racial diversity of their respective universes and hence cannot be considered completely representative of either Brazil or the United States. Yet the fact that they were drawn from the most industrialized and populous sections of their respective countries is a source of strength in two ways. First, it enhances their comparability and, second, it increases the likelihood that they reflect the attributes of a sizable portion of the population of either country. Nonetheless, the regional nature of these samples means that the generalizability of our findings to other sections of either country remains an open question which only further research can answer.

The achievement motivation of the boys from both countries was measured through the use of a Thematic Apperception-type test. This test involved showing the subject four ambiguous pictures and having him tell a story under time pressure about each one. The same pictures were used in both countries. An intensive effort was made to discover whether these pictures, which had been developed in the United States, possessed any cultural characteristics that might bias the subject's responses. Careful pretesting in Brazil failed to reveal any problems; the pictures appeared as natural to Brazilians as they did to Americans, although of course there was always the possibility that biases existed which could not be uncovered through a direct questioning of the subject. The subject's imagery was then scored for evidences of concern with achievement and evaluated performance in situations involving competition with standards of excellence.[4] After the projective testing had been completed, the boys in U.S. sample "B" were given a highly structured, group administered, hour-long questionnaire, which was designed to provide information on the boy's perception of his parents: e.g., the extent to which his parents emphasized self-reliance, competition, and excellence, and their willingness to grant him autonomy. At a later date this questionnaire was translated into Portuguese and administered to Brazilian boys; only a portion of the data derived from the questionnaire will be reported in this paper. Data on child-rearing practices in the United States and Brazil were obtained through personal interviews with American mothers and by means of a questionnaire in Brazil.

* * * * *

Findings and Interpretation

Family Structure and Socialization

In contemporary Brazil, family characteristics vary with the social classes, with rural and urban environments, and by region. . . .[5]

The family with which we will be concerned might be called "husband-father centered." In this type of family, the husband is truly a privileged person: in all matters of importance his word is final. The dominant and privileged position of the husband in the Brazilian family is perhaps most striking in the double standard of sex morality, common at all class levels, which condones the infidelity of the husband while imposing strict moral standards for the wife.[6] The woman's role is primarily that of housekeeper and mother. She is not expected to be a companion to her spouse; rather, her major activities center around child rearing and providing services for her husband. She expects, and receives, virtually no help from her husband with either housekeeping or child rearing. Her position in the family, moreover, is distinctly inferior, socially and psychologically, to that of her husband, toward whom she is expected to be submissive, deferential, and passive. In some families, women appear to be little more than servants —they have been observed standing during mealtime while their husbands were seated.[7] There are of course exceptions to this pattern. Strong, dominant women or weak, subordinate men are not unknown in Brazil. Furthermore, the authoritarian, father-dominated family is more likely to be found in rural than in urban areas; it is also more often found in the upper and middle classes than in the lower class. Nonetheless, families in which women are treated as equals by their husbands are

---

[4] Since we were interested in relating family structure to child rearing and achievement motivation, orphans or boys from broken or incomplete families were *not* tested for achievement motivation. This screening process reduced the number of Brazilian boys tested for achievement motivation to 245 persons: 167 from São Paulo, seventy-eight from Rio Claro. All of the American boys examined in this study had also been screened by these criteria. The boys were tested privately and individually. . . .

[5] Emilio Willems stresses this point in his article "The Structure of the Brazilian Family," *Social Forces*, 31 (May, 1953), 339-345. See also, Oracy Nogueira, "A Organizacão da Familia No Municipio de Itapetininga," *Educacão e Ciencias Sociais*, 5 (Agosto, 1959).

[6] Emilio Willems, *op. cit.*, 341. For the historical origins of this culture pattern, see Gilberto Freyre, *The Masters and the Slaves* (New York: Alfred A. Knopf, Inc., 1956).

[7] Donald Pierson noted this situation among lower-class families in a village near the city of São Paulo. See his *Cruz das Almas* (Washington, D.C.: Smithsonian Institute, Social Anthropology Publication #12, 1948). The writer observed a similar situation in a middle-class family in a remote city in North-Central Brazil.

far from common in most regions of Brazil.[8]

The relationships between parents and child in Brazil are ordinarily warm and openly affectionate, perhaps more so than in the United States. To this observer, it appeared that the child in Brazil is fondled, coddled, hugged more often and to a later age than is general in the United States. There is a strong tendency for parents to be overprotective and indulgent as well, behavior which is reflected in the cultural conception of the child as "the protected one"—a fragile creature ("his bones are soft") who needs constant warmth, care, and protection. Brazilians justify their indulgence of children by arguing that life is harsh and painful, hence childhood should be made as pleasurable as possible.

While Brazilian parents take great pleasure in the development of their children, there is relatively little emphasis upon training the child in achievement and independence. The Brazilian mother, for example, is less likely than the American mother to laud those activities and qualities of the child that tend to make him independent of his mother: for example, how fast he walks, how energetic he is, or how quickly he learns to do things by himself. Brazilians, moreover, tend to couple their nurturance with a high degree of authoritarian control. Children are taught to be submissive and deferential toward their father at all times. Indeed, Brazilian fathers often expect deference to paternal wishes even after their children are grown and have families of their own. Brazilian mothers, while more nurturant than fathers (as might be expected in a society where women have virtually no role outside of the family and where maternal involvement in children, particularly sons, is extremely intense), tend also to dominate their children. Throughout her life, the Brazilian mother, like the father, will continue to exert strong influence upon her children. She is quite capable of expressing her opinions forcibly when the occasion requires. It is not unknown for a mother to beat an erring son, even though he be a grown man. The mother, it should be noted, is the principal disciplinary agent in the Brazilian family. Only when the child is unusually disobedient will the father become involved in this aspect of socialization, although the mother will often threaten the child with punishment by the father as a way of securing conformity to her wishes.

Few aspects of the child's behavior evoke more repressive discipline in Brazil than displays of hostility. Aggression is far more severely controlled in Brazil than in the United States. The child in Brazil, while indulged in many ways, is not permitted to express aggression toward parents, siblings, and peers with anything like the freedom that is tolerated in the American child. The American mother may hesitate to curb her child's aggressiveness out of the fear that she may damage his initiative. The Brazilian mother, much less concerned with this effect, tends to regard aggression as a wholly disruptive force and a threat to her authority. In this she is fully supported by the father, who if anything is even less tolerant of aggression from his children. Fighting, even between peers, is severely discouraged, partly out of fear that the child will be

---

[8] There appears to be a movement, particularly in the large cities, toward a more democratic family structure. Even in remote areas of Brazil, the writer has encountered men who, reacting against what they themselves described as "dictatorial" and "tyrannical" parents, were endeavoring to create a more democratic environment in their families. The transition, however, was a painful one, and they often expressed doubt as to the wisdom of the change.

hurt and partly because such fights may lead to feuds between families.

* * * * *

Independence Training as Perceived by the Boy

Up to now our analysis of family structure and socialization in Brazil has been based primarily upon data obtained through observation of parent-child interaction and from the mothers by means of interviews and questionnaires. We turn now to an examination of the boy's *perceptions* of parental behavior and expectations as data on socialization in Brazil. This approach was prompted by Ausubel's argument that the parents' behavior, although an actual event, affects the child only to the extent and in the form that he perceives it.[9] These data were obtained through an hour-long, group-administered questionnaire given to all Brazilian boys and to American boys in sample "B." The subject was asked to evaluate many of his parents' personal qualities, their expectations of him and reactions to his behavior in a number of situations. In general, the questionnaire was designed to provide information on the boy's perception of his parents and of the socialization practices which they employed.

Given the authoritarian structure of the family and the tendency for Brazilian parents to be overprotective and indulgent, one would expect that Brazilian boys would be less likely than their American counterparts to perceive their parents as stressing independence training. Indeed, this is largely the picture which develops out of the data. Thus in reaction to the statement "My father lets me work things out for myself," 21 per cent of the Brazilian boys

said "never" while only 2 per cent of the Americans gave this response. When mother was substituted for father in an identical question, 29 per cent of the Brazilians said "never," as compared with 1 per cent of the Americans.[10] And to cite still another example, 26 per cent of the Brazilian boys strongly agreed with the statement "My mother tells me what I can do and what I can't do most of the time," as compared with 13 per cent of the Americans. These data indicate that Brazilian boys are more likely than their American peers to feel that their parents interfere too much and are inaccessible to argument —both of these are attitudes which suggest that Brazilian boys do not perceive their parents as placing much emphasis upon training for self-reliance and autonomy.

Achievement Training as Perceived by the Boy

The data support our contention that achievement training is stressed less in Brazil than in the United States, but the picture is more complex than in the case of independence training. So far as *aspirations* for achievement are concerned, they show that Brazilian boys perceive their parents as placing less stress upon achievement training than is reported by American boys. But when the parents' *evaluation* of the boy's performance is considered, the problem becomes complicated—as we shall see.

The boy was asked first how well his parents *wanted* him to do, and then how well they thought he *actually was* doing, with regard to nine different kinds of activities. Some of the activities were associated with explicit, culturally imposed standards of excellence,

---

[9] David P. Ausubel, *et al.*, "Perceived Parent Attitudes as Determinants of Children's Ego Structure," *Child Development*, **25** (September, 1954), 173-182.

[10] Wherever percentages are reported, the differences between Brazilians and Americans are statistically significant at the .05 level or better.

while in the case of others the standards were more likely to be implicit and idiosyncratic. The activities about which the boys were questioned were as follows: school work, saving money, competitive sports, noncompetitive sports, "intellectual" games, hobbies where the boy collects things, hobbies which involve building things, aesthetic-expressive activities, and repairing things. Questions were first asked with respect to mother's expectations and evaluations, and then on a separate page identical questions were asked about father. Parental expectations were rated by the boy on a six-point scale, ranging from "doesn't care how well I do" to "wants me to be excellent."

The data show that for seven out of nine activities (eight out of nine for father) the American boys, on the average, perceived their mothers as having higher aspirations than are reported by Brazilian boys. For example, 64 per cent of the American boys reported that their mothers expected them to be excellent or almost excellent in competitive sports as compared with 47 per cent of the Brazilian boys. The differences between Brazilians and Americans for the other activities followed a very similar pattern. However, when the boy was asked how well his parents thought he actually was doing, in contrast with how well they wanted him to do, the earlier pattern is reversed. The Brazilian boy tended to perceive his parents as having a higher evaluation of his actual performance, so far as these activities are concerned, than was the case with American boys. Using a six-point scale ranging from "poor" to "excellent," Brazilian boys reported higher paternal evaluations of their performance on five and higher maternal evaluations on four activities. For example, 52 per cent of the Brazilian boys reported that their mothers thought their work in school was excellent,

while only 20 per cent of the American boys reported so high a parental evaluation.

This finding that Brazilian fathers and mothers were perceived as having lower aspirations for excellence as regards specific activities, while at the same time they were thought to be more content with their son's performance, suggests that Brazilian parents exert less pressure for achievement on their sons than do American parents. We were surprised therefore to discover that Brazilian boys perceived their parents as having higher generalized expectations for achievement than were reported by American boys for their parents. For example, 55 per cent of the Brazilian boys said that their fathers (57 per cent said the same of their mothers) "always expect me to be on top in whatever I do," as compared with 20 per cent of the Americans who made this comment about their father, or 19 per cent about their mother. Or again, 41 per cent of the Brazilian boys "strongly agreed" with the statement "Even when I was very young, mother expected me to do things better than other kids my own age"; only 7 per cent of the American boys gave this response. And in reaction to the statement "My parents expect me to do most things better than other kids my own age," 45 per cent of the Brazilian boys answered "strongly agree," as compared with 6 per cent of the Americans.

Indulgence, Aspirations, and Motivation

There seems to be a contradiction here. For if we are to believe their own reports, Brazilian boys tend to perceive their parents as having high general aspirations despite the fact that they report lower parental aspirations as regards specific activities and higher parental evaluations of actual performance than do American boys. And we know from the mothers' reports that Brazilians do not make demands for self-reliant mastery upon their children as early as do American mothers. What is the explanation of this apparent contradiction? Possibly the answer can be found in the indulgence and overprotectiveness Brazilians experience during infancy and early childhood, which may in some instances set in motion a process of ego expansion and distortion of perception. Let us pause now to consider this process and its origins, for we believe it bears critically (and adversely) upon the development of achievement motivation in Brazil. The description of the process which follows is admittedly hypothetical and should be regarded as primarily a working hypothesis. But it has a measure of psychological coherence in that it is consistent with what is believed to be the psychodynamics of ego development and, as we shall see, is supported at points by data obtained from the boys.

The process begins with the intense involvement and permissiveness which characterize mother-child relations in Brazil. This is especially likely to be the case when the child is a male. Boys in Brazil are often pampered and indulged. They are likely to receive more attention and are permitted far more leeway than their sisters. A Brazilian physician told the writer wryly, "When a child is born, they look at its genitals. If it's a boy, they spoil it; if it's a girl, they discipline it." The data show that boys appear to sense their mothers' intense involvement. For example, 40 per cent of the Brazilian boys said that their mothers "always" become "excited when I get cut or scratched," while only 16 per cent of the Americans gave this response.

This initial overindulgence and intense parental involvement may cause the child to develop an exaggerated impression of his importance and power.

He may begin to fantasize about future exploits; achievement takes on a magical aura in that there appears to be no limit to what he can accomplish. *In some cases these high self-expectations and evaluations are then projected upon his parents.* He comes to believe that they have the same exaggerated opinion of his ability and future as he does. Where his aspirations are related to activities which have empirical referents, such as school work, saving money, or winning at games, the boy's fantasies may be somewhat more realistic. In these areas he is perhaps better able to gauge accurately his parents' aspirations and evaluations of him, but where they concern achievement in some diffuse and unspecific way, his fantasies are less subject, at least initially, to reality testing. In terms of broad goals, he will tend to perceive his parents as having very high expectations for generalized achievement and a high evaluation of his ability. Some confirmation of this point is found in the boy's reaction to the statement "My mother thinks I'm going to be an important person someday." More than half of the Brazilian boys (54 per cent) strongly agreed with this statement, as compared with 19 per cent of the Americans. Of course this is not entirely a function of perceptual distortion. Ordinarily a high degree of parental approval is associated with early indulgence, although, as we shall soon see, the child may come to doubt the sincerity of this approval. Thus in 40 per cent of the cases the Brazilian boy said that his parents "always" gave him "the feeling I'm somebody special," while only 15 per cent of the American boys gave this response. Also, 39 per cent of the Brazilians reported that their parents "always tell me I'm bright"; only 8 per cent of the American boys gave this response.

But for many children in Brazil this period of indulgence is soon ended.

Childhood in the lower class—a category into which the vast bulk of the population falls—is a much briefer period than is generally the case in the United States. . . .

The abruptness and severity of the transition from childhood to quasi-adult status may shake the boy's faith in the benevolence of his environment. Moreover, this transition occurs at a time when he is beginning to realize that the opportunities for advancement in his society are severely limited. Brazil is a highly stratified society with very limited vertical mobility. A lower-class, or even a middle-class, boy who perceives his parents as expecting him "to be on top" or to become "important" may very well come to feel that such aspirations are unrealistic and unreasonable. Possibly at this point the boy begins to question the accuracy of his parents' evaluation, or what he perceives to be their evaluation, of his abilities. Thus the data show that 26 per cent of the Brazilian boys strongly agreed with the statement "My parents think I'm smarter than I really am." Only 13 per cent of the American boys strongly agreed with this statement. He may also wonder whether his parents' interest in achievement is genuine. For one thing, they tend not to provide him with a model. Illustrative of this point is the finding that Brazilian boys, when asked to describe their parents, were less likely than American boys to perceive their fathers as successful or ambitious. Moreover, his parents do not appear to be truly concerned with standards of excellence. For example, 31 per cent of the Brazilians answered "strongly agree" to the statement "when I do a job poorly my mother hardly ever notices," as compared with a similar response from only 3 per cent of the Americans. It is true that his parents reward him when he does something well: 66 per cent of the Brazilians report that their parents always "praise me when I do a good job"; only 33 per cent of the Americans gave an "always" response to this item. But the value of this reinforcement may well be vitiated by the apparently indiscriminate way in which it is given. "My mother tells me I'm doing a good job no matter how I do" is a statement more strongly agreed to by Brazilians (26 per cent) than Americans (13 per cent). Praise so easily given often loses its savor. The child may also wonder, perhaps not unreasonably, whether his parents' approval is sincere, for while they tend to praise him indiscriminately, they react very sharply to his failures. Thus when asked how their parents respond to their mistakes, 46 per cent of the Brazilians said their parents "always get upset," while only 8 per cent of the Americans gave this response.

Probably the boy does not doubt the genuineness of his parents' interest in achievement. Their interest appears real enough, but excessive and unreasonable; thus 42 per cent of the Brazilian boys strongly agreed with the statement "I love my parents, but they expect too much of me"; only 8 per cent of the American boys gave this response. Perhaps the boy begins to feel that his parents do not really understand him. He wonders whether they value him as a person or . . . prize him merely as someone whose achievements will add luster to the family's name. Apparently a large proportion of Brazilian boys come to believe the latter, for they were more likely than Americans to believe that parental approval was contingent upon achievement. In response to the statement "The *only* time I get any praise or reward from my parents is when I do a job well," 40 per cent of the Brazilians answered "strongly agree" as compared with 15 per cent of the Americans. Again, when asked to react to the statement "If I were the smartest kid in my school, my parents would like me better than they do," 49 per cent of the Brazilians said "strongly agree," while only 10 per cent of the Americans gave the same response.

Believing that he is not accepted for himself, the boy feels rejected. "My father," he says, "acts as though I were in the way" ("always or almost always," Brazilians, 23 per cent; Americans, 9 per cent). "His mother," he says ruefully, "doesn't say much about the good things I do, but she is always talking about the bad things" ("strongly agree," Brazilians, 20 per cent; Americans, 9 per cent). It is perhaps understandable therefore that he is inclined to agree strongly with the statement "My parents don't understand my problems" (Brazilians, 27 per cent; Americans, 4 per cent), or that he says "I'm not appreciated at home the way I deserve" ("strongly agree," Brazilians, 28 per cent; Americans, 6 per cent).

The boy's perception of his parents as deeply interested in his success and having high aspirations for, and evaluations of, him is not in itself detrimental to the development of achievement motivation. On the contrary, this perception should be a positive factor, *provided it is accompanied by actual training in standards of excellence, self-reliance, and autonomy.* Brazilian parents, however, tend to be excessively protective and overindulgent. Children who are reared in this fashion may develop exaggerated self-evaluations and expectations whose frustration could generate feelings of being excessively pressured and rejected. A boy in this situation will often lose interest in the actual working process of competition and achievement, although he may continue to fantasize about success. Indeed, the data show that boys who perceive their parents as "expecting them to be on top" and "important," who report that rewards are contingent on

achievement and who feel rejected do, in fact, tend to have low achievement motivation.

Clearly this process of ego inflation and consequent perceptual distortion does not apply to everyone. Not every boy in Brazil is overindulged, not every boy feels excessively pressured or rejected. In fact, the data show that only a minority feel this way. Nor do we regard this process as the determining variable in the development of achievement motivation. Rather, we believe it to be only one factor—albeit a significant one—responsible for the markedly low achievement motivation in Brazil. Let us now turn to an examination of the data, obtained through a Thematic Apperception Test, on achievement motivation in Brazil and the United States.

Achievement Motivation and Nationality

Given the relatively weak emphasis which Brazilian parents place upon independence and achievement training, we expected to find that Brazilian boys, on the average, were lower on achievement motivation than their American peers. This is, indeed, what an analysis of the fantasy stimulated by four pictures shown to Brazilian and American boys revealed. The data in Table 1 show that the mean score (6.5) for American boys in sample "B" is more than twice as large as the score (2.5) for Brazilians—the statistical difference between these two means is highly significant ($P < .001$). The findings for sample "A," not shown here, . . . are comparable to those reported for sample "B."[11]

---

[11] David C. McClelland reports a similar finding in a study of upper-class Brazilian adolescents, approximately sixteen years of age, in the city of São Paulo. See *The Achieving Society* (Princeton: D. Van Nostrand, Inc., 1961).

TABLE 1   Mean Achievement Motivation Scores by Social Class in Brazil and the United States

Social Class	Brazil	United States
I	2.1	7.0
II	3.9	7.3
III	2.8	7.3
IV	1.9	5.4
V	2.5	4.7
$\bar{X}$	2.5	6.5
N	245	367
Nationality	$F = 70.3$	$P < .001$
Social Class	$F = 2.27$	$P < .08$

* * * * *

Even when social class is controlled, the direction of the difference between Americans and Brazilians remains unchanged: upper-, middle-, and lower-class Americans tend to have higher motivation scores than Brazilians of a comparable class. But what is more startling is the finding that the mean score of American boys in *any social class* is higher than the motivation score of Brazilians, whatever their class may be. That is, not only do upper-, middle- and lower-class American boys have higher mean scores than Brazilian boys of the same social class, *but lower-class American boys have a higher mean score than upper-, middle- or lower-class Brazilian boys.* Thus the mean score for lower-class American boys (Class V) is 4.7, as compared with 2.1 for Class I (upper), 3.9 for Class II (upper-middle), or 1.9 for Class IV (upper-lower) Brazilian boys. Nationality seems to be more important than class in determining achievement motivation, as the analysis of the variance shows.

Conclusion

Not all of our Brazilian subjects are from authoritarian, father-dominated families. But the data indicate that the socialization practices (as reported by the mothers and perceived by their sons) associated with this type of family structure are more often employed by the Brazilian parents in our sample than is the case with the American subjects. Children in an authoritarian, "father-centered" family structure ordinarily receive little training in two areas which are important for the development of achievement motivation: that is, achievement and independence.

The authoritarian father, far from encouraging independence, tends to thwart his son's efforts to be self-reliant and autonomous. The child learns that toward a severely authoritarian father only revolt or submission is possible. And submission, in the form of ingratiation and obedience, is the dominant adjustment to authority in Brazil. But persons who deal with the outer world on the basis of submission do not learn to exercise their manipulative powers, nor are they likely to acquire a sense of responsibility for their own fate. Often the result of this situation is not the development of self-reliance but excessive dependence. Nor is the father in this setting inclined to stress achievement training for his sons. On the contrary, a pronounced concern with a son's achievement in a "father-centered" home may be perceived as a threat to the hegemony of the father. He is not accustomed to sharing the limelight with other members of the family, and may, indeed, regard his son's competitive and achievement-oriented behavior (which normally tends to have some aggressive overtones) as an expression of hostility. Since aggression against the father is perhaps the most heinous sin in the Brazilian family and ordinarily evokes harsh reprisals, children often learn to avoid even the appearance of aggressiveness which competition suggests.

A dominant mother, however, is not necessarily a hindrance to the development of achievement motivation in boys. Indeed, this quality in a mother could be a positive factor for the development of achievement motivation, *provided she is a strong person and does not couple dominance with overprotectiveness.* But we have seen that on both these scores, power and protectiveness, the Brazilian mother in an authoritarian, father-dominated family acts in ways which are detrimental to the development of achievement motivation. As a wife, she is expected to be submissive and deferential. Hence she tends not to interpose herself between father and son to provide the boy with more autonomy, another model, other values and directions. As a mother, she is authoritarian; moreover, she tends to be excessively protective and indulgent. An overprotective, "helpful" mother who is constantly doing things for her son tends to keep him from developing the skills necessary for mastering a task on his own. Her high levels of involvement, protectiveness, and nurturance—when not associated with a commensurate degree of autonomy for the child—will be experienced as just another form of maternal domination. Her excessive indulgence, when combined with a certain discontinuity in socialization, may generate a process of ego inflation and perceptual distortion which is ultimately inimical to the development of achievement motivation.

Doubtless, other factors and other aspects of family structure besides those examined here affect the development of achievement motivation in Brazil. Extreme poverty, the rigidity and hierarchical nature of the social system, marriage instability in the lower classes, even disease—all may play a role in the origins of the individual's need to excel. Clearly, further research is indicated. Nonetheless, the combination of authoritarianism, excessive protectiveness, and early indulgence which boys experience in a type of structure very common in Brazil—the authoritarian, father-dominated family—must be considered as partly responsible for the finding that Brazilian boys, on the average, have markedly low achievement motivation when compared with their American peers.

family
and larger
kin
groups

extended kin networks in the united states

twenty-three

One of the myths about the United States family of the past is that it was a large, extended unit living under one roof. A nearly as common myth is that the urban family is entirely independent of its kin network. A mass of research has accumulated over the past fifteen years to prove that, in spite of ideals of independence, most families actually exchange services and help, advice and persuasion, with a wide range of kin. These ties of kinship are not so formalized as in primitive societies, since we have no clans or lineages. Moreover, exactly what obligations and rights go with which kin positions is not known. The reader may compare the findings in this article with his own experience, and contrast them with those from other societies in subsequent sections of this volume.

Kin Family Network: Unheralded Structure in Current Conceptualizations of Family Functioning

MARVIN B. SUSSMAN

LEE BURCHINAL

* * * * *

The major purpose of this paper is to reduce the lag between family theory

Marvin B. Sussman and Lee Burchinal, "Kin Family Network: Unheralded Structure in Current Conceptualizations of Family Functioning," *Marriage and Family Living*, **24** (August, 1962), 231, 235-240. We are grateful to the authors, *Journal of Marriage and the Family*, and the National Council on Family Relations for permission to quote.

and research insofar as it concerns the functioning of the American kin family network and its matrix of help and service among kin members.

* * * * *

One assumption of the isolated nuclear family conceptualization is that the small nuclear family came into existence in Western Europe and the United States as a consequence of the urban-industrial revolution. Furthermore, its small size is ideally suited for meeting requirements of an industrial society for a mobile work force. The effect of the urban-industrial revolution is to produce a small-sized family unit to replace the large rural one. This assumption can be challenged. A study of different societies reveals that industrialization and urbanization can occur with or without the small nuclear family.[1]

If household size reflects in any way the structure and characteristics of the joint extended family in India, then [few] changes have occurred in this system during the period of industrialization in India from 1911 to 1951.[2]

The uprooting of the rural family, the weakening of family ties, and the reshaping of the rural family form into a nuclear type as a consequence of the industrial revolution are disclaimed for one Swiss town in a recent investigation. On the contrary, many fringe rural families were stabilized and further strengthened in their kin ties from earning supplementary income in nearby factories. Able-bodied members obtained work nearby and no longer had to leave the family unit in search of work. Families which moved closer to their place of employment were accommodated in row houses; these units facilitated the living together of large family groups. These findings question the impact of industrialization upon the structure and functioning of the preindustrial family.

It is difficult to determine if the conditions of living during the transition from a rural to an industrial society ended the dominance of the classical extended family and replaced it with a modified kin form, or if it was replaced by the nuclear one. The question is whether the modified extended family has existed since industrialization occurred; is it a recent phenomenon or an emergent urban familism, a departure from the traditional nuclear form; or is it nonexistent? The evidence to support either of these positions is inconclusive. It remains, however, that the family network described variously as "an emergent urban familism" or "modified extended family" exists and functions in the modern community.

The family network and its functions of mutual aid [have] implications for the functioning of other social systems. With the growth of large metropolitan areas and concomitant occupational specialization, there is less need for the individual to leave the village, town, city, or suburb of the urban complex in order to find work according to his training. Large urban areas supply all kinds of specialized educational and occupational training. The individual can remain in the midst of his kin group, work at his specialty, and be the recipient of the advantages or disadvantages preferred by the kin family network. If individuals are intricately involved within a kin family network, will they be influenced by kin leaders and be less amenable to influence by outsiders; will they seek basic gratifications in kin relationships in lieu of the work place or the neighborhood; will they modify drastically current patterns of spending leisure time, thus affecting current leisure forms and social systems?

Empirical evidence from studies by investigations in a variety of disciplines substantiate the notion that the extended kin family carries on multitudinous activities that have implications for the functioning of other social systems of the society. The major activi-

[1] Sidney M. Greenfield, "Industrialization and the Family in Sociological Theory," *American Journal of Sociology*, **67** (November, 1961), 312-322.

[2] Henry Orenstein, "The Recent History of the Extended Family in India," *Social Problems*, **8** (Spring, 1961), 341-350.

ties linking the network are mutual aid and social activities among kin-related families. Significant data have been accumulated on the mutual aid network between parents and their married child's family in a number of separate and independent investigations.[3] The conclusions are:

TABLE 1   Direction of Service Network of Respondent's Family and Related Kin by Major Forms of Help*

| | Direction of Service Network | | | | |
Major Forms of Help and Service	Between Respondent's Family and Related Kin (Per Cent)†	From Respondents to Parents (Per Cent)†	From Respondents to Siblings (Per Cent)†	From Parents to Respondents (Per Cent)†	From Siblings to Respondents (Per Cent)†
Any Form of Help	93.3	56.3	47.6	79.6	44.8
Help During Illness	76.0	47.0	42.0	46.4	39.0
Financial Aid	53.0	14.6	10.3	46.8	6.4
Care of Children	46.8	4.0	29.5	20.5	10.8
Advice (Personal and Business)	31.0	2.0	3.0	26.5	4.5
Valuable Gifts	22.0	3.4	2.3	17.6	3.4

* Marvin B. Sussman, "The Isolated Nuclear Family: Fact or Fiction," *Social Problems*, 6 (Spring, 1959), 338.

† Totals do not add up to 100 per cent because many families received more than one form of help or service.

1. Help patterns take many forms, including the exchange of services, gifts, advice, and financial assistance. Financial aid patterns may be direct, as in the case of the young married couples Burchinal interviewed, or indirect and subtle, such as the wide range of help patterns observed by Sussman, Sharp, and Axelrod. [See Table 1.]

2. Such help patterns are probably more widespread in the middle- and working-class families and are more integral a feature of family relationships than has been appreciated by students of family behavior. Very few families included in available studies reported neither giving nor receiving aid from relatives. However, these relationships until recently have not been the subject of extensive research.

3. The exchange of aid among families flows in several directions, from parents to children and vice vera, among siblings, and, less frequently, from more distant relatives. However, financial assistance generally appears to flow from parents to children.

4. While there may be a difference in the absolute amount of financial aid received by families of middle- and working-class status, there are insignificant differences in the proportion of families in these two strata who report receiving, giving, or exchanging economic assistance in some form.

5. Financial aid is received most commonly during the early years of married life. Parents are probably more likely to support financially "approved" than "disapproved" ones, such as elopements, interfaith, and interracial marriages. Support can be disguised in the form of substantial sums of money or valuable gifts given at the time of marriage, at the time of the birth of children, and continuing gifts at Christmas, anniversaries, or birthdays. High rates of parental support are probably associated with marriages of children while they are still in a dependency status;

[3] Marvin B. Sussman, "The Help Pattern in the Middle Class Family," *American Sociological Review*, 18 (February, 1953), 22-28.

those among high school or college students are examples.

6. Research data are inadequate for assessing the effects of parental aid on family continuity and the marital relations of the couple receiving aid. Few studies report associations between the form and amount of aid given with the parents' motivations for providing aid. Additional studies on these points are necessary before the implications of aid to married children can be better known.

Social activities are principal functions of the kin family network. The major forms are interfamily visitation, participation together in recreational activities, and ceremonial behavior significant to family unity. Major research findings are:

1. Disintegration of the extended family in urban areas because of lack of contact is unsupported, and often the contrary situation is found. The difficulty in developing satisfactory primary relationships outside of the family in urban areas makes the extended family *more important* to the individual.

2. Extended family get-togethers and joint recreational activities with kin dominate the leisure time pursuits of urban working class members.

3. Kinship visiting is a primary activity of urban dwelling and outranks visitation patterns found for friends, neighbors, or coworkers.

4. Among urban middle classes there is an almost universal desire to have interaction with extended kin, but distance among independent nuclear related units is a limiting factor.

5. The family network extends between generational ties of conjugal units. Some structures are identified as sibling bonds, "occasional kin groups," family circles, and cousin clubs. These structures perform important recreational, ceremonial, mutual aid, and often economic functions.

Services performed regularly throughout the year or on occasions are additional functions of the family network. The findings from empirical studies are:

1. Shopping, escorting, care of children, advice giving and counselling, cooperating with social agencies on counselling and welfare problems of family members are types of day-to-day activities performed by members of the kin network.

2. Services to old persons, such as physical care, providing shelter, escorting, shopping, performing household tasks, sharing of leisure time, and so on are expected and practiced roles of children and other kin members. These acts of filial and kin responsibility are performed voluntarily without law or compulsion.

3. Families or individual members on the move are serviced by units of the family network. Services range from supplying motel type accommodations for vacationing kin passing through town to scouting for homes and jobs for kin, and in providing supportive functions during the period of in-migration and transition from rural to the urban pattern of living.

4. Services on occasions would include those performed at weddings or during periods of crisis, death, accident, disaster, and personal trouble of family members. A sense of moral obligation to give service or acknowledgement of one's kin appropriate to the occasion is found among kin members. The turning to kin when in trouble before using other agencies established for such purposes is the mode rather than the exception.

5. General supportive behavior from members of the kin family network facilitate[s] achievement and maintenance of family and community status. Supportive behavior of kin appears to be instrumental in affecting fertility

rates among component family members.

A convergence of many of these findings occurs in the work of Eugene Litwak. In an extensive study of a middle-class population, Litwak tests several hypotheses on the functional properties of the isolated nuclear family for an industrial society: (a) occupational mobility is antithetical to extended family relations; (b) extended family relations are impossible because of geographical mobility. His findings summarized briefly are: (1) The extended kin family as a structure exists in modern urban society at least among middle-class families; (2) Extended family relations are possible in urban industrial society; (3) Geographical propinquity is an unnecessary condition for these relationships; (4) Occupational mobility is unhindered by the activities of the extended family; such activities as advice, financial assistance, temporary housing, and the like provide aid during such movement; and (5) The classical extended family of rural society or its ethnic counterpart [is] unsuited for modern society, the isolated nuclear family is not the most functional type, the most functional being a modified extended kin family.[4]

Conclusions

There exists an American kin family system with complicated matrices of aid and service activities which link together the component units into a functioning network. The network identified by Litwak as extended family relations is composed of nuclear units related by blood and affinal ties. Relations extend along generational lines and bilaterally where structures take the form of sibling bonds and ambilineages, i.e., the family circle or cousin club.

As a consequence of limited historical work and particularistic developments in theory and research in sociology, there is uncertainty concerning the impact of industrialization upon the structure and function of the pre-industrial family. Was the extended classical type found in rural society replaced by a nuclear one, or did it evolve into the modified kin form described in this paper? It is suggested that the notion of the isolated nuclear family stems from theories and research on immigrant groups coming into the city to work during the period of urbanization in Western society. Anomie in family behavior resulted from individual and institutional failure to make appropriate adjustments required by this migration. The coldness and indifference of the workplace and the city as a steel and concrete bastion contributed to a feeling of aloneness and isolation. The basic concern of the in-migrant was survival in an unknown manmade jungle. Survival was related to dependence upon small family units. These could make quicker and more complete adjustments to the new ways of urban life. The ethos of a competitive and expanding industrial society supported the flexibility of movement now possible by an atomistic unit. Every man is for himself, every man should be unencumbered by ties that will hinder his economic or social progress, and every man should seize opportunities to better himself. One assumption of this position is that early urban man had little time for concern or activity with kinsmen. A more logical assumption is that isolation, a depressive workplace, and uncertainty produced greater reliance upon kin.

[4] Eugene Litwak, "The Use of Extended Family Groups in the Achievement of Social Goals: Some Policy Implications," *Social Problems*, **7** (Winter, 1959-60), 177-187; "Occupational Mobility and Extended Family Cohesion," *American Sociological Review*, **25** (February, 1960). "Geographical Mobility and Family Cohesion," *American Sociological Review*, **25** (June, 1960).

Once new immigrants became established in the city, they served as informants, innkeepers, and providers for later kin arrivals. Once these followers arrived, the kin family network then functioned most effectively to protect and acculturate their members into urban ways.

Major activities of this network are that members give to each other financial aid and good[s] of value and a wide range of services at specific times and under certain conditions. The aid and service provided within the network supplement rather than displace the basic activities of nuclear family units. Kinship behavior assists more than negates the achievement of status and occupational advance of component families and their members.

The main flow of financial aid is along generational lines, from parents to young married children and from middle-aged parents to aged parents. Such aid is not restricted to emergencies but may be given at various occasions, such as support for education, to start a family, at time of marriage, to begin a career, and the like.

The network is used among middle-class families as a principal source of aid and service when member families or individuals are in personal difficulty, in times of disaster and crisis, and on ceremonial occasions. There are some indications that established working-class families are following the same pattern. Some situations cannot be handled by the nuclear unit alone, e.g., destruction of the family home by a tornado; while other situations involve more than one nuclear family or individual member, e.g., the death of an aging parent. In such situations these are mutual expectations of going to the aid of kin. Aid is sought from the most immediate kin chiefly along sibling or generational lines. Then it is followed by help from more distant kin.

In many instances everyday or weekly activities link together the members of the kin family network. Joint participation in leisure time activities are possible because of reduction of the work week. Visiting among kin is facilitated by high speed highways and other conveyances of a modern transportation system. Constant communication among kin members is possible by the widespread adoption on all class levels of the telephone as a household necessity.

The feasibility of the kin network in modern society is due to the existence of modern communication and transportation systems, which facilitate interaction among members; a bureaucratic industrial structure suited to modern society, which removes the responsibility for job placement from the network [but] will still permit the network to concentrate on activities intended to aid the social and economic achievement of network members; and expansion of metropolitan areas, in which individuals can obtain educational, occupational, and status objectives without leaving their kin area. Kin members can live some distance from each other within the metropolitan area and still have relationships within the network. Nuclear units function autonomously. Decisions on what and when to act are responsibilities of the nuclear family. Influence may be exerted by the kin group upon the nuclear units, so that the latter may make the "right" decision. However, the kin group seldom directs the decision or action of the nuclear family in a given situation. Immunity from such control is guaranteed by legal and cultural norms which reaffirm the right and accountability of the nuclear family in such situations. The role of the family kin network is supportive rather than coercive in its relationship with the nuclear family.

* * * * *

extended kin in an arab village

twenty-four

In this analysis of the marital and extended kin ties in a Muslim village in Lebanon, note that the household is not a large, complex group of relatives, but the lineage ties with the smaller family unit are stronger and more formalized than United States kin ties. In turn, these Arab patterns now surviving in village life are less specific obligations and rights than once were reported in classic descriptions of Arab Bedouin life.

The World of Kin in Lebanon

ANNE H. FULLER

Kinship, marriage, sex—these are related topics of conversation with which the peasants of Buarij are continually occupied. The division of humankind into male and female is by ordinance of God. The Koran contains injunctions on marriage, incest regulations, and duties of children to parents. The emphasis on bonds of blood and the habit of close kin marriage, particularly on the paternal side, are a part of Muslim tradition.

The small child is called a "bridegroom" or "bride" as a term of endearment. Young unmarried girls confide that they are continually preoccupied

Anne H. Fuller, *Buarij: Portrait of a Lebanese Muslim Village*, *Harvard Middle Eastern Monograph Series*, No. 6 (Cambridge, Mass.: Harvard University Press, 1961), pp. 60-65, 69-70. Distributed for the Center for Middle Eastern Studies, Harvard University. Copyright 1961 by the President and Fellows of Harvard College.

with the thought of their marriage day and the delights of love. Youths, working or waiting for the bride price, grow impatient, and the village wit among them cries "May it rain brides from heaven and each one bring with her her bedding!"

But back of, and beyond, this individual preoccupation with sex and marriage is the deep sentiment that the blood line and lineage must continue. As lineage extends backward into time, so it must continue forward into time. It is in a sense greater than the individual, and within it the individual must play his prescribed role.

The blood bond is the significant kinship factor. The closer the blood ties, the greater the sense of identity between persons, since they partake most closely of the same essence. Blood, moreover, is conceived of as possessing a peculiar import of its own. It is a basic life property. When a new house is completed, a cock is slaughtered, its blood dripping over the threshold. Thus the welfare and longevity of the house are assured. At the time of the sheep slaughter, the blood from the animals' throats is poured over household herbs and flowers. Blood is a fertilizer, promoting life. At the time of the spring festival, girls stain their heels and hands with henna, a substitute for blood and a sign of the renewal of all life. Blood may become contaminated and unclean. Its flow cleanses the body of impurities. Menstrual blood performs this function. Leeching and cupping are means of draining the body of the polluted flow which, left to itself, can cause illness.

The concept of blood as an essence of life relates to lineage. Blood is extended through inheritance. As a life property it finds new embodiment through successive generations. The male is its chief vehicle and transmitter, just as the male is the dominant sex within Muslim society. Women's blood by reason of menstruation cannot possess the same purity of essence or the same life force.

Blood and land ownership intersect, reinforcing one another. For the peasants of Buarij count their respective lineages from the first male ancestor who came to the mountain side, while previous genealogy is lost track of except for hazy outlines. The present owners of land are not only the descendants of these ancestors, but own and work the land in accordance with close blood ties. As the peasants conceive of themselves as stewards of the land, passing it on from generation to generation, so they conceive of themselves as links in a blood chain, passing on its essence as well from one generation to another.

The village clans or paternal lineages derived through blood from a common male ancestor may, as has been seen, possess certain properties in common, such as threshing floors, communal ovens, or a segment of the village cemetery. It is not these properties, however, that the clan regard as their most important asset, but rather the living strength of the clan in terms of total male members and the sum total of land owned by clan members. These two attributes, combined with the past glory of clan ancestors, give a lineage its feeling of importance. The largest clan with the greatest number of adult male members tends to hold the greatest influence in the village, despite the rule that important village offices rotate from clan to clan. Conversely, the smallest clan tends to have least influence.

The importance of the clan to the individual lies in its protective powers. It is the body to which the individual may turn for aid in times of crisis, insult, or injury. It is of greater protective value to the peasant than lesser kin units, since it possesses the largest numerical strength. Injury to a clan member by a nonvillage member or by a member of another clan immediately rallies all clan members together in common concern for a member of the common blood line. A sense of pride and loyalty centers about the clan name, wherein the common pool of blood is identified with a common emotion.

The clan has more meaning for men than for women. This is not only because men are the vehicles through which the blood line is transmitted, but because clan strength is considered in terms of male fighting strength. For this reason the clan with the greatest number of adult males feels an innate strength over the lesser clans of the village.

Women, in contrast, if they have made an interclan marriage, have ambivalent feelings toward the clan. Throughout their lifetime they are considered to be a member of the clan into which they were born, but by marriage into another clan they bear children belonging to the clan of their husband. Thus their allegiance is less well defined and finds orientation in terms of the circumstances with which they are faced. For their own individual welfare they look toward members of their own clan, or more particularly its lesser units —to close paternal kin or to father and brother. For their children's welfare, however, they look to the lineage of which their children are a part.

The cliques formed by village youths often fall into clan patterns, the young unmarried men carrying on banter and verbal rivalry in terms of clan membership. Evening parties during the winter include largely clan members. Engagements, weddings, and funerals always include a full quota of clansmen, though others may be invited as well. The smallness of the village, combined with the linking of clans through marriage, tends to diminish an extreme sense of the clan as a separate entity. Nevertheless, all villagers retain a strong sense of the clan to which they belong, are aware that it is a protective body, and are concerned with preserving its honor and good name.

The clan is composed of joint families and immediate families. No hard and fast rule can be given for the composition of the joint family nor for its exact functions, despite the important role that it plays. The joint family is primarily an economic group banded together for the better welfare of its members or for the better utilization of land. The joint family may consist of a couple and their children, who share in an economic enterprise with the paternal grandparents. The couple and their children may share a compound house with the grandparents or live near them. Or two or more couples, married brothers with their children, may set up a similar household. Usually a share of the parent's land is turned over to a man at the time of his marriage. Yet it may prove advantageous for married sons and their father to continue working all land in common, each caring for a specific area, but all sharing in the produce. The paternal grandparents may or may not eat from the same common plate as the couple and their children, according to their abilities to care for themselves. The old widow or widower, however, is always absorbed into the household of one of the sons, or moves from son's house to son's house, and is there given care. If there are no sons, the widow or widower is cared for by a married daughter. There is no greater disgrace than to abandon the old.

A number of married sons and their families, especially if living close at hand, may share in the common enterprise of caring for certain of the lands belonging to each. This, however, need not be a permanent arrangement, or more than a seasonal one. The pattern of the joint family and its functions remains at all times fluid. Still there is a great sense among the villagers that close kin may be called upon to band together for mutual aid whenever the occasion demands. This may entail no more than a single enterprise of short duration. Or again it may be a longterm bond between brothers or between fathers and sons who work land in common for a number of years.

The immediate family inhabits a single room or more of a compound house, or possesses its own small dwelling. Its members eat from a common plate. The hard cash they earn from work in the outer world or the share of produce they earn as sharecroppers is theoretically considered a family fund. The produce from the family's lands is also its own, unless the family makes some arrangement by which its members work the lands in common with a larger kin group.

Kinship terms are in the main descriptive, differentiating between paternal and maternal kin and indicating degrees of relationship. Kinship terms are used fictitiously. Men and women, and especially growing boys and girls in the village, address each other as brother and sister, irrespective of relationship. For village men are expected to treat all village women as sisters, observing the proper sexual restraints. Women, in turn, should be able to look on all village men as brothers, with the same regard that they have for their true brothers. Persons, particularly old women, talk much of genealogies, describing or placing an individual within his kin framework. The stranger on entering the community is asked to whom he is related, a known relationship helping to establish his credentials. Gossip and talk of persons in the foothill communities are accompanied by reference to kin. That a person should be devoid of close kin ties is almost impossible for the peasant to imagine. To the orphan or half-orphan there is an attitude of pity, since such a child lacks the closest of kin and therefore the background of family and kinship security.

Degrees of relationship, whether on the paternal or the maternal side, define kin obligations and duties. Children are beholden to their parents and they in turn to them. Paternal uncles stand next to the father as the child's guardian and next in male authority over the child. Paternal first cousins stand next to a girl's brother as protectors within her own generation. This close interrelation of persons on the paternal side involving two generations is an intensification of the sense of paternal lineage contracted into a lesser segment—the offspring of brothers possessing the same paternal grandparents, back of whom are the generations leading back to the ultimate ancestor, who is the focal point from which paternal kin sentiments are derived.

In accordance with the degree of distance of relationship, the same general sentiments are projected to other paternal kin, but in diminishing degree. To the maternal kin, except toward maternal grandparents who because of their age are owed deference, a similar set of general sentiments is shown, although lacking the feeling of deep allegiance and the same demand for reciprocal obligations as found on the paternal side.

The paternal lineage or clan prefers to keep itself free from infiltration of other blood. This finds best expression in the conventional Muslim marriage of first paternal cousins. By this system of marriage, not only is the blood kept the same through both partners' possessing the same paternal grandparents, but also the close allegiance felt between members of the existing generations within the lineage is reinforced and strengthened. In first cousin paternal marriage, kin on both the wife's and the husband's side of the family are of the same degree of relationship, the sentiments directed toward either side of the family therefore being the same and so establishing an equilibrium and balance. Through marriage of first paternal cousins, land and the working of land remain within a close group of persons bound to one another in allegiance. Through first paternal cousin marriage, furthermore, the stability of the marriage itself is better assured, since it is reinforced by the security of close kin bonds and of lands derived from a common source.

Marriages within the village of Buarij are between first paternal cousins (the conventional Muslim marriage), to more distant paternal cousins, to cousins on the maternal side, to individuals of other clans, or to women from outside the village, related or not. Village girls sometimes marry into neighboring communities, usually where attenuated ties of kin already exist. Marriage of first paternal cousins remains the ideal. First paternal cousin families, however, may not possess offspring for suitable pairing in terms of age and sex. The small size of the village, moreover, bringing all persons in contact with one another, tends to diminish the claims of lineage alone and fosters marriage to more distant kin or even between clans. The sum total of intervillage marriages to other than first cousins far outweighs that of marriages to first paternal kin.

* * * * *

Attitudes toward kinship, marriage, and sex relate to the concept of the larger life process, which in the peas-ants' minds must persist above and beyond the individual life of man. The sense of lineage in itself relates to the sense of the continuity of life over and above that of the individual. This sense of a lifeline coincides with that of the continuity and permanence of land since the blood line [was] founded on the first male ancestor who came to the mountainside. Through close ties of kinship, particularly on the paternal side, both the blood line and the land receive greater protection. Land is necessary to life. Life in itself is the essence of creation. By stressing kinship ties, by knitting person to person in a close fabric of mutual obligations, and by preoccupation with marriage and sex, life itself is better assured, sustained, and fortified by land.

extended kin ties in a mexican town

twenty-five

Tepoztlán, a small, ancient town not far from Mexico City, was studied by Robert Redfield a generation ago. Oscar Lewis recently carried out an extensive reinvestigation of its social relations. It must be emphasized that the family patterns described in this section are not Indian, but represent a variation of the family behavior to be found in other Western countries.

The Extended Family in Mexico

OSCAR LEWIS

During the time a married couple lives with the husband's parents, they

Oscar Lewis, *Tepoztlán, Village in Mexico* (New York: Holt, Rinehart & Winston, Inc., 1960), pp. 65-68. Reprinted by permission.

have little contact with the wife's family. When they live alone, ties with the wife's family become closer and often supersede those with the husband's family. In any case, however, the closest kinship tie is with the grandmother, whether on the paternal or the maternal side. The importance of the grandmother, especially as a mother substitute, has already been pointed out.

Aunts, particularly maternal aunts, frequently have an affectionate relationship with nieces and nephews and in emergencies may act as mother substitutes. A boy who has eloped often brings his sweetheart to live with a favorite aunt. Uncles have a respect relationship with their nieces and nephews which may also be an affectionate one. Many children have a favorite uncle who singles them out for an occasional gift or favor. Work exchange between uncles and nephews occurs more often than between married siblings, but quarrels also are apt to occur, particularly over inheritance. After a man's death, a brother will sometimes claim a portion of the property from the widow, especially if her children are still small.

Cousins often have a relationship that resembles that of brother and sister. Parents encourage their children to play with their cousins, especially if they are neighbors; often a person's best and only friends turn out to be one or two favorite cousins. Cousin marriage is forbidden although some cases have occurred.

In-laws

Because of patrilocal residence, the mother-in-law and daughter-in-law relationship is the most important of all in-law relationships. When a young bride goes to live with her husband's family, she is expected to take the role of a grown daughter and give her parents-in-law the same respect and obedience she gave her own parents. The mother-in-law assigns her work . . . ; generally it consists of the most burdensome tasks —grinding corn, making tortillas, and washing and ironing clothes for the entire family. In the past, when girls married at twelve or thirteen, they were unskilled and the mother-in-law taught them housework. The mother-in-law for her part must look after her daughter-in-law when she gives birth and must chaperone the daughter-in-law and see to it that she remains a faithful wife. Many jokes depict the mother-in-law as a "policeman."

Although many mothers-in-law and daughters-in-law manage to get along fairly well, the relationship is a charged one and is recognized as such by Tepoztecans. Both women approach it with apprehension. Girls hear their mothers and other married women say that the daughter-in-law is the mother-in-law's "slave." They are afraid that they will not be able to please their mother-in-law and that they will feel like an outsider in a strange house. The mother-in-law fears that the girl her son brings home will be lazy, just another mouth to feed, or that she will be critical of the way the family lives.

Often the fears are justified, and quarrels are the result. Perhaps this is even more true today than in the past because of the different standards of dress, cleanliness, and personal freedom held by younger and older women. Increasingly, the way out of an unpleasant situation for both is to separate the households. If the wife cannot persuade her husband to move and if her situation becomes intolerable, she returns to her parents' home. It is believed in the village that many marriages have been broken because the mother-in-law and daughter-in-law could not get on together. Father-in-law and daughter-in-law relations are similar to father-daughter relations but even more reserved.

Relations between the wife's parents and their son-in-law depend more on personal factors than on formal obligations, with the exception of the usual respect obligations. In the past, the son-in-law was required to provide his father-in-law with wood and water for two years as part of the bride price. Now any work done by the son-in-law is voluntary and usually is limited to times when the father-in-law is ill or in need. If the mother-in-law is widowed and has property, the son-in-law may help her farm; if she has no means of support, a good son-in-law may help support her or invite her to live in his home.

Tepoztecan men are wary of their mothers-in-law. They think of [them] as meddlesome, trouble-making figure[s] and prefer to keep the relationship a distant one. Actually, most mothers urge their married daughters to try to please their husbands and to bear up under domestic difficulties. Fathers are more apt than mothers to feel a personal affront if their daughter is ill-treated by a son-in-law.

Relations between sisters-in-law and brothers-in-law are not formalized and depend largely on personal factors. Sisters-in-law, whether the wives of two brothers or the husband's wife and sister, are thrown together more often than brothers-in-law. In some families the wives of brothers compete for the esteem of the mother-in-law and carry tales about each other to her. Quarrels over inheritance involve the sisters-in-law as much as the siblings.

Godparents, Godchildren, and Co-parents

The system of *compadrazgo* establishes two sets of formal relationships between nonrelatives: the one is between "spiritual" godparents (*padrinos*) and their godchildren (*ahijados*); the other a relationship known as *compadres*, or co-parents, is between the parents and the godparents. The general purpose of godparents is to provide security for the godchild. The godparents are in effect an additional set of parents

who will act as guardians and sponsors of the godchild, care for him in emergencies, and adopt him if he is orphaned. In Tepoztlán, however, the relationship between *compadres* is much more functional and important than that between the godparent and godchild.

Godparents address their godchildren in the familiar *tu* and are addressed by the respectful *Usted*. Traditionally the godchild kissed the godparent's hand at each meeting, but this is no longer common. The godparent usually gives the child a few centavos when they meet, but many children actually never receive anything from their *padrinos*. *Compadres* address each other with the respectful *Usted*; theirs is a reciprocal respect relationship and in this lies its strength, for such a relationship is highly desirable to Tepoztecans. By respect, Tepoztecans mean a recognition of high and equal status and the avoidance of intimacy or undue familiarity. The latter includes joking and discussing sex or any other subjects of a personal nature. *Compadres* also may not drink together. They do often exchange favors, and borrowing between them is probably more frequent than between kin. At the death of one *compadre*, the other is supposed to contribute toward the funeral expenses. *Compadres* . . . treat each other with special deference. Tepoztecans prefer *compadres* who are neither neighbors nor relatives. . . .

The three most important types of godparents in Tepoztlán are those of baptism, confirmation, and marriage. Reliable persons are sought as godparents of baptism. The husband's parents usually select the godparents of baptism for the first child, but as the couple grows older, the husband may make the selection, and often friendship rather than higher economic status dictates his choice. The godparents of baptism are obliged to assist at the baptism, to buy the infant's clothing for the occasion, and to pay the priest's fee. They also accompany the mother and child to the *sacramisa*, or first Mass, forty days after the birth. If the child dies, the godparents arrange for the wake, dress the body for burial, and contribute to the funeral expenses. An important obligation of godparents is to urge their *compadres* to send the child to school when the time comes. If the child needs punishing, the parents may ask the godparents to scold him. The godparents of confirmation are usually selected by the godparents of baptism; occasionally the latter accept both roles. The godparents of marriage assist at the wedding and act as mediators if the couple later quarrels or separates.

One of the distinctive aspects of the *compadre* system in the village, and in fact in Mexico as a whole, is the way in which it has been extended far beyond the original Catholic forms. In most of Spain, only two or three types of godparents, popularly those of baptism, communion, and confirmation, are known. In Tepoztlán, in addition to the three above, there are the following: godparents of *miscotón* (a Nahuatl term which refers to a small sweater which the godparent puts on the child to protect him from illness), of *medida* or *listón* (these terms refer to a small piece of ribbon, blessed by the priest, which is placed on a sick child as a charm), of *evangelio* (a woman of "bad" reputation is asked to become godmother to a sick child and to pray in the church for his recovery), of *scapulary*, of the Child Jesus, and so on. The godparent system has been extended to secular activities as well. At soccer and basketball games, each team has its godmother, who dresses in white, carries flowers, acts as the sponsor, and hands out prizes to the winners. At social dances, godmothers act as chaperones.

Social, economic, and political factors may enter into the operation of the *compadre* system. Poor families look for better-to-do godparents for their children. Similarly, it is thought desirable to have a *compadre* from the city, for it is assumed that a city family can be of greater help in time of need. The more godchildren a man has, the more *compadres* and the wider circle of persons who can be counted on for favors. For this reason, anyone who aspires to a position of leadership in the village must have many godchildren. There is some feeling against using the *compadre* system in this fashion, however, and some villagers consider having many *compadres* as a burden. In this case, they try to limit their *compadre* relations by asking one or two families to serve as godparents for several children.

Part 8

interplay
between familial
and other
role
behavior

moving the young man into the larger society

twenty-six

The following study is an example of an increasingly frequent type of inquiry, the test of a hypothesis by the use of cross-cultural data. Note the problems of classifying societies and family systems. Attempt also to evaluate the two conflicting hypotheses in light of the data. Is a further alternative hypothesis possible? What additional data would be necessary to demonstrate rigorously the consequences of such male initiation ceremonies?

The Function of Male Initiation Ceremonies: A Cross-Cultural Test of an Alternative Hypothesis

FRANK W. YOUNG

*   *   *   *   *

Many "culture and personality" studies depend on theories which characterize personality as a system of intervening variables or mechanisms by which one aspect of culture—usually child-training practices—influences another aspect, such as religious beliefs or particular institutions. Although this view has been criticized and contradictory evidence on some points has been published, it has been difficult to put the theory to a decisive test because so

Frank W. Young, "The Function of Male Initiation Ceremonies: A Cross-Cultural Test of an Alternative Hypothesis," *American Journal of Sociology*, **67** (January, 1962), pp. 379-385, 391. Reprinted by permission of The University of Chicago Press. Copyright 1962 by The University of Chicago Press.

much of its support is in the form of clinical or anthropological evidence that cannot be replicated. There is need for a test which differentiates between a Freudian hypothesis and an alternative, and which, in turn, rejects one but not the other under conditions that are rigidly controlled.

The opportunity for such a test is provided by the appearance of a study by John W. M. Whiting, Richard Kluckhohn, and Albert Anthony, in which they test on a sample of fifty-six societies a hypothesis that links certain childhood situations to the presence of male initiation rites.[1] They assert that when the infant sleeps on its mother's bed for a year or more, strong feelings of dependency develop. Similarly, if there is a postnatal taboo of a year or more on the mother's sex relations, when the husband finally returns to his wife the displacement of the dependent boy from his mother's close care generates deep hostility. Both these emotions may become disruptive to society when the boy matures. Adolescence is a particularly dangerous period, because at that age the boy is called upon to participate in men's work, independent of his mother's support. At this age he also handles weapons. Since all societies must maintain social control of disruptive behavior, an institutional mechanism of control is functionally necessary. The initiation ceremonies of primitive peoples may be . . . interpreted as such a mechanism. Hazing and genital operations assert the authority of men over the adolescent boy; the separation of boys from women and submission to tests of fortitude break the boys' psychological dependency. A demonstrable association exists between the four initiation customs and the two child-training practices.

It is clear that the foregoing "disruptive emotion" hypothesis follows the classic Freudian framework of impulsive man assailed by a frustrating culture. Although Whiting [and his associates] reject a specific Oedipal explanation, their modification is still in the Freudian tradition, and the many general criticisms that have been made of that framework still apply. For instance, it is assumed that the emotions generated in childhood somehow maintain themselves until adolescence, despite the great variety of experience[s] between the two periods. It is further assumed that the two- or three-year-old boy is capable of the complex emotions and perceptions that are postulated by the theory; that is, when the father returns, the displaced boy is able to infer that the father is to blame, even though it was the mother who allowed the father to return. Third, it is assumed that initiation ceremonies are primarily inhibitory and that this function is almost completely determined by the peculiar patterning of two small aspects of family organization.

Before introducing an alternative explanation based on symbolic interaction theory, it should be acknowledged that Whiting has already abandoned the disruptive emotion hypothesis (a shift that became known to the author after the termination of the study reported here) and has substituted what may be called a "sex-role conflict" hypothesis. The latter explanation of the empirical association between initiation ceremonies and child care employs some concept of identification, namely: "the process of identification consists of the covert practice of the role of an envied status. In learning-theory terms, identification consists (1) of learning a role by rehearsal in fantasy or in play rather than by actual performances, and (2)

---

[1] "The Function of Male Initiation Ceremonies at Puberty," in E. Maccoby, T. M. Newcomb, and E. L. Hartley (eds.), *Readings in Social Psychology* (New York: Holt, Rinehart & Winston, Inc., 1958), pp. 359-370.

such rehearsal is motivated by envy of the incumbent of a privileged status."[2] The initiation ceremony is now interpreted as an institution which resolves a cross-sex identification. The child having a close sleeping relation with his mother (the postnatal taboo is disregarded in the second interpretation) comes to envy her status, which in turn leads to a feminine identification. If he lives in a society where the rule of residence is patrilocal, however, at five or six years of age he perceives that men have the enviable status, which leads him to a male identification. The resulting conflict must be resolved with the help of a social institution.

* * * * *

An Alternative Formulation

According to the symbolic interaction explanation, the function of initiation is to stabilize the boy's sex role at a time when it is particularly problematical, although not in the manner suggested by Whiting. Thus one's sex role becomes problematical insofar as its definition does not provide sufficient guidance in the diverse social interactions allowed or prescribed by society. Inasmuch as societies have a sexual division of labor and some form of marriage, a well-defined sex role becomes functionally necessary when the boy nears the threshold of participation in such social patterning. However, some societies pose still another socialization problem, which is that sex role must conform to more specific requirements imposed by a high degree of male solidarity. Such solidarity may be defined as the cooperation of the men in maintaining a definition of their situation as

---

[2] Roger V. Burton and John W. M. Whiting, "The Absent Father: Effects on the Developing Child," paper read at the 1960 meeting of the American Psychological Association.

one which is not only different from that of women, but which involves organized activities requiring the loyalty of all males. Although solidarity is a matter of degree, a crucial threshold develops when the men of a village come to see themselves as a consciously organized group with the power to exclude or discipline its membership. . . .

In societies with a high degree of male solidarity, stabilization of sex role is not complete until the boy identifies with the male group, since such identification is a major component of the sex role. Identification is here defined as the process of taking as one's own the cluster of social meanings held by a person or group. Identification requires first that the identifier have sufficient skill in symbolic interaction (usually not acquired until early adolescence) to comprehend the symbolic environment and, second, that he recognize that his society requires him to learn certain specific clusters of social meanings, such as those involved in one's sex role. Strength of identification is determined by the degree to which the identifier cooperates in creating and maintaining the definition of the situation and by the degree of clarity given the social meanings by the group or person generating them.

Given the foregoing assumptions, it might appear that identification with a solidary male group is easy compared to learning the relatively vague attitudes required for participation in work and the family, and hence that initiation ceremonies should be unnecessary for the more organized male structure. But the relative clarity of meanings held by the cohesive males is not apparent to the candidate. Typically, the male activities are hidden from the uninitiated. Moreover, once the meanings of the male group are accessible, internalization must be achieved rapidly and precisely. There is no long period of inculcation by way of games, sharing in sex-segregated work, or the differentiated expectations of others. Neither is there the allowable deviation that occurs in most family and work organization. Therefore the social meaning of male solidarity must be dramatized in a memorable way, and the candidate must participate intensely in the presentation. Furthermore, the rest of the community must be alerted to his new status so they can respond appropriately. What could be more impressive to both the youth and the community than to be publicly subincised or to be the center of attention of a group of village men intent upon beating him severely? It is a mistake to interpret initiation ceremonies in terms of culture-bound notions of pain or mutilation. The ethnographic accounts strongly suggest that, given the proper attitude, these are probably accepted with the same equanimity that a woman submits to beauty care or a man to being tattooed. Similarly, tests of fortitude and social separation (the ethnographic accounts give no basis for Whiting's phrase "separation from women") are another way of dramatizing the boy's new status. Not only does he give a performance to the community, but his separation before or after the performance reminds the community by his absence of his new presence.

The solidarity hypothesis may be empirically tested by cross tabulation of the child-training items and initiation ceremonies when male solidarity is controlled. Although this hypothesis ultimately requires a recoding of both the child-training items and Whiting's empirical definition of initiation rites, they are adequate for the present test. The only new factor, then, is male solidarity. Empirically it is defined by the pres-

TABLE 1   Relation of Male Initiation Ceremonies to Exclusive Mother-Son Sleeping Arrangement and Postnatal Taboo When Presence of Exclusive Male Organization Is Controlled

Exclusive Male Organization	Mother-Son Sleeping	Postnatal Taboo	Number of Societies Having at Least One of Four Initiation Customs*	
			Present	Absent
Present	+	+	11	1
	+	−	1	1
	−	+	2	0
	−	−	2	0
			16	2
Absent	+	+	3	4
	+	−	0	2
	−	+	1	4
	−	−	0	22
			4	32

* Genital operations, hazing, seclusion from women, and tests of manliness.

ence of an organization in which all adult males are expected to participate and from which women are excluded. The organization must be institutionalized to the point of having its own building or a taboo that protects open meetings from the perception of women or uninitiated boys. The definition includes the cases of the Hopi and Dahomeans, where there are a number of male organizations of essentially the same type. It is assumed that such re-duplication occurs in larger communities simply as an adaptation to the larger population. When the organizations develop differentiated purposes, they do not qualify.

The cross tabulation of these three factors is shown in Table 1 and follows the format of the Whiting . . . article. It is clear that when male solidarity is controlled, no relation remains between the typology of child-care items and the presence of initiation ceremonies.

* * * * *

A Reconceptualization of Initiation Ceremonies

The cross tabulation in Table 1 shows that when male solidarity is controlled, the association between the child-care items and initiation ceremonies is dissolved. But the indicators of the initial association were based on the rejected hypothesis. It remains now to reconceptualize both of these in terms of the new framework and to show that male solidarity is an even stronger determinant when these variables are re-coded.

The solidarity hypothesis would define initiation ceremonies as the more dramatic forms of sex-role recognition. So conceived, initiation ceremonies involve a patterned performance designed to convey a particular impression to an audience. Such dramatization of sex role takes a variety of forms, combining particular customs, like tattooing, tooth filing, beatings, fasting, special taboos, social isolation, gifts, dances, participation in raids, circumcision, subincision, and so on, in ways that have always attracted the attention of anthropologists. Examples of undramatic sex-role recognition are the informal delineation that results from differentiated

subsistence activities among Koryak men and women, the adolescent boy's shift of residence to a youth camp among the Nyakyusa, and the formal-ized—but undramatic—coeducation in our own society. However, not all customs of the adolescent period are relevant to the social recognition of sex role, and the following rules delineate the limits: (1) the custom must occur periodically in the same general form and be supervised at least in part by the adults of the society, (2) it must apply to all adolescent males and only to these—ceremonies including females do not qualify, and (3) of a series of initiation ceremonies, only the most elaborate, as measured by the scale, is to be coded. Such rules would exclude the tooth filing among children in Alor, the festivities surrounding the young men in wartime Japan who went into the military, the unpatterned hazing of Maori warrior novices, and the marriage-initiation pattern of the Khalapur Rajputs. . . . One major implication of these operational rules is the rejection of the view that initiation marks the attainment of full adult status. There is of course an intimate connection between sex role and responsible adulthood, and in a few societies the recognition of the two statuses merges. But in the large majority, consensual validation of responsible adult status is withheld by prohibitions on marriage, speaking in councils, full participation in warfare, and so on until late adolescence.

* * * * *

In the picture of society suggested above there is little that is new. The novelty lies in the application of this conceptual framework to the phenomena of initiation. Male solidarity has . . . been defined as the consensus of the men regarding the purpose and activities of the group. Although the present study does not directly index these shared meanings, the ethnographic accounts strongly suggest that definite religious, military, and fraternal attitudes exist and are expressed in the ritual activity, regalia, and mythology. These meanings must be maintained by adults inasmuch as, quite aside from the taboos barring the uninitiated, children cannot comprehend these meanings fully until after early adolescence. Granted that games, observation, and conversation serve as an introduction to adult symbolic structures, the inculcation of these is weak and partial. Certainly this line of thought would reject the unconscious learning asserted by the Freudians to occur during the first several years of life.

Initiation ceremonies are viewed as a mechanism for maintaining the consensus of the males. If the boys did not undergo initiation or if some were allowed to avoid it, the male definition of the situation might be distorted or weakened. It is for this reason that initiation is required of all boys in a community. The ceremony insures conformity by involving the candidate in an intense cooperation with men in the symbolic process. Initiation is the first and perhaps most memorable step in a continued participation in an organized symbolic structure. So long as a man participates in it, the social meanings he has internalized remain strong and he plays his sex role with confidence in diverse situations. The rituals themselves only remind him of what it means to be a man in his society; in themselves they contain no meaning. On this view circumcision ·is not different in kind from a gift, a new name, a dance, and so forth. It differs in degree only insofar as its acquisition has a more dramatic and emotional context. Thus almost anything can figure in the initiation ceremony. The sound of a bull roarer or some test of endurance have an intrinsic dramatic quality. Lacking such, the effect may be heightened by hiring a specialist to direct the ceremony or by encouraging the women to wail.

An initial implication of this conception of initiation ceremonies is that empirical work on ritual must allow for the wide variety of symbolic contents; it may not be limited to particular customs. More generally, it suggests that other rituals might profitably be viewed in terms of a dramaturgical framework. The essence of this approach, it should be noted, is the analysis of the function of rituals for groups, not individuals.

the breakdown of a society into separate family units

twenty-seven

Some studies have hinted (note the section by Goode on illegitimacy) that a population may be classed as a nation or province, but be only little integrated, have little sense of solidarity. Here is a brief section from a study of a village in southern Italy, long noted as a region of poverty, lack of loyalty to the nation, and disobedience to the law. The author suggests that, in effect, everyone looks out for his own little family unit and gives as little as he can to any larger collectivity (school, church, kin network, state). Note that the family unit itself may continue to function, but that its exchanges with other social units are curtailed to its own ultimate disadvantage.

A Predictive Hypothesis

EDWARD C. BANFIELD

A very simple hypothesis will make intelligible all of the behavior about which questions have been raised and will enable an observer to predict how the Montegranesi will act in concrete circumstances. The hypothesis is that the Montegranesi act as if they were following this rule: "Maximize the material, short-run advantage of the nuclear family; assume that all others will do likewise."

One whose behavior is consistent with this rule will be called an "amoral familist." The term is awkward and somewhat imprecise (one who follows the rule is without morality only in relation to persons outside the family—in relation to family members, he applies standards of right and wrong; one who has no family is of course an "amoral individualist"), but no other term seems better.

. . . It will be seen that some logical implications of [this] rule describe the facts of behavior in the Montegrano district. The coincidence of facts and theory does not "prove" the theory. However, it does show that the theory will explain (in the sense of making in-

Edward C. Banfield, *The Moral Basis of a Backward Society* (New York: The Free Press of Glencoe, Inc., 1958), pp. 85-90. Copyright 1958 by The Free Press, a corporation. Reprinted with permission of the publisher.

telligible and predictable) much behavior without being contradicted by any of the facts at hand.

1. *In a society of amoral familists, no one will further the interest of the group or community except as it is to his private advantage to do so.* In other words, the hope of material gain in the short run will be the only motive for concern with public affairs.

This principle is of course consistent with the entire absence of civic improvement associations, organized charities, and leading citizens who take initiative in public service.

A teacher who is a member of a leading family explained:

I have always kept myself aloof from public questions, especially political ones. I think that all the parties are identical and those who belong to them—whether Communist, Christian Democrat, or other—are men who seek their own welfare and well-being. And then too, if you want to belong to one party, you are certain to be on the outs with the people of the other party.

Giovanni Gola, a merchant of upper-class origins, has never been a member of a political party because "it isn't convenient for me—I might lose some business."

Gola does not think of running for office because:

I have all I can do to look after my own affairs. I do enough struggling in my business not to want to add to it in any political struggling. Once in office there would be a constant demand for favors or attentions. I'd have to spend all my time looking after other people's affairs . . . my own would have to be neglected. I don't feel like working hard any more. I am no longer young. [He is in his late forties.]

Those who run for office, Gola says, do so for private advantage.

They get the office, and then they look after themselves. Some take office so as to be able to say, "I am the mayor." But really there isn't much honor attaching to an office; people here don't even respect the President of the Republic. In F—, the mayor wants to be mayor so that he can keep the population down.

2. *In a society of amoral familists, only officials will concern themselves with public affairs, for only they [will be] paid to do so. For a private citizen to take a serious interest in a public problem will be regarded as abnormal and even improper.*

Cavalier Rossi, one of the largest landowners of Montegrano, and the mayor of the nearby town of Capa, sees the need for many local public improvements. If he went to the prefect in Potenza as mayor of Capa, they would listen to him, he says. But if he went as a private citizen of Montegrano, they would say, "who are you?" As a private citizen he might help a worker get a pension, but as for schools, hospitals, and such things, those are for the authorities to dole out. A private citizen can do nothing.

The trouble is only partly that officials will not listen to private citizens. To a considerable extent it is also that private citizens will not take responsibility in public matters. As Rossi explains,

There are no leaders in Montegrano. People's minds are too unstable; they aren't firm; they get excited and make a decision. Then the next day they have changed their minds and fallen away. It's more or less the same way in Capa. There is lots of talk, but no real personal interest. It always comes to this: the mayor has to do it. They expect the mayor to do everything and to get everything—to make a world.

Farmuso, the director of the school district and formerly the Communist mayor of a town in another province, is earnest, energetic, and intelligent. He listed several things which might be done to improve the situation in Montegrano, but when he was asked if he could bring influence to bear to get any of them done, he said that he could not. "I am interested only in the schools," he explained. "If I wanted to exert influence, with whom would I talk? In Vernande there are six teachers in two rooms, but no money for improvements. I have talked to the mayor and others, but I can't get anything even there."

The feeling that unofficial action is an intrusion upon the sphere of the state accounts in some measure both for Mayor Spomo's haughty officiousness and for the failure of private persons to interest themselves in making stopgap arrangements for a school and a hospital. In nearby Basso a reclamation project will increase vegetable production and make possible the establishment of a canning factory. The large landowners of Basso will not join together to build a factory, however, even though it might be a good investment. It is the right and the duty of the state to build it.

3. *In a society of amoral familists, there will be few checks on officials, for checking on officials will be the business of other officials only.*

When Farmuso, the school director, was asked what he would do if it came to his attention that a public official took bribes, he said that if the bribery were in his own department he would expose it at once. However, if it occurred outside his department, he would say nothing, for in that case it would be none of his concern.

A young school teacher, answering the same question, said that even if he could prove the bribery he would do nothing. "You are likely to be made a martyr," he explained. "It takes courage to do it. There are so many more dishonest people than honest ones that they can gang up on you . . . twist the facts so that you appear to be the guilty one. Remember Christ and the Pharisees."

A leading merchant would not expose bribery, because "sooner or later someone would come to me and tell me it would be good if I didn't."

4. *In a society of amoral familists, organization (i.e., deliberately concerted action) will be very difficult to achieve and maintain. The inducements which lead people to contribute their activity to organizations are to an important degree unselfish (e.g., identification with the purpose of the organization), and they are often nonmaterial (e.g., the intrinsic interest of the activity as a "game"). Moreover, it is a condition of successful organization that members have some trust in each other and some loyalty to the organization. In an organization with high morale, it is taken for granted that they will make small sacrifices, and perhaps even large ones, for the sake of the organization.*

The only formal organizations which exist in Montegrano—the Church and the State—are of course provided from the outside; if they were not, they could not exist. Inability to create and maintain organization is clearly of the greatest importance in retarding economic development in the region.

Despite the moral and other resources it can draw upon from the outside, the Church in Montegrano suffers from the general inability to maintain organization. There are two parishes, each with its priest. Rivalry between the priests is so keen that neither can do anything out of the ordinary without having obstacles placed in his way by the other, and cooperation between them is wholly out of the question. (On one occasion they nearly came to blows in the public square; on another the saint of one parish was refused admittance to the church of the other when the *festa*-day procession stopped there on its route.) When some young men tried to organize a chapter of Catholic Action, a lay association to carry Catholic principles into secular life, they encountered so much sabotage from the feuding priests, neither of whom was willing to tolerate an activity for which the other might receive some credit, that the project was soon abandoned.

The Montegranesi might be expected not to make good soldiers. However brave he may be, the amoral familist does not win battles. Soldiers fight from loyalty to an organization, especially the primary groups of "buddies," not from self-interest narrowly conceived.

Lack of attachment even to kindred has impeded emigration and indirectly economic development. In the half century prior to 1922, there was heavy emigration from Montegrano to the United States and later to Argentina. In general, however, ties between the emigrants and those who remained at home were not strong enough to support "chains" of emigration. Hundreds of Montegranesi live in the hope that a brother or uncle in America will send a "call," but such calls rarely come. People are perplexed when their relatives in America do not answer their letters. The reason is, probably, that the letters from Montegrano always ask for something, and the emigrant, whose advantage now lies elsewhere, loses patience with them. The relative absence of emigration, as well as as of gifts from persons who have emigrated, is a significant impediment to economic development. Some Italian towns, whose ethos is different, have benefited enormously from continuing close ties with emigrants who have prospered in the New World.

* * * * *

the family as a training ground for political participation

twenty-eight

In this selection, the writer states the general conformity between the individual member of the family and the rest of the family with respect to political attitudes, by pointing out that this is but one element in the more general process of *socialization*. As the young person grows up in the family, he comes to acquire the attitudes of his parents as well as his siblings: he is socialized into the political orientation of his family. Hyman also raises the important technical problem that we do not have data on how this process takes place. Instead, we have correlations between attitudes of parents and children at various ages. How the agreement comes about, or why it is weak or strong, is a problem yet to be clarified.

Agencies of Socialization into Politics

HERBERT HYMAN

Foremost among agencies of socialization into politics is the family. Thus Gillespie and Allport, on the basis of a large scale study of about 2000 youth between the ages of seventeen and twenty-two representing ten different countries, remark:

Youth in all nations anchor their documents within a basic family frame. . . . To be sure, the mode of mention differs in different cultures. . . . But the unquestioned fact remains that the family is the primary social institution in all lands, and our data clearly reflect this cultural universal.[1]

We turn to specific evidence on the problem.

Herbert H. Hyman, *Political Socialization* (New York: The Free Press of Glencoe, Inc., 1959), pp. 69, 71-75. Copyright © 1959 by The Free Press, a corporation. Reprinted with permission of the publisher.

[1] J. Gillespie and G. Allport, *Youth's Outlook on the Future* (New York: Doubleday & Company, Inc., 1955), p. 8.

The Family and Political Orientation

A major class of studies which provides evidence on agents of socialization of the individual into politics involve[s] the determination of intrafamily correlations in attitude or behavior. When children and their parents are measured *independently* and agreements in political view are established, it supports the inference that the *family* transmits politics to the children. While this might appear obvious, it nevertheless needs careful documentation. Furthermore, the degree of such influence can be established, and by proper comparison of these correlations under varied conditions, for example, for children of different ages, one can establish subtle features of the socialization process. A central difficulty in such studies using heterogeneous populations has to do with the *expected value* of correlations between pairs of *unrelated* individuals, who might be in the same social stratum, place of residence, and so on, for this may well be a component of the total agreement found, which has nothing to do with intrinsic family influences. In the instance of most of these studies, this factor is impossible to estimate, and the absolute magnitudes must be somewhat discounted.

* * * * *

These and other studies establish very clearly a family correspondence in views that are relevant to matters of political orientation. Over a great many such correlations from the different studies, the median value approximates .50. The signs, almost without exception, are *never negative*. The only negative findings bear on the area of war, where we might expect the larger social climate to be powerful, and these are but two correlations out of a total of perhaps one hundred. The import is clear. While influence might conceivably flow from child to parent, what is much more likely is that parents are the agents who transmit politically relevant attitudes to their children. The almost complete absence of negative correlations provides considerable evidence *against* the theory that political attitudes are formed *generally* in terms of rebellion and opposition to parents. While positive, the *moderate* magnitude of the correlations, however, leads to the formulation that parents are only one of the many agents of such socialization and that their influence is not that great. One finding . . . deals with authoritarianism, rather than with political orientation. In contrast to most other findings, the correlation was negligible, underscoring the interpretation . . . that authoritarianism may well emerge in adult life for reasons independent of parental factors. Admittedly, the sample is very specialized and many factors of experience may have attenuated an earlier correspondence between parent and offspring in authoritarianism. However, in this same group, parental influence on ethnocentrism shows itself in the C of .57. If the unusual finding on authoritarianism were due to some basic attenuating influence in this sample, one would expect both correlations to be zero.

Any single correlation in one of these studies simply establishes a correspondence between parent and child with respect to a *discrete* attitude. By contrast, our concern is with the socialization of the child on a larger realm of attitudes, since only then would he be equipped with a sufficiently general orientation to cope with the variety of future political issues. The series of studies presented, however, if taken together, do establish that such correspondence is achieved not merely for one attitude, but for many attitudes. Whether this more general orientation deriving from the parents is produced piecemeal by imposing one attitude on top of another until a structure is present, or by a more synthetic process of transmission of clusters of attitudes, is not clear from most such studies. . . .

One other finding is worthy of special emphasis. The one study in which intrafamily correlations in *party preference* are available yields a median value of .90 in contrast with the usual value of .50 for attitudes. . . . Again, we have suggestive evidence that the socialization of the individual into a *party* is a much more direct process than the socialization of the logically congruent area of ideology. Inquiry is called for into the simplicity of such experienced memberships, or the greater intensity of indoctrination, or the larger consensus and summation of such influence over both family and wider environ-

ment, or the lesser number of alternative options. Perhaps it is as West put it: "A man is born into his political party just as he is born into probable future membership in the church of his parents."[2] But we might well add the query, "Why then is a man not born equally into the political *ideology* of his parents?" West also implies a larger consensus and pressure on this special aspect of political orientation when he notes . . . that "changes in politics occur, . . . but a change of party breeds suspicion regarding a man's stability of character."

* * * * *

[2] James West, *Plainville, U.S.A* (New York: Columbia University Press, 1945), p. 89.

Part 9

family dissolution: internal and external factors

social structures and high divorce rates

twenty-nine

Several investigators have recently attempted to ascertain which types of social or kinship structures generate high or low divorce rates. Eventually, an adequate theory may be developed that will apply to both primitive and civilized societies, as well as to class differences within them. In this selection, taken from a longer description of the Kpelle, the investigator outlines a set of factors which, he asserts, determines the rates of marital dissolution. In reading it, consider whether other factors are also pertinent, and whether the author's set will explain known differences in rates among major Eastern and Western countries.

Marital Instability Among the Kpelle: Toward a Theory of Epainogamy

JAMES L. GIBBS, JR.

After only a few months of field research among the Kpelle of Central Liberia, it became quite apparent that

James L. Gibbs, "Marital Instability Among the Kpelle: Toward a Theory of Epainogamy," *American Anthropologist*, **65** (June, 1963), 552-559. We are grateful to the author and the *American Anthropologist* for permission to quote.

marital instability was not uncommon and that litigation over rights in women —"woman palaver"—was widespread. It was only after a detailed analysis of the field data that the writer could arrive at a hypothesis which it was felt could explain the relatively high incidence of marital instability among the Kpelle. However, for ease of communication in this paper, the order will be reversed. The hypothesis which was ultimately formulated will be presented and, following this, the supporting data in the form of a description and analysis of marriage among the Kpelle.

The Gluckman-Leach-Fallers Hypothesis

One of the best known hypotheses purporting to explain marital stability has been offered by Max Gluckman in his analysis of marriage among the Lozi and Zulu.[1] Gluckman suggests that "father-right" or patriliny is associated with low divorce, and "mother-right" or matriliny, with high divorce. Leach and Fallers have both taken issue with Gluckman and offered modifications of his original hypothesis. Leach holds that the transfer of jural authority over a woman to her husband's lineage is not, as Gluckman has suggested, an indication of a high degree of patrilineality, but that *retention* of these rights by the woman's own lineage is such an indication.[2]

Fallers, in his analysis of marital stability among the Soga, takes a complementary view, suggesting that patriliny is not all of a piece. In forms of patriliny in which a woman's patrilineage retains some rights over her after marriage, it does not support marital stability. In other forms, it does.[3]

Juxtaposing Leach's and Fallers' modifications of Gluckman's original hypothesis, we conclude that extreme lineality—*either* matrilineality or patrilineality—leads to instability in marriage because it results in divided jural authority over a woman, with some rights in her vested in her lineage, and some in that of her husband. It is this view—that marital instability can be explained mainly by divided jural authority, or, more broadly, ambiguous normative expectations—that the present study questions.

This hypothesis, although widely accepted, is not comprehensive, for it ignores several factors which systematically influence marital instability. Marital stability can probably be better explained by a frame of reference which views marriage in a matrix of social control, influenced by many social institutions and elements of social structure rather than [by] any single one.

An Alternative Hypothesis: The Paradigm of the Epainogamous Society

John Embree's duality of tightly and loosely structured social systems[4] provides such a frame of reference, and it can be applied by analogy in such a way that it increases our understanding of marital stability. In applying this polar concept to the analysis of marital stability, the writer has coined the short-cut term *epainogamy* to refer to that condition of marriage which is societally supported, praised and sanctioned—indeed, almost enforced.[5] Justification for the neologism emerges in the body of the paper. Epainogamy is derived from the Greek verb *epaineō* —meaning "to praise, approve, or publicly sanction" and the stem—*gamy*, pertaining to marriage. An epainogamous

---

[1] Max Gluckman, "Kinship and Marriage Among the Lozi of Northern Rhodesia and the Zulu of Natal," in A. R. Radcliff-Brown and Daryll Forde (eds.), *African Systems of Kinship & Marriage* (London: Oxford University Press, 1950).

[2] E. R. Leach, "Aspects of Bridewealth and Marriage Stability Among the Kuchin and Lahkar," *Man*, 57 (1957), 52.

[3] L. H. Fallers, "Some Determinants of Marital Stability in Busoga: A Reformulation of Gluckman's Hypothesis," *Africa*, 27 (1957), 106-123.

[4] John F. Embree, "Thailand: A Loosely Structured Social System," *American Anthropologist*, 52 (1950), 181-193.

[5] I am indebted to Mr. Harold Haizlip of the School of Education of Harvard University for suggesting this term.

society is one in which divorce is rare and marriage is stable. A nonepainogamous society is the obverse of this, one in which marriage is unstable and divorce is common. These are obviously ideal, polar types which do not exist in reality but are delineated for heuristic purposes.

The hypothesis detailed below holds that the epainogamous society is a tight society, more precisely, one which is tightly structured with regard to marriage. Implicit in Embree's tight society concept is the notion that the tight society must be defined in terms of both structure *and* process. Similarly, it is hypothesized here that marriage in the epainogamous society is stabilized through the presence of *structural* features in the social system (particularly the system of kinship and marriage), which minimize marital deviance through the activation of one or more of the three basic *processes* of social control. These processes are the elimination of normative ambiguity, the rewarding of conformity to norms, and the punishment of deviance from norms.

This analytical refinement makes explicit what is implicit in Embree's original scheme. To explain the operation of the three social control processes, five conceptual categories of rubrics have been constructed, each of which is a cluster of empirical features of social systems. Each cluster serves one of the three social control functions noted above.

Elimination of Normative Ambiguity in the Epainogamous Society

The first way in which an epainogamous society stabilizes marriage is to attempt to eliminate deviance which is generated through misunderstandings as to what behavior is expected. Such legitimate misunderstandings occur when more than one norm or set of norms applies to an action situation. Some institutions in an epainogamous society serve to define a situation so rigidly that no more than one norm properly applies to it. Two of the conceptual rubrics operate in this way. One of them is termed the "fixed and focused allocation of matrimonial rights," which shall be referred to simply as "fixed allocation."

Fixed and Focused Allocation of Matrimonial Rights. The concept of fixed allocation requires that the analyst view marriage as a relationship resulting from the acquisition of personal rights over a spouse. Those rights have usually been viewed as rights over women. They are the right of sexual access, the right over reproductive capacities, the right to laboring capacity, and the right to determine residence.

These rights are the focus of the discussion of marital stability by Gluckman, Leach, and Fallers briefly summarized above. They are correct in their view that fixing the locus of rights over a woman in her spouse or his lineage serves to remove uncertainty or ambiguity from marital norms. Here I would simply add that there are attributes of allocated rights other than their locus or permanence of transfer which also clarify or pinpoint normative expectations. In addition there are social control processes essential to epainogamy which are noted below.

There are seven features of kinship systems subsumed under fixed allocation. Let us see how each contributes to the clear definition of marital norms:

1. Weak conjugal band. Richards[6] and Leach[7] have both correctly held that a high divorce rate is usually found

---

[6] A. I. Richards, "Some Types of Family Structure Amongst the Central Bantu" in A. R. Radcliffe-Brown and Daryll Forde (eds.), *op. cit.*

[7] Leach, *op. cit.*, 53.

in societies where the sibling bond is more important than the conjugal one; for in a case of conflict, the conjugal bond will be viewed as the more dispensable. In such societies, notably matrilineal ones, *complete* rights over a woman are not transferred to her husband, hence inclusion under this rubric.

2. Preferential marriage. The stabilizing effects of preferential marriage as an obligatory form are frequently mentioned in the literature. It operates, first, to remove uncertainty in mate selection and, secondly, to minimize matrimonial strain through marriage of persons who already have strong social bonds in kinship.

3. "Alternative marriage." "Alternative marriage" is a form of union which is recognized as marriage, but is less prestigeful than the normal form. It conveys fewer rights than the normal form and weakens epainogamy. An example would be an optional form of marriage in a patrilineal society based on suitor service and uxorilocal residence where the union is fully recognized as marriage from the end of the period of bride service. Here the groom does not acquire the right to determine his wife's residence, nor does he have rights over her labor. In fact, the woman's family acquires rights over *his* labor for a period which is usually specified. If such a young man is called upon by his lineage for labor or a contribution of farm produce for a ceremony, the friction arising over how much of his labor, or fruit of his labor, is still claimable by his kinsmen can endanger his marriage.

4. Continuation marriage. . . . The levirate and sororate and other forms of secondary or continuation marriage can be interpreted as indicating that the rights transferred in marriage are transferred permanently. The rights do not end with the death of the spouse but continue in a union entered with the deceased spouse's sibling.

5. Polygamy. Conceptually, polygyny involves—for a woman—the sharing of rights in her husband with her co-wives. This leads to ambiguity as to what is an equitable arrangement and frequent dissension as to whether a given culture's notion of equitability is being met. Polygynous marriage does not, in and of itself, necessarily bring discord. However, in the absence of tension-reducing mechanisms, such a sororal polygyny or provision of separate houses for each wife, polygyny tends to produce marital instability. A parallel feature, polyandry, may result in conjugal instability, if not in marital instability.

6. Incest regulations. In some kinship systems the rules of incest are such that the right of sexual access is merged in a man and some of his kinsmen. Where a man must share his wife with his brothers or other kinsmen, sexual rivalries are brought into the family, sometimes causing quarrels between the male kinsmen. Such dissension over the husband's right to sexual access results in termination of many unions.

7. Filiation of children. The filiation of children is a measure of the firmness with which the right *in genitricem* is held by the husband. Where adulterine children are not unequivocally filiated with their pater rather than their genitor, an element of dissension and instability is introduced. A similar divisive element is introduced when illegitimate children are not unequivocally filiated with their mother's group rather than with that of their genitor. Similar results may occur in the allocation of children at divorce, because a wedge for discord is found where children may be alternately allocated to either in kin group.

In sum, seven discrete features of systems of kinship and marriage, logically related by the concept of type of allocation of marital rights, contribute to marital stability by minimizing normative ambiguity in marriage. The reduction of normative ambiguity can be understood when we view allocated rights *in personam* not only in terms of their unitary locus and their intended permanence, but in terms of the exclusiveness with which they are exercised.

Ceremonialization of the Marriage Bond. A second set of features which contributes to the clear defining of normative expectations is the "ceremonialization of the marriage bond." The relevant empirical features include the elaboration of the marriage ceremony, the participation of kinsmen and others in the ceremony, and the prominence of ritual in the ceremony. Their stabilizing functions are readily apparent. These features of marriage ceremonial call attention to the union, drive its meaning home in terms of ritual symbolism, and dramatize important elements in the roles of spouses and involvement of the two kin groups. Moreover, ceremonial emphasis of the act of marriage underlines its significance and stresses the fact that some sort of consensus or complementarity of expectations must be found by the couple because their relationship is important. Sacralization, or the inclusion of elements of supernatural beliefs and acts, implies that the union will be supported by supernatural sanctions as well as secular ones.

Both the ceremonialization of the marriage bond and the fixed allocation function to eliminate ambiguity in the norms regulating marriage.

The Rewarding of Conformity to Marriage Norms

The second major way in which marriage in an epainogamous society is stabilized is through rewarding conformity to marital norms. This is done mainly by restricting access to valued personal rights to marriage so that a married person can get something which is desirable and not available elsewhere. Homans, writing on social control, has made a statement which explains why this action can work effectively.[8] Broadly paraphrased, he has said that a person who conforms for the rewards which compliance brings will continue to conform only as long as he cannot get those rewards elsewhere. One rubric, "the relative scarcity of matrimonial rights," explains the operation of this process.

Relative Scarcity of Matrimonial Rights. Several specific features of systems of kinship and marriage can be discussed under this rubric.

The right to sexual access available *in* marriage may be scarce *outside of* marriage. This is the case where premarital intercourse is rare and adultery is also uncommon.

Reproductive rights may be viewed in the same light. The ability to acquire children to be filiated with one's kin group may not be possible short of marriage. This is the obverse of the situation where a man can claim his illegitimate or adulterine child through the transfer of a fee.

A matrimonial right seldom discussed with regard to marital stability is the right to a woman's labor. However, its relative availability may be crucial. As P. M. Worsley and Ronald Cohen have both shown, in a society in which women are a major source of labor and thereby contribute to their husbands' economic and social standing, that access to women's laboring capacity may be as much valued as access to their sexual or reproductive capacities.[9]

[8] George Homans, *The Human Group* (New York: Harcourt, Brace & World, Inc., 1950), p. 290.
[9] P. M. Worsley, "The Kinship System of the Tallensi: A Revaluation," *Journal of the Royal Anthropological Institute*, **86** (1956),

Where these valued rights are scarce outside of marriage, they function as positive sanctions for those who conform to the norms of marriage—that is, to those who marry and stay married. The scarcity value of these rights may be even further enhanced where they are difficult to acquire even *in* marriage, i.e., where access to marriage is restricted. There are several specific features of kinship systems which serve to restrict access to marriage itself. They include late age for marriage and high bride price, especially where it is customarily transferred in one lump sum. Even the amount of bride price returned at divorce may affect the possibility of *re*marriage, as will the senior levirate, which can restrict the number of women available to bachelors.

Thus the scarcity of matrimonial rights within and outside of marriage stabilizes marriage because spouses will be more tolerant of any strains that develop, viewing them as the price to be paid for the desserts of marriage, the rare benefits at hand. Marital conformity thus brings its own reward. [In psychological terms, one might say that the lack of alternative means of gratification indicates that goal-seeking behavior (in marriage) is not easily frustrated.]

The Punishment of Deviance from Marital Norms

The third way in which the epainogamous society stabilizes marriage is through punishing deviance from marital norms. This is done by shutting off access to valued ends, or by subjecting the spouses to group controls, or by both. Such punishment is particularly effective when the deviant cannot escape the social field. . . . Two rubrics, "the mode of access to scarce ends" and "group involvement," show the operation of this principle.

Mode of Access to Scarce Ends. The rubric, "mode of access to scarce ends," refers to the fact that in some kin-oriented societies, access to valued rights, privileges, resources, and office and rank is based primarily on the ascriptive criterion of unilineal descent; while in other groups, access to such ends is primarily by achievement. Where a man is dependent on his kin group for land, labor, ritual support, selection for political office and bride price, he is firmly bound to it and will not cross it lightly. They can withdraw their labor from those tasks which are too much for one man alone, bypass him for political office, or refuse to perform rituals on his behalf if he does not comply with their wishes. Each of these actions by the group is a negative sanction. If he persists in an unpopular divorce or acquiesces in his daughter's divorce, he causes the group either to forfeit or to return bride price. He may thereby risk the application of the series of negative sanctions listed above; for then the descent group can punish him by shutting off his access to these valued ends.

A contrasting type of kin-oriented society is one in which a man may achieve valued social ends through the operation of the achievement principle. Several specific features of social systems show the operation of this principle and a relatively broad mode of access to valued ends. Some of these features are primary, others secondary. The first of the primary features is the allocation of political office on the basis of personal allegiance rather than a consanguineal link. Second is a division of labor which allocates most of the primary subsistence roles to women. The presence of the concept of adultery damages and the recognized use of wives

37-70. Ronald Cohen, "Marriage Stability and Its Determinants Among the Kanuri of Northern Nigeria." Mimeographed paper given at the annual meeting of the American Anthropological Association (November, 1958).

marital instability among the kpelle   **201**

as a source of such income is third. Although these three are the most important or primary features in determining a broad mode of access to valued ends, there are other relevant features, such as cooperative work groups based on the territorial or associational principle rather than the descent principle and farms worked by nuclear families rather than small-scale descent groups.

Where the three primary features occur together, a man is dependent on his wives as a source of income and labor, enabling him to accumulate the wherewithal to attract clients and, ultimately, power. The man is then freer from dependence on, and control by, his kin group. However, where the mode of access to valued ends is through dependence on the role of women rather than through the descent group, marital instability increases. This is because in such a society a woman is an asset and need not tolerate a marriage that she views as stressful, . . . for she can readily find another husband. A woman is quick to leave a marriage and a man is not solicitous to preserve it, because obtaining another wife is not difficult.

I conclude that where access to valued ends is narrow, via the ascriptive mode of corporate descent group membership, deviance from marital norms can be punished by such groups through shutting off access to valued goals. Where access to goals is broad, via the achievement mode, especially through dependence on women, deviance in marriage is less easily sanctioned and marital instability consequently is greater.

Group Involvement. The second cluster of empirical features of kinship systems which serve to punish deviance from matrimonial norms are classed under the rubric "group involvement." By this is meant the extent to which the spouses' two kin groups have a stake in the marriage. Mother-in-law jokes notwithstanding, the greater the *institutionalized* involvement of other individuals in marriage, the more stable it is likely to be, because those who have a stake in a marriage will attempt to hold it together. Several specific features of kinship systems are subsumed under this rubric.

Preferential marriage can be considered again in this connection. Such a marriage, especially cross-cousin marriage, does not simply link two kin groups, but it reduplicates ties which grew out of an earlier marriage. Thus one marriage cannot end without endangering others. Therefore kinsmen of estranged spouses who are both consanguines and affines to each will act to reconcile the couple and to apply sanctions to those who are considered wayward.

Suitor service and infant betrothal where the bride is raised in her husband's household both serve to bring one spouse into the household of the other for long periods of time. This acts to create bonds of sentiment between the in-marrying spouse and his or her affines, whose threatened withdrawal can serve as a sanction against marital deviance.

Betrothal in adulthood where it is not primarily self-determined by the couple but by their kinsmen is patently an earmark of group involvement. It is most often epainogamous, because the families arranging the engagement usually consider factors such as economic skills and emotional stability more than romantic attraction.

A pair of features which indicate group involvement are the levirate and sororate; their presence indicates not only that marriage endures longer than the lifetime of the spouses, but that it links groups rather than simply linking individuals.

As Leach has indicated, high bride

price is relevant not in and of itself, but because it means that a man must depend on his kinsmen to help him to accumulate it.[10] When bride wealth is substantial, it is usually shared among the members of the receiving kin group. These kinsmen will exert conciliatory pressures on estranged spouses lest they, the kinsmen, have to return their portion of the bride wealth in case of divorce. Yet high marriage payments are sometimes associated with easy divorce. Leach has noted that high payment may be a fruitless attempt to "consolidate the intrinsic weakness" of the af-

final tie in its competition with the sibling bond.

Conclusion

I conclude that the epainogamous society is one in which marriage is stable because of the presence of a series of specific features of kinship and social organization which separately an jointly serve not only to define norma tive expectations in marriage sharply and unequivocally, but to sanction those expectations both positively and negatively.

---

[10] Leach, *op. cit.*

* * * * *

the factors generating higher divorce rates among the lower social strata

thirty

In his larger report, from which this section was taken, the author summarizes the overwhelming evidence of an *inverse* correlation between class and divorce rate, i.e., toward the *lower* strata the divorce rate is *higher*. This seems to be a nearly universal pattern when the divorce procedure becomes easily available to all strata. (See the author's article, "Marital Satisfaction and Instability: A Cross-Cultural Class Analysis of Divorce Rates," *International Social Science Journal.*)

In the present selection, the author assumes the availability of divorce and focuses on the factors within the various social strata that might create greater tensions, lesser cohesion, or greater approval of divorce as a solution. The author suggests that we view the family as a boundary-maintaining unit and that we ask which kinds of forces might or might not support it in the different social strata.

The Meaning of Class Differentials in the Divorce Rate

WILLIAM J. GOODE

Considerable evidence [has been presented] that the lower classes have a higher divorce rate, and that the Negro divorce rate is higher than the white. A class differential divorce pattern is not . . . to be found only in our own data. We have returned to previous studies which contained similar data, although to our knowledge no one has previously taken theoretical account of the fact, or even noted that the fact was contrary to previous assumption. . . . It seems useful to pursue . . . the *meaning* of these apparently economic facts.

* * * * *

. . . Socioeconomic factors doubtless exert general structural pressures on marriages, in different degrees at different class levels. Consequently, one may not ignore them. The results of empirical study seem to demonstrate what common sense asserts, that economic factors are of importance in marital stability. . . .

Students of marital conflict once thought sexual conflict was very important in marital troubles, but they have come in recent times to believe that sexual problems are usually an *index*, rather than a cause, of basis interpersonal conflicts. Thus when a wife complains that she finds no pleasure in her sexual relations with her husband, one begins to probe for deeper conflicts between the two individuals, with the expectation that these con-

William J. Goode, *After Divorce* (New York: The Free Press of Glencoe, Inc., 1956), pp. 57, 60-63. Copyright 1956 by The Free Press, a corporation. Reprinted with permission of the publisher.

flicts actually cause the sexual incompatibility.

Naturally, then, similar transformations have been suggested for conflicts about economic matters. More particularly, conflicts about economic factors may sometimes be interpreted as *personality* failures: a "mature" personality will not be affected by such things, and the apparent conflict is simply thought to hide a more basic personality weakness. It cannot be denied of course that an "economic complaint" may indeed hide something deeper. It is nevertheless a poor research practice to *assume* the deeper meaning without analyzing the matter. The parlor Freudian dictum, "things are never what they seem; indeed, the opposite" seems almost a cynical response to observation.

Unfortunately, then, "personality" assumptions often lead into the same kind of stultifying pseudo-explanations that were characteristic of the heyday of instinct theory. Having pointed to personality problems as a possible cause, the search can stop.

It is at least possible to maintain that since (1) those who obtain divorces represent such a large segment of the population, and (2) the cultural structure of our time contains so many factors reducing the stability of the family, we ought not to search *first* for personality causes. Whatever contribution personality "weakness" makes to marital instability—and no study has achieved such a measurement—the *social meaning* of the economic can nevertheless be studied with some profit. This is not, to repeat, a substitute for personality analysis; it is on an entirely different theoretical level. If we can show through what avenues the socioeconomic seems to affect marital relations, we are at least a step further toward an adequate understanding of divorce and postdivorce adjustment. We shall attempt at many points to present data toward this end.

. . . Now "stability" may be defined in purely economic terms, but of course it has sociological dimensions: not only are the stabler incomes to be found in (1) particular kinds of occupations, but stability of income is likely to be associated with (2) a different way of life. Furthermore, stability of income is associated with (3) *size* of income, particularly over longer periods of time. And the latter factor is also one of the determinants of larger social patterns in our society.

Finally, neither stability nor size of income, even when viewed sociologically, exhausts the social *meaning* of the economic. *Who earns* the income and *who controls* the income are further aspects of the economic factors which must be considered when we look at the American family. We have called the association between socioeconomic factors and divorce a "rough" one. We have done so to call attention to the fact that the economic factor does not act directly, but is mediated through other factors, mainly sociological. We can more easily measure the socioeconomic than these other factors, but we suppose that when we have better techniques we shall have higher correlations between these social factors and divorce than between any purely economic indices and divorce. That is to say, it will be the social *meaning* of these factors which will discriminate between instability and stability. The socioeconomic, then, *is* important, but *interactionally*, and not as a simple, direct, causal element. We cannot of course present a sophisticated analysis now, but we can at least point to some of the sociological dynamics that appear to play a role. Later on we shall document these assertions further.

Perhaps the most fundamental set of symbolic relationships is that between the stability of the family, the unity of the family, the role of the husband as breadwinner, and his role as family head. Now during the 1940's there was a large increase in the porportion of married females actively working; the increase in 1940-46 was about 50 per cent. By 1953, of the female labor force, married females formed 56.6 per cent. There is certainly more toleration of the working wife. Further, there is no widespread opinion that a family will not survive even if the male head fails in his role as breadwinner. Nevertheless, there is little evidence that the female *as breadwinner* is beginning to emerge as a social role. To the extent that there is folk belief about the matter, on the other hand, it is phrased in a negative fashion: the expectation is that failure of the husband in this respect may help to make the family unstable. When the married woman works, the work generally carries a negative social evaluation in contemporary America (1) except under specifiable conditions of need or (2) unless redefined in *nonbreadwinning* terms.

For example, a crisis situation justifies such work. If the husband, say, is incapacitated for a long or short while, the wife may work. For many strata the wife's work may be defined in terms of need: "saving a nest egg," or "to pay off the furniture," or even "we can't get along without it."

In the upper educational strata, the work may be defined in nonbreadwinning terms: "expressing the wife's personality," or "giving the family a wider range of experiences," or "to keep the wife from stagnating." As we might expect, when such verbal responses express a genuine conviction, it is possible that for such groups we may find as high a "happiness score" as in other families in the same strata.

We believe, then, that toleration or

even approval of the working wife are most often given a justification of (1) necessity or (2) essentially *non*bread-winning aims. By contrast, no explanation at all is called for and no redefinition in terms of "higher" values is required if he *is* earning an adequate income, i.e., is fulfilling his role and his wife is *not* working. Even in those small circles in which it is felt that the wife *ought* to hold a job, this is an ethic that is carefully distinguished from the mere earning of money.

Now as to the *use* of the money, the husband's income is supposed to be earned for *all* the family. The male head of family is responsible, according to our values, for the support of the entire group, and legal prescriptions underscore these values. This legal responsibility carries correlative headship rights with it, and while the actual patterns of domination are much more complex and often contradictory, open and public failure to keep this headship must be explained or husband and wife will be censured. There are, indeed, various deprecatory terms in our slang to describe a husband in this situation (e.g., "henpecked," "Milquetoast").

If certain earlier comments may now be placed in this context, it is obvious that personality problems can be displaced into economic problems. As the simplicist formulation of parlor psychoanalysis has it, the "stable personality" will not be affected by such economic strains as we have just noted or by any others, while the immature will complain of economic factors in the marriage when the "real" trouble is emotional. Nevertheless, in our society the material goals of comfort, medical care, style in clothing, homes, and furniture, and size and newness of automobiles are widely accepted, while the actual distribution of *income* is far more skewed. Put in another way, although the material and other aspirations of

lower socioeconomic strata *are* lower than those of the upper, the *income* of lower strata is relatively even lower. Consequently, the feeling of socioeconomic strain is greater in the lower strata. . . .

If the foregoing considerations are correct, then in some cases *economic strain may also be displaced onto noneconomic relationships,* such as sex and marital adjustment. Perhaps a general theory of personality will finally emerge which will be able to describe the psychodynamic patterns even when the source of strain is economic, or hunger, or glandular deficiency, not alone when it is "sexual."

Tracing the pattern of strain further, whenever discord from whatever source becomes chronic, the withdrawal of economic support can be one major expression of waning loyalty. This denial of breadwinning obligations and of family unity may be met by a denial of headship. It may be supposed that these changes are economically less catastrophic in the lower economic strata. The upper and lower may be contrasted in this fashion: (1) A higher proportion of the upper-strata income is committed to long-time "investment" expenditures, such as annuities, insurance, houses, and so forth, and thus has little flexibility; (2) a higher proportion of the lower-strata income, when it is committed at all, is given over to consumer goods, such as cars, television sets, and so forth; (3) consequently, there is less censure and less catastrophe at withdrawal of support in the lower than in the upper [strata]. Moreover, the difference between the husband's earnings and the wife's potential earnings is on the average greater toward the upper strata; thus she is more helpless, and withdrawal of support creates far more problems.

* * * * *

unwilled major role failure in the family

thirty-one

In a group of related reports, Bernard Farber and his colleagues have studied one type of marital dissolution intensively: what happens to the family when a child is severely mentally retarded. The student may note that this is one of several catastrophes of this general variety—mental disease, severe neurosis, chronic physical illness—which prevent one individual from fulfilling others' role expectations and require others to assume additional burdens. Guilt and love usually prevent parents from placing the retarded child in an institution until major role problems have been created. Consider how other types of unwilled role failures might affect the family.

Family Organization and Crisis

BERNARD FARBER

The aim of the research was to investigate various ways that families organize themselves to counteract the disintegrative effects of having a severely mentally retarded child.

Sample

The sample consisted of 233 families living in the Chicago area in which both husband and wife were interviewed. The parents were (1) Caucasian, (2) predominantly middle class,

Bernard Farber, "Family Organization and Crisis: Maintenance of Integration in Families with a Severely Retarded Child," *Monographs of the Society for Research in Child Development*, **25**, No. 75 (1960), 85-91. We are grateful to the author and the Society for Research in Child Development for permission to quote.

(3) married and living together at the time of the study, and (4) had been in contact with a parents' association for promoting the welfare of the mentally retarded. The mentally retarded children were (1) aged sixteen or under, (2) born in the present marriage, and (3) predominantly of the "trainable" classification.

Procedure

In the collection of data, two interviewers visited each family in their home at an appointed time. While one interviewer talked with the husband, the other interviewed the wife.

The interview, which lasted about two and one-half hours, consisted of two parts. The first section was an oral interview in which the parents were asked to elaborate on various matters pertaining to the family and the child's handicap. Interviewers recorded the responses verbatim.

The second section of the interview consisted of a questionnaire which was completed in the presence of the interviewer. This section included an index of marital integration, a sibling role-tension index, a social mobility scale, and a neighborliness scale, in addition to questions on parents, friends, and basic social data.

In the analysis of the quantitative data, statistical techniques utilizing nonparametric assumptions were applied. The .05 probability of chance occurrence was used as the basis for accepting or rejecting hypotheses.

Discussion

The research centered around the following questions:

1. What are the conditions or circumstances which influence the potential severity of the disintegrative effects of the retarded child on the family?

2. What are the effective courses of action which the family may take in order to maintain its integrity?

3. As specific courses of action: (a) Is it necessary to place the retarded child in an institution? (b) How does the relationship between normal and retarded siblings affect the personal adjustment of the normal siblings?

The Conceptual Model

To organize the data in a way which would relate the various questions, a conceptual model was developed. The basis for the model was the von Neumann and Morgenstern theory of games of strategy. The analogy regarded the family as being involved in a game of strategy against nature. The range of nature's strategies was indicated by the degree of severity with which specific conditions potentially affected family integration. Certain kinds of family organization which could potentially counteract the strategies of nature were regarded putatively as integrative family strategies. The major payoff or reward for the family was the degree of marital integration at the time of the study. The role of the investigator was that of a judge whose task was to discover those strategies which had a utility either for the family or for nature.

Aside from the simple game characteristics, the model assumes "an original state of nature," or a situation in which the game is not played. That is, if nature makes no move to undermine the integrity of the family, the family will develop according to a life cycle considered desirable according to the culture of the community. However, should nature make a "move" against the orderly development of the family life cycle, family integrity would be threatened, and counteracting strategies [would have to] be developed.

At any given point in time, the family life cycle is defined by the domestic values of the members and the specific roles in use at that time. (Here a specific role is regarded as a given point in the development of a career.) These define the present stage of development (roles) and the desired direction of movement (values). But agreement by husband and wife on values and coordination of roles is, by definition, the degree of marital integration. Hence if there is disruption in the development of roles or a confusion in domestic values, this disturbance in life-cycle development should be reflected in the degree of marital integration.

Inasmuch as the domestic value hierarchy defines the direction of movement in the family life cycle, in an integrated marriage there is implied a clear-cut focus of the parents on a single aspect of family life—the development of children, the welfare of the parents, or the promotion of the home.

Furthermore, at any given point in time in the integrated marriage, the roles of the family members are so organized [as] to direct the family members consistently toward gratification in the chosen aspect of family life. When the family life cycle is disrupted by the presence of the severely retarded child, the family must reorganize its activities to maintain a consistent focus upon a given aspect of family life.

The major hypothesis of the study was that, especially where the strategies employed by nature against the family were potentially severely disruptive to marital integration, a consistent orientation by the parents toward the welfare of the normal children, the home, or the parents themselves was necessary to maintain a high marital integration.

In the investigation, the orientations included in the hypothesis were defined on the basis of (1) whether the parents sought emotional support from within or outside the nuclear family, (2) valuation of the normal children by the parents, (3) the parents' tendencies in daily interaction and division of labor as reflected in their value systems, and (4) the parents' attitudes toward community participation as a reflection of their priorities in developing their life career. The orientations were:

1. The integrative child-oriented family was one in which both husband and wife were favorably inclined toward high social mobility; the husband emphasized traditional rather than companionate values in family life; the wife identified highly with at least one of her normal children; under certain conditions, interaction between normal and retarded siblings was limited; and emotional support was provided by the wife's mother or the community.

2. The integrative home-oriented family was one in which either the husband or wife cared little about social mobility; the husband stressed companionate values in family life; under certain conditions, interaction between normal and retarded siblings was limited; and either the parents were highly integrated in the neighborhood or the husband identified highly with his wife.

3. The integrative parent-orientated family was one in which the parents were favorably inclined toward a high degree of social mobility; the husband stressed companionate rather than traditional values in family life; and the husband identified highly with his wife.

All families which lacked any of the characteristics required for classification in one of the above three categories were placed in a fourth category. In the first three categories the families were regarded as having a focus around which to organize the lives of the family members so that the husband and wife could achieve mutual gratification with respect to their goals. The families in the fourth, or residual, category, however, were regarded as either (1) lacking in focus or common orientation or (2) being organized in its system of roles in such a way as to impede gratification pertaining to a common orientation. Hence the residual category was considered as the grouping of kinds of family organization[s] not conducive to high marital integration of the parents.

The strategies of nature were classified as favorable, unpredictable, or unfavorable. Two criteria were used to classify sets of circumstances according to favorableness. The first criterion for classification was the size of the mean marital integration score for parents in that set of circumstances. The second was the internal consistency among each set of circumstances. Each set of circumstances was classified on the basis of the sex of the retarded child, marital prediction score of the parents, religion, social class, and birth order of the child. Internal consistency was determined by the degree to which the set of circumstances met the conditions specified in the following propositions:

1. The marital integration of parents with severely mentally retarded boys tends to be lower than that of parents with retarded girls.

2. Parents whose marital integration had been low prior to the birth of a severely retarded child tend to have a lower marital integration at the time of the study than parents whose early martial integration had been high.

3. Middle-class parents of severely mentally retarded boys tend to have a higher marital integration than lower-class parents of retarded boys.

4. Marital integration of Catholic parents of retarded boys is affected less severely than that of non-Catholic parents of retarded boys.

5. Among Catholics, a firstborn mentally retarded boy affects the parents' marital integration *less* severely than does a nonfirstborn boy.

6. Among non-Catholics, a firstborn mentally retarded boy affects the parents' marital integration *more* severely than does a nonfirstborn boy.

7. Among middle-class families, the marital integration of non-Catholic parents of retarded girls is affected *less* severely than the marital integration of Catholic parents of retarded girls.

8. The marital integration of parents of nonfirstborn retarded girls is affected *less* severely than the marital integration of parents of firstborn retarded girls.

* * * * *

Results

The findings pertaining to the relationship between the use of child-oriented, parent-oriented, and home-oriented strategies and marital integration were:

1. When parents who used consistent parent-oriented, child-oriented, or home-oriented strategies were compared with those who did not, the parents who utilized one of the three consistent orientations were found to have a higher marital integration than the others. This results was statistically significant for families in favorable, unpredictable, and unfavorable circumstances, respectively. However, the difference in marital integration between parents who used one of the three strategies hypothecated as integrative and those who did not was greatest for families faced with unfavorable circumstances.

2. For each level of favorableness of circumstances, parents of children in institutions who used the putatively integrative strategies had a higher marital integration than similar parents who used other strategies. Similarly, parents of retarded children at home who utilized the hypothetically integrative strategies tended to have a higher marital integration than those who did not.

3. Among those families using the putatively integrative strategies, there was no statistically significant difference in marital integration between parents with a retarded child in an institution and parents with a retarded child at home. Although these results were not statistically significant among families who used the putatively integrative orientations, the difference in mean marital integration between parents with a retarded child in an institution and parents with a retarded child at home *increased* with the decrease in favorableness of circumstance. As a result, for families faced with unfavorable circumstance, the mean marital integration of parents with a child in an institution was substantially higher than that of parents with a retarded child at home. In contrast, parents who did not utilize one of the putatively integrative strategies showed no consistent difference in degree of marital integration

between families with a retarded child at home and those with a child in an institution.

4. Because of imperfections of theory and technique, the investigator can take into account only a few of the major strategies—he must regard the remainder as idiosyncratic and not in accordance with the rules of the game as the investigator defines them. The data were examined to determine some of these unanticipated strategies. The analysis revealed that:

a. When families faced with favorable circumstances had only one child (the retarded child) and kept this child at home, they generally had high marital integration. If parents faced with unfavorable circumstances kept their only child (who was retarded) at home, they generally had very low marital integration.

b. When the family met all the criteria for the child-oriented integrative strategy except that the mother did not identify with any of her normal children, by improvising compensating acts or moves, the parents were able to maintain high marital integration. These compensating moves included hiring a full-time maid or the wife's taking a part-time job.

5. In dealing with the relationship between normal and retarded siblings at home, it was found that:

a. When the retarded child was young, interaction between normal and retarded children of approximately the same age tended to be on an equalitarian or playmate basis. For older children, the normal sibling (especially if this normal child was a girl) tended to assume a superordinate position in the relationship.

b. Normal girls who interacted frequently with their retarded sibling tended to be involved in more tense role relations with their mother than did normal sisters who engaged in little or no interaction with the retarded child. The results were inconclusive for the normal brothers of retarded siblings at home. Since these findings were based upon judgments of open-ended responses which were sometimes vague, the results should be verified with more adequate instruments.

Practical Implications of the Research

The results of the study seem to have the following implications for families with a severely mentally retarded child:

1. *Type of Family Orientation Rather than Institutionalization per se Seems Important for the Marital Integration of the Parents.* Whether or not to place the child in an institution is necessarily a decision which the parents themselves must make. In making this decision, the parents should consider institutionalization not as a solution *in itself* of problems regarding the retarded child and other family members. Rather they should contemplate institutionalization or keeping the child at home in the context of the various other steps that must be taken to maintain a healthy family life for themselves and all of their children. Institutionalization may be important insofar as it increases the opportunity for the parents to develop a consistent family orientation.

2. *The Degree of Marital Integration of the Parents of Severely Mentally Retarded Children Is Not a Function of Either (a) the Severity of the Crisis Situation or (b) the Strategies Used by the Family, but Is a Resultant of the Combination of the Two.* The result implies that in treatment the counselor or social worker must consider both the severity of the crisis and the procedures for developing integrative strategies to provide adequate therapy. Although common sense would indicate in general that such a procedure should be

followed, common sense does not specify the importance of the sex of the child, the social class of the parent, or the religion of the parent as important determinants of the severity of the crisis. Nor does common sense specify the necessary steps to be taken by the individuals as family members in counteracting the crisis. Steps should be taken to increase the agreement of the parents on their values pertaining to family life. Then recommendations can be made as to the appropriate actions to be taken with respect to matters of social mobility, neighboring, relations with own parents and in-laws, division of labor between the parents, the place of the normal children in the family, and the solution of specific husband-wife problems.

3. *Normal Sisters (but Not Brothers) Are Given Parent-Substitute Responsibilities and Are Seen by the Mother to Be Affected Adversely.* The mother whose daughter interacts frequently with the retarded child tend[s] to view the daughter as moody, stubborn, easy to anger, or having other negative traits more often than mothers whose daughters do not interact frequently with the retarded child. We assume that this difference in perception grows out of the conflicts and anxieties generated between mother and daughter when many responsibilities for the retarded child are placed upon the daughter. Both the present sample and other studies have indicated that a close mother-daughter relationship facilitates the daughter's later marriage and personal adjustment. Hence the results suggest that the parents of retarded children should be aware of the possible consequences to the mental health of the normal daughter if she is given a surrogate (or parent-substitute) role in relation to the retarded child.

Theoretical Implications of the Research

* * .* * *

In the testing of generalizations related specifically to family life, the research suggests that:

1. Variation in the development of the family life cycle can explain differences in both the marital integration of parents and the role of normal siblings (especially girls) in the family.

2. A consistent organization of the parents' source of emotional support, their interaction with and valuation of children, their daily routine and division of labor, and their community participation around a given aspect of family life provide a basis for high marital integration.

3. The mother's expectation that her normal daughter frequently assume a surrogate role may prevent the girl from developing a healthy personality. Stated in terms of feminine role expectations, the findings suggest that placing much emphasis upon the instrumental (e.g., care, protection, and training the retarded child) aspects of the daughter's family role inhibits the girl's development of social-emotional aspects of behavior. Since in American culture girls are supposed to be social-emotional role specialists, the daughter cannot assume this social-emotional role adequately when she is expected to do so in ordinary social relations.

in-laws and marital conflict among jewish families

thirty-two

In an earlier report, Hope J. Leichter described the problems of family casework with a group of New York Jewish families when the caseworkers (themselves mainly Jewish) held very different views about *proper* family behavior. For example, most of the clients (63 per cent) thought children should not leave home until they married, but only 3 per cent of the caseworkers approved of so close a tie between parents and older children. In general, the caseworkers believed that "normal" or "mature" behavior was close to the ideals of the independent nuclear family; their clients approved of much closeness between adult generations and among families in the in-law and kin network.

Conflict, like homicide, is most likely to take place between people who interact intimately. Characteristic of these families is a great reluctance to restrict the closeness of family ties. The authors explore the direction of conflict and some of its causes, while contrasting these patterns with kin network systems in other societies.

Laterality and Conflict in Kinship Ties

CANDACE L. ROGERS

HOPE J. LEICHTER

* * * * *

The idea that the marital bond is affected by the way in which the family is integrated with its kin network has been noted by many. The question is not simply with which *side* of the net-

Candace L. Rogers and Hope J. Leichter, "Laterality and Conflict in Kinship Ties," unpublished paper delivered at the National Conference on Social Welfare, New York (May 28, 1962), pp. 5-13, 15-17. We are grateful to the authors for permission to quote.

work a nuclear family is involved, but whether, and how much, the family is involved with both sides, with neither, or with one and not the other. Regardless of what the pattern is, it will have consequences for the marital bond. Parsons has observed that in the contemporary United States the relative isolation of the nuclear family from both husband's and wife's kin, and the general shift of residence at marriage for both husbands and wives to a new, separate household, places a special priority on the marital bond, making it the key tie in the kinship system.[1] This goes together with romantic love and individual, rather than family, choice of marriage partners. Some time ago Thomas and Znaniecki noted that the contractual relationship between the husband's and wife's kin in the traditional Polish peasant's marriage tended to strengthen the marital bond; it was in the interest of both sides of the kinship network to solidify the couple's relationship.[2] Those brought up in peasant society were not geared to individual mate selection and a marital tie based on romantic love, so that marriages were weakened when immigration to the United States disrupted the traditional supports of kinship.

In all societies there are laterality norms prescribing the extent and kind of involvement which the nuclear family should have with the husband's and the wife's sides of the kin network. These norms may define the kin with whom the marital pair will live, inherit from, work with, give assistance to, and owe primary loyalty to. In traditional China, for example, husband and wife were affiliated with the husband's paternal kin, to whom they owed a loyalty which in many situations was greater than that they owed each other.

* * * * *

The kinship system predominant among urban middle-class families in the contemporary United States has been described as bilateral or multilineal: . . . we consider ourselves descended equally from our maternal and

<hr>

[1] Talcott Parsons, "The Kinship System of the Contemporary United States," in *Essays in Sociological Theory*, rev. ed. (New York: The Free Press of Glencoe, Inc., 1954), pp. 177-196.

[2] William Thomas and Florian Znaniecki, *The Polish Peasant in Europe and America* (Boston: The Gorham Press, 1920).

paternal kin, although we are patronymic in that the wife takes the husband's family name at marriage. We affiliate formally with neither one nor the other side of the kin network; unlike the Chinese, when couples marry they do not automatically become part of one partner's kin group. No commonly acknowledged rule requires a couple to live near the husband's family rather than the wife's, or to inherit one side but not the other. Instead, couples in our society belong to three family systems: the husband's family of birth, the wife's family of birth, and the family established by their own marriage. No hard and fast rule exists defining the nature of the couple's obligations to the husband's as compared to the wife's family.

Among the client families of Eastern European Jewish origin, there is a greater involvement with the wife's than with the husband's kin in most areas of activity. Clients were asked to list any kin who dropped in unannounced, who had a key to their apartment, with whom they gave and received baby-sitting assistance, with whom they shared a household at present or in the past, who lived in the same building, and who lived within walking distance. In all of these cases the majority of kin listed came from the wife's side of the family. With one

TABLE 1   Proportion of Wife's Kin Listed in Answers to Questions on Interaction and Proximity*

	Per Cent
Drop in unannounced	78
Have a key	86
Share present household	54
Share past household	93
Live in same building	91
Live within walking distance	66
Give baby-sitting assistance	86
Receive baby-sitting assistance	76

* This table should be read as follows: Of all the kin listed as dropping in unannounced, 78 per cent were wife's rather than husband's relatives.

exception, two-thirds or more of the kin listed were on the wife's side of the family. Kin sharing a present household are almost equally divided between husband's and wife's relatives; these are most likely to be elderly parents of husband or wife, and illness, economic need, or widowhood are likely to play a major part in determining who will move in with the couple. Past residence with kin, however, was most often [true] of young couples in the homes of the wife's parents.

There were also certain exceptions in the lateral direction of kin interaction which appear to relate to the type of activity. Seventy-five per cent of the kin with whom husbands were in business were their own kin. Thus in the man's occupational role he is involved more often with his own kin than with his wife's. Husbands also listed more of their own kin, 86 per cent, as those with whom they maintain phone contact. In most areas of interaction, however, particularly those defined as part of the woman's role, there is a predominance of interaction with the wife's kin. Moreover, there are more wife's than husband's kin in geographic proximity, and this is set for the household [and] not merely [for] the individual action of the husband or the wife.

Therefore there are definite tendencies for client families to be more heavily involved with the wife's than with the husband's kin. Other data, dealing with sentiments rather than interaction, support this interpretation. When asked which relatives clients feel they have most in common with, which relatives they feel closest to, and which relatives they would want to care for their children if something should happen to them, wives give priority to their kin and husbands most often mention theirs. But husbands mention their own kin less often than wives mention kin on their side. Thus there are more husbands who give priority to their wives'

TABLE 2   Proportion of Own Kin Listed by Husbands and Wives on Sentiment Items

	Husbands (Per Cent)	Wives (Per Cent)
Most in common with	58	76
Feel closest to	61	91
Would leave orphaned children to	58	85

side of the family than there are wives who lean toward the husbands' side.

This tendency for client families to lean toward the wife's side of the kinship network may be related in part to the different roles of husband and wife in maintaining their own household. . . .

* * * * *

This suggests there is more reason in the day-to-day life of the household for a woman to maintain close contact with her side of the family, particularly the women in her family, than for a man to keep in constant touch with his kin.

Whatever the individual motivations for the matrilateral tendency found in client families, there is also reason to believe this was the traditional pattern among Eastern European Jews and may at one time have been more extensive than it is now.

In their description of life in the Eastern European Jewish village or "shtetl," Landes and Zborowski assert that the son-in-law is warmly received into the bride's family; the marriage is arranged by the parents, and "it is a commonplace that a man prefers his son-in-law to his son." If the son-in-law is a promising scholar, the wife's father has an obligation to support the young couple, who may live with her parents for several years after marriage while he pursues his studies. "This is known as supporting the young couple in *Kest*, and is regarded by the bride's parents as an ideal arrangement."[3]

In contrast, the parents of a son—particularly his mother—are much less ready to welcome a daughter-in-law, since it often means losing their son to the family of the girl he marries. Landes and Zborowski quote a proverb saying, "when a son marries, he gives the wife a contract and the mother a divorce." The son's mother never acknowledges any girl is good enough for her son and is continually critical of her appearance, her housekeeping, her child-rearing practices, her cooking. . . .

There is reason to believe, then, that the tendency for a couple to be drawn into the wife's circle of kin is not simply a matter of common household interests between the wife and her mother. In addition, the attitudes of the couple's parents toward both husband and wife traditionally contribute to the pattern: her parents are warmly disposed toward him, while his parents, and particularly his mother, are less likely to accept her. Now we turn to the next part of the analysis: How is the marital relationship affected by this pattern of matrilateral involvement.

In a total of 147 client families, husband, wife, or both answered the conflict questions in the questionnaire with sufficient detail to permit further analysis. The 234 conflict situations they described were classified according to which spouse's kin were listed and whether or not the conflict with kin led to marital conflict. In all, husbands and

wives listed 467 kin in various categories. . . .

When conflicts which led to marital discord are separated from those that did not, it is clear that the relatives involved in the two types are different. Husbands and wives both tend to name their own relatives in nonmarital conflicts. But in conflicts that led to marital discord, both husbands and wives list more kin on the husband's side of the family.

Some of the themes which emerged from the write-in questions on conflict, and from interviews, may help clarify this tendency for husband's kin rather than wife's to stimulate marital conflict.

One of the most prevalent themes has to do with the wife's complaint that her husband's relatives neglect, exclude, or criticize her and that her husband fails to defend her sufficiently; that is, his family rejects her and, under the cross pressure of his divided loyalties to them and her, the wife feels he wavers. A few quotes from interviews and questionnaire data will serve to illustrate these themes:

Mrs. 247: [It was about] the marriage of their daughter—we were annoyed that we weren't asked to the ceremony. . . . We told them how we felt. . . .

Mr. 247: [Says of the same situation, it was] not our business to say anything.

This problem of invitations, particularly to weddings, occurs frequently and vividly documents the feelings of exclusion on the wife's part. In one case, a client wife blamed her husband's sister for not making sure she and her husband were told where an anniversary party was to be held. Mrs. 014 says she feels the incident was "proof" that "I was never accepted as a member of the family." The wife's feeling of rejection may not be due to a sense of exclusion

---

[3] Ruth Landes and Mark Zborowski, "Hypothesis Concerning the Eastern European Jewish Family," *Psychiatry*, 13 (1950), 447-464.

but rather to a feeling that she is constantly being criticized by her husband's kin, as the examples below suggest:

Mrs. 104: My husband's sister is always making remarks of anything I do that she thinks is not right and he comes home arguing with me. . . . Example: children's underwear not white enough. . . . My mother-in-law always agrees with her.

Mrs. 238: When my husband was put on a salt-free diet, my sister-in-law thought it would be best not to kosher meat for my husband. I continued to do what I thought best about food in my house [despite the fact that her husband agreed with his sister].

Sometimes the wife feels that not only she but her husband is being rejected by his kin. As Mrs. 148 put it:

It began between me and my father-in-law about him not caring when his son was emotionally ill. He went on his vacation and didn't even call till he was home several days. [She says her husband took his father's side.] I shouldn't butt in with him and his parents' treatment of him, but I get so angry and frustrated that he treats them so regally when they're so indifferent and cold to him and his family.

A related theme in these conflicts is the wife's feeling that her husband devotes too much time and affection to his relatives, neglecting her:

Mr. 265: Wife felt time I used visiting sister should be devoted to spend more time at home.

Mrs. 264: Whether or not to visit father-in-law on Saturday in preference to going out together. Husband went alone.

Mrs. 073: He wants me to go to his relatives. He goes to them without me, has given gifts without my knowledge, and used to spend his days in aunt's house and take her by car on errands

which he has found hard to do for me (I mean the car favors).

A final succinct statement of this theme: "I think my husband spends too much time for his father," says Mrs. 026. . . .

* * * * *

A central theme therefore is the wife's feeling that her husband's relatives reject, exclude, neglect, exploit, or criticize her or her husband. Related to this is the complaint that the husband devotes too much time and attention to his relatives at the expense of that to his wife and children. Conflicts with the wife's kin also occur, but they are much more frequently between the wife and her mother or other kin and do not become a source of marital conflict; husbands generally do not appear to feel excluded from the wife's family or to resent the wife's involvement with her kin in the same way that wives resent the husband's involvement with his.

An emphasis on a strong tie with the wife's family, specifically a mother-daughter tie, has also been observed in East London by Young and Willmott, but the focal point of conflict with kin is different. They report, "the great triangle of adult life is Mum-wife-husband," describing the frequent resentment which husbands have of their mother-in-law's influence, claiming that the husband may feel "excluded from the feminine circle."[4] They report, moreover, that "the first visit of a man to his future bride's family is thought more of an event than that of the girl to his family."[5]

Despite certain similarities in the

---

[4] Michael Young and Peter Willmott, *Family and Kinship in East London* (New York: The Free Press of Glencoe, Inc., 1957), pp. 46-47.
[5] *Ibid.*, p. 51.

matrilateral emphasis in the East London study, the focal point of conflict presents a contrast to that found among the Jewish clients. One factor of importance in the structuring of conflicts among the client families is undoubtedly the high value placed on maintaining interaction with kin. Data on kinship values revealed a strong emphasis on obligations to interact with kin, much stronger than that found among caseworkers, of whom the majority also come from Jewish families. One values item included in [our] questionnaire was, "It's selfish for someone to cut himself off from his relatives." Most agreed: 65 per cent of the husbands agreed, 64 per cent of [the] wives agreed. Some clients linked the obligation to maintain kin ties with Jewish cultural values:

Ideology stresses in the Jewish family the fact that you are related; in some form or another, you must be close. . . . If I come in, I ask Milton how he is. But Milton doesn't ask me how I am. This is a different view already; I'm interested in him, I ask him, but he didn't ask me. I'm not going to be petty about it and not ask him next time. I'm not that kind of individual. . . . Truthfully, if he wasn't a brother-in-law, the next time I saw him I wouldn't ask him either. But I was brought up with the idea of relatives' closeness . . . the closeness of the family. So if he comes up, I'll ask him again. But if he was a stranger, I'd never ask him again because he's not interested in me. But that's my background. That's why I say in a Jewish family this here business of ideology.

The importance of maintaining close ties with kin means, then, first, that the husband's family is likely to resent his tendency to move away from them into the wife's kinship circle, and second, that it is difficult for the husband to reduce potential conflicts with relatives by avoiding them altogether; the obligation to continue interacting is too strong. It is this obligation to maintain close kin ties with all relatives, combined with a tendency for client families to be matrilaterally involved, which appears to pull the husband in two directions, with a consequent strain on the marital tie.

Conclusions

We have examined the concept of laterality—the ways in which the nuclear family is integrated with one or both sides of its kin network—as it applies to the analysis of interaction and conflict found among client families and their kin. Data on Jewish Family Service clients indicate that client families tend to be more involved with the wife's kin than with the husband's, that this matrilateral focus places a strain on the couple's relations with the husband's kin, and that this strain in turn appears to strain the marital bond.

Structural predisposition to strain is of course only one of the multiple factors contributing to the conflicts suffered by any one family. Nevertheless, it offers the social worker a useful guide in mapping out the ways in which external systems may shape the internal workings of the family group.

Part 10

interaction
between
familial
and societal
factors
in social change

the machine as a factor in family change

thirty-three

In this classic of a century ago, Karl Marx points out that the machine is not defined as the use of steam engines or water power, but as the creation of a substitute for the human hand. Once the machine can perform the action formerly carried out by the hand, then power can be applied. However, this means that human skill is reduced in market value. Consequently, the unskilled may be ›hired at low wages. Economic competition then—Marx followed the thinking of classical economics, in the main—forces everyone to work at the lowest wages, and the total wages of all members of the family become equal to the wages once earned by the head of the family alone. Note that he utilizes a substantial body of *social research* available at that time (albeit of a crude variety) to buttress his assertions about the effect of the machine on women, children, and the family.

The Approximate Effects of Machinery on the Workman

KARL MARX

The starting point of modern industry is, as we have shown, the revolution in the instruments of labor, and this

Karl Marx, *Capital* (New York: Modern Library, Inc., n.d.), pp. 430-437. Reprinted by permission of Random House, Inc.

revolution attains its most highly developed form in the organized system of machinery in a factory. Before we inquire how human material is incorporated with this objective organism, let us consider some general effects of this revolution on the laborer himself.

Insofar as machinery dispenses with

muscular power, it becomes a means of employing laborers of slight muscular strength and those whose bodily development is incomplete, but whose limbs are all the more supple. The labor of women and children was therefore the first thing sought for by capitalists who used machinery. That mighty substitute for labor and laborers was forthwith changed into a means for increasing the number of wage laborers by enrolling, under the direct sway of capital, every member of the workman's family, without distinction of age or sex. Compulsory work for the capitalist usurped the place, not only of the children's play, but also of free labor at home within moderate limits for the support of the family.[1]

The value of labor power was determined, not only by the labor time necessary to maintain the individual adult laborer, but also by that necessary to maintain his family. Machinery, by throwing every member of that family onto the labor market, spread the value of the man's labor power over his whole family. It thus depreciates his labor power. To purchase the labor power of a family of four workers may, perhaps, cost more than it formerly did to purchase the labor power of the head of the family, but in return, four days' labor takes the place of one, and their price falls in proportion to the excess of the surplus labor of four over the surplus labor of one. In order that the family may live, four people must now not only labor, but expend surplus labor for the capitalist. Thus we see that machinery, while augmenting the human material that forms the principal object of capital's exploiting power,[2] at the same time raises the degree of exploitation.

Machinery also revolutionizes out and out the contract between the laborer and the capitalist, which formally fixes their mutual relations. Taking the exchange of commodities as our basis, our first assumption was that capitalist and laborer met as free persons, as independent owners of commodities, the

[1] Dr. Edward Smith, during the cotton crisis caused by the American Civil War, was sent by the English Government to Lancashire, Cheshire, and other places, to report on the sanitary condition of the cotton operatives. He reported that from a hygienic point of view, and apart from the banishment of the operatives from the factory atmosphere, the crisis had several advantages. The women now had sufficient leisure to give their infants the breast, instead of poisoning them with "Godfrey's cordial." They had time to learn to cook. Unfortunately the acquisition of this art occurred at a time when they had nothing to cook. But from this we see how capital, for the purposes of its self-expansion, has usurped the labor necessary in the home of the family. This crisis was also utilized to teach sewing to the daughters of the workmen in sewing schools. An American revolution and a universal crisis in order that the working girls, who spin for the whole world, might learn to sew!

[2] "The numerical increase of laborers has been great, through the growing substitution of female for male and, above all, of childish for adult labor. Three girls of thirteen, at wages of from six shillings to eight shillings a week, have replaced the one man of mature age, of wages varying from eighteen shillings to forty-five shillings." [Thomas de Quincey, *The Logic of Political Economy* (London, 1845). Note to p. 147.] Since certain family functions, such as nursing and suckling children, cannot be entirely suppressed, the mothers confiscated by capital must try substitutes of some sort. Domestic work, such as sewing and mending, must be replaced by the purchase of readymade articles. Hence the diminished expenditure of labor in the house is accompanied by an increased expenditure of money. The cost of keeping the family increases and balances the greater income. In addition to this, economy and judgment in the consumption and preparation of the means of subsistence become impossible. Abundant material relating to these facts, which are concealed by official political economy, is to be found in the Reports of the Inspectors of Factories, of the Children's Employment Commission, and more especially in the Reports on Public Health.

one possessing money and means of production, the other labor power. But now the capitalist buys children and young persons under age. Previously the workman sold his own labor power, which he disposed of nominally as a free agent. Now he sells wife and child. He has become a slave dealer.[3] The demand for children's labor often resembles in form the inquiries for Negro slaves, such as were formerly to be read among the advertisements in American journals. "My attention," says an English factory inspector, "was drawn to an advertisement in the local paper of one of the most important manufacturing towns of my district, of which the following is a ccpy: Wanted, twelve to twenty young persons, not younger than what can pass for thirteen years. Wages, 4 shillings a week. Apply &c."[4] The phrase "what can pass for thirteen years," has reference to the fact that by the Factory Act, children under thir-teen years may work only six hours. A surgeon official appointed must certify their age. The manufacturer therefore asks for children who look as if they were already thirteen years old. The decrease, often by leaps and bounds in the number of children under thirteen years employed in factories, a decrease that is shown in an astonishing manner by the English statistics of the last twenty years, was for the most part, according to the evidence of the factory inspectors themselves, the work of the certifying surgeons, who overstated the age of the children, agreeably to the capitalist's greed for exploitation, and the sordid trafficking needs of the parents. In the notorious district of Bethnal Green, a public market is held every Monday and Tuesday morning, where children of both sexes from nine years of age upward, hire themselves out to the silk manufacturers. "The usual terms are 1s. 8d. a week (this belongs to the parents) and '2d. for myself and tea.' The contract is binding only for the week. The scene and language while this market is going on are quite disgraceful."[5] It has also occurred in England that women have taken "children from the workhouse and let any one have them out for 2s. 6d. a week."[6] In spite of legislation, the number of boys sold in Great Britain by their parents to act as live chimney-sweeping machines (although there exist plenty of machines to replace them) exceeds 2000.[7] The revolution effected by machinery in the judicial relations between the buyer and the seller of labor power, causing the transaction as a whole to lose the appearance of a contract between free persons, afforded the English Parliament an excuse, founded on

---

[3] In striking contrast with the great fact that the shortening of the hours of labor of women and children in English factories was exacted from capital by the male operatives, we find in the latest reports of the Children's Employment Commission traits of the operative parents in relation to the traffic in children that are truly revolting and thoroughly like slave dealing. But the Pharisee of a capitalist, as may be seen from the same reports, denounces this brutality which he himself creates, perpetuates, and exploits, and which he moreover baptizes "freedom of labour." "Infant labor has been called into aid . . . even to work for their own daily bread. Without strength to endure such disproportionate toil, without instruction to guide their future life, they have been thrown into a situation physically and morally polluted. The Jewish historian has remarked upon the overthrow of Jerusalem by Titus that it was no wonder it should have been destroyed with such a signal destruction, when an inhuman mother sacrificed her own offspring to satisfy the cravings of absolute hunger." ("Public Economy Concentrated." Carlisle, 1833, p. 56.)

[4] A. Redgrave in "Reports of the Inspectors of Factories for 31st October, 1858," pp. 40-41.

[5] Children's Employment Commission, Fifth Report, London, 1866, p. 81, n. 31.

[6] Children's Employment Commission, Third Report, London, 1864, p. 53, n. 15.

[7] *Ibid.*, Fifth Report, p. 22, n. 137.

judicial principles, for the interference of the state with factories. Whenever the law limits the labor of children to six hours in industries not before interfered with, the complaints of the manufacturers are always renewed. They allege that numbers of the parents withdraw their children from the industry brought under the act, in order to sell them where "freedom of labor" still rules, i.e., where children under thirteen years are compelled to work like grown-up people and therefore can be got rid of at a higher price. But since capital is by nature a leveller, since it exacts in every sphere of production equality in the conditions of the exploitation of labor, the limitation by law of children's labor, in one branch of industry, becomes the cause of its limitation in others.

We have already alluded to the physical deterioration as well of the children and young persons as of the women, whom machinery, first directly in the factories that shoot up on its bases, and then indirectly in all the remaining branches of industry, subjects to the exploitation of capital. In this place therefore we dwell only on one point, the enormous mortality, during the first few years of their life, of the children of the operatives. In sixteen of the registration districts into which England is divided, there are, for every 100,000 children alive under the age of one year, only 9000 deaths in the year on an average (in one district only 7047); in twenty-four districts the deaths are over 10,000, but under 11,000; in thirty-nine districts over 11,000, but under 12,000; in forty-eight districts over 12,000, but under 13,000; in twenty-two districts over 20,000; in twenty-five districts over 21,-000; in seventeen over 22,000; in eleven over 23,000; in Hoo, Wolverhampton, Ashton-under-Lyne, and Preston, over 24,000; in Nottingham, Stockport, and Bradford, over 25,000; in Wisbeach, 26,000; and in Manchester, 26,125.[8] As was shown by an official medical inquiry in the year 1861, the high death rates are, apart from local causes, principally due to the employment of the mothers away from their homes and to the neglect and maltreatment consequent on her absence, such as, amongst others, insufficient nourishment, unsuitable food, and dosing with opiates; beside this, there arises an unnatural estrangement between mother and child, and as a consequence, intentional starving and poisoning of the children.[9] In those agricultural districts, "where a minimum in the employment of women exists, the death-rate is on the other hand very low."[10] The Inquiry-Commission of 1861 led, however, to the unexpected result that in some purely agricultural districts bordering on the North Sea, the death rate of children under one year old almost equalled that of the worst factory districts. Dr. Julian Hunter was therefore commissioned to investigate this phenomenon on the spot. His report is incorporated with the "Sixth Report on Public Health."[11] Up to that time it was supposed that the children were decimated by malaria, and other diseases peculiar to low-lying and marshy districts. But the inquiry showed the very opposite, namely, that the same cause which drove away malaria, the conversion of the land from a morass in winter and a scanty pas-

___

[8] Sixth Report on Public Health, London, 1864, p. 34.

[9] "It [the inquiry of 1861] . . . showed, moreover, that while, with the described circumstances, infants perish under the neglect and mismanagement which their mothers' occupations imply, the mothers become to a grievous extent denaturalized towards their offspring—commonly not troubling themselves much at the death, and even sometimes . . . taking direct measures to insure it," *ibid*.

[10] *Ibid.*, p. 454.

[11] *Ibid.*, p. 454-463. "Report by Dr. Henry Julian Hunter on the Excessive Mortality of Infants in Some Rural Districts of England."

ture in summer into fruitful corn land, created the exceptional death rate of the infants.[12] The seventy medical men whom Dr. Hunter examined in that district were "wonderfully in accord" on this point. In fact, the revolution in the mode of cultivation had led to the introduction of the industrial system. Married women, who work in gangs along with boys and girls, are, for a stipulated sum of money, placed at the disposal of the farmer, by a man called "the undertaker," who contracts for the whole gang.

These gangs will sometimes travel many miles from their own village; they are to be met morning and evening on the roads, dressed in short petticoats, with suitable coats and boots, and sometimes trousers, looking wonderfully strong and healthy, but tainted with a customary immorality, and heedless of the fatal results which their love of this busy and independent life is bringing on their unfortunate offspring who are pining at home.[13]

Every phenomenon of the factory districts is here reproduced, including, but to a greater extent, ill-disguised infanticide and dosing children with opiates.[14] "My knowledge of such evils," says Dr. Simon, the medical officer of the Privy Council and editor in chief of the Reports on Public Health, "may excuse the profound misgiving with which I regard any large industrial employment of adult women."[15] "Happy

indeed," exclaims Mr. Baker, the factory inspector, in his official report, "happy indeed will it be for the manufacturing districts of England, when every married woman having a family is prohibited from working in any textile works at all."[16]

The moral degradation caused by the capitalistic exploitation of women and children has been so exhaustively depicted by F. Engels in his *Lage der Arbeitenden Klasse Englands,* and other writers, that I need only mention the subject in this place. But the intellectual desolation, artificially produced by converting immature human beings into mere machines for the fabrication of surplus value, a state of mind clearly distinguishable from that natural ignorance which keeps the mind fallow without destroying its capacity for development, its natural fertility, this desolation finally compelled even the English Parliament to make elementary education a compulsory condition to the "productive" employment of children under fourteen years, in every industry subject to the Factory Acts. The spirit of capitalist production stands out clearly in the ludicrous wording of the so-called education clauses in the Factory Acts, in the absence of an administrative machinery, an absence that again makes the compulsion illusory, in the opposition of the manufacturers themselves to these education clauses, and in the tricks and dodges they put in practice for evading them.

For this the legislature is alone to blame, by having passed a delusive law, which, while it would seem to provide that the children employed in factories shall be *educated,* contains no enactment by which that professed end can be secured. It provides nothing more than that the children shall on certain days of the week,

---

12 *Ibid.*, p. 35, 455-456.

13 *Ibid.*, p. 456.

14 In the agricultural as well as in the factory districts the consumption of opium among the grown-up laborers, both male and female, is extending daily. "To push the sale of opiate . . . is the great aim of some enterprising wholesale merchants. By druggists it is considered the leading article," *ibid.*, p. 459. Infants that [took] opiates "shrank up into little old men," or "wizzened like little monkeys," *ibid.*, p. 460. We here see how India and China avenged themselves on England.

15 *Ibid.*, p. 37.

16 "Reports of the Inspectors of Factories for 31st October, 1862," p. 59. Mr. Baker was formerly a doctor.

and for a certain number of hours (three) in each day, be inclosed within the four walls of a place called a school, and that the employer of the child shall receive weekly a certificate to that effect signed by a person designated by the subscriber as a schoolmaster or schoolmistress.[17]

Previous to the passing of the amended Factory Act, 1844, it happened, not unfrequently, that the certificate[s] of attendance at school were signed by the schoolmaster or schoolmistress with a cross, as they themselves were unable to write.

On one occasion, on visiting a place called a school, from which certificates of school attendance had issued, I was so struck with the ignorance of the master that I said to him: "Pray, sir, can you read?" His reply was: "Ay, summat!" and as a justification of his right to grant certificates, he added: "At any rate, I am before my scholars." The inspectors, when the Bill of 1844 was in preparation, did not fail to represent the disgraceful state of the places called schools, certificates from which they were obliged to admit as a compliance with the laws, but they were successful only in obtaining thus much, that since the passing of the Act of 1844, the figures in the school certificate must be filled up in the handwriting of the schoolmaster, who must also sign his Christian and surname in full.[18]

[17] Leonard Horner in "Reports of the Inspectors of Factories for 30th June, 1857," p. 17.

[18] Horner in "Reports of the Inspectors of Factories for 31st October, 1855," pp. 18-19.

*   *   *   *   *

the family as an independent factor in industrialization

thirty-four

Within roughly half a century after the Meiji Restoration in 1868, Japan had built heavy industries almost without foreign capital, achieved a high rate of literacy, established many high-profit plants whose yield permitted further economic expansion, and modernized many of its basic economic relations. Both China and Japan were in a similar situation in the last half of the nineteenth century—threatened by Western powers superior in war technology, governed by a corrupt and incompetent bureaucracy, torn by rural-urban and class dissension, and giving highest respect to a type of learning that was essentially irrelevant to modern technological problems. Yet China did not achieve a solution for its difficulties. In this section, the sociologist points to certain crucial family differences between China and Japan that contributed to the very different pace of modernization in the two countries.

Contrasting Factors in the Modernization of China and Japan

MARION J. LEVY, JR.

*   *   *   *   *

As in China, the governmental structure [in Japan] was a combination of highly centralized and highly decentralized elements. The system of controls set up by the Tokugawa rulers [1603-1867] was certainly in its initial stages one of the most tightly and effectively controlled feudal systems the world has ever seen. The strong men of the Tokugawa regime were well aware of the sort of trouble nobles could give if they were permitted to get out of hand, and they set about deliberately to make this impossible. . . . Nevertheless, in the local areas controlled by the *daimio*, the discretion of the *daimio* [feudal noble] was virtually unlimited as long as it did not threaten in any conceivable way the precedence and power of the *Shogun* [Premier]. Neither the centralized elements nor the decentralized ones were of the same sort as those in China, however. One of the main differences in these respects lay in the fact that decentralization went all the way down the hierarchy in China, stopping in essence only with the family head, whose powers were not decentralized though they were sometimes delegated. In Japan the decentralization lay in the scope of power left to the *daimio* (as in the case of the scope of power left to the governors in China), but the *daimio* did not necessarily de-

Marion J. Levy, Jr., "Contrasting Factors in the Modernization of China and Japan," Simon Kuznets, Wilbert E. Moore, and Joseph J. Spengler (eds.), *Economic Growth: Brazil, India, Japan* (Durham: Duke University Press, 1955), pp. 515-521. We are grateful to the author and Duke University Press for permission to quote.

centralize their control further. Certainly the system in Japan was not such that the position of family head was in general as strategic as in China.

As in China, there was in fact a bureaucracy that conducted, and was held responsible for, major administrative functions, but it was not in anything like the Chinese sense a single bureaucracy for the country as a whole. As in China, there was considerable need for, and emphasis on, ability on the part of the persons who fulfilled these administrative roles. Unlike the Chinese bureaucracy, that in Japan was not set up as a separate concrete organization with members chosen for ability and insulated, ideally speaking, from other concrete organizations in the society. In this sphere, the Japanese resorted to a most interesting social device, and this device was one that had considerable adaptive value in the period of modernization. In Japan the family system was also a major focus of loyalty despite the fact that it did not take the same order or type of precedence as that taken by the Chinese family system. Unlike the case in China, the major administrative posts were hereditarily determined. In China this was only true, ideally speaking, of the Emperor's position.

This situation also obtained among the merchants. Among the merchants of Japan there was not the possibility of leaving merchant roles that existed in China, . . . and since the rule of equal inheritance on the part of all sons that held in China was not characteristic in Japan, there was not the tendency for a man's successor in these roles to inherit something less than the estate that he had left intact. The Japanese worked out, either deliberately or not, a sort of civil service system by adoption. Sometimes these adoptions would even cross the ordinarily closed class lines. A *daimio* might adopt as his successor an exceptionally able young man from among his *samurai* [feudal warriors], who in general performed administrative functions for him. He would ordinarily seek an able man from within his own family if possible, but he could and sometimes did go outside the family or the kinship structure as a whole. Furthermore, he could, and sometimes did, supplant his actual eldest son with a person adopted as eldest son. Such adoptions were generally made only after the previously legitimate successor, if any, had shown himself to be conspicuously unable. When such an adoption took place, one had an administrator picked for ability. But one did not have to seek vainly to insulate this man from a sea of nepotistic and similar conflicting pressures. He was put in a role such that all of these pressures motivated him to use his abilities to the utmost for the administrative purpose for which he was chosen. Family, friends, feudal loyalties, everything he had been taught to respect, in both fact and ideal, required the maximum objective use of his talents in the role for which he was selected. The conflict between the betterment of one's family and the proper fulfillment of office so common in China was not to nearly the same degree a problem here because one's family and one's office were combined.

This was done by the merchants as well as by the feudal lords. Japanese merchants, unlike Chinese ones, were not preoccupied with the use of merchant status to abandon merchant roles. They were rather much concerned to recruit, on the basis of competence, family members who would in fact remain in merchant roles and preserve the welfare of the family thereby. This particular technique was continued by the successors of the merchants in the modernization of Japan. The *zaibatsu* [great industrial clans], who in strategic numbers developed directly out of Tokugawa merchant families, were well known for this. These families instituted a sort of business civil service within their companies, and those men most successful in the competition and destined to become major figures in the various enterprises of the family were frequently brought into the family membership itself. It was, in a sense, the Japanese equivalent of giving a particularly important member of the administration of a stock company a major block of stock in the company, presumably tying thereby his self-interest and the interest of the owners of the company as tightly together as possible.

There were two major differences between Chinese and Japanese family structure that are relevant for present purposes: (1) the manner in which family considerations entered the total social picture and (2) the fact that there was not in Japan a single ideal type of family for the entire membership of the society. The first of these turned on the difference in manner of integrating the two societies; the second turned on the marked differences in class structure in the two societies.[1]

A third difference that was probably strategic for present purposes lay in the emphasis on primogeniture in Japan. It was not always true that the oldest son in fact succeeded to the family property or rights. He could be, and

---

[1] This had many implications. For example, in Japan the possibilities of alternative employment were even more restricted than in China because of the closed class situation and because of the relations of the peasants to their lords.

sometimes was, replaced by someone adopted as an oldest son, or he could even be replaced by a younger brother, but the rule practiced in China of equal inheritance among all the sons was not followed in Japan. This made possible at one and the same time the continued concentration of wealth in a single family line and the creation of a cadet class. Both of these are closely related to the feudal social structure. . . .

Despite many similarities between "traditional" China and "traditional" Japan, the total structures of the two societies were markedly different. "Traditional" Japan was a feudal society . . . , or at least a very close approach to one, and this was not true of "traditional" China. Furthermore, when one looks into the history of Chinese and Japanese experience, one is struck by the contrast between Chinese and Japanese attitudes toward general social control and the maintenance of social stability. The Chinese had an attitude much like that attributed to Locke. The structure of society would function to the best interests of everyone if it were set up in accord with the Will of Heaven and left as much alone as possible, with occasional interference only to restore the Will of Heaven. The rulers of Japan, however, often seem to have been preoccupied with the possibilities of manipulating social structure for purposes of control, and with the strategic role of those who know how to plan and execute such manipulations. There is certainly evidence that the strong men of the Tokugawa knew what they were about in these respects, and there is at least good reason to suspect that those in power during the modernization of Japan were up to the same sort of thing.

The founder of the Tokugawa regime, Iyeyasu, and his followers, especially Iyemitsu and Yoshimuno, seem certainly to have been conscious so-cial engineers. The early Tokugawa (Iyeyasu and Iyemitsu) were well aware of the vulnerabilities of social control in a feudal system. It was one thing to order a power hierarchy and tie land distribution to it in the feudal manner. It was quite another to retain control over the nobles once great power had been allocated to them. Iyeyasu's predecessors and colleagues, Nobunaga and Hideyoshi, and subdued just such a set of nobles and thereby made the Tokugawa regime possible. Iyeyasu and Iyemitsu had no intention of having to do it again. At a time when the nobles were still relatively weak and they strong, the Tokugawa set up a system intended to defy the decay so common in feudal systems. For one thing they set up an official capital city in the form of a court at Yedo. Then they made it clear that, although they were not the emperors of Japan, they were not merely the first among equals as far as the nobles were concerned. Each feudal lord of any consequence, the *daimio* in this case, was required to spend a definite portion of his time at the *Shogun's* court, and when he was not there, he had to leave members of his family (preferably his wife and heirs) in his place. The only solidarity in Japanese social structure that offered any threat to the primacy of the obligation to one's overlord was the family bond, and by this hostage system the Tokugawa tied the two together as far as the *daimio* were concerned. One might . . . meritoriously sacrifice one's family to fulfill one's obligations to one's overlord, but to sacrifice one's family in the attempt to defy one's overlord was sin itself in that society. Even if one lord did attempt revolt, the pressures that the *Shogun* could bring to bear upon the rest through their own feelings of loyalty and the hostage system were enough to guarantee the *Shogun* overwhelming allies in addition to his own strength.

Having established their regime, the Tokugawa attempted to guarantee its security into perpetuity. This was of course futile in the long run, but the thoroughness of the attempt and the relative stability it achieved for some two and a half centuries are illuminating. The Tokugawa attempted in every way possible, at first, to prevent change. There were detailed regulations as to what was expected of virtually every type of person in the society. These regulations were made as minute as possible, the more so the more an individual's role was likely to be one in which deviance on his part could be significantly disruptive of order in the society. The regulations covered dress and deportment to such an extent that deviant activity was likely to be immediately and visually obvious. Individuals failing to offer the proper homage in a given situation could be, and were on occasion, cut down by the *samurai* without further question. On one occasion in the nineteenth century, the automatic application of such measures involved the Japanese in a serious incident with the British—an incident that brought home radically to the Japanese their utter defenselessness before the Western powers.[2]

---

[2] The Namamugi incident (1862) involved a British subject named Richardson, who was overwhelmed by the magnificence of an approaching *daimio's* retinue, remained mounted, and stared. It was gross insolence and lèse majesty from the Japanese point of view, something every person of low social status knew better than to do. The *daimio's samurai* cut down the offender. The British in reprisal made their first punitive use of a breech-loading naval rifle to pound to pieces certain Japanese forts which had perhaps the most modern artillery in Japan. The Japanese were most impressed. They learned far more from the incident than the fact that Westerners were not sensitive to the intricacies of feudal respect and the like.

Whatever their methods or whatever the foundations on which they built, subjects of the Tokugawa both knew and, of their own will apparently, came to accept the tremendous emphasis placed on loyalty to the various positions in the feudal hierarchy. Every man's first duty was to his overlord. This obligation surpassed even the family obligation, and it was in considerable part because of this that the role of the family in Japanese social structure was so markedly different from that in China. The extreme emphasis placed on this sort of loyalty is well illustrated in the case of the nobility by the Tale of the Forty-Seven Ronin and in the case of the peasants by certain of the phenomena associated with the peasant revolts under the Tokugawa regime. In the case of the Forty-Seven Ronin, the facts are perhaps not as important as the legend that immediately sprang up about them. Much was made of this legend in the transitional and resultant stage of Japan. In brief, the legend has to do with a group of retainers who sacrifice all other goals to avenge the death of their immediate overlord. In order to throw their master's enemy off guard, they are credited with virtually every act held evil, especially the ruination of their own families. After he has relaxed his guard, they slay him. Their vendetta, however, has been at least superficially in defiance of the *Shogun's* law against vendettas, so they fulfill their obligation to the *Shogun* by peacefully surrendering themselves with never a plea for mercy. The *Shogun*, despite his own respect for their extreme regard for loyalty, cannot let their breach of the law go unnoticed. Their fate is sealed, but the *Shogun* does permit them to atone for their crime by the honorable ceremonial suicide of the *samurai*. All of them commit *seppuku* [hari-kiri] and complete thereby all of the responsibilities they bear. Their master is avenged, their duty to the *Shogun* is fulfilled, and . . . their family obligations are satisfied because they leave their families a most honorable heritage. They have sacrificed everything to the ideal of feudal loyalty, and in so doing they have realized everything.

The peasant revolts sometimes furnished an equally impressive example of the emphasis placed on loyalty to one's masters. During the Tokugawa regime, the exactions placed upon the peasants sometimes were such that the peasants took matters into their own hands and backed their demands for reform by a show of force. It was quite clear in some of these cases that they in fact commanded the force necessary to carry their points, and . . . their demands were granted. Even after their power had been clearly demonstrated, however, once their demands were granted, their leaders on more than one occasion either were taken by, or themselves surrendered to, the very authorities against whom their use of force had been successful. These leaders usually suffered most painful deaths apparently without ever becoming the cause for a further demonstration of force on the part of the peasants. The peasants seemed to feel that, while they had had no choice but to revolt, someone had somehow to pay for this violation of things as they "should be."

In Japan, loyalty to the feudal hierarchy took clear precedence over loyalty to one's family. This did not mean that loyalty to one's family was unimportant. It was tremendously important. It did mean, however, that one had two means of control over the deviance of individuals, control as in the Chinese case through the family organization and direct control through the feudal hierarchy. One of the implications of this dual hold on the individual was that the possibility of individualism by default was minimized. Even if an in-

dividual were to lose or be separated from his family, he could not lose or be separated from the entire hierarchy of persons in positions of power over him. One of the most important arguments used in the amazingly peaceable deposition of the *Shogun* was of course to the effect that the *Shogun* had himself violated his loyalty to his overlord, the Emperor. The emphasis on loyalty was never denigrated. The people were simply told that this loyalty was due directly to the Emperor and his officials and hence to the Japanese nation and not to the *Shogun*.

* * * * *

Some of the differences between the "traditional" Chinese social system and that of "traditional" Japan have . . . been mentioned. . . . One of the most important . . . is the difference in class system in the two societies. . . . China had *ideally speaking* almost an entirely open class system. In the Japanese case, the picture was almost exactly the opposite with regard to the ideal patterns. Ideally speaking, the class system was completely closed. One was born to the social position of one's parents. It was expected that one stay in that position and that one's children and children's children stay in it as well. Actually there was some mobility, but it was rather carefully hedged so as not to disturb the general or the ideal patterns. There was some mobility within the class distinctions. One could, for example, rise higher or fall lower in the scale of *daimio* or peasant families, for example. There were also occasional cases of families that were demoted, though these were more likely to be wiped out. There were cases of elevation in status by the *Shogun*, but again these were probably rare. Certainly the most strategic form of mobility as far as its bearing on the present problem is concerned is one that appeared to involve no interclass mobility at all. This was the mobility involved in the peculiar "family civil service" mentioned above. But it is the essence of the adoption procedure that one's past position is in theory wiped out; the adopted son is at least in fiction held always to have been what he has just been made. Furthermore, such elevation was neither so frequent nor was it conducted in such a way that it could be made the goal of achievement by others generally in the society. It was a bonus that came occasionally; it was not something that could or should be striven for. This lack of general motivation to compete no doubt resulted in a failure to realize many human resources in the society, but at least in the Tokugawa period the strategic significance of relatively small differences in skill was not such as could be met only by large-scale motivation of this sort. In the modern period, when such differences did assume importance, an embryonic pattern of mobility that could be adapted to new conditions was in existence. Furthermore, the basis for such mobility in Japan was specifically relevant to the position for which the person was chosen. This was in marked contrast with the system of China, which had more of the character of the old British civil service, in which persons were selected primarily on the basis of examinations on a general intellectual background that was not necessarily germane to the roles that a person would fulfill after selection. For this purpose there was a sort of "on the job training" or none at all. In Japan those selected for advance by adoption were not selected until they had already shown the specific abilities for which their services were desired, and this in turn gave a precedent of sorts for later selection of persons on the basis of germane abilities in the modern period in which such a basis became so important.

* * * * *

changing patterns of child rearing in russia

thirty-five

Since children are effectively socialized to become like their parents, social change is impossible. This is obvious. But equally clear is the fact that social change takes place. Does all this change occur, then, after children leave home? Here Alex Inkeles deals with the special case of Russia, in which the attempt was made to transform the society from one generation to another. Some parents resisted, and some of these did so successfully. The author here explores the possibility that, though Russian children do become like their parents, their parents have also been changing their system of child rearing. Note especially the problems of research design that he raises.

Social Change and Social Character: The Role of Parental Mediation

ALEX INKELES

* * * * *

. . . These studies . . . seem to have one element in common in their approach to the role of the parent as "child rearer" under conditions of social change. Implicitly, if not explicitly, the parent is conceived as having available a relatively fixed repertory of child-training procedures provided by his culture and learned by him in the period of his own childhood. Two main alternatives as to his utilization of those techniques are then generally considered. On the one hand, the parent is seen as acting as the passive agent of his culture, raising his children according to the procedures he had learned earlier in his own childhood, even though these techniques may have lost their appropriateness. It is assumed in that case that as his children grow up the gulf between parent and child will rapidly grow great, and relations will become strained as the child meets and learns the conflicting behavior patterns and underlying values of his "own" new culture. On the other hand, the parent may know enough not to try to apply the training procedures under which he was raised, and in that case he either surrenders to other cultural surrogates, such as peer group, teachers, mass media, and so on, or borrows, and of course generally ineptly applies, some prefabricated set of rules. In the lower

classes the borrowing might be from the local baby clinic, and in the upper classes from books and lectures on child rearing. In short, the parents will manifest what Mead terms "disturbed and inconsistent images of their children's future."[1]

Without doubt these descriptions are faithful to the facts in many situations. Nevertheless, they seem to have made inadequate allowance for the positive adjustive capacity of human beings and for the process of continuous interaction that goes on between them and their sociocultural environment. Very often the global impact of Western contacts on a nonliterate people may be almost totally disorienting, but parents need not be either unimaginative and passive agents of their culture, raising their children by rote, or so disorganized and disoriented as is suggested by Mead's discussion. Although parents are adults, they may nevertheless still *learn*, and learn what they feel to be major "lessons," from their experiences under conditions of social change. This learning, furthermore, may influence the parents to seek purposefully to bring their children up in a way different from that in which they were raised, and in a manner intended better to suit the children for life in the changed social situation. This has been clearly recognized by Aberle and Naegele, who in a passage not easily duplicated elsewhere in the literature affirm that:

Alex Inkeles, "Social Change and Social Character: The Role of Parental Mediation," *Journal of Social Issues*, 11 (1955), 13-14, 16-22. We are grateful to the author and *Journal of Social Issues* for permission to quote.

[1] Margaret Mead, "The Implications of Culture Change for Personality Development," *American Journal of Orthopsychiatry*, 17 (1947), 633-646.

All in all child rearing is future oriented to an important extent. The picture of the desired end product is importantly influenced by the parents' experiences in the adult world, as well as by their childhood experiences. When adult experience changes under the impact of major social change, there is reason to believe that there will ultimately, although not necessarily immediately, be shifts in the socialization pattern as well.[2]

* * * * *

When we consider the profound differences, during their years of child rearing, in the life experience of the revolutionary generation as contrasted with that of its parents in the tsarist generation, what differences may we expect in their values with regard to child rearing? The revolutionary upheaval of 1917 and the subsequent programs of forced social change struck a great blow at the traditional structure of Russian society and profoundly altered it. Massive programs of expansion were undertaken in industrialization, in urbanization, in formal organization and administration. The pattern of rural

[2] D. F. Aberle and K. D. Naegele, "Middle-Class Fathers' Occupational Role and Attitudes Toward Children," *ibid.*, **22** (1952), 366-378.

life, in which the bulk of the population was involved, was drastically revised through the forced collectivization of agriculture. Centralized political control and political terror were ruthlessly imposed. Opportunities for mobility increased greatly. Under these circumstances we might well expect the traditional values to suffer the greatest loss of emphasis, with a consequent shift to stress on either simple successful adjustment or the more secularized morality represented by the personalistic values and the pursuit of knowledge as an end in itself. In addition, our knowledge of the growing opportunities for advancement, associated with the generally expanded development of the formal occupational structure, leads us to anticipate that greatly increased weight would be given to achievement. Finally, the central role played by the state in Soviet affairs, the existence of the political terror, and the additional fact that our respondents were disaffected from the political system, lead us to anticipate heightened concern with political considerations in child rearing.

In Table 1 we have indicated the distribution of emphasis among the di-

TABLE 1   Child-Rearing Values of Parents in Russian Prerevolutionary and Postrevolutionary Times

Areas	Distribution* of Emphasis in	
	Tsarist Period (Per Cent)	Postrevolutionary Period** (Per Cent)
Tradition	75	44
Achievement	60	52
"Personalistic"	32	44
Adjustment	16	21
Intellectuality	12	22
Politics	12	20
Number of Respondents	77	78

   * These percentages total more than 100, since respondents were scored for as many themes as cited, but percentaging is on the basis of total respondents.
   ** The percentages in this column have been adjusted to equalize for the effect created by the larger number of responses given by our informants in describing their own activity as parents, as against the manner in which they had been raised by the Tsarist generation.

mensions in our set of dominant value orientations. The relative stability of the gross rank order is testimony to the fact that both generations of parents represented a common cultural tradition which they carried forward through time. Nevertheless, it is clear that there have been very substantial shifts in the relative weight of several value orientations, and they go largely in the expected direction. Perhaps the most striking finding is the sharp decrease in emphasis on the traditional values, accounted for overwhelmingly by the decreased emphasis on religious training and belief. Under the impact of industrialization and urbanization, perhaps abetted by the antireligious and "proscientific" propaganda conducted by the regime, parents in the revolutionary generation clearly shifted toward an emphasis on more secular values. This shift is reflected in the increased emphasis on learning (intellectuality) and positive personal qualities as *ends in themselves* rather than as *means* to the attainment of the good life lived, as it were, "in the sight of God." Thus secular morality replaced traditional and religiously based morality.

Perhaps most directly and explicitly related to the intervening experience of the parents under conditions of social change is the increased attention paid to political considerations in the education of one's children. The greater emphasis on political problems arises from the fact that the Soviet regime has progressively "politicized" more and more areas of human activity that in most western societies fall outside the political realm. A person at all alert to his situation and surroundings could therefore hardly fail to realize that if he wished to prepare his child adequately for life under Soviet conditions, he must train him to an awareness concerning the political realities of the sys-

tem, even though such training had not been important in his own childhood. This interpretation is borne out by the statements made by our interviewers.

Finally, it is necessary to comment on the major instance in which the data fail to confirm expectation, namely in regard to emphasis on achievement values. This failure is of course only relative, since achievement was the most emphasized value in the rearing of children by those in the revolutionary generation. Nevertheless, in absolute weight it declined in importance even though it had been expected to increase. It might be that since our respondents were refugees from the system, and since many of them looked upon too active pursuit of a career as suggesting involvement with the regime, they did not admit fully the importance they actually attributed to inculcating achievement strivings in their children. On the other hand, it may be that the expectation was unrealistic quite apart from specific Soviet conditions. There is some evidence that values such as security, adjustment, and personal attractiveness are becoming ever more important foci in child rearing in the United States and that stress on achievement as *an end in itself*, although still prevalent, has become somewhat old-fashioned. This pattern may be associated with the combination of mass industry, education and communication, and the consumer culture of which the Soviet Union is but one example.

All told, however, the data certainly seem strongly to support the assumption that the experience of extreme social change that the revolutionary generation underwent did have a marked effect on that generation's approach to the rearing of its children. As compared with the way their parents raised them, they can hardly be assumed to have merely "recapitulated" the earlier pattern of child rearing. On the contrary, having experienced marked social change, they adjusted their child-rearing practices, the better to prepare their children for the life they expected those children to lead.

To test the effectiveness of the changed general child-rearing orientations of the revolutionary generation, we would need data on the personality patterns prevalent among their children in the third generation, which we unfortunately do not have. Nevertheless, we can make a very approximate approach to our second question concerning the effectiveness of the changed child-rearing emphases if we shift our attention to the realm of occupational choices. In that area we have data not only on the values stressed by parents, but we also have information on the values which the individual held in regard to himself. In treating value orientations relative to the occupational world, we are of course dealing not with personality patterns in a psychodynamic sense, but rather with something more closely akin to "social character" as it has been defined by Riesman and Inkeles.[3]

[3] David Riesman, *The Lonely Crowd* (New Haven: Yale University Press, 1950) and Alex Inkeles, "Some Sociological Observations on Culture and Personality Studies," in C. Kluckhohn, H. A. Murray, and D. M. Schneider (eds.), *Personality in Nature, Society, and Culture*, 2nd ed. (New York: Alfred A. Knopf, Inc., 1953), pp. 577-592.

The influence of their experience with social change on the child-training practices adopted by the revolutionary generation is perhaps even more strikingly evident in the area of occupational choices. In addition to asking about the specific occupations for which parents wished to prepare their children, we asked the reasons for the selection. The reasons cited provide us with a guide to the values that were dominant in the home atmosphere created by the parent for the child. Considering the nature of the social change experienced by the revolutionary generation . . . , we might again well expect that as part of the general weakening of the traditional way of life there would have been a decline in the importance of family tradition, as against self-expression or free choice, as values emphasized in orienting the child toward the occupational world. In addition, it is reasonable to assume that economic and material rewards would have come to be much more stressed among the goals set before the child, as would the necessity of finding work that permitted an appropriate accommodation to the highly politicized occupational structure in Soviet society.

As a comparison of the first and second columns of Table 2 indicates, three of these four expectations are rather strongly supported by the responses of our interviewees. We see, to

TABLE 2   Changing Values Concerning the Occupational Realm

| | Distribution of Emphasis Among Values Stressed | | |
| | In Child Rearing by: | | In Hypothetical Choice by |
Value Areas	"Tsarist" Generation (Per Cent)	"Revolutionary" Generation (Per Cent)	"Soviet" Generation (Per Cent)
Rewards	41	25	14
Tradition	35	14	11
Self-expression	21	38	62
Politics	3	23	13
Number of Responses (equal to 100 Per Cent)	58	63	931

begin, a sharp decline in the importance of family tradition as a criterion in shaping the child's occupational orientation, along with a marked increase in the role played by self-expression or free job choice. In addition, we may note the much greater emphasis on guiding the child toward a job that is politically desirable, which for our respondents generally meant one safe from danger of political arrest and not too directly involved in the regime's political objectives. Finally, it should be observed that here again the data fail to support our expectation that the material and psychic rewards on the job . . . would be more emphasized by the revolutionary generation than by the tsarist generation. Indeed, the relative weight of such rewards as values to be emphasized in orienting children toward the occupational world declined markedly from the one generation to the next.

Now to return to our original research design, do we have any evidence that the different child-rearing patterns utilized by the middle generation as a response to their experience of social change actually were effective? Or did the parents in that second generation, despite their apparent intention, act in fact as passive agents of the culture and, *nolens volens,* raise their children in their own image and much as the first generation would have done the job? For a proper answer to this question we should have access to the children of the revolutionary generation and to data on their job choices coded by the same categories used to describe the child-training values of their parents. Unfortunately we can only approximate each requirement. Respondents on both our written questionnaire and oral interview remained anonymous, and we therefore have no way of identifying the actual children of the revolutionary generation. But we can secure a reasonable equivalent of that third group, which we call the "Soviet" generation, by taking all respondents under thirty-five in 1950. Most of them were raised and reached adulthood in the same period in which the revolutionary generation was acting in the parental role and could well have been their children. As for the values that governed their job choices, we are obliged to draw on our written questionnaire, which presented the respondents with a choice of pre-coded categories not strictly comparable with those used in assessing child-training values. For example the check list included the omnibus category "I feel suited to it," which we have equated here with "self-expression," but which obviously could have meant many more things to the respondents.

Quite apart from such methodological difficulties, it would be naïve to expect a near-perfect correlation between the values that the parents in the revolutionary generation stressed while they reared the Soviet generation and the ones which that generation emphasized in its own job choices. Such training always produces only an approximation of the parents' desire. More important, those in the Soviet generation have had their values shaped by many influences other than those exerted by their parents. Nevertheless, our expectation is that on the whole the pattern of value orientations of the Soviet generation will be quite close to those that were stressed in child training by their parents in the revolutionary generation as contrasted with those inculcated in an earlier era by the tsarist generation. The relative degree of fit between the two sets of orientations may be taken as a rough measure of how successful the revolutionary generation was in training the Soviet generation to orient in new directions.

The appropriate comparison may be obtained by examining the third column of Table 2—which contains the distribution of emphasis in the operative values guiding the job choices of the younger generation—in relation to the first and second columns. The over-all comparison strongly suggests that those in the revolutionary generation were highly successful in their purposive effort to shape the values their children would carry into adulthood. This is most evident in the marked emphasis that the Soviet generation places on self-expression rather than family tradition as a criterion for its job choices, much in keeping with the lesser emphasis that its parents had put on tradition in orienting their children's thoughts about the world of jobs and work. Even if we make allowance for the strong pull of the actual code category, "I feel suited for it," this interpretation would clearly not be materially affected.

It will be noticed, further, that in raising children, those in the tsarist generation gave extremely slight attention to political considerations, whereas those in the revolutionary generation stressed it very heavily, indeed more heavily than tradition. In their own job choices, those in the Soviet generation again show the apparent influence of their parents' concern for this dimension, although in their own value scheme it does not loom quite so large as it did in their parents' efforts at socialization. Finally, we may note that material and psychic rewards, such as income and prestige, had roughly similar relative weight, as compared to politics and tradition, in the child-rearing practices of the revolutionary generation and in the actual job choices of the Soviet generation.

It seems reasonable to conclude again, therefore, that the revolutionary generation did not merely act passively as the agent of the old culture, recapitulating in its own parental activities the socialization practices that had earlier been used by *its* parents. On the contrary, it may be said that the middle generation, responding to its experience of social change under the Soviet regime, in large measure turned away from the pattern of child rearing under which it had been raised earlier and in its approach to the new Soviet generation stressed goals and values of a different sort. It appears, furthermore, that this training of the youth in new value orientations was relatively successful.

Because the numbers are small and the sample unusual, the material presented here is perhaps little more than suggestive of the results that might be yielded by research specifically designed to increase our knowledge in this area. Indeed, a stronger case could have been made with the material at hand had not rigorous limits of space precluded the presentation of quotations from our interviews that show graphically the way in which conditions of social change experienced by the parents influenced their approach to raising their children. Nevertheless, the material presented should serve to alert us to the role that the parent plays, through both purposive and unconscious adjustments in his child-rearing practices, in mediating the influence of social change to his children, and consequently in better adapting them for the changed social conditions they may meet as adults. Furthermore, although the demonstration presented above dealt only with the more surface level of attitudes and value orientations, there is reason to believe that similar processes operate with regard to the development of personality at deeper levels.

changing role relations of the japanese wife

thirty-six

Since World War II, Japanese sociology has made great progress. Social research has paid especially great attention to the family, since it was viewed as expressing the traditional spirit of the nation. At the same time, not only did the many forces for change well up that had been kept under tight control during the previous fifteen years, but a new element also entered. Japan leaders had linked the nation's success with its old myths and traditions; consequently, when defeat came instead, many people began to question the old customs. Thus the attempts by the United States administration to press both law and social practice toward democracy, especially in the family, were aided by Japanese leaders. Here a noted Japanese sociologist of the family summarizes many of the indices of family change to be observed in contemporary Japan.

The Changing Social Position of Women in Japan

TAKASHI KOYAMA

*   *   *   *   *

The Wife's Role in Housework

Housework represents an . . . important task which women perform in the family. Formerly, it was generally understood that men have nothing to do with housework. This laid a heavy burden upon women. Since the last world war, the idea of "democracy," which is penetrating gradually into home life, and technological changes, in the form of modern appliances and conveniences, which are lightening housework are being diffused, and they have contributed to reduce women's burden in housework in both rural and urban areas. But it must not be forgotten that current economic conditions impose upon the housewife a much heavier financial burden that offsets the gains from technological inventions.

In relation to the housework of today, we shall first treat opinions on the question of the husband helping the wife in her housework. In 1951, the National Opinion Research Institute

Takashi Koyama, *The Changing Social Position of Women in Japan* (Paris: UNESCO, 1961), pp. 62-65, 67-75. We are grateful to the author and UNESCO for permission to quote.

TABLE 1 Opinions Concerning a Man Assisting in Kitchen Work

Opinion	Men (Per Cent)	Women (Per Cent)	All Japan (Per Cent)
Approve	31	34	32
Disapprove	42	46	45
It depends on the situation	11	8	9
Don't know	16	12	14

conducted a survey.[1] One of the questions asked was: "Do you approve or disapprove of a man assisting in kitchen work?" The answers were as shown in Table 1. According to this finding, nearly half of all Japanese people disapprove of a man assisting in kitchen work. But a slightly higher percentage of women than of men approved of the man assisting in kitchen work, and the same situation existed in replies of those who "disapprove." It is a striking fact that only one third (31 per cent for men and 34 per cent for women) of men and women approve of a man helping in kitchen work; also, more married or older persons disapprove of a man helping in kitchen work than single or younger persons.

It can be seen from a review of other studies of this kind that the majority of wives are often unaware of the amount and burdensomeness of their work in connection with housekeeping. Their minds are preoccupied with the problem of how to escape from poverty. The survey of the "Wife's Wishes of this Year" conducted by *The Mainichi* in 1953 asked this question: "What do you desire most of your husband?" Many wives who replied desired their husbands to improve the present financial and living conditions of their homes. "Increasing income," "stable living," and "saving money"—these were desired of their husbands by 30 per cent of all women respondents. Next in importance were the problems of

[1] National Public Opinion Research Institute, *Research on Women and Youth* (Tokyo: The Institute, 1951).

finding a place to live and keeping the house constantly in good repair—22 per cent of the women respondents desired these of their husbands. Thus financial considerations and housing conditions formed the subject matter of slightly over 50 per cent of the wishes expressed. The remaining half of the replies showed that excessive drinking and smoking, lavish spending and failure to keep regular time (32 per cent in all) were things that wives would wish their husbands to do something about.

Wife's Work for Income

According to the traditional notions of Japan, it is [as] absolutely right for a woman to look after domestic affairs and children as it is for men to do outdoor work. It is just as undesirable for a wife to work outside the home in order to earn a cash income as it is for her husband to do the housework. After the last world war, a large number of women entered a variety of occupations. As a result, the traditional notion of women's role as being exclusively concerned with housekeeping is changing.

. . . [As for] the attitude of Japanese people toward married women working outside the home, if we look at the survey on women and youth conducted by the National Public Opinion Research Institute in 1952, we see that about the same number of persons . . . intimated their agreement with each of the four replies, namely, "I approve of her working outside" (23 per cent), "I disapprove of her working outside" (25 per cent), "It depends on the occasion" (25 per cent), and "I don't know" (27 per cent).

The traditional notion seems to be definitely crumbling, and the majority of those who approve of married women working outside regard such work as a necessary evil, an evil which has been forced upon them by the difficulties of present-day life. The fundamental attitude is still that "the woman's place is in the home." On the other hand, a comparison by age shows that the younger the respondents, the larger the extent of approval for women working outside the home. The postwar change has induced many women to engage in economic activities to help to support the family. According to the investigation of 1949 by the Ministry of Labour, 40 per cent of women were reported to add one half or more to the amount of the family income by doing part-time work, by helping in the family business, or by taking up a regular occupation. There were only 22 per cent who "added nothing." As the research was conducted at the time of the business depression, a period when any member of the family who could work at all was called upon to supplement the family income, these figures are perhaps not representative of the women of today. But one cannot overlook the fact that the wife's economic activities during that period greatly influenced the role she plays.

Women's economic activities are now not restricted to the occupational field, for their growing concern with investments is also a remarkable trend of recent times. The legal code of prewar days laid down that women were incompetent to deal with property, and they did not take any positive interest in the management of property. Even when a stockholder's name happened to be that of a woman, this did not in most cases represent her ownership nor her own will; her name appeared because her father or husband, who was the real holder, used her name. Today many women study the stock market for themselves and invest in stocks and make money in preparation for their daughter's marriage or for their own use. Large joint-stock companies are now issuing periodicals for women investors, and the number of copies is increasing rapidly every month. Though this phenomenon is still confined to urban districts, such publications indicate the very significant change that has occurred in recent times.

* * * * *

Women's Status as Observed in the Customs of Life

However great and substantial changes in laws and regulations may be, the ways and customs of the people do not, for their part, change easily in a nation like Japan. To be sure, changes in law do have an educational value in modern society. Therefore some important aspects of the customs of Japanese society which have a bearing on the status and position of women must be described and analysed.

Appellation of the Husband

When a wife speaks of her husband to a third person, she speaks of him as *shujin* (master). In the old patriarchal family, the husband was, indeed, the "master of the *iye*," because the office of the headship of the household was assigned to him, whence came the appellation, *shujin*. In the context of present-day Japanese society, a term with such a social derivation may sound highly inappropriate now that the old family system has, from the legal standpoint, been abolished. Today, in the private letters of women or in their contributions to the reader's columns of magazines and newspapers, the term "my husband" instead of *shujin* is very often intentionally used. But in their daily conversation, *shujin* is still widely used. Although there are other terms in use today to designate the husband, the word *shujin* is still used very frequently (*shujin* is used to the extent of 50 per cent in terms of frequency). This practice should not be taken too seriously, nor should the use of this term be taken to show the submissive position of the wife. Many wives use it unconsciously as a customary pronoun for "husband." . . .

* * * * *

Equality in Meal Taking

In the patriarchal family system, the existing patriarch, whether the husband's father or the husband himself, and the eldest son, who was to be patriarch in the coming generation, were served better meals, while the wife, daughters, and other sons had to be content with poor meals. If the husband was fond of a drink at supper, the wife had to prepare sake and some eatables, see to the warming of the sake, and wait on him while he leisurely enjoyed his supper. If nice food was sent as a present from a distant place, it was first offered to the spirit of ancestors and then to the patriarch's table. If this procedure was not conformed to, the wife was reproached.

[One] report . . . shows that today those wives whose families in their childhood offered nice food first to the father or grandfather make up 49 per cent, as compared with 30 per cent who adhere to this practice at the present time. On the other hand, those who grew up in a family where there was equal sharing of nice food with no priority for any specific member of the family amount to only 14 per cent, whereas at present 38 per cent practice equality in regard to meals. In the case of farming families, 50 per cent still adhere to the old custom.

* * * * *

Husband and Wife Going Out Together

According to the old Japanese custom, the husband and wife never sat together in the drawing room, nor were they seen together in places of recreation or culture. In the survey by the Ministry of Labour, in which respondents were asked if the wife went with her husband to the cinema or other place of amusement, only 3 per cent in rural areas answered "Yes," and 22 per cent of Tokyo women answered "Yes." In contrast, those who replied "Absolutely not" to the same question amounted to 21 per cent in Tokyo and as much as 60 per cent in rural areas.[2]

Expression of Conjugal Affection

In the patriarchal family of the past, the focus of married life was on the security of the family as a whole, rather than on that of the individual. Here conjugal affection was overshadowed by the *iye*. Moreover, as people were taught to restrain from giving any outward demonstration of their feelings and affections, they were less inclined to express their affection. Accordingly, the idea of a husband and wife going out together for recreation became a subject for ridicule. A number of husbands went so far as to imagine that they could gain personal credit by speaking ill of their wives to others, even though in their own private life they were tender to their wives.

What changes have occurred in regard to conjugal affection? In addition to the reform of laws and regulations and the change in ideas, the growing influence of the media of mass communi-

2 Women's and Minors' Bureau, Ministry of Labour, *The Life and Opinions of Housewives* (Tokyo: The Ministry, 1957).

cation results in people in general becoming acquainted with the customs of other countries and with the manners of the whole world, and this contributes to remove the psychological barriers imposed by society. Formerly, "the affection of husband and wife" was not even to be spoken of in the presence of others. But this is no longer the case. In this regard, the survey by the Department of Domestic Science, Ochanomizu Women's University, shows that 26 per cent of those questioned do not hesitate in the frank expression of conjugal affection in public, as compared with 40 per cent who can express such affection only if nobody sees them.[3]

The Turn of Getting Up, Going to Bed, and Taking a Bath

Where the status of the members of a group is firmly determined by considerations of age and sex, there emerges a pattern of ceremonial behavior and observance which recognizes differences in status. In the traditional Japanese family, there were many of these ceremonial relationships and patterns of etiquette prescribing who should go to bed first in the evening, who should get up first in the morning, and who should take a bath first. These patterns of etiquette were observed. The wife was expected to get up first and not after her husband so that she might make herself neat and presentable to him. The saying was that she must "get up early so that he might not catch sight of her dishevelled appearance." She was expected to make preparation for her husband and other members of the family to begin their day's work. Likewise, she could not go to bed earlier than her husband; if she did, she was called "an idle wife." In taking a bath, the proper turn was strictly observed,

and the idea of a woman taking a bath before a man was inconceivable.

How far have these patterns of etiquette changed? Some studies on this matter have been made, and their findings may be summarized as follows. In rural areas, rather more than 50 per cent of the wives are regularly the first of all the members of the family to rise in the morning, as compared with only 4 to 5 per cent of husbands who get up first. The vast majority of husbands, or family heads, especially in rural areas, go to bed first. In most urban families, this priority is not given to any specific member of the family. In the matter of taking a bath, the majority of husbands enjoy priority in rural areas.

The priorities noted above are of course partly influenced by various considerations of convenience as well as by the complexity of modern life. Thus in urban society, these traditions are in fact rapidly becoming obsolete.

* * * * *

Attitude Toward the Position in the Family

. . . How do wives feel about their own position in the family?

In the survey of 1955 by the Ministry of Labour, 70 per cent of those questioned answered, "the further improvement of women's position in society is necessary," and only 18 per cent replied, "the position as it now stands is satisfactory." The younger or the more educated the respondents, the higher the proportion of responses which stated, "improvement is necessary."[4]

In Mrs. Suehiro's investigation, the women questioned were asked about their position in two respects, namely,

[3] Yoshitomo Ushijima, *et al.*, *Psychology of Married Life* (Tokyo, Makishoten, 1954).

[4] Women's and Minors' Bureau, Ministry of Labour, *On the Status of Women* (Tokyo: The Ministry, 1955).

in the family and in society.[5] . . . The vast majority [79 per cent] held the opinion that "women's position has to be improved further" in society. But in regard to the position of women in the family, a considerable number of the women questioned said that they are "satisfied with their position as it stands now [55 per cent]."

. . . Comparison in the light of the husband's occupational background reveals that the wives of professional and clerical workers give the highest rate of those who are satisfied with their present position in the family (60 per cent), and the wives of agricultural workers give the lowest rate (42 per cent). As to women's position in society, the need for improvement is insisted on by many wives of agricultural workers as well as by those of professional and managerial workers. This may be regarded as reflecting the present position of women in contemporary Japanese society.

Subjectively, a feeling of satisfaction with the position of women is not always determined by the position a woman holds in her own life. Under the patriarchal family system with prescribed status, the members of the family of lower status found pleasure in fulfilling their assigned roles, whatever hardship might be imposed upon them. Accordingly, women, though objectively their position was far from satisfactory, were able to find a pleasure in living. Now, when people have become conscious of the equality inherent in the individual, the person assigned to a lower position often finds his inferior status very frustrating. According to the survey of the Ministry of Labour, a wife's satisfaction with her present life tends to be associated with the following circumstances: the husband assists with the housework; the husband and wife often go out together; the husband esteems her housework highly; the husband and wife enjoy their daily life; the husband and wife together manage the household economy; the husband and wife both have a good knowledge of the family estate; and so forth. Each of these circumstances is a concrete situation according to which we can accurately assess the position of women in the family.

* * * * *

---

[5] Kazuko Suehiro, "Research for the Domestic Science," 1958 (unpublished).